THE
EAST COAST
MAIN LINE
1939-1959

THE EAST COAST MAIN LINE 1939-1959

—VOLUME 2—

B.W.L. BROOKSBANK AND PETER TUFFREY

FONTHILL

Fonthill Media Limited
Fonthill Media LLC
www.fonthill.media
books@fonthill.media

First published in the United Kingdom and the United States of America 2022

British Library Cataloguing in Publication Data:
A catalogue record for this book is available from the British Library

Copyright © Peter Tuffrey and B. W. L. Brooksbank 2022

ISBN 978-1-78155-749-5

The right of Peter Tuffrey and B. W. L. Brooksbankto be identified as the author of this work has been asserted by him in accordance with the Copyright, Designs and Patents Act 1988.

All rights reserved. No part of this publication may be reproduced, stored in a retrieval system or transmitted in any form or by any means, electronic, mechanical, photocopying, recording or otherwise, without prior permission in writing from Fonthill Media Limited

Typeset in 10pt on 13pt Sabon
Printed and bound in England

Contents

1	The East Coast Main Line's Principal Points	7
2	Alterations to the Way and Structures (1939–1959)	122
3	Locomotives of the ECML (1939–1959)	147
4	ECML Locomotive Depots, their Allocations and Workings	163
5	Passenger Rolling Stock on the ECML	191
6	Management and Staff of the ECML	196
7	ECML Stations and Signal Boxes in 1939	210
8	ECML Wayside Stations and Closure Dates	218
9	ECML Tunnels and Principal Overbridges	225
10	Gradients and Speed Restrictions on the ECML	236
11	Staff Distribution (October 1939)	239

Endnotes   246
Bibliography   251

1

The East Coast Main Line's Principal Points

Introduction

In this section, the whole of the East Coast Main Line between King's Cross and Edinburgh Waverley stations will be examined closely, with a particular emphasis on the ways and structures: the line, stations, connections, yards and other physical features. Interposed will be accounts of the traffic at the principal stations (including connecting and branch line services) with observations on changes over the period 1939 to 1959. Some emphasis is placed on freight traffic on account of its importance and—perhaps—its relative unfamiliarity to the reader. The lines, stations and many other elements are described as they were in August 1939, but as some plans on which they are based are dated before the late 1930s, there may be marginal differences from the precise layout in 1939.

King's Cross

King's Cross was by no means London's largest station and only handled 60,000 passengers a day in 1939, along with 7.5 million parcels per year. The whole station covered 155¾ acres and had 15 platforms, the longest being 981 feet. The main line station was contained in Lewis Cubitt's original structure of 1852—the largest station in Britain at the time—with a roof comprising two arches, each 105 feet wide and 71 feet high, separated down to the ground level by an array of wide brick arches, which formed a partition between platforms 1 to 5 and 6 to 10. Footbridges spanned the platforms halfway along.

The frontage (set back from Euston Road and later partially obscured) was surmounted by a clock set in an Italianate turret. There were eight platforms in the main station: Nos 1 to 10 (there being no Nos 3 or 9) of which 1, 2, 4, 5 and 6 were used for arrivals, although not exclusively as demonstrated by platform 1, which was primarily dedicated to parcels traffic. The centre platforms—Nos 5 and 6—particularly were used for intermediate distance trains, such as the Cambridge Buffet Expresses. Platform 10 was the famous principal departure platform (not protected by a ticket barrier) and was lined with the main public facilities. The platform, being slightly longer than the others, was also the main congregation point for railway enthusiasts.

York Road station platform, which was situated a short distance away from the rest of the station on the east side, was served by Up local trains proceeding to Moorgate via the London Passenger Transport Board's Metropolitan Widened Lines. Down trains came up out of the tunnels on a curved gradient of 1:50 into platform 16, which was 1:37 and often caused a difficult start for drivers of Down local trains. This line was also known as Hotel Curve after the Great Northern Hotel on the surface. Platform 16, with platform 17 on its western side and 11 to 15 on its eastern side, constituted King's Cross suburban station. This rather grim establishment, with largely wooden platforms, was somewhat separate from the main station (although platform 11 was contiguous with no. 10) and had its own booking office and buffet which was modernised in 1939. Beyond the suburban platforms were four more bays, used for unloading milk churns, horses and other purposes. As well as the cramped locomotive yard on the west side of the station throat, there were several spurs set between the running lines in that area, where pilot locomotives could stand.

Recently, certain improvements had been made to King's Cross. In particular, the removal of No. 9 carriage line enabled the widening of island platforms 7 and 8. New barriers and indicators were constructed behind the buffer-stops and the refreshment rooms were considerably improved with a sumptuous new lounge for first-class ladies. Further modernisations would not occur for several decades subsequently despite plans being prepared in the 1950s.

The most important upgrade under LNER stewardship concerned the station's signalling system, which was electrified in 1932. In the station and through Gas Works Tunnel, the signals were operated by an all-electric power frame of 232 levers housed in a box located just off the end of platforms 5 and 6. Many of the cables were carried from the box over the tracks on gantries to platforms 10 and 11 as a precaution against floods.

There remained very awkward arrangements of tracks in the short throat leading to the three two-track Gas Works Tunnels, which were positioned in accordance with the necessity for the lines to pass under Regent's Canal just outside the station.[1] The easternmost tunnel carried the Up Slow line (used by trains to the Widened Lines and platform 1) and the Up Fast (leading to platforms 1 to 5). The middle contained the Up relief (leading to all platforms) and Down Fast No. 1 (accessible from all platforms); normally all empty stock movements used this tunnel. The lines running through the westernmost Gas Works Tunnel comprised Down Fast No. 2 (platforms 6 to 17) and the Down Slow (from platforms 11 to 17). Problems were exacerbated by conflicting movements between Up and Down trains and the positioning of the locomotive yard on the western side. Engines released from Up trains had to execute a series of manoeuvres to reach this area, which allowed servicing to be conducted more efficiently than running through the tunnels to King's Cross shed, and there were quite elaborate rules of working to be followed by staff.

Approximately 45 long-distance trains (including parcels and newspaper trains) left King's Cross on a normal weekday in 1939, with about the same number of arrivals. During the war, the number declined to 30, then 20 by summer 1944, and in post-war years rose back to the pre-war level. For these services, the stock had to be brought to

The East Coast Main Line's Principal Points

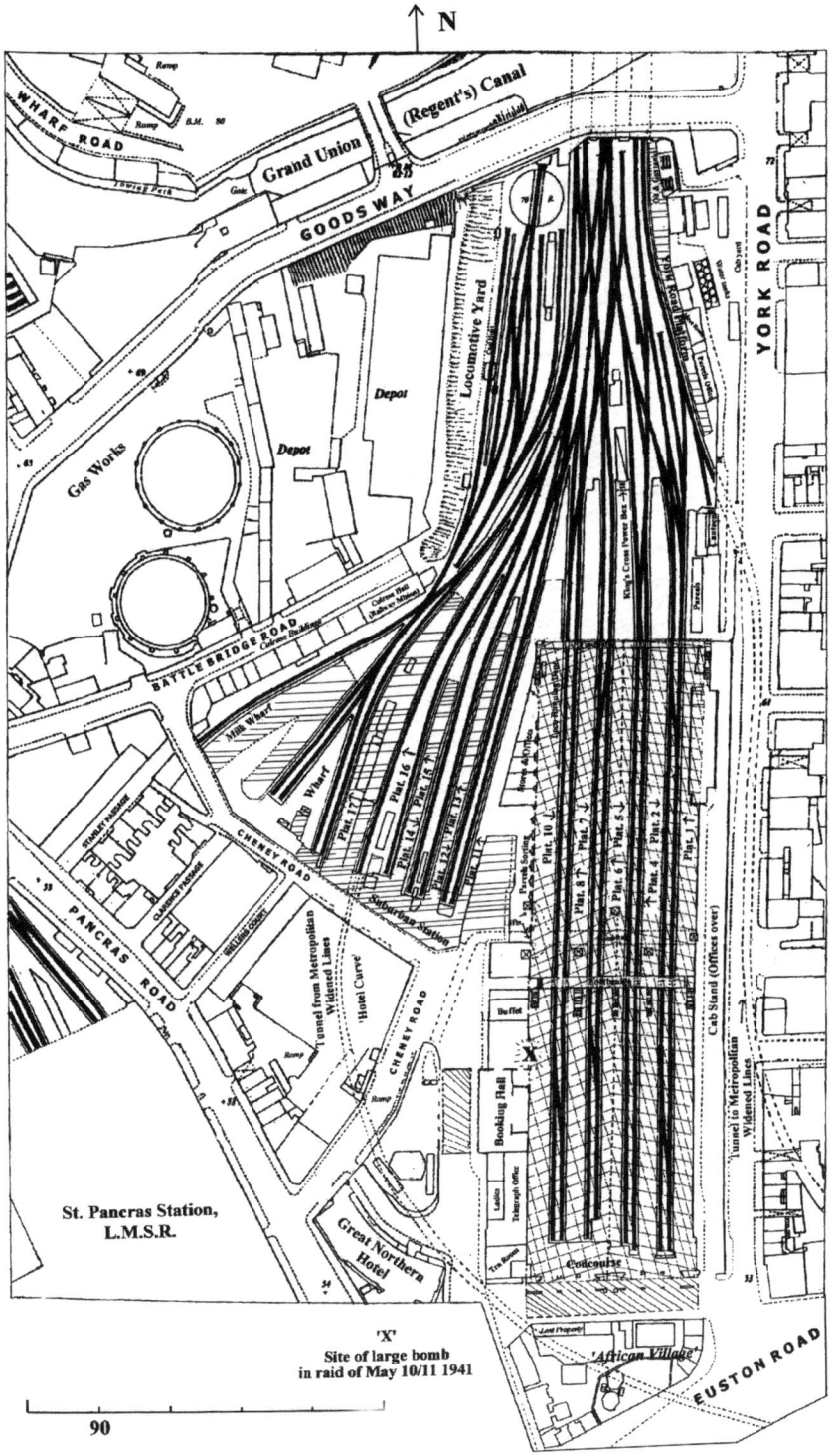

The layout of the station in 1939, scale 1:1250.

King's Cross station frontage, c. 1960. The area between the station entrance and Euston Road in the foreground was occupied by shops for many years, but has recently been cleared for a pedestrian zone as part of a large redevelopment project.

Parcels are loaded in the night-time gloom of King's Cross station's platform 10.

and taken from King's Cross from the carriage sidings a distance away which doubled the amount of workings. There were also around 100 local and outer suburban trains running and 40 daily goods services each way on to the Widened Lines, all of them having to run outside peak hours. Over 400 trains could be handled at King's Cross in 24 hours.

Services continued during the night, including sleeping car, parcels, mail and newspaper trains, which left in the late evening, and equivalent trains also arrived in the early hours. Platform 10 was often nearly impassable with trolleys used to convey the goods to the vans forming the trains, and No. 1 was similarly congested with the incoming goods and mail. Several overnight sleeping car arrivals also loitered in several platforms, allowing passengers to continue their slumber (if they wished) until 07.30, when they would be ejected.

Local Services in the London Area

The outer suburban trains from King's Cross missed most of the stops between Finsbury Park and Potters Bar, then called at most stations to Hitchin, Letchworth, Baldock, Royston, Cambridge and Peterborough. Some of the Cambridge services were fast with limited stops and buffet facilities, being dubbed the 'Beer Trains' by students at Cambridge. Before and during the war, the outer suburban trains were worked most often by C1 Class Atlantics from Hitchin and King's Cross sheds, but also by B17 4-6-0s, Claud Hamilton (D15, D16/2 and D16/3) 4-4-0s from Cambridge and occasionally B12/3s; there were also rare appearances by Pacifics, mainly on the 'Beer Trains'. Quite frequently during the war and afterwards, locomotives from GE section sheds (particularly March) would appear on the Cambridge line trains. The Cambridge allocation included the Royal engines, which were kept in excellent condition for use on Royal Trains to Sandringham. In 1944–45, some of the very first B1 Class 4-6-0s worked regularly on the Cambridge trains, presaging the almost wholesale takeover by these locomotives in 1946.

Motive power for the LNER inner suburban trains was almost exclusively Gresley N2 Class 0-6-2Ts, assisted occasionally by Ivatt N1s or Gresley N7s. These trains provided a frequent service from King's Cross down the main line as far as new Barnet, Potters Bar or Hatfield, or branching off at Wood Green, they ran to Gordon Hill, Cuffley or Hertford North. With certain trains skipping stops, the Hertford line was better served before the war than in the 1950s, until dieselisation towards the end of the decade. Although the rest of the 'Hertford Loop', on to Langley Junction between Knebworth and Stevenage, had no regular local service between September 1939 and March 1962, it was much used by freight as a diversionary route and at times by some regular through expresses.

Until the war, there was a separate service northward from Hertford North to Hitchin or Letchworth, usually worked by a steam railcar. Additionally, before the war, there were frequent trains via Highgate to Alexandra Palace and via Finchley (Church End) Central from April 1940 to High Barnet, connecting at Finchley with a shuttle service to Edgware. Before the war, a large proportion of the inner suburban trains ran from Moorgate via the Metropolitan Widened Lines, but Moorgate station and the surroundings were shattered during the Blitz. Consequently, these services were suspended in October 1940 and were

N2 Class 0-6-2T No. 69534 waits to depart from platform 12 with a local service to Potters Bar on 7 January 1957. *Picture: B. W. L. Brooksbank*

not restored until May 1946 (following an interim period of operating from Aldersgate, beginning October 1945) and then only in the rush hours.

Many inner suburban trains started at Finsbury Park, with London, Midland and Scottish Railway (LMSR) trains from Broad Street (formerly North London Railway) also joined the line here. Worked by LMSR 0-6-0Ts or 2-6-2Ts, these trains ran to New Barnet or Potters Bar, to Gordon Hill on the Hertford North line, and to High Barnet via Finchley, but were also suspended in October 1940 due to war damage. When reinstated in June 1945, they were worked by LNER locomotives, and like the Moorgate trains, ran only in rush hour.

In July 1939, the connection of the High Barnet line to the London Underground (LPTB) system was inaugurated with the completion of the new tunnel from Archway to the surface near East Finchley, where a connection was made with the LNER lines. The High Barnet line was then electrified from Highgate where it was connected to and taken over by the LPTB (Northern Line) in April 1940.[2] The LNER then ran a steam service between Finsbury Park and East Finchley, but only until March 1941. During September 1939, the Edgware shuttle train was substituted by a bus service, then in May 1941, a rail service was reinstituted in the form of Northern Line trains which ran just to Mill Hill East. After electrification, LNER steam-hauled goods trains continued to run to High Barnet until October 1962 and to Edgware until August 1964; the line remained open for freight as far as Highgate until October 1970. The daily trains comprised four coal trains to Mill Hill Gas Works, two trains to Edgware and one to High Barnet, all but one starting from Highbury Vale Yard. They were limited in length on account of the steep gradients and were hauled by N2s fitted with special catches to operate the Underground's automatic signals.

The Alexandra Palace branch was not electrified and the service was cut back in 1940 to a push-pull train from Finsbury Park; from September 1946, it operated in rush hours only. This shuttle was first worked by ex-Great Central Railway F2 Class 2-4-2Ts until late 1950 and thereafter there were periods when C12 4-4-2Ts returned, having worked the service in earlier years, and when ex-GCR 4-4-2Ts were tried. Finally, some N7s were converted to haul the train and were used until the branch closed in July 1954.[3]

During the first few years after the war, suburban services from London were gradually restored to peacetime frequency and speed. The restorations included the fast Cambridge Buffet Expresses and even one or two locals from Moorgate, which did not stop at King's Cross. Soon after the war, there were some fairly major changes in locomotive types employed on secondary passenger services, such as the King's Cross outer suburban trains. Although B17s and ex-Great Eastern Railway 4-4-0s continued to run into King's Cross on trains from Cambridge, the Ivatt Atlantics were dwindling in numbers due to withdrawals. The replacements were mainly B1 Class 4-6-0s and L1 2-6-4Ts, but during the immediate post-war period (when sufficient numbers of these classes were not available), Pacifics, V2s, K3s and even J39 Class 0-6-0s were used on the Cambridge trains. The L1s proved feeble and could only manage the lighter and slower workings. During the mid-1950s, other locomotive types—including A5 4-6-2Ts, LMSR Fowler and BR Standard Class 2-6-4Ts, LMSR and BR Standard Class 5 4-6-0s and BR Class 4 2-6-0s—were observed on the outer suburban services, although only for short periods. The employment of the Class 5 4-6-0s early in 1955 was mainly in connection with trials preceding the general introduction of BR's automatic warning system (AWS), but from 1957, three of the class were allocated to King's Cross.

In October 1958, some of the King's Cross inner suburban services began to be worked regularly by diesel multiple units (DMUs) based at Cambridge, but the whole local timetable

Thompson B1 Class 4-6-0 No. 1005 *Bongo* at New Southgate with a train heading north to Cambridge on 20 April 1946.

was not altered, to take advantage of the DMUs and the New Barnet to Potters Bar widening, until summer 1959. At this time the suburban services were completely recast and greatly improved as a result of the removal of steam locomotives, with half-hourly services offered at all stations. In addition, semi-fast trains ran to Welwyn Garden City, calling only at Finsbury Park before Oakleigh Park. Extra peak-hour services included trains from Broad Street and Moorgate, although many of these were made up of ordinary stock hauled by the new Type 2 diesels. By the end of 1959, these locomotives were operating most of the outer suburban trains on slightly faster schedules, omitting the Finsbury Park stop, and they also sometimes worked through to Cleethorpes with express trains.

Further out at Hatfield, branch services ran west to St Albans Abbey and east to Hertford North (diverging at Welwyn Garden City), and west to Luton Bute Street and Dunstable North where interconnection was possible with the LMSR service to Leighton Buzzard on the West Coast Main Line. In 1939, there was one through train from King's Cross to Dunstable on weekdays and five on Sundays. In the early part of the war, more trains ran on weekdays through to Dunstable and also some via Hatfield to Hertford North, but these all ceased by 1942 and were not restored after the war, apart from the 07.35 Hertford North–Broad Street. In the 1950s, many of the Hatfield trains were extended to Welwyn Garden City, where many of the Dunstable and Hertford North branch trains then commenced.

During a weekday, mainly at night, some 30 or so heavy freight trains, which were principally hauled by K3 2-6-0s or V2 2-6-2s (and occasionally Pacifics), came out of King's Cross Goods Yard through Copenhagen Tunnel and up Holloway Bank or out of Clarence Yard. An equivalent number of up trains slipped in to East Goods Yard and King's Cross Yard. Around 20 unbraked coal or brick trains arrived from Peterborough New England at Ferme Park Yard and the equivalent empty trains departed; these trains were predominantly hauled by 2-8-0s of Gresley and War Department Austerity designs, along with BR 9F 2-10-0s in the 1950s.

At King's Cross, Finsbury Park and Ferme Park, there were countless short goods trains hauled by J52 (later J50) 0-6-0Ts or N1 Class 0-6-2Ts between the former GNR yards and others around London. A substantial portion of the goods passing through the aforementioned yards were destined for those operated by other companies, notably across the Thames to the Southern Railway. Before the war, there were approximately 35 trips each way (with necessarily short trains of 20 to 30 wagons because of the steep gradients) from Ferme Park or East Goods Yard/Clarence Yard to the SR using the Widened Lines and eight depots in East London by the North London line through Canonbury; exchange traffic westbound to Willesden, Acton and Feltham Yards was also routed via Canonbury.

Early in the war, this traffic was very much augmented, requiring the loop north to west from Harringay on to the Tottenham & Hampstead (T&H) line (built during the First World War) to be reopened, along with the connection with the North London line at Gospel Oak. The working timetable for 1944 shows no fewer than 77 LNER trips each way over Blackfriars Bridge (12 being 'Q' workings) during the week and 47 on Sundays—the peacetime restriction during weekday rush hours was no longer applied. By the Canonbury loop on weekdays, there were 15 trips (two 'Q') to East London and two to Acton, while five weekday trips were routed over the T&H loop. In 1951, the weekday trips over Blackfriars Bridge had fallen to 40–45 (none on Sundays, except when required), but there were now seven (one 'Q') over to the T&H and still 15 to East London. In addition to all these workings, there were numerous local trips between the main GN yards in the area and the GN suburban yards.

King's Cross to Hitchin

The first 50 yards of Gas Works Tunnel had a falling gradient of 1:100, but the next 1½ miles to Holloway rose at 1:107, forcing the locomotive to work hard, with the result of the tunnels being especially smoky and unpleasant places. In a few hundred yards before Copenhagen Tunnel, Belle Isle Up signal box was passed, followed shortly by Copenhagen Junction box, while on the Down side was Goods and Mineral (G&M) Junction box. The last controlled the entrance to King's Cross Goods station and its yards and the locomotive shed, which was in the middle of the goods sidings and hemmed in by these on both sides. From a passing train, the yards and shed were not visible, though on occasions J52 Class locomotives could be seen shunting or an engine was coming on to the main lines to travel down to the station.

The combined track-work of all the goods, coal and locomotive yards amounted to approximately 130 roads. The greater part of the goods depot (potato depot, Inwards and Outwards sheds together with the Coal and general sidings) was situated on the south side of 'Top Shed'. King's Cross Goods dispatched and received 20 to 25 long-distance trains daily, mostly during the night. At the heart of the goods station was the six-storey granary building of 1850, facing Regent's Canal to the south and having on the flanks two transit sheds, the intervening tracks—partly covered by goods offices—serving for the assembly of trains. Until 1938, this complex had formed the Inwards sheds, but afterwards constituted the Outwards sheds. Lateral and longitudinal tracks were connected by wagon turntables worked by hydraulic capstans, and many of the tracks had access to cart roads, as well as some of the basins of the canal. Some 120 dray horses lived in stables below. Other goods offices were on the eastern side of the complex and beyond was the former Midland locomotive shed[4] and its sidings. To the north, and parallel to York Way was the substantial potato market above Gas Works Tunnel. The market had 40 'runs' at right angles from the main tracks, into which hundreds of wagons of potatoes, mainly from Lincolnshire, were unloaded daily.

West of the 1850 complex were sets of coal-drops and their associated sidings, some with access to the canal basins. Ranged along the south bank of Regent's Canal were the large group of Camley Street coal-drops, which were at right angles to the tracks of the King's Cross Yards and served by a line that crossed from the Yard over the canal. Beyond Camley Street was the LMSR main line out of St Pancras with its associated yards. Further to the west in King's Cross Yards was the Inwards shed (previously Outwards shed), with tracks and unloading bays at a higher level. On the north-west side of the Inwards shed was the locomotive depot with its ancillary sidings and extensive coal stacks. To the north of these again was the goods empties shed (usually known as Four Arch) flanked by 20 siding roads, mainly devoted to coal deliveries to private traders. Lastly came the sidings to the Engineer's yard and manure wharf, above which the single North London Incline climbed up to the LMSR at St Pancras Junction, Maiden Lane. On the other side of the main line at Belle Isle the remains of Cemetery station could be seen and this had previously been used by funeral trains to New Southgate but had closed in 1873.

Access to and from King's Cross Goods Yards was complicated. For traffic travelling to and from Finsbury Park, the co-operation of G&M Junction, Belle Isle Up and South Holloway Down signal boxes was necessary. Until February 1935, there had been a Belle Isle Down box, but afterwards King's Cross signal box worked directly with Copenhagen Junction box on the down side and with Belle Isle Up box. There was the exception of light engine movements to King's Cross station, which entailed conflicting movements across the Down Fast and Down Slow lines.

On emerging from the western Gas Works Tunnel at the site of the former Belle Isle Down box, the Down Slow line split off a 'Down South London Goods' line, which in turn joined (at G&M Junction) the Up and Down Goods lines of the main yard. These lines connected with at least 10 others, including Nos 1 and 2 Goods arrival roads, Down Goods, Down and Up coal roads and Up and Down engine roads, also with access to the empties and coal yards. All were handled by G&M Junction working to Holloway South Down and Up boxes. Just inside King's Cross Goods Yard, a ground frame (designated Five Arch box) further controlled the fans of sidings of the main (southern) part of the yard. While shunting operations continued almost incessantly, using several spurs, they were hampered by the bends and narrow gaps between the arches of York Way bridge.

After G&M Junction box, the lines from King's Cross Goods connected with the Down South London Goods line coming from the western Gas Works Tunnel and entered their own bore on the western side of Copenhagen Tunnel. G&M Junction box also controlled the North London incline and a spur that ran back from King's Cross Coal Yard and curved round over Copenhagen Tunnel to run eastwards parallel to the North London line, serving the coal yard off Caledonian Road (this depot lasted until October 1967). Finally, crossing high above the ECML near the south end of Copenhagen Tunnel was the four-track North London line, just east of the site of the former Maiden Lane station.

Near the country end of the three Copenhagen Tunnel bores was a flyover to carry the Up Goods line over the main lines and through the western bore into King's Cross Goods Yard alongside the Down Goods Line. Further north was Holloway South box and a short distance onward was Holloway North box; both consisted of two boxes for Up and Down[5] line traffic.[6] On the Down side between the North and South boxes was Holloway Carriage Sidings, consisting of 17 dead-end lines catering for short turnaround trains. The six lines through Copenhagen Tunnel expanded at Holloway South into four lines in each direction. The Down Goods line divided again before reaching Holloway North Down box and beyond gave off a Down Carriage line that connected with the Up Canonbury Carriage (bi-directional) and Goods lines near Finsbury Park No. 2 box, which was hidden from the main line by the Carriage Shed. Opposite this box were no fewer than 56 parallel tracks, including the sidings of Clarence Yard, Western Carriage Sidings, East Goods Yard and Highbury Vale Yard. All of the sidings in Clarence Yard debouched northwards, most of them on to the through lines at Finsbury Park No. 2 box, but the top end (consisting of six sidings) and the Western Carriage Sidings (five roads with two under cover) joined at Finsbury Park No. 3 Box at the south end of Finsbury Park station.

On the Up side at Holloway South, there was the old Holloway & Caledonian Road station, which was opened by the GNR, primarily as a ticket platform, and closed by the company in 1915. Under the LNER, the Cattle Dock[7] remained in use, with a group of

The East Coast Main Line's Principal Points

The complex of lines leading to the King's Cross Goods Depots and the engine sheds, scale 1:1250.

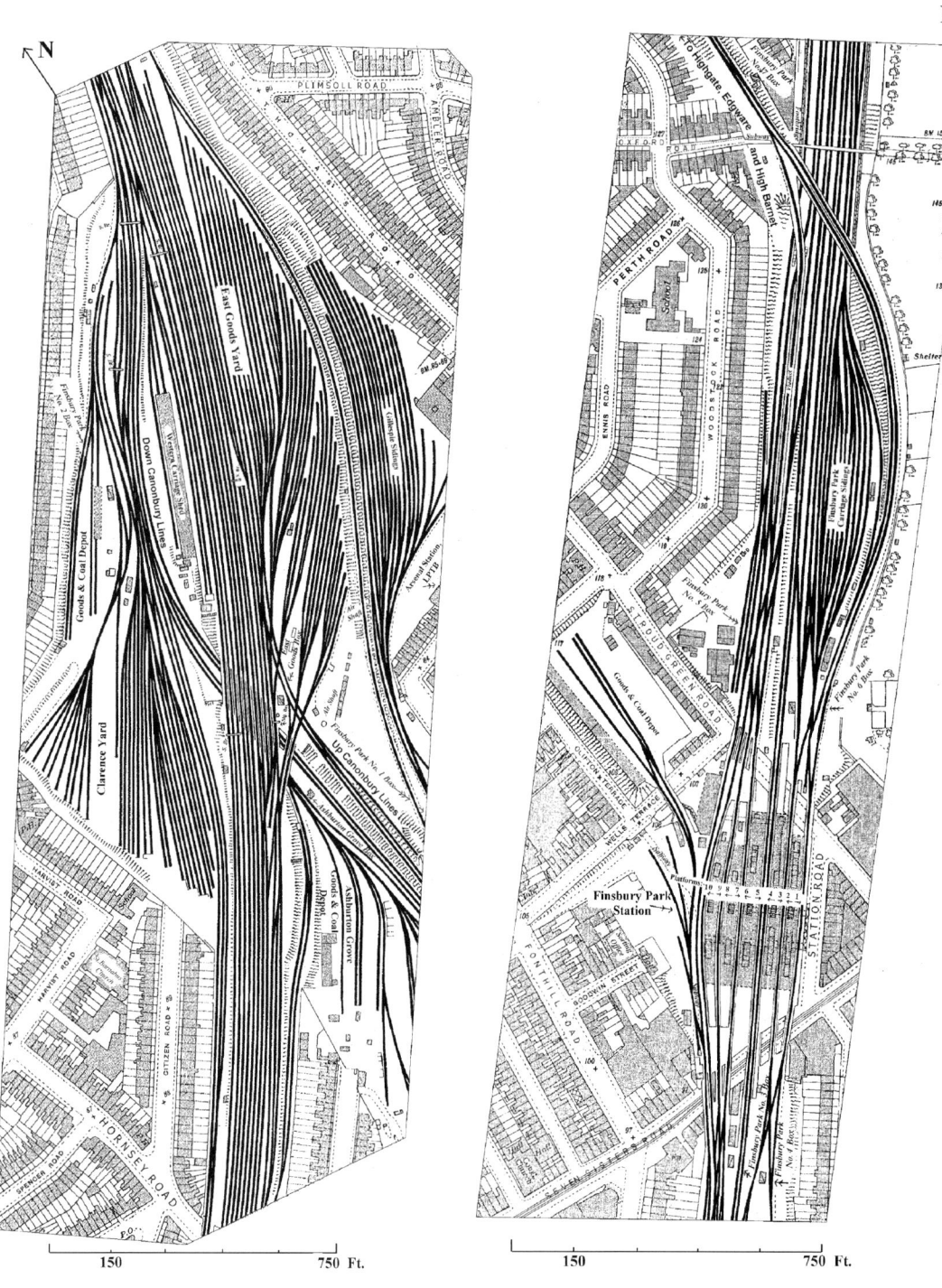

Above left: The layout of Clarence Yard and East Goods Yard in the mid-1930s.

Above right: Finsbury Park station and Carriage Sidings, 1936.

six sidings and cattle pens for unloading livestock for the Metropolitan Cattle Market and Abattoir, which was located to the west of the main line. Next to the Cattle Sidings was the prominent Islington Electric Light Works (later CEA Power Station) with attendant sidings and also those of Star Brush Works. At Holloway South Up box, the Up Goods joined the Up Slow line while the Up coal line continued over the flyover to enter Copenhagen No. 1 Tunnel and gain access to King's Cross Goods Yard. Holloway North Up box controlled the constriction of three Up Goods/coal lines into two. This box also managed the multiple exits of the East Goods Yard complex, which comprised 36 southward dead-end roads in six groups (the main group having 14 roads), with two lines from Finsbury Park No. 4 box (Nos 1 and 2 Up Eastern Lines) passing between the two groups.

Just north of Holloway North boxes, the main lines crossed over the four lines to/from Finsbury Park No. 1 box and the important Canonbury line that led to the North London line, East London, etc. The westernmost of these four was called the Up Carriage line as it was used to run stock for King's Cross from Western Sidings by a curve on to the Up line at Holloway North Up box. Up Canonbury line passenger trains ran from Finsbury Park station entirely on the Up side, passing between East Goods and Highbury Vale Yards. The latter comprised Gillespie Sidings (10 southwards roads), the goods and coal depot on the Up side at Drayton Park, together with Ashburton Grove Yard (29 northward roads, including those serving the goods and coal depot, the Corporation refuse incinerator and other works), were on the Up side of the ECML at a lower level; their access from the Canonbury lines was controlled by Finsbury Park No. 1 and Ashburton Grove boxes.

Finsbury Park station (2½ miles from the terminus) had five island platforms, seven platform lines and a Down (Independent) Goods line, all straddling the busy Seven Sisters Road at the south end and Stroud Green Road at the north end. The main entrance was on the Up side in Station Road, but there was an entrance on the Down side through a long subway from Wells Terrace. The Down Goods line continued through to Ferme Park Yard and beyond, and from it branched spurs to the MacFisheries Depot, the milk depot and the substantial goods and coal depot off Stroud Green Road. On the Up side, there was a group of ten through carriage sidings for local trains and also two dead-end sidings beyond the flyover. A short distance from the north end of the station on the Down side was the Stone Yard Engineer's Sidings, then the branch to Highgate, and on to High Barnet, Edgware and Alexandra Palace climbed up and curved off by a single line flyover above the Down Slow No. 2 and Down Goods lines. In the Up direction, the flyover was double track, with one track a carriage road, both converging on No. 1 platform road.

The seven Finsbury Park signal boxes were concerned principally as follows: No. 1, connections Down to Canonbury; No. 2, Clarence Yard; Nos 3 and 4, connections south of the station on the Down and Up sides respectively; Nos 5 and 6, those north of the station on the Down and Up sides; and No. 7, the approach from Highgate. In addition, there were Ashburton Grove and East Goods boxes for controlling the exits from those yards.

Finsbury Park was an important stopping and interchange station for GNR line suburban services, comparable almost with such centres as Stratford and Clapham Junction—and unusual in having local lines arranged with platforms on both sides of the trains to facilitate a dash from one train to another. Thus, the platforms were numbered 1 to 10 (east to west): Nos 2 and 3, Up Slow line; Nos 6 and 7, Down Slow No. 1; Nos 8 and 9, the Alexandra Palace line; No. 1, Up Canonbury line; No. 10, Down Slow; and No. 2, Down Canonbury line. Underneath ran the Piccadilly line, bringing more people from the suburbs to the east of the ECML—Southgate and out to Cockfosters, and providing LNER passengers a direct route to the West End and beyond, but there was only a short spiral staircase to and from the main platforms.

Finsbury Park also saw a great deal of freight traffic. During the day, these trains were mainly local, principally the feeder services on their way to and from Ferme Park Yard. At night most of the main line freights came through from King's Cross Goods and the other yards to the south of Finsbury Park station.

Harringay station was reached a mile further north after a modest climb from Finsbury Park, but then 8¼ miles at 1:200 began at Hornsey and ended at Potters Bar. As far as the north end of Wood Green station, there were five passenger lines, namely: Down Slow No. 2; Down Slow No. 1; Down Fast; Up Fast; and Up Slow. Supplementing these were the Down Goods, which continued to Wood Green Tunnel Box north of the station, and Up Goods Nos 1 and 2. On the Up side immediately before Harringay station was a small goods yard and on the Down side the formation of the single-track bi-directional north to west spur from the Down Goods line to the LMS & LNE Joint (Tottenham &Hampstead) line at Harringay Junction. To reach this spur from the Up side of Ferme Park Yard, trains had to reverse from Harringay Up Goods Box over the flyover to Ferme Park North Down box, then go forward again on the Down Goods line under the aegis of Ferme Park South Down box, which handed them over to Harringay Junction box.

The Ferme Park Yards spread on each side of the main line for a mile between Harringay and Hornsey. Between Ferme Park South and North Down boxes, there were two extra through Goods lines, while on the Up side between Ferme Park North and South Up boxes as far as Harringay Up Goods box there were the Nos 2 and 3 Up Goods lines.

Ex-GNR C12 Class 4-4-2T No. 7374 moves from a siding to Finsbury Park station with a local train for Alexandra Palace in 1947.

On the Down side, the Ferme Park Yards comprised the through Down Yard (25 roads) and the dead-end Western Sidings (12 roads), with several additional single-ended sidings for the Carriage & Wagon department and Hornsey Goods Yard. On the Up side were the Low Yard (four through and 18 dead-end roads) and the dead-end Top (15 roads), Klondyke (12 roads) and Harringay (nine roads) Yards. Low Yard mainly dealt with coal for the Southern Railway, Top Yard with traffic for Clarence, East Goods and King's Cross Yards and Harringay Yard with coal for King's Cross locomotive depot and local yards. There was a through engine line between each of these yards, and also double engine lines from Hornsey shed skirting the yards on the far east side. In the Up direction, Hornsey locomotive depot was accessed at Hornsey Up Goods box, from either the Up Carriage line or by an engine line from No. 1 Yard.

The yards on each side of the main line at Ferme Park were connected by the Down and Up viaduct lines on a flyover (crossing ten through lines) used for the transfer of wagons between the Up and Down yards and for main line freight locomotives taking up Down workings after being serviced at Hornsey shed. These viaduct lines connected with the Up Goods lines at Harringay Up Goods box and with the Down Goods line at Ferme Park Down box.

From Hornsey to Wood Green, there were still eight running lines: Down Goods, Down Slow Nos 2 and 1, Down Fast, Up Fast, Up Slow, Up Goods and Up Carriage. Shortly after Hornsey station on the Down side, there were the two contiguous groups of Waterworks Carriage Sidings (three and one roads respectively debouching northwards and one through road). These were accessed by reversal at Wood Green No. 1 box and here certain empty trains from King's Cross were serviced. Otherwise, empty stock went over the Wood Green flyover (across five main lines and a siding) to Bounds Green box or Bowes Park station and then reversed to reach the Carriage Depots on the Up side. Stock was placed in one of the 12 roads (greatest capacity 15 bogies) between the repair shed and the Up Hertford line or the three roads (from five) of the Old Yard on the other side of the latter. The stock of the majority of long-distance trains and some of the suburban trains exercised this manoeuvre. Many of the trains were passed through the washing plant before being accepted into one of the two reception roads near Wood Green No. 4 (Up) box and then stabled in one of the 32 tracks of the Hornsey Nos 1, 2 and 3 Yards. The latter had seven southward roads (four under cover in the 'Coronation' Shed), where a redundant C12 4-4-2T was employed to warm up the sleeping car stock. No. 2 Yard had nine southward roads and two through reception roads. No. 1 Yard (14 southward roads) also gave access to Hornsey Gas Works on the east side by means of wagon turntables. At Bounds Green, there was also a large carriage repair facility built in 1939[8] with 16 roads, many being taken up by reserve stock. Between them, these carriage yards accommodated over 900 coaches and dealt with 1,600 to 2,500 trains a week.

Four Wood Green boxes (Nos 1 and 3 on the Down, Nos 2 and 4 on the Up), Wood Green Tunnel box and Bounds Green box (on the Hertford branch) were necessary to control the complex traffic in the area, including empty stock workings. No. 4 box also dealt with the goods yard, which was on the Up side. From Bounds Green box, a sidings connection led to the adjoining Palace Gates Goods Yard, where there was a two-road engine shed. This siding was upgraded to a running line in 1944 to allow the working of through trains from the Hertford Loop to Temple Mills and other goods yards on the Great Eastern Section.[9]

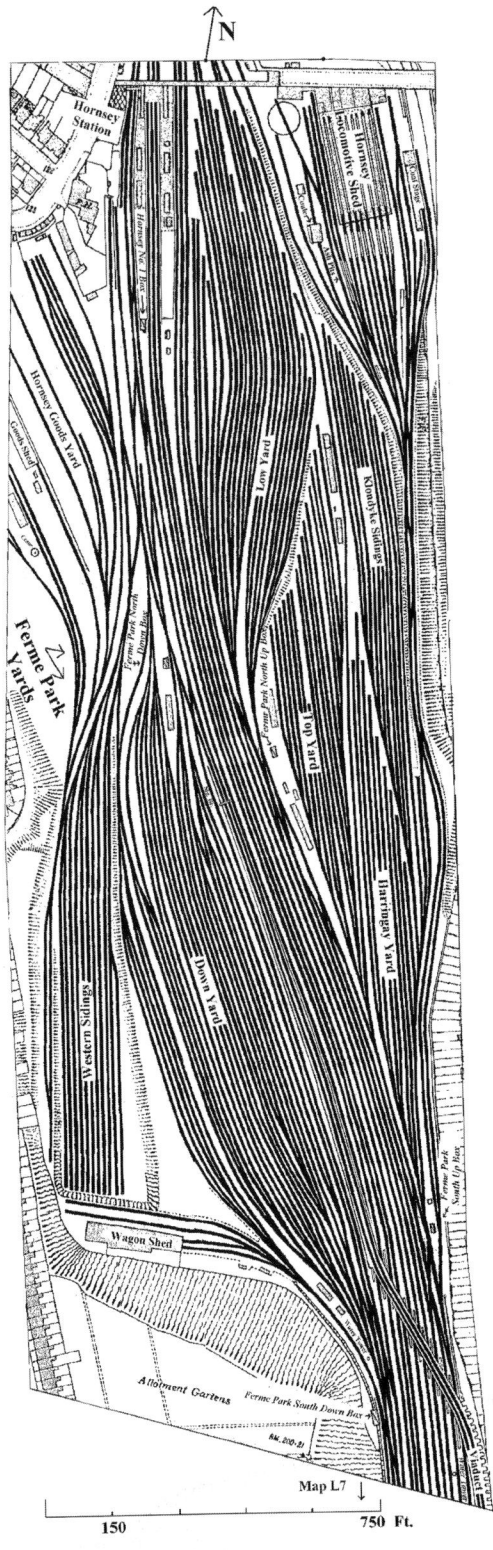

Several groups of goods sidings either side of the main line form Ferme Park Yard. Hornsey station was located top left and the locomotive shed top right.

View south in Ferme Park Down Yard with the flyover to the left and the main lines on the extreme left, *c.* 1935.

Wood Green station had three islands and five platforms. Branching off to the right at Wood Green was the Hertford Loop (the suburban line to Hertford North via Gordon Hill), which extended through Watton-at-Stone to rejoin the main line at Langley Junction, south of Stevenage. The Down Hertford line connected off all three Down lines at Wood Green No. 3 and passed over the main lines by a flyover, which was steeply graded and a source of trouble. The loop was a useful relief route in times of emergency and for the double-track bottlenecks through Hadley Wood and over Welwyn Viaduct. Capable of handling main line expresses, the line was also used regularly for certain main line freights and by one regular Up through passenger train during the war.

The Down Goods line skirted Wood Green station, and while Down Slow No. 2 became the Down Hertford line and climbed up over the flyover, the Goods line passed through a defile known as the 'Khyber Pass' before eventually converging with Down Slow No. 1 at Wood Green Tunnel box. The Up Hertford line, which from Bounds Green box was separated from its Down counterpart, connected only with the Up Carriage line at Wood Green No. 2. Thus, Up Hertford trains had their own platform on the far side of the easternmost island, while Up local trains in the Slow line had a platform face on each side; as at Finsbury Park, their passengers could alight on either side of the train. The Up Hertford line connected with the Up Slow and Fast main lines at the south end of the station adjacent to No. 4 box, after which it became the Up Goods line. Skirting all on the left was the Up Carriage line from Bounds Green Depot.

As soon as the Hertford Loop diverged, and past a group of seven carriage berthing sidings on the Up side, the end of the series of busy sidings and relief lines down from King's Cross had been reached. Then, only four running lines entered Wood Green Tunnel, the first of five

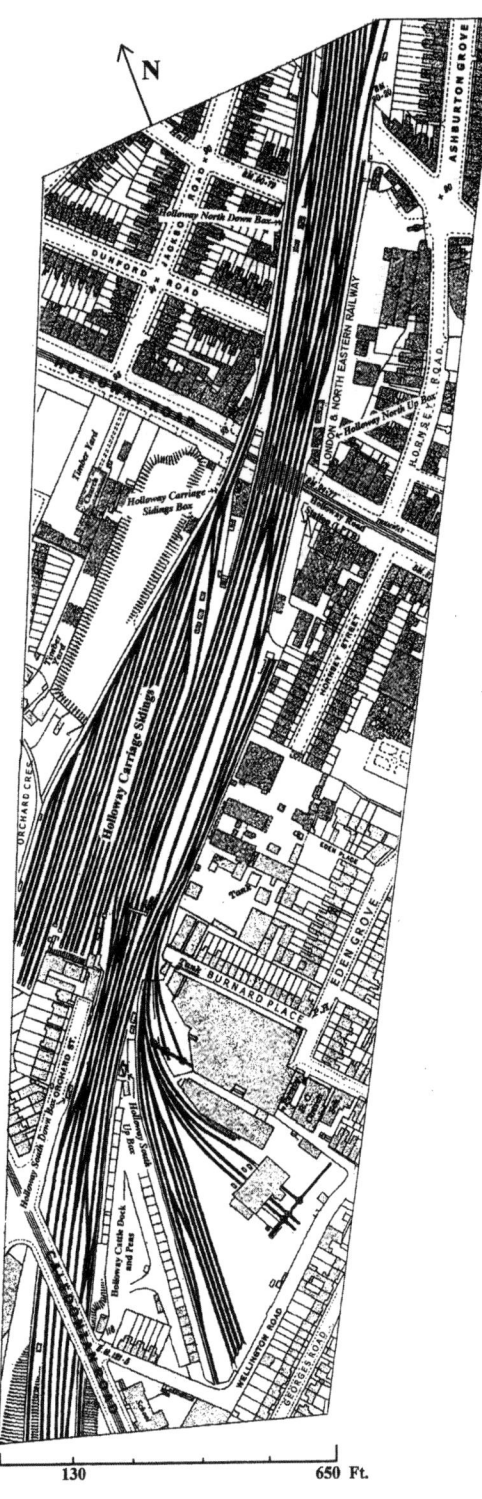

Holloway Carriage Sidings.

tunnels on the climb to Potters Bar. The other four on this stretch were: Barnet, south of Oakleigh Park station; Hadley South and North, on each side of Hadley Wood station; and Potters Bar, about ¾ of a mile south of the station. Between Wood Green and Hatfield (17¾ miles from King's Cross) there were stations at New Southgate & Friern Barnet (for Colney Hatch), Oakleigh Park (for East Barnet), New Barnet, Hadley Wood, Potters Bar & South Mimms, and Brookmans Park—the last being a modern station opened in 1926.

A mile north of New Southgate station was Cemetery box, situated where there had at one time been a terminal for unloading coffins brought from the Necropolis station at Bell Isle outside King's Cross. After Wood Green the four-track main line had one extra Goods line in the Down direction past Oakleigh Park as far as Greenwood box (¾ mile north of New Barnet) and also an extra Up Goods line past New Barnet to Oakleigh Park and from Cemetery box to the south end of New Southgate station. Soon after Wood Green Tunnel, the line swept high on a substantial bridge above the valley. At new Southgate there were sidings on both sides. The 15 or so on the Up side comprised the coal yard and others normally used for storing old coaches and succeeded at Cemetery by another four sidings. On the Down side, the sidings served Southgate Gas Works and the large Friern Mental Hospital. Just north of Oakleigh Park were sidings on the Up side devoted to traffic from Vauxhall Motors at Luton. There were quite extensive facilities at New Barnet: Down and Up Independent Goods Loops, and four sidings on each side (those on the Down used for carriages); on the Up, there was a run-round siding as well as access to the Gas Works—the goods shed was on this side, while on the other were loading platforms on the independent Down Goods line.

The Down Relief line was not available to passenger trains north of New Barnet, and from Greenwood box to just beyond Potters Bar was a two-track bottleneck. At Hadley Wood, the main station buildings were on the road overbridge; at Welwyn North, there were only two platforms, which caused delays when trains stopped. The same also applied at Potters Bar, but the station had refuges and a run-around loop for local trains; on each side, there were limited goods facilities but with loading docks. An indication of the

A4 Class Pacific No. 14 *Silver Link* passes Greenwood signal box with an up express around 1947. The box was later lost during the widening scheme.

problems the bottleneck could cause is that (in 1955) on a weekday 185 passenger trains (many stopping) and 70 freight trains passed through Potters Bar and the station had an average of 1,600 season ticket holders and 630 other passengers per day.

The end of the fully built-up London area was reached at New Barnet, the line passed through Middlesex from Finsbury Park and reached Hertfordshire past Potters Bar. From the latter, through Brookmans Park, to Hatfield, the gradient fell at 1:200 and there were signal boxes at Marshmoor and Red Hall, with sidings at Hawkshead and Marshmoor serving the depots of leading civil engineering firms. In recent years, Hatfield New Town has spread south and spawned a new station at Welham Green, 2¼ miles south of Hatfield, opened in September 1986.

The platforms at Hatfield were partially staggered, the Down one being an island. There was an Up Fast line running between the Down and Up main platform lines. At one end of the Up platform was a bay for London locals separated by the main station buildings from a bay at the north end used by trains off the branch from Hertford North. Trains for the Dunstable and St Albans branch used the outer face of the Down island, although the western face had no connection at the south end with either the Down Slow or Down Fast lines until August 1942. The Down Goods line ran between No. 1 and No. 3 boxes independently over on the west side, giving access to the Down Yard and the two-road locomotive depot. Hatfield had to handle much of the goods traffic of the branches, especially during the war. The Down Yard had four northward and two southward roads, while the Up Yard (with the main goods shed) had nine southward and five northward roads; the Up Yard was just north of the station. Access to all main lines and the St Albans branch was controlled by No. 2 box.

The branch to St Albans (Abbey station) from Hatfield quickly diverged to the left, but on to Welwyn Garden City (three miles), there were six running lines, the outermost on each side constituting the beginning of the branches to Dunstable (Down side) and Hertford North (Up side), which both diverged north of Welwyn Garden City. Halfway along this stretch the extensive Twentieth Mile Gravel & Brick Works was passed, with its sidings on the Up side and fed by a tramway that crossed over the ECML from the works on the west side. Welwyn Garden City station was built in 1926 (previously being a halt) with a fine neo-Georgian building in keeping with the town's architecture. There were two island platforms with four tracks between them, carrying on for nearly a mile to Digswell Viaduct. There were several substantial factories, each with private sidings, on the east side of Welwyn Garden City and on the branches—one of the prominent ones being Shredded Wheat Mills. Before the war, the traffic was handled by a modest goods yard on the Up side, but this was overwhelmed by the intense usage (as well as at Hatfield) and a new marshalling yard (with seven through roads) had to be built on the Up side.

The passenger service on the Hertford branch from Hatfield ceased in June 1951, while the track and signalling were maintained for some years subsequently for handling private sidings traffic, before coming to an end in September 1963. The passenger service to St Albans, which had no through trains except during the war, stopped in October 1951 and that to Dunstable (LMSR) in April 1965. When the Hertford branch was closed, there were still six trains per day, although on the St Albans branch just one—compared to ten in 1939. The branch to Luton and Dunstable had many private sidings—not least Vauxhall Motors—

Welwyn Garden City station—seen here looking north in the 1930s—was opened on 20 September 1926 as a result of the development of the area, although a halt had been in use since 1920.

and consequently, goods traffic was active until closure in January 1966, although trains continued between Luton and Dunstable from the Leighton Buzzard direction until 1989. After Nationalisation, the sections west of Hill End and of Harpenden East, on the St Albans and Dunstable branches respectively, went over to the London Midland Region in April 1950, but ex-LNER locomotives continued to work through to Leighton Buzzard during the 1950s.

The 14¼ miles from Hatfield to Hitchin climbed mainly at 1:200 to a summit near Woolmer Green box, passing over the substantial Digswell (Welwyn) Viaduct, high over the Mimram Valley south of Welwyn North station, and then through Welwyn South and North Tunnels. These features are the reason for the persisting 2½-mile bottleneck, relieved only by the Hertford Loop. Many passenger and freight trains called at the two-platform Welwyn North station, with the latter traffic being handled in two small goods sidings located on each side of the south end. The convergence and crossover at Digswell were worked remotely from Welwyn North box, while Woolmer Green box operated the crossover and divergence of the line to four tracks at the other end of the bottleneck.

A long descent at 1:200 then began for the next 20 miles, taking the line through Stevenage, Hitchin and Arlesey. At 25 miles from King's Cross was Knebworth station after which came the junction and crossovers at Langley. Here, the Hertford Loop joined from the east side as the Down line burrowed under the main lines to join on the left just before Langley water troughs. This facility[10] (27½ miles from King's Cross) was the first of six sets on the main line, the others being: Werrington, 80 miles from King's Cross, near Werrington Junction; Muskham, 122¼ miles from King's Cross, north of Newark; Scrooby, 146 miles, between Ranskill and Bawtry; Wiske Moor, 219¾ miles, north of Northallerton; and Lucker, 316½ miles, north of Newham. Each was provided with water-softening apparatus and a siding for the wagons (usually old tenders) to receive the sludge produced by the treatment of the water.

B1 No. 61099 hauls a King's Cross-bound train from Cambridge through Welwyn North station on 2 June 1951. *Picture: B. W. L. Brooksbank*

Ivatt C1 Class Atlantic No. 3284 collects water from Langley troughs while working an unidentified Pullman service—either the 'West Riding' or 'Queen of Scots' Pullman trains, which were operated by King's Cross C1s between 1925 and 1935.

At Langley, the sludge siding was outside the Down line from Hertford and connected to two long sidings for sorting main line carriages and ambulance trains during the war. Northwards from the junction was a goods and coal yard with wharf and long refuge siding. Stevenage (and Knebworth before the junction) was well endowed with goods facilities, including loading docks and refuge sidings. Beyond Stevenage on the Down side were a couple of sidings at Wymondley. The Down Relief line was goods only[11] between Stevenage North and Hitchin South boxes. Hitchin was the limit of outer-suburban services from King's Cross.

On the Up side at Hitchin South (and slightly elevated) was a large Engineer's yard consisting of four roads each way from the working site in the middle. Here, track was fabricated for the ECML in the London area, although in 1954 much of the work was lost to Chesterton Yard at Cambridge. Between Hitchin South box and the station were carriage sidings on the Down side with four tracks, cattle pens and loading docks; on the Up side were a number of dispersed goods roads and a long locomotive yard stretching from the shed behind the Up platform. Hitchin station's entrance was on the Down side and there were platforms on the slow lines only, which sloped down to the station buildings. There were four tracks between the Down and Up sides, the Fast lines passing through the centre; an Up Goods and extra siding passed behind the station buildings.

Varying from the LNER locomotives that predominated in the area were engines from the LMSR, which arrived at Hitchin on local passenger and goods trains off the ex-MR branch from Bedford. The local trains (about four a day) to Hitchin from Bedford Midland Road were worked by MR 0-4-4Ts (before the war) or 2-6-2Ts from Bedford shed. A diesel railcar took over in September 1958, giving a more frequent service through from Northampton until it ceased in January 1962; goods services stopped in December 1963. Exchange traffic with the LMSR at Hitchin amounted to some 200–400 wagons per week during the war.

At the north end of the station, the important secondary line to Cambridge branched off on the Up side at Cambridge Junction. The MR branch to Bedford also diverged at this point on the Down side. There were substantial yards on both sides dealing with the considerable freight traffic off these lines. Hitchin Yard box controlled movements in and out of the Down Yard (12 roads) and Cambridge Junction the Up Yard (10 lines and Gas Works) that curved round parallel to the Cambridge line. The LMSR Yard[12] was nearby off the Bedford branch and controlled by its own box—Hitchin LMS.

Hitchin to Peterborough

The next stretch of 44¼ miles of the ECML to Peterborough was a high-speed section, as the only slight difficulty was the 1:200 from Huntingdon North to Leys, just south of Abbots Ripton station. At Arlesey and Sandy stations, there were short two-track bottlenecks because the Down Relief line north of Hitchin was only a Goods line, as was the Up relief line, most of the way from Huntingdon, except from Paxton Box to Sandy (exclusive), from there to Biggleswade South and from Arlesey (exclusive) to Cadwell box. Turn-outs to the Fast lines were provided at each station and also at Paxton (full crossover), Sandy North Junction (from 1940), Langford and Cadwell (both full crossovers).

The flat farming country between Hitchin and Peterborough required few connections and facilities to be offered with the ECML, although at Cadwell there was an Up siding, unlocked by Three Counties box. Further on, there was a substantial brickworks on the Down side and a limeworks on the Up, each served by sidings and a tramway. Then, at Three Counties station, the remains of a branch trailed in on the Up side, which had served a large lunatic asylum situated one mile away to the east. At Langford Bridge (between Arlesey and Biggleswade), there was a goods station on the Down side with several sidings. Biggleswade and Sandy had sizeable goods yards on each side of the main line for handling the district's substantial sugar beet traffic.

At Sandy, the quite important LMSR Bletchley–Cambridge line crossed by a single-line overbridge to the north and shared the station; the line to Cambridge then turned quickly away to the east. This line was single-track from Bedford, and while double east of Sandy, it managed to cope with a great increase in traffic during the war, with no more than a doubling for a half-mile out of Bedford and the installation of passing loops at intermediate stations. An LNER goods yard was on the west side and that of the LMSR on the east—both to the south of the station—and between the yards, there were two long, northward-facing sidings where exchange traffic was handed over before the war.

In 1944, these were upgraded to fully-signalled connections between each track of the two major routes. Westbound trains of the LMSR took the outer face of the Up island platform at Sandy, while eastbound trains had their own platform complete with London & North-Western Railway-style signal box at the south end. There were about seven stopping trains per day in 1939, with five on Sundays, and this level remained high during the war as well as into the 1950s when the motive power was ex-GER 4-4-0s and LMSR Classes. The service improved with dieselisation in the 1960s, but the line was closed in January 1968 nevertheless.

Nearly 1½ miles north of Sandy was Sandy North Junction (from September 1940) where the west to north loop converged from the LMSR line. Next was Everton box and then Tempsford (with Down side goods yard), followed by St Neots. Between Tempsford and St Neots, Little Barford power station was built in 1941–1942, with half a dozen reception sidings laid at a slightly lower level than the main line. As they were on the Down side, coal trains had to perform a complicated series of manoeuvres to gain access to the Up ECML. St Neots had extra goods independent lines in each direction, and on the Down side a substantial goods yard with loading dock, granary, etc. Between St Neots and Offord & Buckden, all four lines were interconnected at Paxton box and northwards, the Up Slow was again only a Goods line from Huntingdon North No. 1 box.

Huntingdon North station had ample passenger facilities, with respectable station house on the Up side and generous canopies over the single Up platform and the Down side, where the Down Slow line had a platform face making an island. This was supplemented by a Down goods independent line, but there were no relief lines. Generous goods facilities were provided by two yards on the Down side and one on the Up. No. 1 box controlled the crossovers and yard movements at the south end of Huntingdon North and No. 2 box those at the north end. Fifteen trains each way on the main line stopped during the week (six on Sundays), but these were all slow trains, taking 1½ to 2 hours to get to or from London, except for one fast Up train in the morning with no similar evening service.

Huntingdon North station looking south on 28 May 1956, with goods yard on the right.
Picture: R. Stephenson, B. W. L. Brooksbank Collection

Huntingdon also had an LMSR branch from Kettering. This passed through from the west about a mile south of Huntingdon North station and went under the ECML before running parallel over the River Ouse, then veering away sharply just before Huntingdon East station. North and east stations almost adjoined and were connected on the Up side of the ECML at the south end (No. 1 box) by a short single-track loop used only once or twice a day by transfer goods. The branch was seldom used, but during the 1940s, ex-MR 2-4-0s worked the line through to Cambridge over LNER lines via St Ives. In 1939, there were additional LNER trains (four) between Huntingdon East and St Ives, worked by engines from the single-line shed at the former. In the 1950s, the motive power was upgraded to Ivatt 2MT 2-6-0s from Kettering or Cambridge. The line was closed in June 1959, although the loop from Huntingdon North remained open for goods as far as Godmanchester until June 1962.

In the 1930s, the LNER increased line capacity on the main lines, by erecting automatic colour-light signals to break up long block sections, at 24 sites between Edinburgh and London. At the time, from Huntingdon North No. 1 box (at the London end of the station), there was only a Down goods line as far as the summit at Leys and onwards to Holme. North of Leys, where there was a turnout remotely controlled from Stukeley box, through Abbots Ripton to Connington South box, there was also an Up Goods line, which eventually was extended to Huntingdon No. 2, leaving one line in the Up direction only through Huntingdon station.

At Abbots Ripton, the island platforms were staggered but only the Down side had one face available for stopping passenger trains, and the goods facilities (on the Down side) were minimal. There were some sidings at Connington on the Up side as well as refuse tips on either side, but during the war, a large yard, comprising 12 through roads, a hump and facilities for locomotives was built at Connington on the Down side, remaining in use after the conflict. Connington Yard was controlled at each end by new Connington South and North boxes. Holme station had a bay on the Up side, used by trains on the branch eastwards to Ramsey North, goods yards on each side—that on the Up having six roads, also an Up Goods loop (built during the war) in addition to a run-around loop. The

An Up express headed by A3 Class Pacific No. 2751 *Humorist*—fitted with Kylchap double blastpipe and chimney and wing-type deflectors—races through Abbots Ripton station around 1939.

Ramsey branch had just three passenger services (two mixed) and three goods workings each day.[13] Most of these ceased as early as June 1947, although goods trains continued until July 1973.

Peterborough

Yaxley & Farcet station, 3¾ miles from Peterborough, signalled the southern edge of the city. From this point to Stoke box (28 miles), four running lines were available, although most of the extra tracks were only Goods lines operated under 'Permissive' or 'No Block' regulations. Extra Down and Up Goods lines—called 'Brick Roads'—ran between Yaxley and Fletton Junction boxes. There was then only one Down Goods line, which continued past Peterborough North station to Spital Junction, where it crossed over to the Up side and in doing so conflicted with both Down and Up main lines. This position continued as far as Werrington Junction, where it reverted to the Down side to become the Down Slow as far as Stoke box.

Between Yaxley and Fletton Junction, there were six sets of sidings off branches on the Down side and five on the Up; the main Up group at Fletton had 11 roads. Yaxley station had its own goods yard on the Down side with cattle pens and loading wharf. The sidings were principally for servicing the vast brickfields of the London Brick Company, Forder's and Eastwoods. There were brickworks on both sides of the ECML, with an aerial ropeway crossing the line near Fletton Junction, all penetrated by miles of railway. At Fletton Junction, there was also a long siding serving a large sugar beet factory, more brickworks and other premises. Trailing in on the Down side was the Botolph branch (or Fletton Loop), which formerly ran to the LNWR line at Longville Junction and had been used by a GNR service to Leicester Belgrave Road until 1916, then for freight until 1929 when the connection was severed. During the war, there were thoughts of reinstating the connection but the line lost out to the Sandy Loop, although in 1947, the decision was reversed and brick traffic to the West Midlands commenced.

The main line entered Peterborough on a pair of long viaducts—one was constructed in 1924—with brick arches and three-span steel girder bridges over the River Nene. Just before the river, the lines from Peterborough East (GER) station ran underneath. These were LMSR lines and included the former LNWR lines to Northampton and Rugby, from which diverged at Fletton Junction the former MR line that then crossed the Nene on its own bridge and went past North station on its way via Melton Mowbray to Leicester and Birmingham or Nottingham and Derby. The MR line, conveying through LNER trains from the east, connected with the ECML by means of Down and Up loops between Nene Junction (LMSR) box and Crescent Junction (LNER) box just south of Peterborough North, then again at Westwood Junction and Wisbech Junction beyond. Once over the Nene bridges, the ECML passed Nene Carriage Sidings (14 dead-end sidings plus three through to the LMSR line), situated on the Down side opposite the power station and the South Yard, which adjoined the goods station and tranship shed on the Up side.

Peterborough North station had just one Up platform (No. 2), at which all main line through passenger trains had to be accommodated. Yet, the prodigious flow of freight on the Up had either to be fitted in between these trains or otherwise pass across the Down main lines to the Up Slow on the western side of the station and then back across at Crescent Junction. As they had to cross all through lines at Spital Junction, finding paths for Down freights was only a little less than a conundrum for the signalmen than was slipping the Up freights through. Moreover, owing to pathing problems in the cramped layout more LMSR lines trains to Leicester called at the North station than did those from Leicester. In 1939, each weekday saw 45 to 50 freight or mineral trains scheduled to be passed on the main line tracks through Peterborough North each way, between about 55 passenger trains; there would also be numerous unscheduled trains.

The Up platform had a short bay (platform 1) at its south end and a loading dock at each end. The main Down platform (No. 3) had two bays (Nos 4 and 5) at the north end and an outer face (No. 6) for excursions, and this was a through line but not signalled for reversible working. Trains originating at Peterborough North for the Lincolnshire and the Midland & Great Northern (M&GN) lines normally used platforms 4 and 5. It was possible for trains bound for Peterborough East and beyond to leave from any of the three through platforms and from No. 1 bay, but in practice, platform 6 was readily available to trains coming from Peterborough East and the GE Section, including the MR line trains. Services to the east had to reverse into platform 6; platform 3 was used rarely for Up trains and then only for those originating. On the west side of the station, there were the Up Slow and Down Goods lines, but no more platforms. Beyond these again were the Up and Down LMS through lines. Peterborough North also featured a sharp curve that necessitated slowing to just 20 mph for even the fastest expresses; Up trains were also restricted to 30 mph over the older Nene bridge. Heavy Down expresses that stopped often had to be banked away by a pilot, though only to the end of the platform. The Down platform could only accommodate 12 bogies and the Up platform 13, which resulted in the long trains prevalent during the war having to draw up to the platforms more than once.

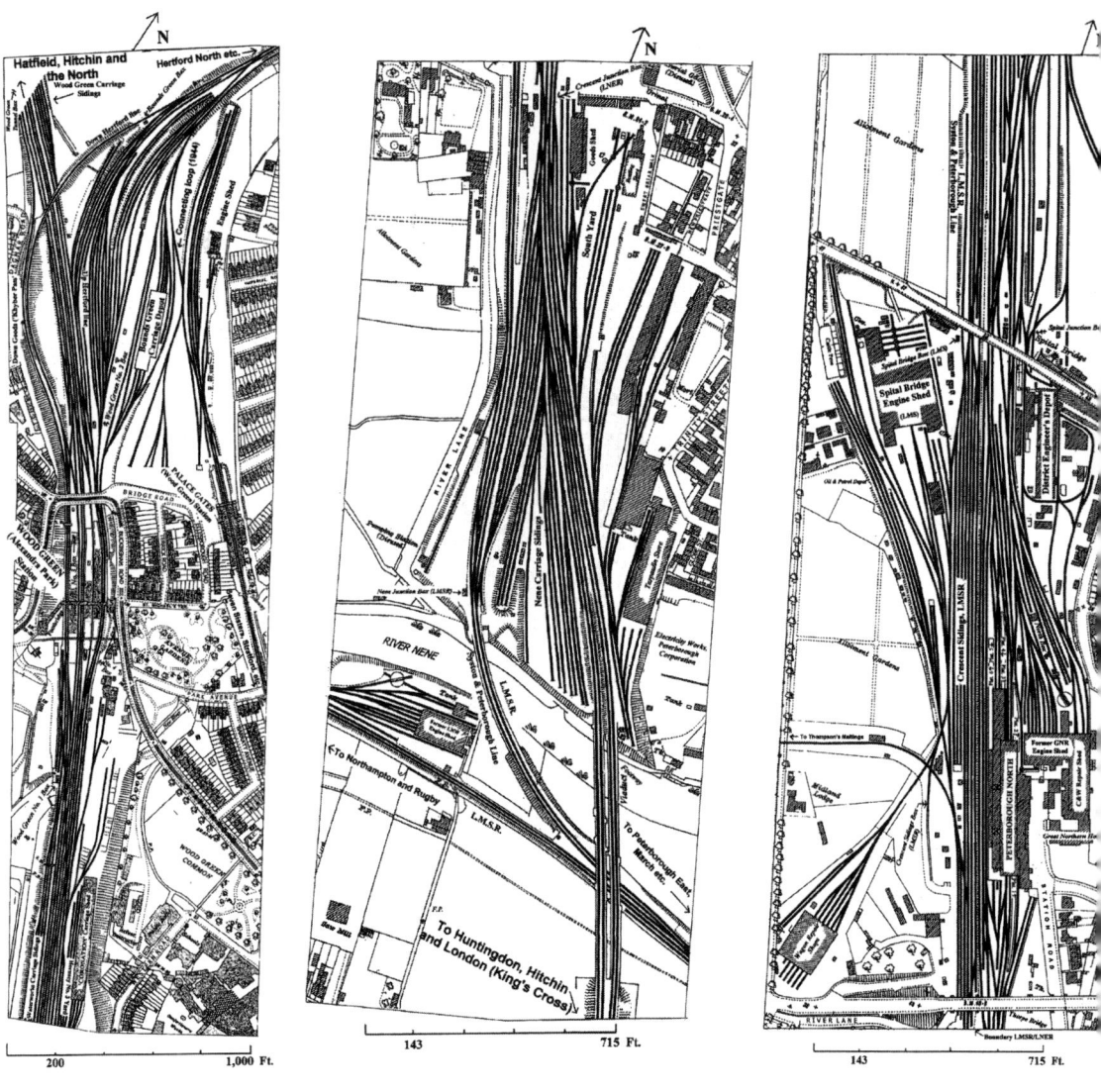

Above left: Wood Green station with the junction for the Hertford line and Bounds Green Carriage Depot to the right.

Above middle: Peterborough Bridge Junction to Crescent Junction, 1926.

Above right: Peterborough North station area just after Grouping.

N2 Class 0-6-2T No. 69579 at the south end of platform 2 (Up) at Peterborough North station on 18 August 1962; the engine would be sent for scrap the following month.
Photograph: B. W. L. Brooksbank

The track layout at both ends of Peterborough North was complex. Crescent Junction (LNER) box regulated the manoeuvres at the south end and North and Spital Junction boxes those at the north end. At this end, there were not only the links between each of the platforms and the Down and Up main lines, but also from the parcels dock, the 60-foot locomotive turntable and the Carriage & Wagon Sidings, all on the Up side. Spital Junction box also had to manage the many other short sidings and spurs just north of the station on the Up side, devoted to the District Engineer's depot and a minor locomotive yard. The LMSR's own Crescent Junction box controlled—along with Spital Bridge (LMSR) box—the access to their Crescent Sidings, Spital Bridge shed, C&W sidings and several private sidings, all being on the west side and independent of the LNER facilities.

Trains to be seen at Peterborough North consisted of several principal flows. First, there were expresses from King's Cross; secondly, there was the main line freight traffic, consisting of fitted and semi-fitted trains running mainly at night and loose-coupled (mainly coal) trains from Peterborough to London; and thirdly, Peterborough North was the junction off the main line for most of Lincolnshire. Much of this secondary traffic for Lincolnshire, by the subsidiary main line of the GNR that branched off at Werrington Junction, started at Peterborough and went to Spalding, Boston, Frisby, Louth and Grimsby. By this route, certain expresses ran through from King's Cross to Cleethorpes regularly and also to Skegness in the summer. Before the war, all the LNER trains from the Peterborough East direction were secondary services from March, Ely, Cambridge or Norwich, while during and after the war, through expresses were run this was from Colchester to the North and Scotland.

To and from East Anglia, there was the North Norfolk traffic of the M&GN until its operations were taken over by the LNER in October 1936. The M&GN ran all the way to Yarmouth and Lowestoft from Peterborough North, joining the MR line at Westwood

Junction and then branching off at Wisbech Junction to climb over the ECML on the 'Rhubarb Bridge', north of New England Yard, and proceeding eastwards to Sutton Bridge, South Lynn (for King's Lynn) and then right across Norfolk to Melton Constable, Cromer Beach, Norwich City and Yarmouth Beach. There were also independent LMSR trains from Peterborough East to Leicester, etc., all of which called at Peterborough North, although after the war some coming from Peterborough and one Down train passed through on the LMSR lines to the west of the station.

From March or Cambridge, the motive power of the LNER passenger trains was usually GER 'Claud Hamilton' 4-4-0s or B17 4-6-0s. The locomotives used on the Lincolnshire services during the 1940s were GNR 4-4-2s and 4-4-0s and GCR 4-6-0s, 4-4-2s and 4-4-0s, stabled at New England, Peterborough (and the sub-shed at Spalding), Boston, Lincoln or Immingham and Gresley K2s and K3s from New England or Boston. After the war, the B1s largely took over, then as early as 1955, the DMUs (based at Lincoln or Norwich) were used on the local services in Lincolnshire and on the line to March, Ely and Cambridge.

By 1939, the basic M&GN passenger services were being worked by 4-4-0s of GNR origin, in addition to those from the GER and GCR, which worked to Peterborough North, mainly from South Lynn shed. In 1949, B12/3s and K2s were also drafted to the M&GN. Then, in the 1950s, a large number of the new Class 4MT 2-6-0s of LMS Ivatt design were brought to the line and took over almost all of the passenger and some of the freight traffic. The motive power originally owned by the M&GN was scrapped before the war (passenger locomotives) and towards the end/after the conflict (freight engines).

The basic service (weekdays only) on the M&GN from Peterborough North comprised two trains through to Yarmouth, one as far as Melton Constable and in 1939, an 'express' (with

M&GN 4-4-0 No. 42 (of MR design) stands with a train at Peterborough North station in the mid-1930s.

through coaches from King's Cross) for Cromer; in addition, there were several stopping trains to King's Lynn via South Lynn. In the war, there were just four trains, all through to Yarmouth.

In peacetime summers—especially Saturdays—the M&GN transformed into a major holiday route as numerous expresses from the Midlands travelled via Saxby and Sutton Bridge onwards to the bracing Norfolk seaside resorts. Despite the many happy memories created on these family outings, the M&GN system was one of the first major rail closures pre-Beeching when the services stopped on 2 March 1959; much of the nightly freight services had ceased in 1954. From the summer of 1959, the loss of the trains on the M&GN was compensated to some extent by running through Midland line trains to the Norfolk Coast via Peterborough East and the former GER line via March and the Ely North Curve. From the outset, many were steam-hauled as far as Spital Bridge, where a new diesel would take charge.

A major part of the main line freight traffic at Peterborough North consisted of unbraked trains in the Up direction and empties in the Down, also of general goods in both directions and bricks from the Fletton brickworks—some of which were carried in distinctive high-capacity bogie wagons. The working timetables (WTTs) show that on weekdays in 1939, some 50 main line freight trains each way were dealt with at the ECML yards at Peterborough; the number in wartime only rose by 20 trains. Peterborough New England shed's large stud of 2-6-0s, 2-8-0s and 2-10-0s were the main motive power of choice for such services; long-distance freight trains usually had a fresh engine attached at Peterborough. Of course, by no means did all freight trains terminate at Peterborough (New England); rather than going along the main line via Grantham, many to/from Doncaster went up the Joint line via Spalding, or else via Boston, also some of those to/from the Nottingham direction and Grantham went via Sleaford.

The normal motive power of the MR line passenger trains on the LMSR in the 1940s were 2P 4-4-0s, on the LNWR-line trains Stanier 2-6-4Ts or 'Black Fives'; in the 1950s, BR Standard 4-6-0s were common. The 4F 0-6-0s also worked some of the trains and were the principal motive power of the summer Saturday and excursion services. The lateral flow of freight traffic at Peterborough on the LMSR lines was heavy: each weekday about 25 Up (westbound) trains were booked to leave Spital or Wisbech Sidings, but there were 30 to 35 arrivals because many Down LNWR-line trains from Northampton and Rugby diverted at Seaton to Luffenham on the MR in order to reach these yards, whence it was tripped to Peterborough East, Bridge and Stanground Sidings. Additionally, around 10 trains each way passed along the LNWR line under the ECML directly to Peterborough East and there were special workings further east, mainly to Whitemoor Yard. Westwood Yard dispatched (and Spital received) approximately seven freight trains each weekday to and from the M&GN line. During the war, the needs of the many East Anglian Airfields in particular led to an even more prolific east to west flow of freight. The LMSR freight trains were hauled by many 3F and 4F 0-6-0s and 7F 0-8-0s from the LNWR lines, some Hughes 5MT 2-6-0s and (from the mid-1940s) Stanier 8F 2-8-0s, while Garratts from Toton also arrived quite regularly. The LMSR/LMR locomotives came from a remarkably wide range of depots in the Midland and Western Divisions.

Northwards from Peterborough North were a succession of yards. On the Down side were the LMSR yards, comprising the Crescent and Spital Bridge coal sidings and adjoined the LMSR Spital Bridge locomotive shed. These were situated just across the LNER relief

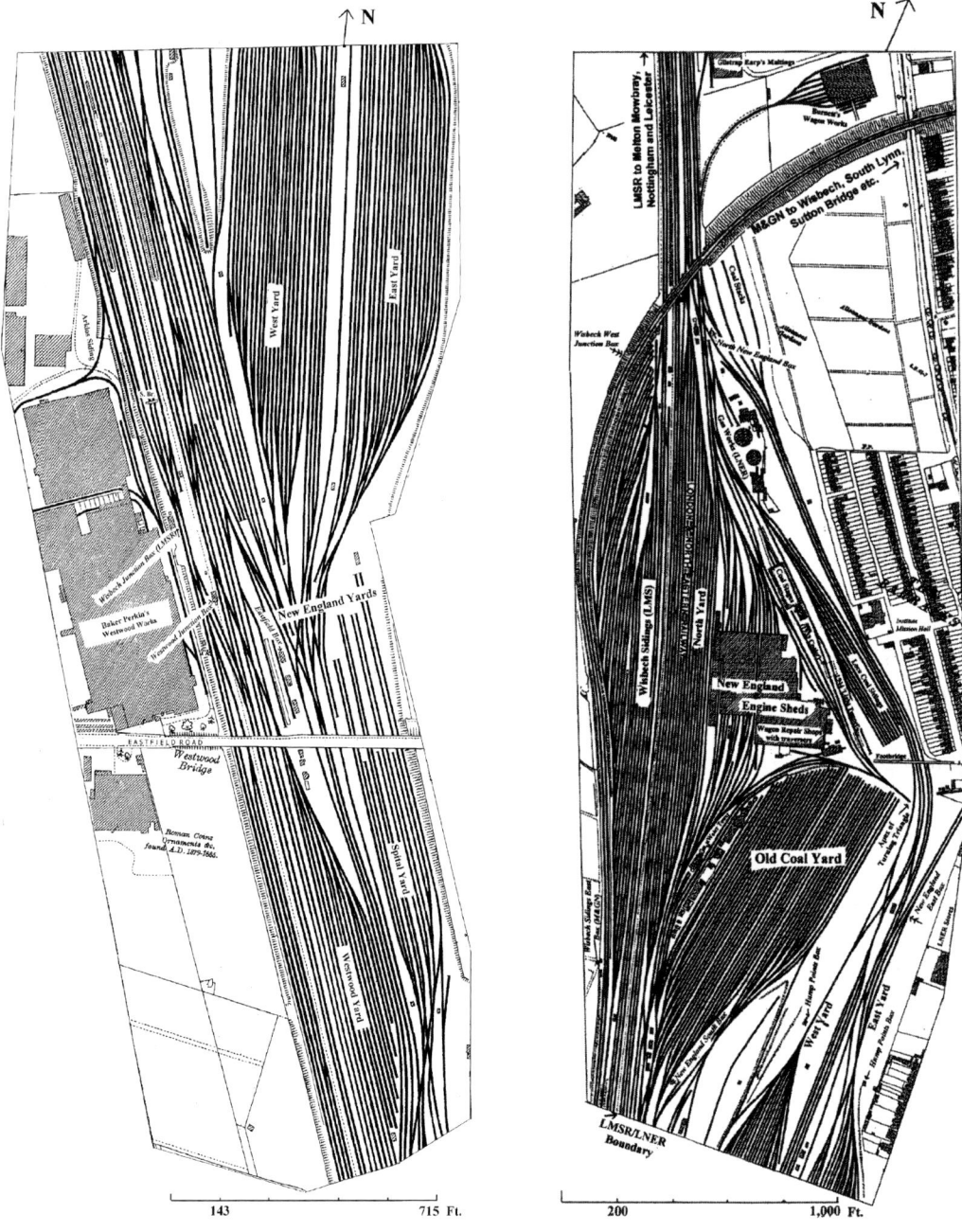

Above left: Peterborough Westwood and New England East and West complexes, 1926.

Above right: The northern group of sidings at Peterborough with New England engine shed sandwiched in the middle.

lines and the LMSR lines skirting the North station and connecting with various industrial premises. Then, at Wisbech Junction (LMSR), the former M&GN double line diverged left to skirt the west side of Wisbech LMSR Sidings: these comprised about 18 through roads and 11 south-facing stops, stretching from Wisbech Sidings East box to Wisbech West Junction box, after which the M&GN crossed over the ECML on the 'Rhubarb Bridge' and headed east. Also at Wisbech Junction, connections converged from the ECML at Westwood Junction, so leading trains from the latter to the M&GN line; the Down (southbound) LMSR line was relieved by a Down Goods between Wisbech West and Wisbech Junction.

On the Up side of the main line were the LNER Yards, which were among the largest marshalling complexes on the ECML. These began at Spital Junction, where the Down Goods line of the ECML, after crossing the main lines, threw off separate lines to serve the four Down Yards, while the Up coal, goods and engine lines converged into the Up main and slow lines for the south. Adjacent to the ECML were Westwood Yard (Down, nine north-facing and three through roads) and Spital Yard (Up, 11 south-facing roads) behind it. These were followed by the extensive New England Yard complex, engaged primarily with the remarshalling of coal trains southbound and empties northbound. The North Yard (Down, with eight through and three reception roads) was next to the ECML beyond Westwood Yard; Old Coal Yard (Up, with 43 south-facing roads) flanked each side of the Up coal and engine lines that ran past the locomotive depot on the west side. Three lines (Up Goods, Up arrival and Down transfer) swept round the whole complex on the eastern side from North New England (later New England North) box to New England East box and eventually to Spital Junction box. West Yard (Down) and East Yard (Up), each with a hump at the north end serving 20 through roads, lay between the Old Coal, Westwood and Spital Yards, separated by the above Up Goods line, which passed through the yards to Eastfield box and then divided into Up Goods and Up coal lines to Spital Junction. Flanking this through Up Goods line were four Down reception tracks, on one side and four Up reception lines on the other, servicing respectively the West and East Yards.

A Down Goods line ran on the Up side of the main line and this was supplemented past North Yard by three additional Down departure lines converging beyond North New England box into the Down Goods going on to Werrington Junction. From there, the Up Goods spawned an Up coal line, and at North New England, the two lines divided again into the more easterly Up Goods and Up arrival lines and the Up coal line through to New England South box and giving access to North Yard, also indirectly the Old Coal Yard and to West and East Yards. Beside these Up lines was a Down transfer line—a departure road from West Coal Yard—also looped around from New England East to North New England. Lastly, north of the M&GN line bridge, on the Up side were three substantial rail-connected factories: Cambrian Wagon Works, Gilstrap Earp's Malthouse and Brotherhood's Engineering Works.

Movements within the New England complex were controlled by four signal boxes, none of which signalled any traffic on the ECML. North New England box worked with Walton box on the main line to the north and also handled traffic on the Up side factories. As well, it controlled all movements of locomotives at the north end of the locomotive depot and trains in and out of North Yard; it worked also with New England East box for the movements through the complex described above. At the other end was New England South box, which controlled the movements southwards from the locomotive depot and the North Yard, also worked with Eastfield and Westwood Junction boxes. The fourth box was Eastfield, which passed Up freights to Spital Junction box and Down ones to New England South or East boxes, while controlling the exit from Old Coal Yard, as well as engines and Up coal trains from New England South and the movements to and from East and West Yards. Westwood Junction box worked the main line with Spital Junction to the south and to the north with Walton box and Werrington Junction box—where ultimate routing was determined. Spital Junction and Westwood Junction between them controlled the traffic in and out of Westwood Yard, which was not really part of the New England complex.

The Peterborough area had a large number of yards, necessitating countless trip workings between them, many of which passed through or beside Peterborough North station. The New England complexes along with the Westwood and Spital Yards dealt with most of the north–south traffic on the ECML, Westwood being particularly important at night dispatching Down ECML freight trains from London with M&GN traffic, while Old Coal Yard dealt with Up rough goods, East Yard with Up coal, Spital with local Up goods, West with Down rough goods and North with Down empties.

The traffic of other Peterborough Yards was: Wisbech (ex-MR, receiving from the M&GN, GNR, LNWR and GER lines, forwarding to LMSR destinations in the Midlands and North), Spital Bridge (ex-MR, receiving from the GER, GNR and MR, forwarding to the M&GN, also local traffic), Peterborough East (ex-LNWR receiving from the GER and M&GN, forwarding to the LNWR), Peterborough Bridge (ex-GER, forwarding to the LNWR, MR, M&GN and GNR), and Stanground (ex-GER, receiving from Spital Bridge and New England, forwarding to Whitemoor). Rationalisation began when Peterborough East and Bridge Yards were joined together in 1952. Then, early in 1954, Crescent, Spital Bridge and Wisbech Yards were closed down. After that a number of freights from the LMR worked straight through to Whitemoor Yard, where spare capacity in the Down Empties yard was employed to make up trains formerly dealt with at Peterborough; new braked services from Whitemoor to Niddrie West and Ardsley were introduced, and—departing in the Up direction—to destinations on the LMR.

Even after this rationalisation, in 1955, 800 wagons passed westwards and 1,100 eastwards, and still over a quarter of the wagons handled at New England had to be tripped to other yards. The numerous yards to be shunted and all the transfer trips still required a large fleet of 0-6-0s and 0-6-0Ts to be maintained at New England, also several at Spital Bridge. The New England yards dealt with between 3,000 and 4,000 wagons per day, and yet only East and West Yards had a hump—otherwise, shunting was the conventional type.

Peterborough to Grantham

Between Peterborough and Grantham, there were 29 miles of undulating countryside, and from Peterborough North to Stoke box, there were four running lines. The relief lines were signalled most of the way for goods trains, and there was a short stretch through Tallington station with no Down Relief line at all. Therefore, the Down Slow through Tallington was signalled for passenger trains only as far as Greatford box (north of Tallington) and at

Corby station, while the Up Slow was so signalled all the way from Stoke box but only as far as Tallington (exclusive). There were connections between the main and relief lines at the four intermediate stations and intermediately on the Down at Lolham and Greatford boxes and at Burton turn-out (near Stoke) and on the Up at Helpston.

At Werrington Junction (three miles from Peterborough North), the lines to Spalding and beyond veered off to the north-east. Directly after Werrington Junction were Werrington water troughs. Shortly beyond and ¾ mile south of Helpston box, there was a siding on the Up side for Peterborough Waterworks at Etton, but with a ground frame released by Tallington box. For the first five to six miles out of Peterborough, the MR line to Leicester ran a separate course beside the ECML on the Down side, then through its station at Walton before turning west at Helpston. Afterwards on the ECML came the wayside stations of Tallington, then Essendine, which had junctions for Stamford and Bourne.

Tallington had a fair-sized goods yard on each side, both with a shunting neck, wharf and private sidings, while its island platforms were islands in name only as stopping passenger trains had to use the fast line faces. A similar situation existed at Essendine, where there was an island platform only on the Down side, with an Up Fast line in the centre. The Stamford branch trains used the outer face of the Down island; the Up platform was a semi-island, formed by the Up bay at the south end and used by Bourne branch trains. The Down side sidings were enlarged during the war into a minor yard of five northward roads, and there was an extra Goods line on the Down side between Essendine South and North boxes. In the 1940s, before the branch from Bourne closed (to all traffic—still six passenger workings) in June 1951, engines might appear from the M&GN sub-shed at Bourne as well as from Boston's sub-shed at Sleaford, although most of the Bourne line workings were covered by New England from its sub-shed at Spalding. Trains to Stamford (LNER, Stamford East after Nationalisation), normally worked by a C12 until the 1950s, were diverted to the ex-MR Stamford Town station in March 1957. In June 1959, the six daily passenger trains[14] and the freight trains ceased altogether.

After Essendine came Stoke Bank, which consisted of nine miles at 1:200/178. On the ascent of the incline, there were stations at Little Bytham and Corby (Lincs. LNE): both had sidings on each side of the line and there were also Sidings at Lawnwood, between the two stations. Apart from refuge sidings, there was an additional Up loop at Little Bytham and two at Corby. The Down Goods line between these two places was set aside for stabling freight trains at times of congestion. At Little Bytham some traces of the earthworks remained on the Up side of the private railway to Edenham, built by Lord Willoughby de Eresby to serve his Grimsthorpe estate, closed since 1865. Just to the north, the western link with the M&GN system—the single-track ex-MR line from Saxby to Bourne—passed over the main line. Only four daily passenger trains and two freight trains were scheduled to use this route, although during the war, use by freight trains was more frequent.

At the summit, 345 feet above sea level, and the highest point of the ECML in England, there was a sign saying 'London 100 miles'. Shortly after Stoke box (at the summit), the line began to fall at 1:200 and plunged into Stoke Tunnel (880 yards). On the Down side, immediately thereafter was the junction at Highdyke for the ironstone branch from Sproxton, Stainby and Colsterworth, preceded by a group of five northward sidings and followed by another three south-facing, two being at a higher level. At Highdyke, there could often be seen a local

View north—in May 1956—from the footbridge over the main line at Tallington station (left) with the goods sidings on the right. *Picture: R. Stephenson, B. W. L. Brooksbank Collection*

Thompson A2/3 Pacific No. 60500 *Edward Thompson* passes Stoke signal box, which marked the end of the 19-mile climb from just north of Werrington Junction, with a train bound for Newcastle in the early 1950s.

industrial locomotive off the branch, as well as one or two LNER 2-8-0s. After Highdyke, there was a relief line only on the Up side and at the next station—Great Ponton—the outer face of the island platform on that side was not available to passenger trains. Great Ponton had its main goods facilities on the Down side, but also a yard of three southward goods and two northwards (Engineer's) sidings on the Up side. The ensuing three-mile stretch to Grantham South was broken by automatic signals at Saltersford, where a long loop (worked electrically from Grantham South box) was put in during the war on the Down side.

Grantham

Grantham—105½ miles from King's Cross—was an important junction with the line to Nottingham[15], Derby and Stafford, while eastwards ran a thriving secondary line to Sleaford and Boston, from which trains to Lincoln branched off at Honington. In 1939, there were also four stopping trains to Leicester Belgrave Road, turning off the Nottingham line at Bottesford East Junction and joining the GN&LNW Joint line, to pass through Melton Mowbray as far as Marefield Junction, thence by the GN branch to Leicester. These Grantham-Leicester trains ceased in 1941, but one or two a day were restored after the war, only to stop entirely when the GN&LNW system was closed to passenger trains in December 1953. The major branches required a locomotive depot and yards at Grantham to work them, the GNR and LNER using Grantham as a mid-way point for engine changes on through ECML expresses.

The approach to this major junction was heralded by Grantham South box, where the Down Goods line separated to serve the extensive South Yard or four through 'back' roads and eight dead-end roads, the 'Field' Sidings, Carriage Sidings (four roads) and locomotive depot. On the Up side was Grantham's sizable goods station, its yard and other sidings from which branches served the adjoining engineering works of Aveling Barford and Ruston & Hornsby.[16] The south end of Grantham was controlled by Grantham Yard box, which was on the Up side at the end of platform.

Grantham station's principal buildings were on the Up side and resembled Peterborough North, having an all-over roof. Grantham also only had a single Up through line and platform (No. 2, which accommodated up to 18 bogies), but an extra Down passenger line, the Down through platform (No. 3 with a capacity of 15 bogies) having an outer face (No. 5). The latter was used for many Nottingham line local trains, and there were also bays (Nos 1 and 4) at the north end of each main platform. In 1942, the western (No. 5) platform line, also the Down Goods line that skirted the carriage sidings between Grantham South and North boxes, were resignalled for reversible working in order to keep locals and Up freight trains from the Nottingham line off the Up main. Nevertheless, freight trains from Colwick and other places still had to be passed at some point over all the main lines to the Up side and the number of scheduled trains involved amounted to around 15 a day each way—out of the 45–50 passing through Grantham. North box controlled all these movements off the Nottingham line as well as the main line itself, the carriage and dock sidings on each side and most of the movements in and out of the locomotive depot. The curve at the north end of Grantham station required a speed restriction for trains not

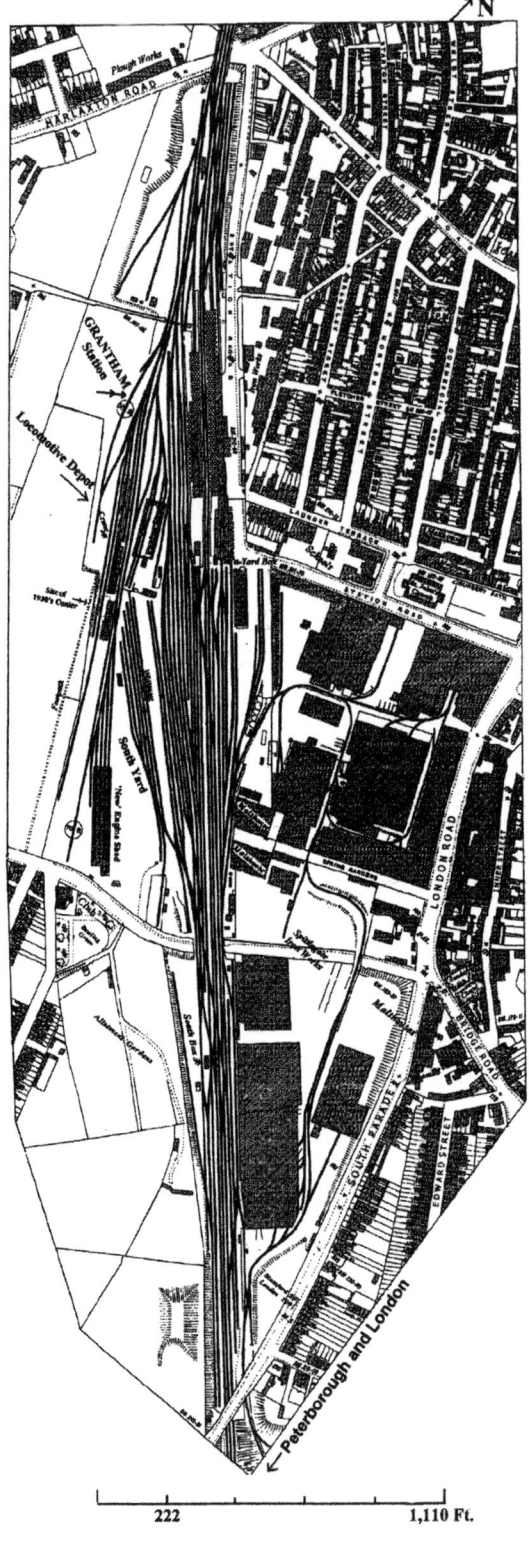

Grantham station, shed and Down Yard in the early 1930s.

Looking south along the main line platforms at Grantham station, May 1956. *Picture: R. Stephenson, B. W. L. Brooksbank Collection*

The busy Grantham North signal box viewed from the north end of the station's Up platform.

stopping; those trains doing so often had difficulty in starting again and on occasions the station pilot was used to provide assistance.

Trains from the Nottingham area were worked mainly by Colwick engines, both of GNR and GCR origins. The most abundant type was the J6 0-6-0, followed by a J1 or J2, a GNR Atlantic or 4-4-0. On eastbound trains the usual locomotives would be GNR or GCR 4-4-2s, 4-4-0s or 0-6-0s from Grantham, Lincoln, Boston or Immingham sheds, while in the 1950s, Grantham shed used B12/3s or L1s. Local services to Lincoln and Boston were converted to operation by DMUs, based at Lincoln as early as mid-1955, while DMUs did not take over the Nottingham line until a few years later.

Grantham to Retford and Doncaster

Northward from Grantham, the double-track ECML and the two tracks of the Nottingham line curved quite sharply to the right—partly on a five-span brick viaduct—for a little over half a mile as far as Barrowby Road box, where the Nottingham line curved away. From 1937, this box controlled Nottingham line trains only, together with the access to Ambergate Yard down on the west side. The actual junction with the ECML was then at Grantham North, although an emergency crossover remained at Barrowby Road. After 1½ miles came Peascliffe Tunnel and the line then went into the Trent Valley at Newark, through wayside stations at Barkston, Hougham and Claypole—the first two with staggered platforms and each with a small goods yard.

At Barkston station was Barkston South Junction, where the lines to Lincoln, Sleaford and elsewhere in Lincolnshire turned off and an extra Down platform was provided on the branch. Just beyond Barkston, a line passed underneath the ECML, connecting the Nottingham line at Allington Junction with the Sleaford line at Barkston East Junction, forming a cut-off that carried holiday trains to the Lincolnshire Coast, in addition to a number of through freights. At Barkston North Junction, a double-track east to north loop came in on the Up side, used by some seasonal or excursion trains from the coast heading northwards. The triangle formed by the junctions at Barkston was regularly used for turning new and repaired locomotives being run-in from Doncaster 'Plant' Works, and both the cut-off and the loops were much used by special traffic during the war. The branch from the Sleaford line at Honington to Lincoln was maintained to a high standard for occasional use as a diversionary route off the ECML. Some local trains conveyed through coaches between Lincoln and King's Cross and the line was also traversed by the Highdyke-Frodingham ironstone trains.

From Grantham, the 46 miles to Rossington (about 5 miles south of Doncaster) were virtually all just double-track, but the traffic density in the 1940s and 1950s remained high, with frequent freights interposed between the expresses, especially north of the junctions at Newark and Tuxford. There were a few loops (those signalled for Absolute Block working are marked '*'), as follows: Down loops at Hougham*, Claypole to Balderton box*, north of Trent box*, Dukeries Junction to Tuxford North Junction (two lines), Lincoln Road box to Markham Siding*, between Retford South and Babworth (two lies as far as Retford North) and between the latter and Canal box, south of Ranskill*, and north of Bawtry; Up loops from Barkston North Junction to near South Junction, from Newark North to

South*, Grove Road to Gamston, Babworth[17] to Retford South, Canal to Babworth, south of Ranskill*, and north of Bawtry.

More loops were created during the war. Otherwise, as along most of the double-track sections of the ECML, there were many refuge sidings, some of which were able to accommodate two or more—even up to five—freight trains. In addition, there were crossovers between the main lines at each station and by the signal boxes at Barrowby Road, Barkston North Junction, Barnby, Trent, Bathley Lane, Lincoln Road, Gamston, Grove Road, Babworth and Scrooby.

Just south of Newark station, an important freight-only line approached on the Down side. After throwing a branch to coal sidings and gas works, it connected to the ECML at Newark South box and the station. Many and varied trains came by this line via the Bottesford Junctions from Colwick Yard and, during the war and afterwards, from the ironstone branches off the GN&LNW Joint line through Harby & Stathern, bound for Doncaster, Hull and elsewhere. Apart from a hiatus during the war, a local passenger service, of just one train per day, ran from Nottingham Victoria to Newark until January 1955, but freight appears to have continued through to April 1987.

Newark had the main buildings of the station (named Newark North Gate from 1950) on the Down side. There was a bay on this side for the Nottingham trains, and the Up platform had a bay at the south end, the Up Slow running behind it between Newark North and South boxes. Between Newark South and the station was the Down Yard (eight roads) and to the west was a small engine shed and turntable; the substantial goods shed was on the Down side just north of the station. An extensive Up Yard (11 dead-end and some through roads), from which branches led to several industrial premises, stretched from North box past the station to south box.

Controlled by Newark North box was the junction with the west to north M&GN Joint connection from the LMSR near Newark Castle station, which trailed in just beyond on the Down side. Worked as a siding, this loop saw several local trip workings daily, between Western sidings at the ECML end and Castle sidings at the other, in addition to various factories. Very occasionally, through goods trains traversed the line and it remained busy until the loss of traffic in the 1960s, but did not close until October 1973. The above loop no longer exists, but a south to east loop opened in March 1965 now allows trains to run from North Gate towards Lincoln; this line has superseded the route from Peterborough via Spalding as the main route from London, etc., to Lincoln, Grimsby and Cleethorpes.

Northwards from Newark, the ECML crossed the Nottingham–Lincoln line of the LMSR at Midland Crossing box.[18] The main line followed the River Trent and near Muskham box spanned Newark Dyke on a large truss bridge, then the other tributaries on two long series of brick arches on each side of five spans over the main river. Directly beyond was Trent box, which had charge of a full crossover, sidings on the Down side for the water-softening plant and a Down loop running beside Muskham troughs on the main line.

The ECML passed through Carlton-on-Trent and Crow Park (for Sutton-on-Trent) stations, each possessing very rudimentary goods facilities, and the singular two-level station 11½ miles north of Newark called Dukeries Junction. This was not a 'junction', but a wayside station on two levels. Only two trains (one during the war) each way stopped at the Low Level (ECML) station. The High Level was on the Lancashire, Derbyshire & East

Coast Railway (LD&ECR), which only ever ran from a terminus at Chesterfield Market Place to Lincoln Central and was absorbed in the early 1900s by the GCR, having failed in its intention to link industrial Lancashire with a new port on the Lincolnshire coast that was never built. As it served a number of thriving collieries in Nottinghamshire, the LD&ECR line, although closed to passenger trains in December 1951 (Chesterfield to Shirebrook North) and September 1955 (remainder), continued to be a busy artery for west to east coal traffic, including that exported via Immingham. In the early 1950s, no fewer than 35 trains a day were scheduled each way: the line served High Marnham power station at Fledborough until 2003, and in 2009, part of the route was recommissioned as a Network Rail Test Track.

Between Dukeries Junction and Tuxford North Junction on the Down side were Tuxford Exchange Sidings, comprising nine through roads including two reception roads. Half a mile to the north at Tuxford North Junction, a well-used west to north spur (later closed in September 1964) came from the LD&ECR round past the four Up reception roads of the LD&ECR Tuxford West Yard (nine roads) and Tuxford shed. Immediately after the junction was Tuxford North station which had a south-facing loading dock in the Down platform adjoining the goods yard; north of the station was another Down loop and one Down and two Up refuge sidings. Consisting of a Down loop as well as Down and Up through lines, the connection with the LD&ECR was important for freight, especially for fish trains and special passenger trains, such as the 'Starlight Special' from Marylebone to Newcastle and Scotland. Over the LD&ECR through Mansfield, it connected the GCR system (thus also the GWR and SR via Banbury) with the ECML and destinations north of Doncaster. In many respects, this was the preferred route for such through traffic—especially during the war—as it bypassed the congested Sheffield area.

The ECML, having climbed up from Crow Park to a minor summit at the very short Askham Tunnel, fell down to the plain of the River Idle, which was crossed by a five-span brick viaduct just before Retford. After a 6½-mile stretch from Tuxford, sectioned by the boxes at Lincoln Road, Gamston and Grove Road—each with loops and crossovers—came Retford (138¾ miles from London). At Retford was another flat crossing where the ECML and the ex-GCR Sheffield-Lincoln/Grimsby line intersected. The large Retford South box (located by the crossing on the Down side of the ECML and aligned parallel with the GCR line) dealt with the traffic at this busy junction.

Mainly because of the heavy coal traffic to the power stations erected along the Trent, in June 1965 the crossing was to be replaced by a dive-under for the former GCR route. Separate Retford Low Level platforms were built on this line and the curve from the Up ECML to the GCR line was removed. Until this date, GCR passenger trains called at the GNR main line station by means of loop lines that curved sharply round to the ECML at Retford North and South Junctions adjacent to each end of the station.

Retford's station building adjoined the Up main platform, which curved round at its south end on the alignment of the GCR tracks; additionally, there was an Up Fast line between that and the Down platform line. There was no connection leading off the Up Fast line at the south end and all trains heading for the GCR line to the east had to stop on the platform line. The Down platform was an island, the outer face of which was used primarily by Down GCR line trains. On the west side, there were carriage sidings between the Western platform and the

Dukeries Junction Low Level station frames the High Level station perched on the bridge above.

Dukeries Junction Low Level station and signal box from the High Level station, *c.* 1947.

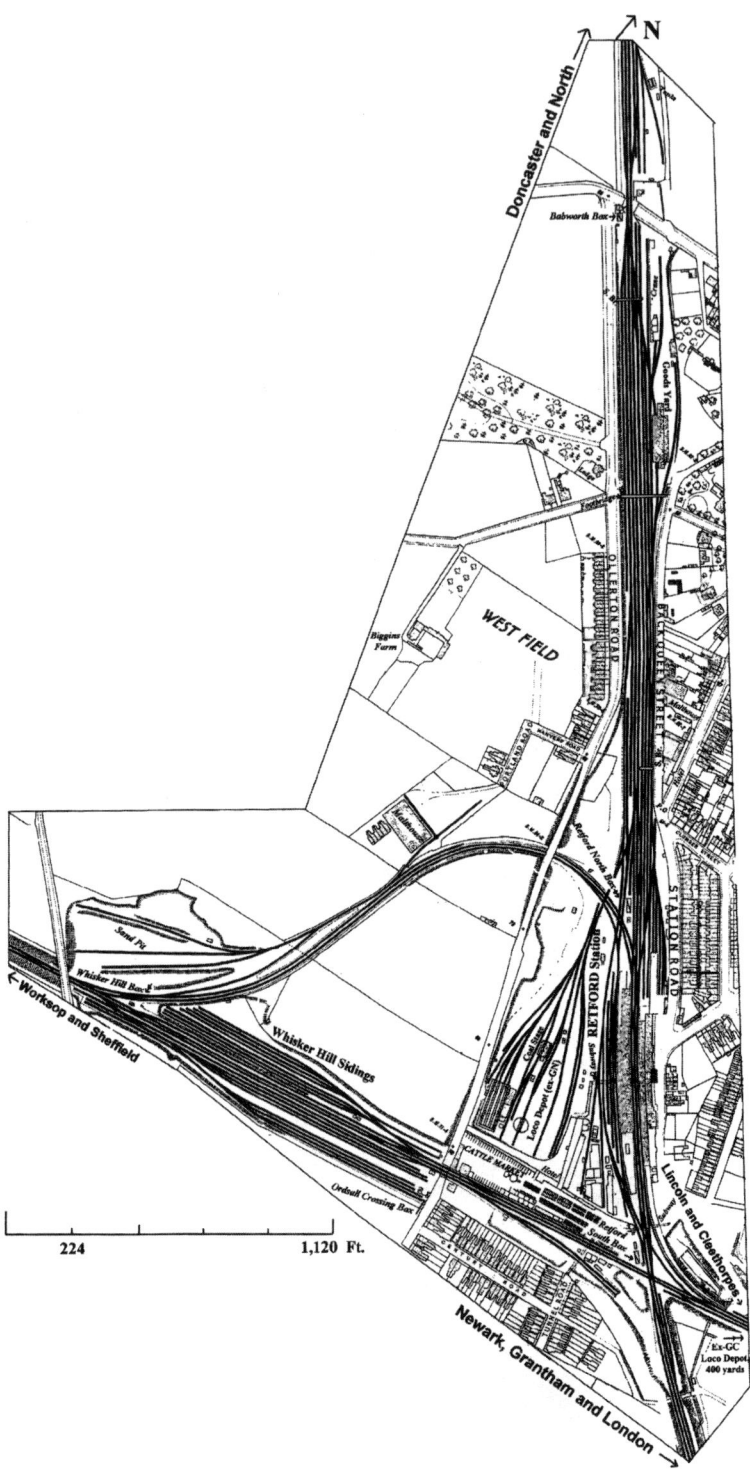

Retford station and the important junction with the GCR line, 1920.

View south from the Down Main platform at Retford station to Retford South signal box, which controlled the flat crossing of the GCR main line over the ECML.
Picture: R. Stephenson, B. W. L. Brooksbank Collection

Down Goods line, and beyond that were the cattle, Engineer's and Carriage & Wagon sidings, as well as the GNR locomotive shed. The Down Goods line and the line from the engine shed crossed the GCR curve on the level and connected with the Down main line north of North Box, while the Goods line continued to Babworth box, where there were again multiple crossovers and the Down and Up lines constricted briefly to two tracks. Then, between the boxes at Babworth and Canal, where the Chesterfield Canal was crossed on a girder bridge, there were again Down and Up Goods loops and other sidings. Apart from cattle sidings near the GNR engine shed, there were ECML Goods Yard at Retford (each with six roads) on the Up side at the north end of the station and half a mile further on near Babworth box.

On the ECML at Retford, the trains were similar to those at Grantham, with workings that joined the ECML at Newark and at Tuxford, compensating for those that turned off at Grantham. On the former GCR line, there were the largely secondary services from Manchester and Sheffield to Lincoln, Boston (and Skegness in the summer) or Gainsborough Central, Barnetby, Grimsby and Cleethorpes, with additional summer Saturday trains to Sutton-on-Sea and Mablethorpe.[19] Before the B1s took over, the passenger trains were hauled by GCR 4-6-0s or Atlantics and GNR Atlantics, K2s and K3s, mainly from Gorton, Sheffield, Lincoln or Immingham sheds. The freight train flow on the GCR line (amounting to 60 trains each way on weekdays, all crossing the ECML at Retford South) was mainly from Manchester, Sheffield and the North Nottinghamshire coalfield to Frodingham Yard for the Scunthorpe steelworks and to Immingham Dock. This was hauled by various GCR types and latterly by O4s and War Department Austerities.

The next station on the ECML was Barnby Moor & Sutton, which was unusual in having no goods yard or even a crossover. Then came Ranskill, ahead of which were Down and Up loops for Torworth Crossing (fully signalled with points worked electrically from

Ranskill box, which was located over the road crossing north of the station). To the east of the Up loop, the LNER had a wagon works before the war, and early in the conflict, a large ordnance factory was built on the site of this. To the south of the station, Ranskill also had a sizable goods yard on the Down side.

Scrooby Sidings followed on the ECML, half a mile from the remains of Scrooby station, which was closed in September 1931. A yard at Scrooby, with four northward and three southward tracks, was the collecting point for coal traffic from Harworth and Firbeck Collieries: this was brought along the branch (closed in June 1965) from Scooby Junction to the South Yorkshire Joint line at Firbeck Junction. Between Scrooby and Bawtry were Scrooby troughs, and a succession of over 30 brick arches took the ECML over the River Ryton and several other small streams.

Bawtry was a very active station. It had a bay platform at the north end of the Down side and several loading and cattle pens in the extensive goods yards, which were situated on each side of the line, also on the Misson branch to serve several industrial premises. During the war, a reinforced building adjoining the Down goods yard housed the Doncaster District Control Office. North of the station were fully signalled Down and Up loops. The goods-only line from Misson[20]—originally from Haxey Junction on the Isle of Axholme (Lancashire & Yorkshire & North Eastern Railway Joint line) route—trailed into the yard on the Up side; this line closed finally in April 1965.

Doncaster

After Rossington, the ECML approached Doncaster's large goods yards and various junctions. At the height of the coal industry, the output of some 52 collieries in the Doncaster district passed through the town's goods yards or left directly by one of the avoiding lines; only Harworth and Rossington Collieries to the south and Bentley Colliery to the north fed directly on to the ECML. In the complex of yards on the Carr Flats, there were the Decoy Down Yard (capacity 1,000 wagons) and Up Yard (1,420 wagons), Wagon Works Sidings, Down Mineral Empties Yard (later renamed Belmont, 1,400 wagons) and Up Mineral Yard (1,200 wagons), each having their own reception lines; finally, there was the large locomotive depot. The principal yards stretched for two miles between Childers Drain and Bridge Junction boxes—at one point, there were no fewer than 76 parallel tracks.

There were Up and Down Goods lines from Rossington as far as Potteric Carr Junction, then at least two relief lines for each direction to and through Doncaster Central station. The first junction was at Loversall Carr, where there were sidings on the Down side for northbound traffic from Rossington Colliery. On the Up side, there were exchange sidings for the traffic with the LMSR Dearne Valley line, to which loops on each side connected at Black Carr East Junction. Just after this point, the ECML passed under the LMSR line,[21] which was an ex-L&YR outlier from Crofton near Wakefield to Bessacarr Junction on the GN&GE Joint line. This latter ran from Lincoln, Sleaford, Spalding and March to join the ECML on the Up side at Black Carr Junction. Shortly afterwards came the overbridge carrying the South Yorkshire Joint (GCR, GNR, L&YR, MR and NER) mineral line, which began at Kirk Sandall Junction on the main lines to Doncaster from Hull and Grimsby to junctions at Brancliffe (west

Above left: Looking east to the closed Barnby Moor & Sutton station on 18 May 1967; the signal box was still in use for the level crossing. *Photograph: B. W. L. Brooksbank*

Above right: Ranskill station and signal box in May 1956. The station closed two years later, but the box remained in use, controlling several level crossings in the area, such as Barnby Moor & Sutton. *Picture: R. Stephenson, B. W. L. Brooksbank Collection*

Bawtry station exterior (Down side) with a relatively large number of early motor cars, *c.* 1920.

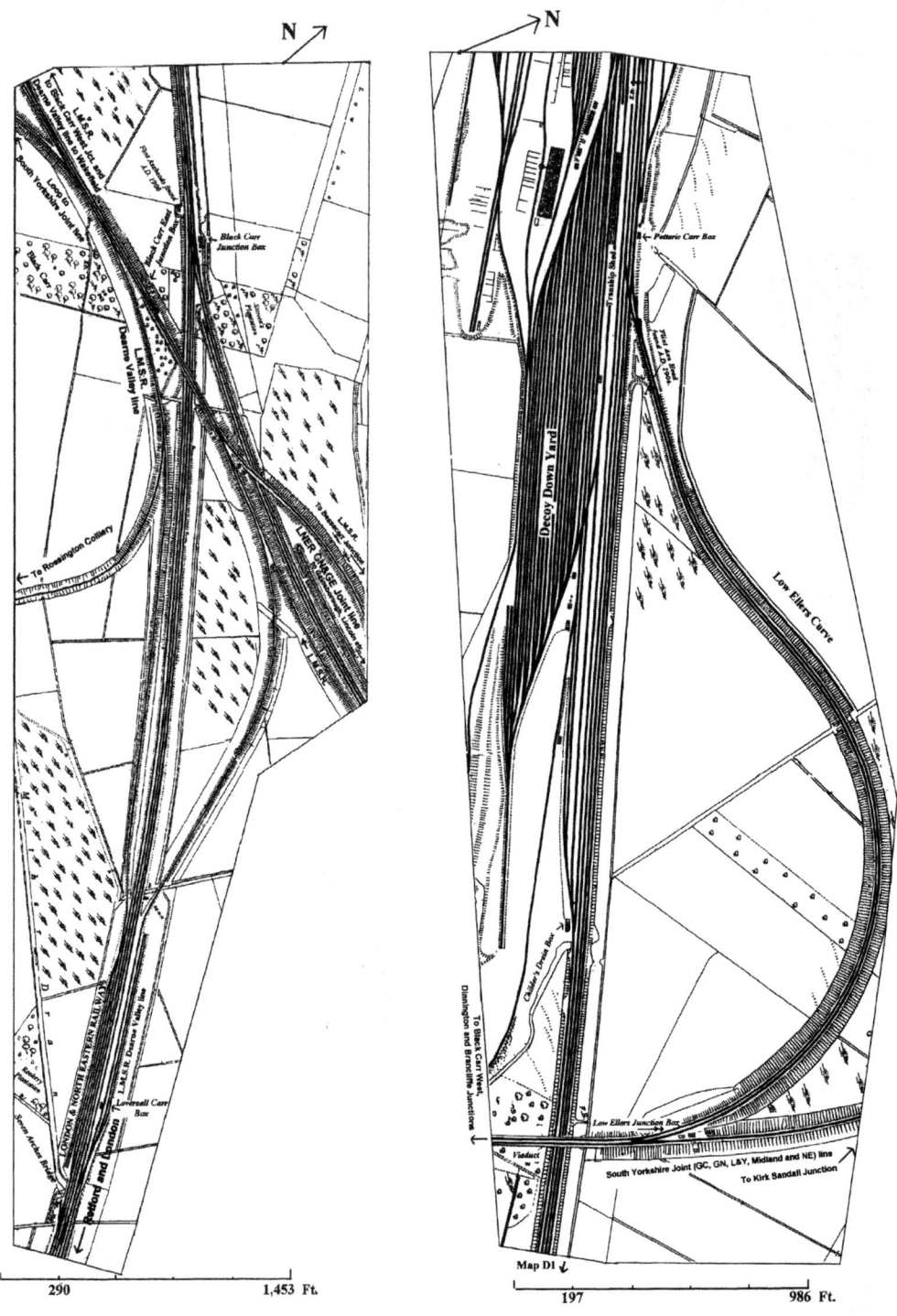

Above left: The lines at Black Carr Junction, Doncaster, 1939.

Above right: Low Ellers Junction and Down Decoy Yard, Doncaster, 1939.

of Shireoaks), with the GCR Retford–Sheffield line. The SYJR also connected to the Up side of the ECML at Potteric Carr box by the double-track Low Ellers Curve. At Childers Drain box—after the above overbridge—the four reception lines of Decoy Down Yard began on the left, with the 17 through roads of the Down Yard behind them and towards the end of the tracks was the tranship stage opposite Potteric Carr box on the other side of the main line.

Potteric Carr also managed the convergence of the Up lines emerging from Decoy Up Yard and its five associated reception and departure roads, as well as the Up fast and slow goods lines that bypassed Decoy Up Yard, on which through freight trains stopped for examination and (usually) changed engines. The next boxes were Decoy No. 1 (Down) and No. 2 (Up): the former controlled the complex exits from Decoy Down Yard, the four reception lines for the Down Mineral Empties Yard and the very extensive sidings (over 25 roads) of the Carr Wagon Works. The two boxes also handled the intricate movements of locomotives and transfer trips over the multiple crossings between the Up and Down sides. Decoy No. 2 co-operated with Carr box in handling trains out of the Up Mineral Yard, and with Red Bank—the next box on the Down side, sited between the Down main and goods lines—the movements of locomotives leaving the depot to work Down goods trains. The shunting of the 19 dead-end sidings (in two separate groups until reorganised during the war) of Decoy Up Yard was regulated from a points cabin under the control of Decoy No. 2 Up box.

In addition to the Down and Up main lines, two extra Down lines (coal and goods) ran through from Decoy No. 1 to Bridge Junction, while on the Up, a Down transfer and four Up lines (Mineral departure, engine, fast goods and slow goods), plus five Up reception lines ran through from Carr box. Northwards from the latter, there was also a Down engine line, making five lines (designated Down transfer, Up fast goods, Up slow goods, Down engine and Up engine) running through between the locomotive depot and the six Up Mineral reception lines as far as Sand Bank box.

After Red Bank, the next main line box was Balby Junction, and in the intervening mile lay the large Down Mineral Empties and Up Mineral Yards (hump yards, with 26 and 18 through roads respectively) on each side of the ECML. Balby Junction box regulated the northern exits from the Down Empties Yard and some factory sidings, together with a complex of main line crossovers. The entry to the Up Mineral Yards was handled by Sand Bank box, located a little north of Balby Junction and having no functions on the main line; shunting of the Up Mineral Yard was regulated from a points cabin. Likewise, Carr box, well off the main line on the Up side close to Red Bank box, regulated the exits from the Up Mineral Yard as well as the locomotive yard.

At the north end of the complex of yards and Doncaster shed on the Carr Flats was Bridge Junction, where the lines converged under a wide road bridge and where within the space of four years two major accidents occurred (1947 and 1951). The signal box there operated the junction of the loop (two Down and one Up Goods lines) on the Down side to St James' Junction, where it joined the GCR South Yorkshire (SYR) line from Mexborough and Sheffield, which itself converged with the ECML at South Yorkshire Junction box. In addition, Bridge Junction box—in conjunction with Sand Bank box—controlled the constant engine movements from the north end of the locomotive yard; northwards, this box handled the reversal from the Up main line of many trains of empty carriage stock into the Garden Carriage Sidings on the

Ivatt Atlantic No. 1455 passes Decoy No. 2 signal box with an Up express before Grouping.

The points box for Decoy Yard.

Down side. Also on the Up side, there was an exit from the GNR goods depot at South Yard and Shakespeare Sidings. The South Yard had a total of eight through roads and at its southern end, Shakespeare Sidings had five southward roads; two of these served the South Dock and at the other end behind the goods shed was another pair facing northwards—Middle Dock.

From Bridge Junction to the next box, South Yorkshire Junction, there was a Down goods independent, which after crossing and being joined from the SYR line divided into separate Down GNR and SYR goods independent lines to pass in between Doncaster Central station and West Yard. Coming away from the station as far as Bridge Junction were three Up Relief lines (Passenger Independent and goods independent Nos 1 and 2). South and South Yorkshire Junction boxes between them handled these independent lines as well as the station lines and movements to and from the SYR line. South box also controlled access to the goods depot from the Up Passenger Independent (platform 1) line which rejoined the ECML at Bridge Junction.

At South Yorkshire Junction, just before the junction between the line from Sheffield and the ECML, was the exit on the Down side from Garden Carriage Sidings, which had six through roads and a northward siding, also a through engine line with ash pit. Here, the Up and Down SYR goods independents formed a double junction with the line from Sheffield—until the remodelling of 1949, without any connection to the ECML—to form a route direct to Frenchgate Junction to the north of Doncaster station, running alongside and to the west of the line serving the Down western platform (later No. 8). These lines enabled goods trains between the routes north of Doncaster and the Sheffield line to avoid the station area, although the bulk of the heavy traffic on the GCR lines west and east of Doncaster used the Doncaster avoiding line just to the north. At South Yorkshire Junction, the Down goods independent crossed the Sheffield route to run alongside the Down SY Independent, these goods lines having a connection with the locomotive works.

Just before the war, the LNER undertook an extensive rebuilding of Doncaster station and remodelling of the layout, including the laying of extra running lines between Frenchgate Junction and the north throat of the station complex and modernisation of the signalling, but this was interrupted during the war. By August 1939, the principal station entrance buildings on the Up side had been rebuilt in a contemporary architectural style and a new Up line was soon to be laid, making the Up platform (Nos 1 and 4) into an island, as was the Down platform (Nos 5 and 8) already. The Down island had two bay platforms (Nos 6 and 7) at its north end and two sidings (accessible from a head-shunt) at the south end, while the Up island had bay platforms (Nos 2 and 3) only at the south end. After the new power signalling came into use in 1949, platform 5 was also used for some departures towards Sheffield. Non-stopping trains took the Down and Up through lines in the centre. The very long express trains of the war were a problem because No. 4 platform could only handle 15 bogies and platform 8 14 bogies, but platform 5 could only take 10—platform 1 was not available at all until November 1941. During this period, the detachment of through coaches for Hull was abandoned.

To the west of the station on the Down side were the goods independent lines and the West Yard, which was a complex of nine northwards roads all used primarily for handling parcels trains and empty coaching stock. Finally, there were running roads, sidings and a 60-foot turntable by which locomotives went in and out of the plant, situated further over to the

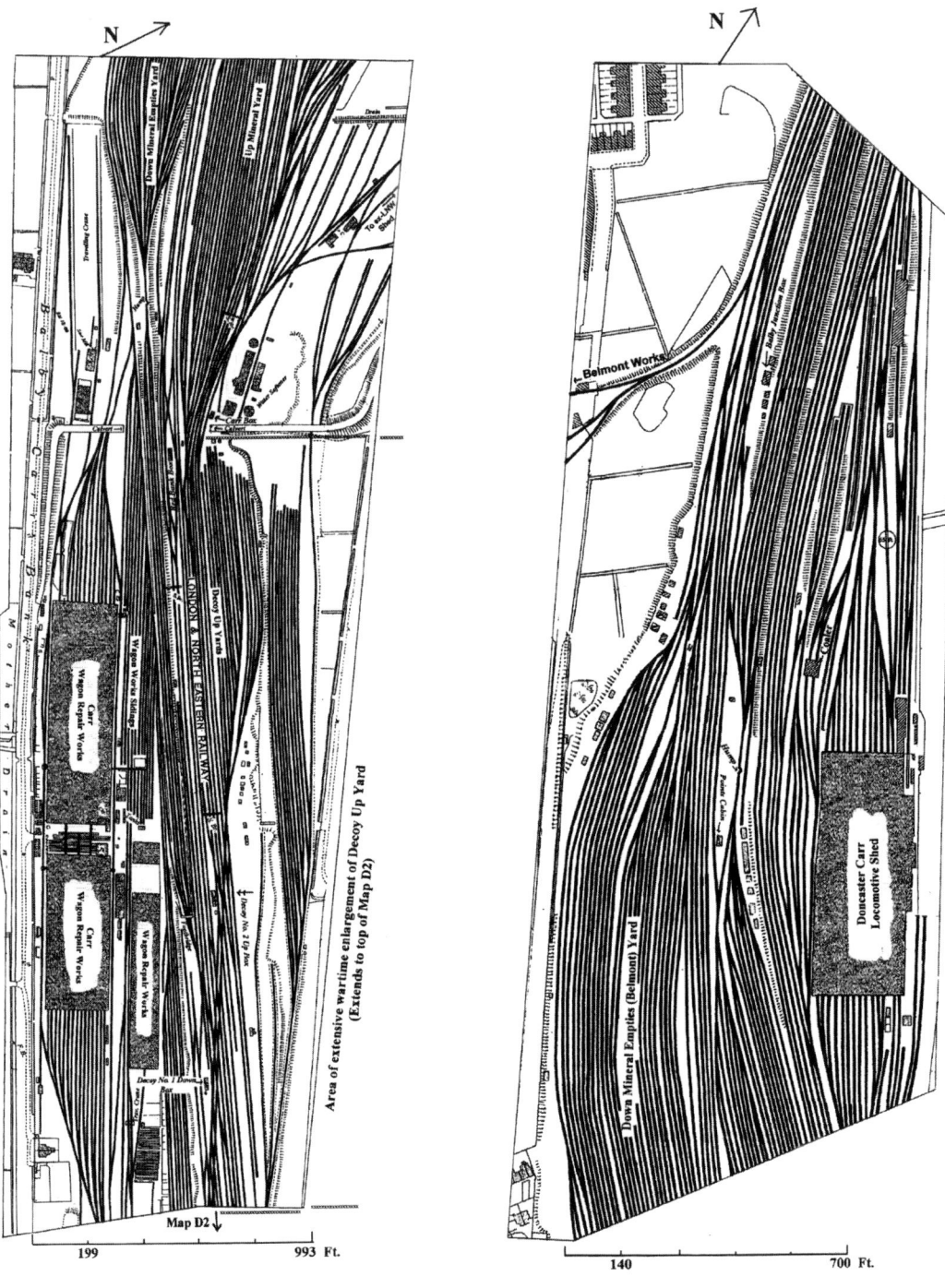

Above left: Up Decoy, Down mineral empties and Up mineral yards with Doncaster Carr Wagon Works, 1939.

Above right: The main line divides the large locomotive shed on the east side from the Down mineral empties (before the wartime alterations) to the west.

The East Coast Main Line's Principal Points

Above left: Sand Bank box to St James's Bridge (south of Doncaster station), including the junction for the Sheffield line, 1939.

Above right: Doncaster station area (before modernisation) and Doncaster Plant Works; the Crimpsall Repair Shop, etc., were located just to the south-west.

View of the area between Balby Road Bridge and St James Bridge, Doncaster, c. 1905. Bridge Junction box is closest to camera and in the distance is Shakespeare box; on the left are Garden Carriage Sidings.

west. The works offices presented an imposing facade towards the station, but, in spite of its 30–40-acre site, the plant was otherwise hidden from the ECML.

Until the resignalling of 1949, the north end of the station had the unusual feature of three separate signal boxes more or less in line, controlling the different segments of the layout. 'A' box on the Up side dealt only with Up trains entering the station and movements to the five Old Yard sidings and North Dock to the north of the Up platforms. 'B' box, alongside the Down Passenger Independent, was concerned with trains on the Down main line plus those from the Down island platform and from the north end bays, and there was a 52-foot turntable adjacent to the box. Lastly, 'C' box, on the Down side of the Down GNR goods independent, controlled movements between that line and the Down (but not the Up) SYR Independent, together with the exit from West Yard and the north end connections into the Carriage & Wagon sections of the plant. The block sections between the boxes on each side of Doncaster station varied according to the lines concerned: the short section between South Yorkshire Junction and Doncaster South applied only to the main lines, and on the Down side 'C' box split the sections on the Down goods independent lines. All this was much simplified from early in 1949, when the new signalling was introduced and the south and north power boxes were brought into use.

The middle sections of the Down and Up platform lines in the station were each protected by a rather austere GNR-style canopy supported by long ranks of cast-iron columns standing between the platform lines and the through lines. In 1940, a subway from the Down side to the station entrance area was constructed, superseding the passenger footbridge. In addition, a footbridge spanned the whole range of the station tracks and those on the west side, which led from the streets on the east side over to the plant.

Doncaster was one of the principal traffic centres of the ECML and also a major junction to Sheffield, Hull, Lincolnshire and Leeds. The traffic at Doncaster was therefore heavy and varied, requiring much to by-pass the town altogether to ease congestion, taking one of four avoiding lines.

Almost all the ECML expresses from London passed through Doncaster. Some of these uncoupled their Leeds/Bradford or Hull portions there, thus involving an engine change. If heavy trains had difficulty getting away, they were allowed rear assistance. The Hull line was a problem, because between Doncaster and Thorne North the line was Route Availability (RA) 7, prohibiting the use of Pacifics or V2s. Expresses off the GN&GE Joint line from East Anglia also arrived at Doncaster for Yorkshire and the north-east. In addition, there was a busy service on the former GCR artery between Manchester, Sheffield (and Barnsley) and South Humberside (Scunthorpe, Barnetby, Immingham Dock, Grimsby and Cleethorpes). Secondary and local passenger services ran on the former GCR lines, on the GN&GE Joint and to Leeds and Hull. There were also many special workings, especially during the war, and in peacetime during Doncaster's annual St Leger Week. Finally, an oddity that ran daily until the 1950s was the workmen's train—the 'Spike Island' Special—to and from the Carr Wagon Works; this comprised six-wheeled coaches hauled by the Wagon Works Pilot (normally a J50 or J52 0-6-0T).

The motive power of the main line expresses in 1939 was Gresley Pacifics, or the occasional K3 or V2. On the GNR and GCR secondary services into Doncaster were a great variety of pre-Grouping types, such as GNR Atlantics, 4-4-0s, 2-6-0s, or GCR 4-6-0s, Atlantics and 4-4-0s. Some Leeds expresses were worked by GCR B3 or B4 4-6-0s, or Gresley K3s and K2s, shedded at Copley Hill, Ardsley or Bradford. Also, in the 1930s and 1940s several GCR B2s and B4s allocated to Lincoln also worked trains ranging from the Parkeston Quay–York, the wartime workers trains to Ranskill Royal Ordnance Factory and main line freights. Working regularly off the GN&GE Joint would be GER 4-4-0s and Gresley B17s. By the late 1950s, BR Standard Class 7 'Britannia' Pacifics were working the through trains from East Anglia via Lincoln and through Doncaster to York.

Local trains from Hull and York brought K3s, D49s, and NER 4-6-0s and 4-4-0s, while Sheffield-Hull trains would often have GCR B5s. Local trains from Leeds had a variety of motive power down to GNR 0-6-0s; those from Penistone via Barnsley would bring GCR C13s or J11s. Finally, there was the LMSR local passenger service of about eight weekday trains from Wakefield via Knottingley (normally worked by L&YR 2-4-2Ts, often push-and-pull) and a few LMSR trains from Sheffield Midland via Swinton. Both LMSR services ceased upon the outbreak of war, but the Wakefield service was revived briefly afterwards until March 1947. The few LMSR trains in 1939 between Sheffield and Hull via Doncaster were worked by LNER locomotives, but in the early 1950s, LMR engines appeared again for a while. The introduction of the B1s reduced the variety of motive power on these workings. Thompson L1s were used on trains from Leeds, while LMSR 4MT 2-6-0s appeared from Hull on stopping trains. From 1957 DMUs operated the local passenger services, both on the GNR and GCR lines to Doncaster.

The yards at Doncaster Carr handled 70–75 scheduled main line freight trains each way on weekdays even in 1939, and about half that number passed through the station; in 1952, 45 freights were booked through the station alone. On freight trains, the motive power could be anything from A4s to J3s or J52s. Mainly, there was a preponderance of 2-8-0s from GNR O1 (O3) and O2 Classes, GCR O4 Class, including the Thompson rebuilds (classified O1) and the 'Austerity' 2-8-0s after the war. Long-distance and fast freights would be worked by V2s, K2s or K3s, and in the 1950s, the new Peppercorn K1s.

Gresley A4 Class Pacific No. 4495 *Great Snipe* backs on to an Up King's Cross train at Doncaster station. Pictured shortly after construction in early September 1937, the engine would be renamed *Golden Fleece* by the end of the month.

Many J39 0-6-0s from Doncaster shed—and others—were to be seen, while O4s and Q4s came from the West Riding sheds. Numerous NER B16s and Q6s visited Doncaster from the north-east and often continued south. From Whitemoor came March's numerous 2-8-0s of several classes and sometimes GER 0-6-0s (J17s, J19s and J20s). Although much of the lateral freight on the GCR artery, including that to Hull, took the avoiding line, GCR workings through the station brought many and varied engines of GCR vintage from sheds such as Mexborough, Frodingham, Immingham and elsewhere. From the mid-1950s, the predominantly LNER scene at Doncaster was modified further by the introduction of LMSR-type and Standard 2-6-0s by BR. Eventually, the BR Standard Class 9F 2-10-0s became prominent, working from Doncaster, Whitemoor, York and the north-east.

Doncaster to Selby and York

Leaving Doncaster for Selby (18½ miles) and York (32¼ miles), Frenchgate box was passed on the Down side, close to the Great North Road overbridge. The line then ran over the New Cut (Dun [*sic*.] Navigation) waterway on a girder bridge. At Marshgate Junction, the main lines to Hull and South Humberside forked to the right, flanked by Marshgate Sidings and goods yard. The connection to the Corporation Yard was on the Down side, then almost immediately the line to Wakefield, Leeds and Bradford veered off to the left at Marshgate Junction and the Down Passenger Independent line also ended. From the junction with the Wakefield line, the recently installed No. 2 Up Passenger Independent line ran over the two bridges on new spans to the north end ('A' box) of Doncaster station and from 1941 served the new No. 1 platform.[22] At Marshgate, the main line crossed the River Don on another girder bridge and went under the principal (ex-GCR) Doncaster avoiding line.

There was a Down loop (fully signalled) before Arksey, an Up relief siding at Heck and two sidings on the Down side at Henwick Hall (1¼ miles before Selby Canal box), but otherwise the ECML was only double-track going forward to Selby. There were crossovers at each intermediate station and also at Bentley Colliery, Shaftholme Junction, Joan Croft Junction, Henwick Hall and Selby Canal boxes. However, traffic of all kinds was heavy between Doncaster and York, and to compensate for the lack of four tracks some of the freight traffic was routed from Shaftholme Junction via Knottingley and Church Fenton, as were special passenger trains, in addition to certain King's Cross to Harrogate services.

Wayside stations on this stretch to Selby—Arksey, Moss, Balne, Heck, and Temple Hirst—were designed using functional architecture. Arksey (the only one of GNR lineage) differed in having a half-timbered structure and only Heck and Temple Hirst had any substantial goods facilities. North of Arksey on the Down side was Bentley Colliery, which was a large installation with extensive sidings. This was situated on a branch just off the ECML and accessed by both north- and south-facing single-track curves which formed a triangle, all being controlled from Bentley Colliery box located midway between the main line connections. Between Arksey and Moss (4¼ miles from Doncaster) was Shaftholme Junction. There the original (until 1871) main line turned off on the Down side to the north, to join the L&YR (later LMSR) line to Knottingley and Wakefield and so to give connections into the Swinton and Knottingley (S&K, MR&NER) Joint at Ferrybridge, so to Church Fenton, York and Harrogate.

Before reaching York, the ECML crossed numerous small streams and waterways leading to the Humber: the River Went between Moss and Balne; the Knottingley and Goole Canal near Heck; the River Aire at Temple Hirst; and the River Ouse at Selby and Naburn. The ECML also crossed the path of several west to east coal-carrying lines. First, above Marshgate Junction was the GCR line, from Hexthorpe Junction on the SYR main line to the Hull/South Humberside line at Bentley Junction. Shortly before Shaftholme Junction, the main line was crossed by the former Hull and Barnsley Railway (H&BR) and the GCR Joint line. This ran from the former GCR&MR Joint line at Braithwell Junction to Aire Junction on the H&BR main line.

About half a mile later, that line passed overhead and the ECML went under the direct line of the former West Riding & Grimsby Railway (GNR&GCR Joint), which cut across from Adwick Junction on the Doncaster–Wakefield line to Stainforth Junction on the Doncaster–Hull/South Humberside line; in addition to freight, this latter line carried seasonal holiday traffic. Half a mile beyond Shaftholme Junction, an east to north spur came in on the Up side at Joan Croft Junction from the GNR&GCR Joint at Applehurst Junction. The signal box at Joan Croft Junction had been closed since 1930; thereafter the points were worked electrically from Shaftholme Junction box and the crossover by a ground frame released by that box. Until 1952, there was Joan Croft Halt, which was only used by railway staff and their families.

On approaching Selby over the Selby Canal a mile or so south, a long-disused cut-off towards Goole was crossed. This had run from the former NER Leeds-Selby line at Thorpe Gates to Brayton East Junction. Next at Brayton Junction, the ECML was joined on the right by the then still active NER branch from Goole, with a small group of sidings there on the Up side of the branch. At Selby Canal box, the running lines expanded to six, with two Down and two Up Goods lines as far as the junction with Selby South, and on the Down side a

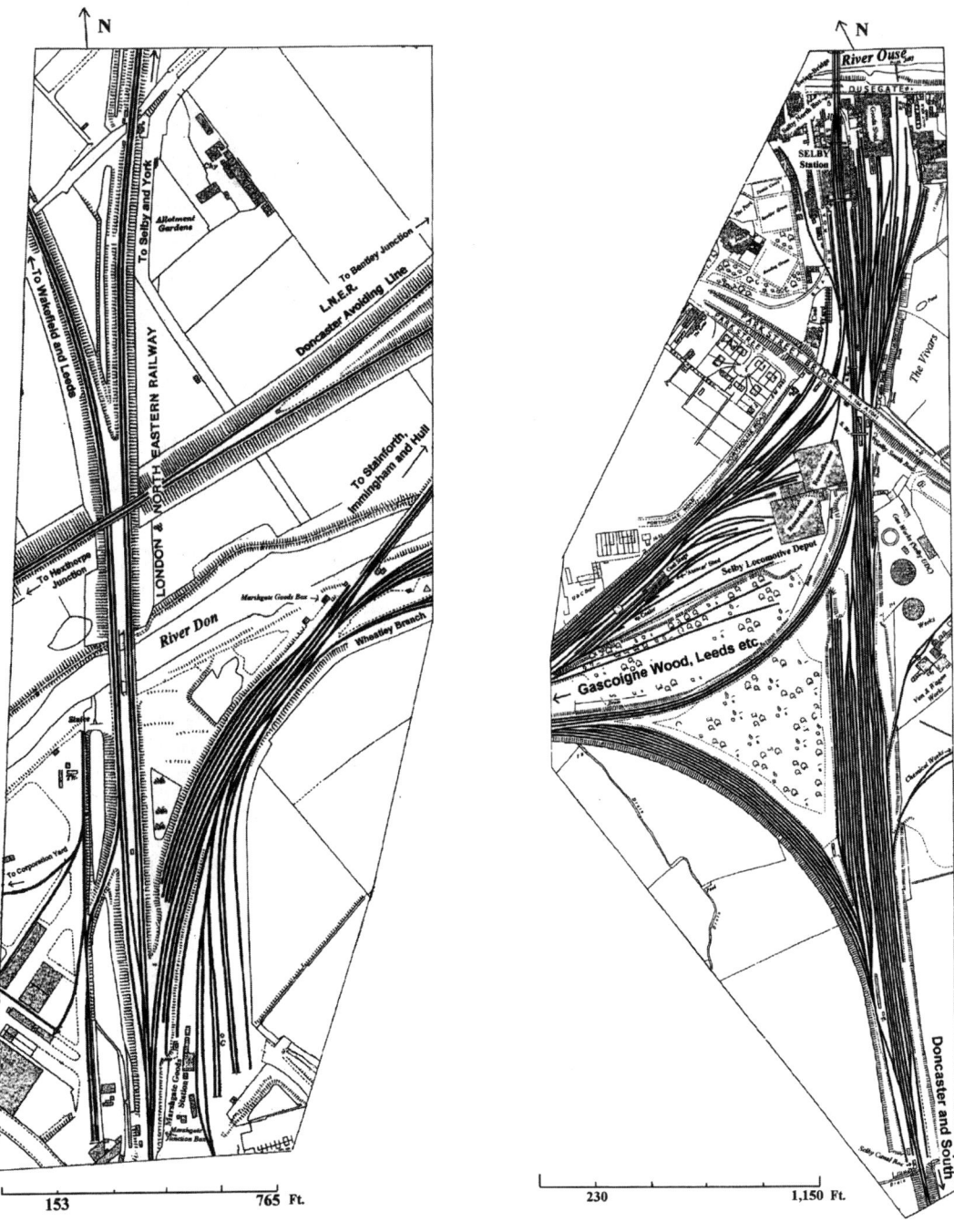

Above left: Marshgate Junction and the junctions for the Leeds and Hull lines north of Doncaster station, 1930.

Above right: Lines to Selby station from the South and Leeds.

reception line led to the ten (partly dead-end) sidings of Selby New Yard which extended as far as the locomotive depot situated in the angle of the lines from Leeds, accessed only from the Leeds direction. The main lines from Leeds joined at Selby South, but the Down Leeds Goods loop, which passed to the north side of the depot, joined nearer Selby station.

Selby station had its own Down and Up through platforms on loops off the main lines. At the south end, there was a parcels bay on the Down side, and on the Up side, a bay used by trains from the Bridlington line that reversed into it and by Goole locals. The goods depot, with 20 roads devoted to various purposes, was behind the Up side of the passenger station. At Selby North box, the Up and Down platform loops merged with the respective main through lines before crossing Selby swing bridge, which had a 40-mph speed limit. Immediately to the north of the bridge were again Up and Down loop lines, and to obviate the need for point rodding to cross the swing bridge, these were adjacent to Selby North box and tracks were gauntleted over the bridge.

There was another cabin athwart the centre of the northern (swinging) span of the bridge, for the man who operated the moveable span and semaphore signals for the river traffic. The arrangements at Naburn swing bridge were similar, and both bridges were liable to be run into by vessels on the river. On occasions of high tide, vessels might be given priority over trains at Selby, as they were entitled by law unless the Act for the railway stated otherwise. In hot weather, cold water had to be sprayed on to the metalwork to counter the expansion that could prevent the bridges being closed after the passage of a vessel. During the war, both Selby and Naburn swing bridges were decked to allow use by road vehicles in an emergency; this was done at a number of railway bridges, especially in Eastern England, at the time of the invasion threat in the summer of 1940.

Apart from the ECML traffic through Selby, a good service of trains ran on the west–east axis from Leeds (some through from Manchester and Liverpool) to Hull, and also trains via Market Weighton to Driffield, Bridlington, Filey and Scarborough. In 1939, the intermediate stations to Driffield were served by three trains only, but these were reduced to two in the

Gresley D49/2 Class 4-4-0 No. 62762 *The Fernie* comes off the swing bridge into Selby station on 5 April 1957. Picture: B. W. L. Brooksbank

1950s and—except for Market Weighton—the stations were closed in September 1954. The through trains to Driffield ceased in June 1965 and freight ceased two months later. In addition, certain trains ran from Hull and Selby via Milford Junction either to Pontefract and Sheffield, or to Castleford and Normanton, or via Church Fenton to Tadcaster and Harrogate. During the war, the local trains on the Tadcaster line were augmented by those bringing workers to the Thorp Arch Royal Ordnance Factory, while after the war, passenger services on that line fell off to about one each way by 1955, before final closure in January 1964. These passenger trains were worked by D20s and D49s until taken over after the war by B1s and LMSR-type 2-6-0s. Summer brought Saturday-only expresses and weekend excursions to the seaside, some of which were hauled by engines of LMSR sheds; in 1939, there were also daily LMSR Sheffield to Hull trains via Selby. Conversion of local services to DMU operation ensued from 1958. The local service (five trains) from Selby to Goole was operated by a steam railcar until the war, when a push-pull fitted G5 0-4-4T took over until DMUs came shortly before the branch closed to all traffic in June 1964. There was also the Cawood branch, which diverged from the Leeds line 1½ miles from Selby and lost its passenger service in 1930 though remained open for goods until May 1960.

Freight traffic on the west to east axis through Selby was considerable, amounting to 20 trains—to be added to the 30 or so on the ECML—each way per day. Much was coal traffic to Hull from Gascoigne Wood Yard (on the Leeds line between Hambleton and South Milford), but the flow of mineral and merchandise trains through Selby to and from Hull also ran to Neville Hill Yard (Leeds), via Milford Junction to Normanton, Castleford, Ardsley and Bradford, or northwards from Gascoigne Wood Junction via Church Fenton to York, Croft, Newport and Heaton.[23] Hull Dairycoates shed provided much of the motive power for these freight flows, employing NER 4-6-0s and 0-8-0s and O4 2-8-0s, 'Austerity' 2-8-0s during and after the war, LMSR 8F 2-8-0s in the late 1940s and 4MT 2-6-0s in the 1950s. Neville Hill locomotives (0-8-0s and in the war USA 2-8-0s) were also prominent, and the trains from the North East brought similar engines from York, Newport and Heaton.

After the swing bridge, there were then four tracks (designated Down duplicate, Down main, Up York and Up Hull), which turned sharply to the east and in half a mile came to Barlby box. From there to Barlby North box there were also two Up Independent lines, only one of which was available from the York direction because the Up Hull line ran through separately and did not converge until Selby North. This stretch was flanked by extensive factory sidings as well on either side, principally for the large British Oil and Cake Mills. At Barlby North Junction, the ECML curved sharply towards the north, while the line to Staddlethorpe and Hull went straight ahead. The line to Market Weighton and Driffield, also a branch to the large sugar beet factory, left the Hull line just east of the box, which was sited in the angle of the divergence of the York and Hull lines. Barlby North was thus a key box, controlling not only the junctions but also the double crossovers between the York and Hull lines and further sidings on each side. The connection from Selby to the Hull line was by a facing crossover between Down and Up main lines and then a further pair of points trailing into the Up main. Thus, Down Hull trains were brought briefly on to the same track as trains on the Up ECML. This arrangement arose mainly from the frequent use, especially during the war, of the route from Market Weighton as far as Everingham as a single line, with trains running on the Down line while wagons were stored on the Up line.[24]

The ECML ran past the Down siding at Osgodby and then through wayside stations at Riccall, Escrick and Naburn (each with goods yards, on the Down side at Riccall and Naburn and the Up side at Escrick), and over Naburn swing bridge half a mile north of the station.[25] Before the war, between Barlby North and Chaloner's Whin boxes, goods trains could get out of the way only in a refuge on the Up side at Escrick, but wartime traffic forced the insertion of lengthy goods loops in both directions and the erection of extra signal boxes between Riccall and Escrick. From Naburn, the ECML was double-track to Chaloner's Whin Junction where the ECML met the four-track main lines from Church Fenton and the west and south—two Leeds line and two Normanton lines.

York

From South Points box (just over half a mile from Chaloner's Whin Junction), the four running lines expanded to six as far as Holgate Bridge Junction—the four main lines being flanked by Down and Up excursion or 'Holgate Loop' lines; crossovers at Chaloner's Whin and South Points enabled interchange between all lines. On the Up side was Dringhouses Up Yard, which in 1939 was of relatively minor importance, yet still had 20 through roads.[26] On the Down side, there were four through reception roads constituting Dringhouses Down Yard. The entries and exits of these yards were controlled by South Points box and in part worked electrically. At this box, the Down Holgate excursion line left the Down Leeds line, and a further four reception lines—for traffic awaiting entry to York Down Yard—commenced there and ran behind the Down Excursion (Racecourse) platform as far as Holgate Bridge, where their exit to the Down excursion/Leeds lines was worked by a ground frame released from the locomotive yard box.

Thus, next to the Holgate Sidings were the Racecourse platforms, just south of the massive Holgate Bridge from which ramps gave access, severed by the Down and Up excursion lines; after the outbreak of war, these platforms were no longer used. Immediately past Holgate Bridge, the five through freight lines curved left past the Cattle Dock Sidings, on their way to York Yard South and the Down and Up Yards; these being situated beside the avoiding line which cut across the junctions at York Yard North and Skelton. These lines at Holgate were designated 'Leeds' and 'Doncaster' Down and Up Goods and Down Independent, and there was also an Up Independent that joined the Up 'Doncaster' Goods line before it and the Up 'Leeds' Goods crossed over the passenger lines. Meanwhile, the five passenger lines (four main and an Up Loop line) made their wide arc the other way through York station—in 1939, York station handled over 360 trains in 24 hours.

On the left of the approach to the station, located within the triangle formed by the main and goods lines, were the three dilapidated York South sheds: these comprised a straight shed used latterly by LMSR engines and two surviving roundhouses occupied by the local LNER pilot engines and other vehicles. On the opposite side was the old Queen Street shed yard, which was only used as a stabling point by 1939. Behind the latter was the former York & North Midland Railway Works, which were used as the York Railway Museum, along with the original refreshment rooms of the old terminal station—located through an archway in the City Walls. Opposite the imposing NER Headquarters building was the

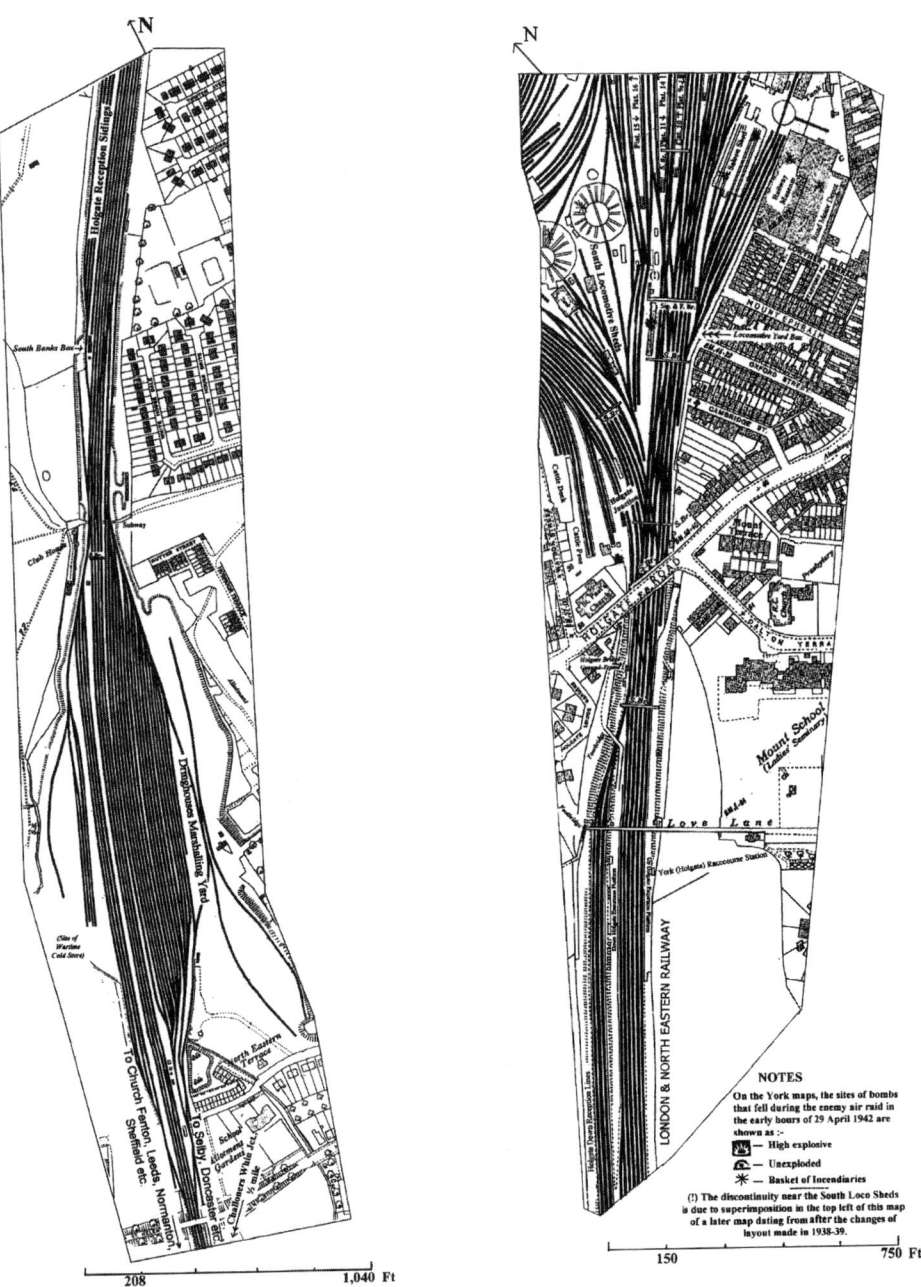

Above left: York Dringhouses Yard, 1937.

Above right: Holgate Platforms to York Yard South, 1937.

original Station Hotel, which was also used as railway offices. The North Eastern Area Main Line Control Office was in the original terminal building on the south-east side of the old station. The old locomotive shed and much of the old station were used for coaching stock, and also on the Queen Street site were the Railway Institute, signal and telegraph depot, lost property depot, and road motor depot, next to which there was—from the 1950s—a loading bay for Motorail services.

The main station had 16 platforms, of which five (Nos 8, 9, 14, 15 and 16) were through platforms. All except No. 14 (and Nos 15 and 16 added on the Down side in the 1938 rebuilding) were spanned for much of their length by the arched, curved roofs, one 48 feet high and 81 feet wide flanked by two 40 feet high (55 and 45 feet wide respectively), and there was another arch of 36 feet spanning the bay platforms (Nos 1 to 3) on the south-eastside of the station. Platforms 8 and 9 were the main through platforms, No. 9 being long enough to accommodate two full-length trains. The two Up and Down through lines between these platform lines were interconnected with them by scissor crossings. There were five bay platforms (Nos 1, 2, 3, 10 and 11) at the south end, available for any southbound train; at the north end were six (Nos 4 to 7, 12 and 13), of which only Nos 4 to 7 were available to trains for the lines over the bridge to Scarborough and Hull and not to main line trains. The bay platforms 12 and 13, with no access to the Scarborough Bridge, were used by some trains down the main line (including to Pickering via Gilling) and by Harrogate trains. The island comprising platforms 15 and 16—separated from platform 14 by a through siding—had been built only in 1938. Until the completion of the modernisation in 1951, platform 15 was accessible from the south end only by light engines and platform 16 was the freight dock with its sidings, and a through engine line that connected to the main York North shed with the group of engine sheds at the south end.

The whole of the operations at the south end were controlled by the enormous locomotive yard box and signalled by some complex NER gantries. The box had 295 levers and was worked by four signalmen and a traffic regulator per shift, and they even had remote control over the junctions at Holgate Bridge and—by electrical release of a ground frame—the exit from the Holgate Reception Sidings. Opposite the locomotive yard box, there were six running lines: Down and Up Leeds, Down and Up main, Up Loop and Carriage Sidings Loop; also on the far side was the Back Road, which branched off the Carriage Loop to give access to some 18 siding roads serving the old shed and old station premises. A profusion of crossovers at the south end allowed relatively easy access to all platforms of the station from all approach lines.

In the middle of the station above the main Up platform (No. 8) was platform box (80 levers). At the north end of the station and opposite each other were the Leeman Road and Waterworks boxes, with 91 and 110 levers respectively. The latter was a 'temporary' structure put up in 1938 in place of the earlier Waterworks box, on a site constricted by the need to double the lines to Scarborough Bridge, it remained until 1951. At Leeman Road, the 'Scarborough Goods' lines curved in sharply from York Yard South and the Branches Yard; along with the exits from platforms 14, 15 and 16 and the Fruit Dock, crossed the main exits from platforms 8, 9, 12 and 13 on the level, to join at Waterworks Junction those from platforms 4 to 9 leading over the double-track Scarborough Bridge. Further round the curve on the Up side was Clifton box (120 levers).

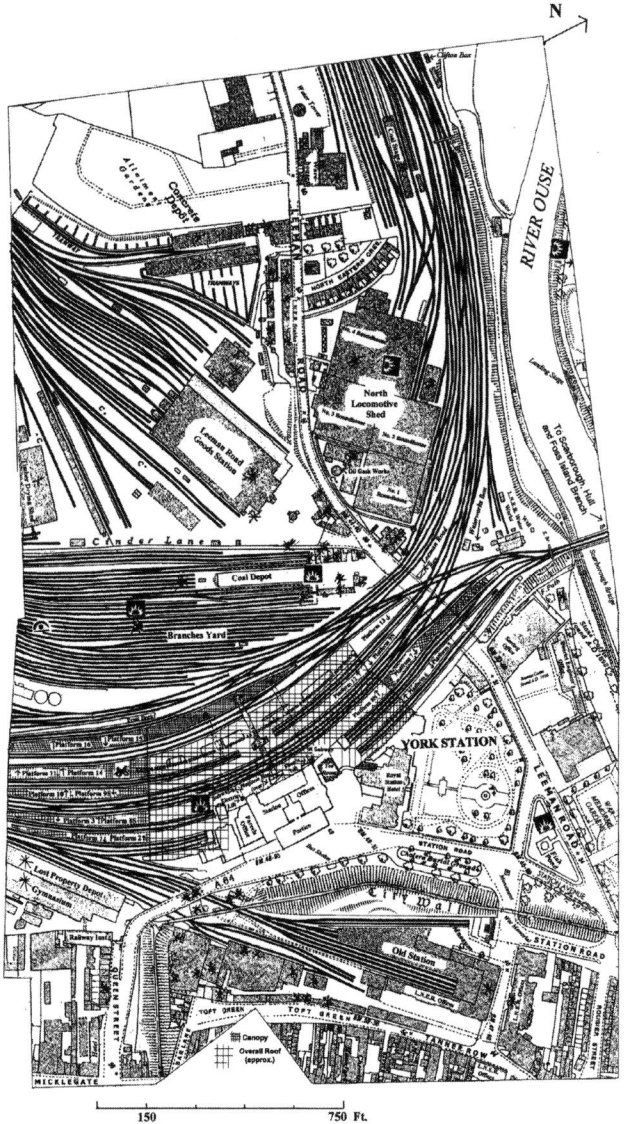
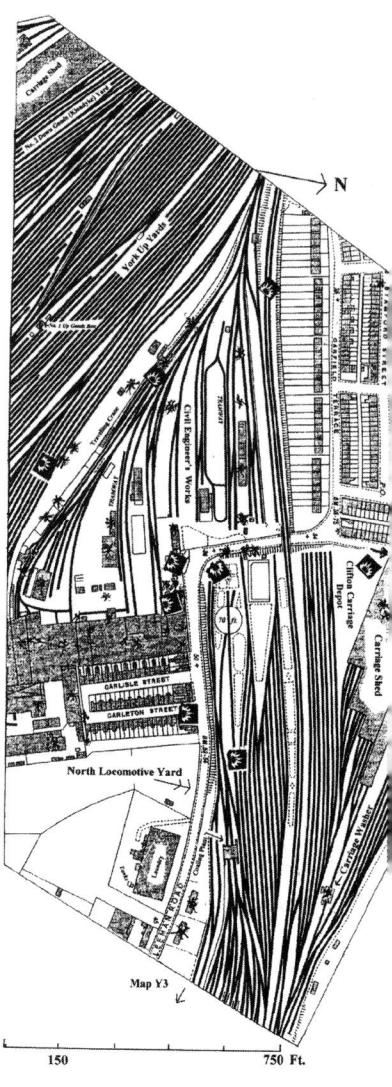

Above left: York station (showing some later alterations), Branches and Leeman Road Goods Yards and North locomotive shed, 1937. Note: York maps have the sites where bombs fell in late April 1942 added to them.

Above right: The area to the west of the station and north locomotive shed.

Through movements along the main platforms 8 and 9 and the centre lines were passed between the locomotive yard, platform and Waterworks boxes, and the last two worked with Clifton box. Platform box was responsible for the central crossovers, Leeman Road for the north end bays Nos 12, 13 and 16, and Waterworks for the 'Scarborough Corner' bays Nos 4 to 7. The Waterworks Crossing was controlled jointly by Leeman Road and Waterworks boxes, by means of electrical releases and slotted signals whereby both boxes had to 'pull off' the appropriate slot before the signal arm would move to 'clear' position. In May 1951, the work of all these mechanical signal boxes, also those at Chaloner's Whin and South Points, was taken over by the new panel signal box; also certain permanent way alterations were made.

At the north end of the station began the severe S-bend, first to the west and then to the north, bringing the main lines serving the 1877 station to run parallel with the Goods lines which were on the alignment of the original railway into York from the north. The tracks north of platforms 12 to 16 converged into the Down and Up 'Station' lines. Along with Goods lines diverging off the Scarborough Goods lines, these ran parallel to the main lines as far as Clifton box, where they joined together to form the main lines northwards to Skelton Junction and beyond. Thus at Clifton, the eight running lines from the station area—the four Up lines having access to platforms 8 to 13—converged to six, to seven after the Up Bank Loop was added during the war. The complex was controlled partly by Waterworks box (Up and Down main lines and the Bank loop) and partly by the Leeman Road box (Up and Down station lines and the Goods lines from York Yard South). Clifton box also directed access to the Clifton Carriage Yard, which consisted of several groups of sidings each side of the main line, the Carriage Shed being on the Up side, and the North shed opposite on the Down side.

Traffic in and out of the York Yards on the avoiding line was regulated by York Yard South and York Yard North boxes and by three further internal Yard boxes—No. 1 Down Goods, No. 2 Up Goods and No. 1 Up Goods. York Yard South box[27], was situated where the six Goods lines, sweeping round from Holgate Bridge Junction, along with eight northward

Leeman Road and Waterworks signal boxes, York.

sidings dealing mainly with livestock traffic on the inside (west side) of the curve, met the Scarborough Goods lines which curved sharply round from Leeman Road to the east. Between these groups of through lines were those giving access to the three south sheds (NER, MR and GNR) mentioned previously, and to the permanent way sidings. The south box also controlled the lines into Branches yard and coal depot, which comprised no less than 30 roads to either side of the Scarborough Goods lines. The lines that continued on through the York Yard complex comprised Down and Up main goods lines and to the east of them three further Up lines (Goods, Goods No. 1 and 'B' departure lines).

Past the Up Yard again were four more lines: the exit from the Up Yard, the 'Frodingham' and 'York' lines, also the Down Mineral line, which became an Up Through line, also giving access to Branches Yard and the Wagon Shops. To continue northwards: No. 2 Up Goods box handled the convergence of Nos 3 and 4 with Nos 1 and 2 Up Goods lines, emerging from the main Up Yards and the subsidiary No. 4 group of sidings. Finally, there was the No. 1 Up Goods box at the south exit of the main (14-road) Up Yard. The hump of the main Down Yard (13 roads) adjoined York Yard South box; trains to be shunted had to be brought back from the two Down reception lines by a loop west of the box. At the north end of the Down Yard was No. 1 Down Goods box, with a coal stage and turntable beside it. This latter box was responsible for movements at this end of the Down Yard, as well as the south end of Klondyke Down Yard (11 roads), the other end of which went under York Yard North box. The distance between York Yard South and York Yard North boxes was 0.47 miles. A prominent feature stretching the length of the York Yards to the west was the Carriage Works, with 15 long roads in and beside the range of workshops. These comprised the principal carriage works of the LNER.

Although parallel with the main lines from the station, York Yard North box did not signal them. It controlled the northern outlets of the York Yards, which on the west side of the Down and Up main goods lines comprised four Down Independent lines, three lines out of Klondyke Sidings and two out of the York Carriage Works on the east side, and an Up Independent and a North departure line. In addition, this large box managed the traffic into the Up Yards by the North arrival line, the 'Frodingham' and 'York' lines going round to York Yard South, the access to the wagon works and lastly the lines into and out of Leeman Road Goods Depot by the Warehouse branch, which in turn, by means of a ground frame, gave access to the extensive Engineer's yard and to Bradley's Sidings.

Northwards of York North box were the nine Down departure and four Up arrival lines, flanking the continuation of the main goods lines on each side, which stretched over half a mile to Skelton Junction. Accessed off No. 9 (westernmost) feparture line through a gate were the extensive sidings of the British Sugar Corporation factory that occupied a large site over to the west. At Skelton Junction, the Goods lines finally joined up with the main lines coming from York station, and the branch to Knaresborough and Harrogate diverged on the Down side. Apart from a small group of sidings next to the Harrogate branch, also the Skelton Engineer's Low Yard there and his High Yard beyond the junction on the Down side, Skelton Junction in 1939 marked the limit of the York goods yards.

The NER had thus evolved a complex of yards sufficient—until the Second World War—for marshalling the goods traffic at York. In addition to the two through Goods lines that passed straight through the York Yards, the Company had built three other Goods lines, which skirted

The East Coast Main Line's Principal Points

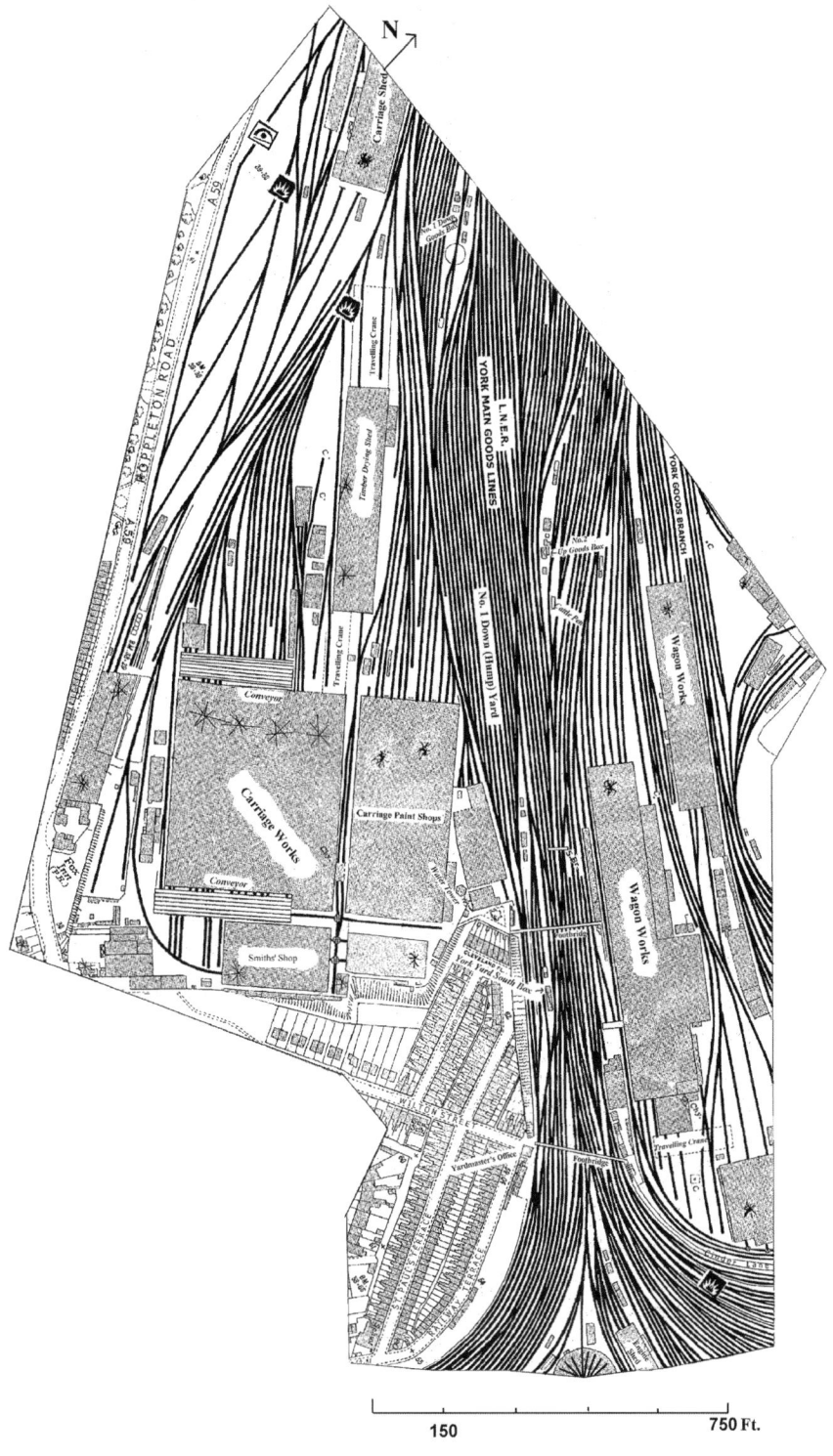

York was also a major engineering centre for the LNER as the Carriage Works were the largest for the company; the Wagon Works mainly dealt with repairs.

the yards on their east side and as well gave access to the Scarborough lines. The latter facility was used principally for goods traffic for Foss Islands and the Derwent Valley Light Railway. In the war, the extra traffic necessitated the addition of another Up Independent line (the Bank Loop) to Clifton and through the passenger station. Only in dire emergencies were passenger trains allowed to run on the Goods lines through York Yard, although special permission was eventually obtained from the Ministry of Transport Inspector for running up to three through trains on summer Saturdays in 1950. Afterwards this practice was unnecessary because the major resignalling in 1951 enabled a freer flow of all traffic.

The Down and Up Independent lines serving York Yards continued—on the Down side—for a further 1½ miles to Skelton Bridge, where the lines converged into a two-track bottleneck over the River Ouse. During the war yet another large yard, Skelton New Sidings, was built along this stretch on the Down side, but for both Down and Up traffic, along with servicing facilities including a 70-foot turntable. Skelton box was entirely rebuilt at the time and converted mainly to power operation. At the northern end of the new Yard the Down Independent was joined on to the Down Slow by constructing a new single-line bridge over the River Ouse, relieving the existing bottleneck. Skelton Junction was also the beginning of the 42½-mile stretch of the ECML to Darlington, which had recently been re-signalled before the war with modern electrical equipment.

The profusion of lines and yards reflects the magnitude of the traffic at York. Major flows of passengers and freight joined the ECML there for onward movement to North-East England and Scotland, coming from the Midlands, Central South and South-West England, Wales, Lancashire and West Yorkshire. The resulting patterns of passenger and freight train services were of great diversity. Apart from main line passenger trains on the trunk ECML from Doncaster, London and the South to Newcastle, Edinburgh and beyond, the passenger traffic from the north end of York station comprised trains to Teesside via Northallerton and Eaglescliffe as well as eastwards to Scarborough, Whitby and Bridlington.

Other than the Up ECML, expresses southwards from York ran to West Yorkshire and Lancashire, routed either by the former NER line to Leeds and thence by the LMSR (ex-LNWR) line via Huddersfield and Stalybridge to Manchester and Liverpool or to Stockport, Crewe, etc., or by the LMSR (ex-L&YR) route via Normanton and Wakefield to Manchester and Liverpool. There were the LMSR Midland Division trains by the S&K line via Pontefract to Sheffield LMSR and southwards on to Birmingham and Bristol. LNER trains also went by the S&K line to the GCR, then west via Wath and Woodhead or south via Mexborough and Sheffield Victoria (or the Darnall Curve) and so eventually to London Marylebone or via Banbury to the GWR and SR. The trains to the LMSR nearly always changed from LNER to LMSR motive power at York—even during the war—while those on the LNER line to Leeds changed engines mainly there. After Nationalisation, LMR engines quite often worked through to Scarborough and not infrequently to Teesside and Newcastle on excursions.[28] During the war, the regular overnight train to Bristol ran up the ECML to serve Selby before turning towards Sheffield. 'Unusual' routings of LMSR engines occurred with troop specials, although this would depend on the route knowledge of the drivers.

As well as stopping services on the main lines, local trains ran from York west to Harrogate, north to Gilling and Pickering (until January 1953) and east to Hull. Tank engines (G5s, N8s or N9s), also on the Harrogate line before the war, steam railcars, worked the shorter runs,

The East Coast Main Line's Principal Points

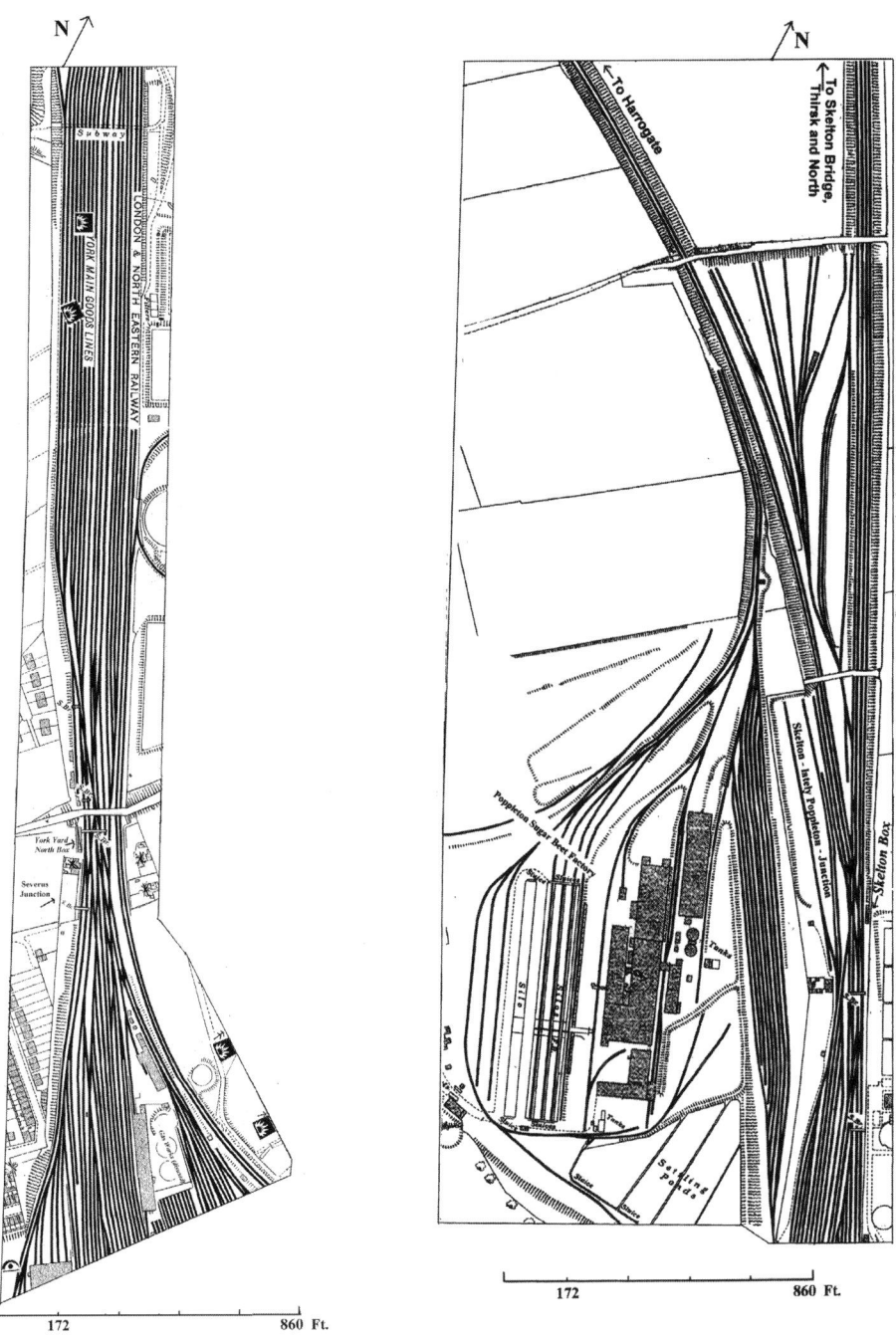

Above left: York North Yard to Skelton Junction, 1937, showing some of the locations where bombs fell during the raid of April 1942.

Above right: Skelton Junction for the Harrogate line and the location of the Poppleton sugar beet factory.

with D20s and D49s made the longer runs, such as to Hull. Starbeck and Hull (Botanic Gardens and Dairycoates) sheds worked to York on these services, adding to the general variety. From mid-1957, many of the local services were passed on to DMUs.

The larger passenger locomotives (Pacifics and V2s) predominated at York on the ECML expresses, helped at busy times by K3s or NER Atlantics and B16s. On the many secondary services to Leeds, Scarborough and Hull, D49s were the mainstay, supplemented by NER D20s and D21s, or by GCR 4-6-0s and 4-4-0s from Lincolnshire. While B17s were generally rare north of Hitchin, they did venture to York before the war via the GN&GE Joint line and on specials off the GCR line, working through from Leicester to Newcastle on trains that took the Darnall Curve, so did not change engines at Sheffield.

After the war, B1s took over many of the secondary services. Holiday trains to the coastal resorts were most often hauled by B16s from York and Neville Hill sheds also by B1s post-war. In the 1950s, LMSR-type and BR Standard 2-6-0s and 2-6-4Ts appeared regularly from Scarborough, Whitby and Hull. The LMSR trains were worked mainly by 'Jubilees', 'Black Fives', Hughes 2-6-0s, and in the 1950s by BR Standard Class Fives.

York's freight traffic comprised a number of major flows of minerals and general merchandise to and from the areas of heavy industry of Yorkshire, Lancashire and the Midlands to the north-east. Many of these trains originated at one of the yards in the York area, while others ran through between the north-east and Scotland and various points in the South and West, also to and from Hull. During and after the war, many more of the trains were scheduled to pass through, stopping only for examination—not marshalling—and for locomotive and crew changes. The many and various yards were certainly kept busy, for the freight traffic through York was extremely heavy. Before the war, they were handling some 160,000 wagons a month, and this figure may well have been half as much again during the war and in the years immediately after it.

With all these regular workings, and during the war countless *ad hoc* workings under 'Control orders', it was to be expected that LNER locomotives would turn up at York from all the main line sheds on the former NER, most of those on the former GNR and GCR and a few (such as March) on the GER, as well as the ex-NBR's St Margaret's and Haymarket depots. LMSR locomotives would turn up from most of the sheds in its Central and Midlands Divisions as well as some in the Western Division. The long-haul freight trains through York were worked by all the larger types of the LNER mixed traffic and freight locomotives, also in particular, B16s. During the war, every conceivable passenger tender engine was pressed into freight work, especially before the introduction of the War Department's 'Austerity' 2-8-0s and 2-10-0s. In the 1950s, LNER 2-8-0s became rarer at York and were replaced by BR Class 9F 2-10-0 locomotives, in addition to an increased use of Pacifics, V2s, B1s and K3s on braked goods trains.

As there was a limited amount of local freight traffic at York, smaller LNER freight locomotives were rather less in evidence, except during the war. The country stations were sources of considerable traffic, and on the line to Scarborough, there were still goods yards, many of which were quite busy during the war, at 10 of the 12 intermediate stations closed to passengers in September 1930. Furthermore, there was the freight branch turning off at Burton Lane Junction, shortly before the Market Weighton line curved off from the Scarborough line at Bootham Junction. This served the Rowntree's Factory Halt and other factories, also goods depots at Foss Islands and Layerthorpe. Unadvertised passenger trains ran to Rowntree's Halt from York until July 1988, having earlier run through from Selby. At Foss Islands Junction, the private Derwent Valley Light Railway used to branch off and run south to a junction with the NER Selby–Market Weighton line at Cliff Common. The DVLR lost its passenger service in 1926, but remained open for freight until 1964 and part survives as a 'heritage' railway.

York to Darlington

When leaving York station, a northbound ECML train had to labour slowly round the sharp left-hand curve passing the locomotive depot of the left. Beyond Clifton Carriage Sidings on the Up side was the Waterworks siding, controlled by a ground frame released by Skelton box. A mile from Clifton box at York Yard North box, the freight-avoiding lines came in on the left, closely followed by the junction at Skelton. Then began the long, level and virtually straight 'racing ground' of the ECML across the plain of York to Thirsk (22 miles) and on slightly rising gradients to Northallerton (30 miles).

In the 1940s and 1950s, the ECML from York to Northallerton had a traffic density as great as that on any other extensive stretch of main line in the country, with freight trains moving in almost every block. Before the war, over 60 freight trains were scheduled each weekday both ways and there would also by numerous unscheduled trains. In this stretch, all these had to share the double-track with about 45 daily passenger and parcels trains each way during the week. In the war, this caused a strangulation of the traffic; even after the conflict, the traffic density continued to increase for at least ten years. Four lines were in use, but with only one Up line between Pilmoor and Alne until 1960, by which time the need for the extra capacity began to decline.

From immediately north of Skelton Bridge almost to Alne, there were four tracks in 1939; thereafter to just south of Pilmoor, an extra Down line had been installed. Also for half a mile south of Thirsk (at Green Lane), there were Up and Down Goods loops. Between the north end of Thirsk and Longlands Junction at Northallerton, there were again four tracks. At Northallerton, a new Up loop had been constructed, connecting the Stockton–Leeds line at Boroughbridge Road Junction and burrowing under the ECML to the Up Slow line at Longlands Junction.

Together with these widenings of the running routes, a completely new signalling system had been installed in the mid-1930s between Skelton Junction and Northallerton, and this was taken through to Darlington South immediately before the war. Included in all this 1930s modernisation had been the complete rebuilding of the stations at Beningbrough and Otterington, and of the Down side at Alne and Raskelf. The two-platform wayside station at Sessay and the larger one at Thirsk remained unaltered at this time, but were to be radically rebuilt during the subsequent widening of the ECML during the war. The rebuilt stations were of a contemporary design in brick with high-pitched tiled roofs having large overhanging eaves. Beningbrough, Tollerton and Otterington had platforms only on the Slow lines. At Alne, where there was already a bay on the Up side for Easingwold trains, a platform was built for the new Down Slow, while at Raskelf the Down platform had been made into an island.

All of the seven wayside stations on this stretch of the ECML had adequate goods facilities. Except at Pilmoor, where they were rudimentary and on the Moor Siding situated off the Boroughbridge branch, they were on each side of the line and embodied coal-drops. There were also goods sidings on the Up side at Sessay Wood Junction (for the Gilling branch) and at Manor House (Otterington). Crossovers between the Fast and Slow lines and between Down and Up Fast lines existed at each intermediate station and also at Skelton Bridge, Sessay Wood, Thirsk Green Lane and the north end of Thirsk Yard.

The resignalling, which at the time was 'state of the art', entailed the replacement of the Hall automatic semaphore signals installed by the NER between Alne and Thirsk in 1903–04 by an electrical system incorporating colour-light signals, power-operated points and electrical route-relay interlocking. New part-power signal boxes had been built at Beningbrough, Alne, Sessay Wood (later called Pilmoor South) and Otterington. At Thirsk, a new power signal box of completely modern design. At Skelton, Tollerton, Raskelf, and Pilmoor station (later called Pilmoor North), the existing manual boxes were converted to partial power-operation, although as at Beningbrough and Otterington, and except for Skelton, they were not in use continuously. The colour-lights were three-aspect (four-aspect where spacing was closer than usual), with position light junction and shunting signals. All sections were controlled by track circuits, and apart from the signals worked at times by the above boxes, which were opened when needed, automatic colour-light signals were sited between the boxes to divide this busy line into shorter sections. The box at Sessay Wood controlled not only the south to east junction onto the line towards Sunbeck Junction and Gilling, but also the east to north connection from the Gilling branch towards Pilmoor, while Pilmoor station box worked the connections from the Boroughbridge branch.

At Thirsk, the box—with a rather novel route-setting panel, now at the National Railway Museum—could control not only the main line from the Sessay Wood direction through towards Otterington, but also the branch coming from Melmerby. Ground frames, in-section or released by the nearest box, were used for access to sidings on the Up side just north of Beningbrough, at Sessay and at Manor House near Otterington, also the siding connection with the Easingwold Railway at Alne.

Just before Beningbrough was the sign 'Edinburgh 200 miles', and just after Alne 'London 200 miles'. Between these was a 'Halfway' sign and it was here, eight miles from York, that the enginemen of the non-stop expresses changed over by means of the corridor tenders fitted to A3 and A4 Class Pacifics. An oddity to be seen at Alne was the ancient little train of the independent Easingwold Railway, the branch curving away north-east just beyond the station. This railway was not nationalised in 1948 and had its own private engine until 1947, when it was withdrawn and a locomotive was hired from BR. Before the war, there were six weekday passenger (or mixed) trips on the Easingwold line each way, cut to two during and after the war until passenger services ceased in November 1948.[29] During the war, the line was so important for servicing airfields that it was completely relaid, thereafter carrying over 60,000 tons of war materials.

A mile or so before Pilmoor, the single-line branch from Gilling, Malton and Pickering joined on the Up side by a triangle of double lines from Sunbeck Junction. The junctions on the ECML here were known as Bishophouse and Sessay Wood, although in the resignalling of 1933, the box at Bishophouse was closed because the new one at Sessay Wood was

Alne station—11 miles north of York—after remodelling in the 1930s.

able to control both junctions. Regular passenger trains (four in 1939, two eventually in the 1950s) were withdrawn from the branch at the end of January 1952 and the south curve was taken out of use in February 1959. The branch continued to be used for school specials to Ampleforth College, occasionally other specials and, being able to take Pacifics and V2s, until September 1962 summer seasonal trains through to Scarborough.

The north curve was then closed—after an accident—while freight traffic (including chalk from Burdale via Malton) lasted until August 1964. At Pilmoor itself, another single-line branch joined on the Down side from Boroughbridge and Knaresborough to the south-west; the station—with no road access and basically an interchange station—had a separate platform for the branch trains.[30] Passenger trains (two a day, four on Saturdays) ceased in September 1950, and the section as far as Brafferton was closed completely, the goods traffic being worked to there from Knaresborough until October 1964. Just south of Pilmoor, there remained the formation of a west to east chord connecting the two branches, but this was not brought into use and the bridge over the main line was demolished during the widening works in 1942. Near the embankment on the west side, four semaphore signals were set up for testing enginemen's eyesight.

Before Thirsk station, there was a small yard of five roads on the Down side and next to it a small engine shed (closed in 1930 though not demolished until 1965), followed by the junction with the double-track Melmerby line. Although part of this line was often reduced to single track for wagon storage, it was still traversed by certain regular trains coming from Leeds via Harrogate and calling at Thirsk. Yet the two wayside stations on the Melmerby line had only one or two trains a day even in 1939, and the line was closed completely in September 1959. A goods line extended eastward from it at Thirsk Town Junction and ran back over the main line for a mile to Thirsk Town; this survived until October 1966.

Until the wartime widening, there were only two tracks through Thirsk station, so there were just two platforms (with northward dock bays on the Down side), but in 1939, there were already Down and Up Slow lines from immediately north of the station through to Northallerton. Adjacent to the Up side, there were the usual goods facilities including a sizable coal yard on a spur, together with small carriage sidings and a wagon-repair yard. The strikingly modern signal box at Thirsk stood prominently on the Down side north of the station. Also north of Thirsk station was a latent marshalling yard, for in 1912, there had been established a Down Yard with four reception roads with a group of six and another of 10 northward roads, plus an Up Yard of four southward roads and five reception and as many as 20 other through roads.

Between the wars, these yards had almost been abandoned, but with hostilities renewed in late 1939, they were revived. The Up Yard especially was then used a great deal, mainly for holding 'convoy' coal trains waiting for paths south. It continued to be used into the 1950s, being controlled from the power box at Thirsk, rather than three manual boxes, which had been used previously.

Eight miles on from Thirsk and after Otterington was Northallerton. On the approaches to it, the secondary (Leeds Northern) main line from Harrogate and Leeds converged from the left, and at Longlands Junction, a single-line connection for Down ECML freight trains bound for Teesside diverged to join the Leeds route at Boroughbridge Road box. In the reverse direction, the corresponding Up Loop burrowed under the ECML just south of the station. From Cordio Junction, the Leeds Northern line avoided Northallerton station on the west, passed Boroughbridge Road box, then the disused Low Level station at Romanby Gates, and continued as the main line to Eaglescliffe and the Teesside conurbation. Passenger trains to and from Teesside calling at Northallerton used the connection between Cordio Junction and Northallerton South Junction and rejoined the Low Level line at Northallerton East Junction, but most Down—and a few Up—through trains used the avoiding line.

Northallerton was a point of divergence for major flows of heavy freight from the south to Teesside. Most of these freight trains ran in and out of Newport Yards, between Thornaby and Middlesbrough, which handled 5,000 to 6,000 wagons per day. Nevertheless, the important Leeds Northern line was closed for passenger traffic between Harrogate and Northallerton in March 1967 and remained open from Starbeck to Melmerby for freight until October 1969. Even the line between Northallerton and Eaglescliffe was closed to passenger trains in October 1990.

Northallerton station was little changed from opening in 1841 and was built on a bridge over a major road from, which the main entrance led to the Up platform. The latter had a bay at its south end, while the Down platform—partially staggered to the north—was an island with two bays at the north end. There were some five sidings on the Down side just north of the station, but the goods yard and substantial coal yard were on the Up side. There was an engine turntable on this side, although the small locomotive shed itself was adjacent to the Low Level line on the Down side.

Being the converging point of two trunk routes, Northallerton was one of the busiest junctions on the whole ECML. Apart from the frequent expresses and countless freights passing through without stopping, there were a number of secondary passenger trains on the Leeds–Harrogate–Northallerton–Stockton–West Hartlepool route. After the war, very few trains called at the wayside stations between Ripon, Northallerton and Eaglescliffe. Newby Wiske and West Rounton Gates were closed in September 1939, and by the mid-1950s, the others enjoyed only one or two trains a day at most—at Sinderby and Pickhill, in one direction only. Then there was the Wensleydale line from Northallerton to Hawes, where a connection was made with the LMSR branch from Garsdale (closed in March 1959). Normally worked by G5s or J21s, the Wensleydale passenger service consisted of three trains through to Hawes and one or two to Leyburn.[31] These lasted until April 1954 but considerable freight, also milk and military traffic from Leyburn and occasional excursions as far as Redmire, kept the Wensleydale line open until April 1964, and for stone traffic from Redmire until 1993. During the war, the line was considered a through Transpennine route by virtue of its connection with the LMSR at Garsdale, but no evidence of its use for this purpose has come to light.

With automatic signalling, Northallerton power box controlled the main line and its junctions, working with power boxes at Thirsk to the south and Eryholme to the north; on the Leeds Northern line, it worked with Newby Wiske to the south and Northallerton East towards Eaglescliffe. The points and signals at Longlands and Cordio Junctions were operated entirely remotely. Northallerton power box also handled the single-line Wensleydale branch as far as Northallerton West Junction (inclusive), although it did not control the Low Level avoiding line. This large signal box (reinforced during the war) was situated on the Up side where the line to Eaglescliffe, Stockton, etc., diverged at High Junction, to join the Leeds Northern line at Low Junction (East) box, which passed under the ECML through the Low Level. The switches for the single-line Hawes branch were also opposite Northallerton box, but this line ran beside the main line for a further 300 yards before curving away to the west. Some 600 yards further on towards Darlington was Castle Hills Junction (controlled remotely from Northallerton box) and a single-line west to north loop from Northallerton West trailed (with an accompanying Up siding) into the Down Slow line. During the war, an emergency double-track loop was built—across the Wensleydale branch—to connect the Low Level line at Romanby Gates with the ECML northwards at Castle Hills.

The next stretch of the ECML to Darlington (14½ miles) took trains into County Durham, crossing the River Tees at Croft Spa by a skew bridge. Two miles from Northallerton were the troughs at Wiske Moor. These were on the Fast lines only, being flanked by Down and Up slow lines that ran from Castle Hills Junction to Wiske Moor Siding. Apart from additional Down and Up Slow lines from north of Cowton to Eryholme, the ECML was otherwise only double-track from Wiske Moor to Black Banks at the beginning of Croft Yard. There were three wayside stations before Darlington, each with a small goods yard: Danby Wiske, Cowton and Croft Spa. There were crossovers at Wiske Moor, Cowton, Eryholme and Croft Spa, but not at Danby Wiske. At Eryholme Junction, halfway between Cowton and Croft Spa, the branch from Richmond and Catterick Camp trailed in on the Down side. Platforms at Eryholme station (closed 1911) were still visible, while the new platforms installed in September 1944 for the use of RAF personnel at Croft Airfield were on the Richmond branch. Goods traffic was handled at Eryholme until 1964, there being a small set of goods sidings on the Up side.

There was a good service of about a dozen trains a day (and a few on Sundays) between Darlington and Richmond, yet the branch was closed to passengers in March 1969; freight continued to Catterick Bridge only until February 1970. There was a subsidiary branch from Catterick Bridge to Catterick Camp Centre to serve the vast military installation. As well as seeing numerous military specials, Camp Centre station was served in the war (from October 1943) by a push-and-pull service, connecting at Brompton Road (near

Catterick Bridge station) with the local trains to and from Richmond, supplemented from May 1944 by a direct service from Darlington, reversing at Catterick Bridge. In the 1950s, through locals were run at weekends between Catterick Camp and Darlington and also through trains (via Darlington) to Birmingham and to King's Cross, supplemented at major holiday times by special trains to various other destinations.

The signalling between Northallerton and Darlington was modernised in 1939 as the final stage of the overall York–Darlington scheme, the work at Northallerton actually being completed on the day war broke out. This stretch of line was then regulated from just three signal boxes: Northallerton, Eryholme and Darlington South, with automatic colour-light signals in between and position light route indicators at junctions. At Northallerton, all signals and points were operated electrically, but the new signal box at Eryholme (opened in June 1939) was an electro-mechanical installation, having both a panel and a lever frame, with the latter operating the junction with the Richmond branch and certain other connections situated nearby. The remote connections at Cowton and the main line colour-light signals were controlled by thumb switches on the panel. Mechanical ground frames were left at certain places where there were sidings: Castle Hills Junction, Wiske Moor, Danby Wiske (North and South), Cowton, Croft Spa (Up and Down), and Black Banks. At Croft Yard, the earlier signal box (with a shortened frame of 50 levers) was retained as a ground frame, subject to control from Darlington South box for movements relating to the main line. Signalling at the Northallerton and Eryholme boxes was operated under the route-relay system by means of thumb switches on the panels with illuminated track diagrams. At Darlington South, where the new system interfaced with the older mechanical and semaphore system onwards on the ECML and the various other lines, there was an all-electric locking-frame with individual working of all points and signals by 155 miniature levers.[32]

Darlington

Over 1¼ miles north from Croft Spa was Black Banks Junction, from which ran a Down Independent line serving as a southern entry to Croft Yard. The Up Independent ended shortly afterwards, having come right through from Springfield—1½ miles to the north of Darlington. After a further 1¾ miles was Croft Junction, before which the large Croft Yard (12 northward roads and six reception sidings) was passed, all being on the Down side. Between there and Darlington South, in addition to the Down and Up Independent lines, there was a crossover each way and the northern access to Croft Yard, which had up to six reception sidings on its northern approaches. The box also regulated the junction with the single-line Croft branch. This was a remnant of the former Stockton & Darlington Railway (S&DR), which ran west of the yard and terminated at a coal depot close to Croft Spa station. Croft Junction box controlled on the Up side the junction with the east to south Snipe House Curve from the Stockton line at Geneva Junction and also led to the large Civil Engineer's central reclamation and storage yard.

Shortly after came Darlington South Junction. Here, from the east and opposite Darlington South power box, the important line from Eaglescliffe, Middlesbrough and Saltburn converged. Indirectly, this also gave access to Stockton and the secondary main line along the

The East Coast Main Line's Principal Points

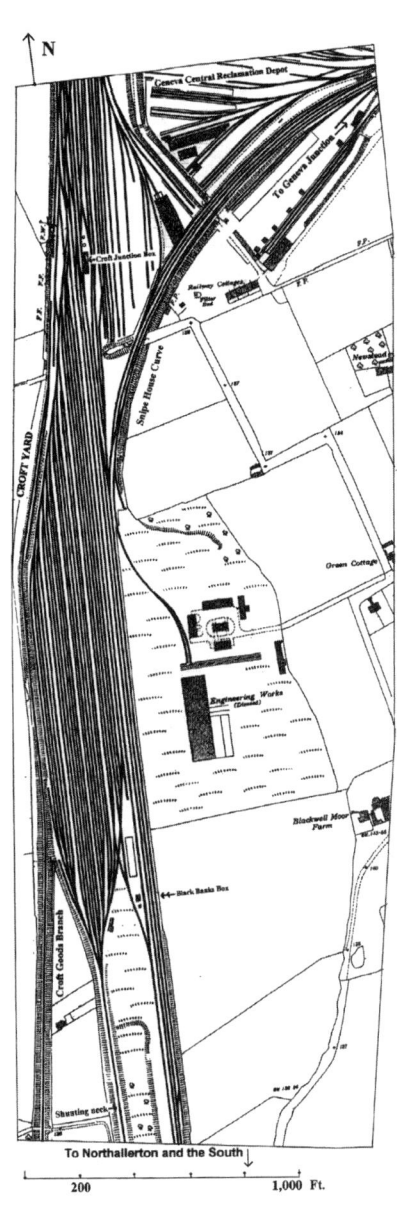

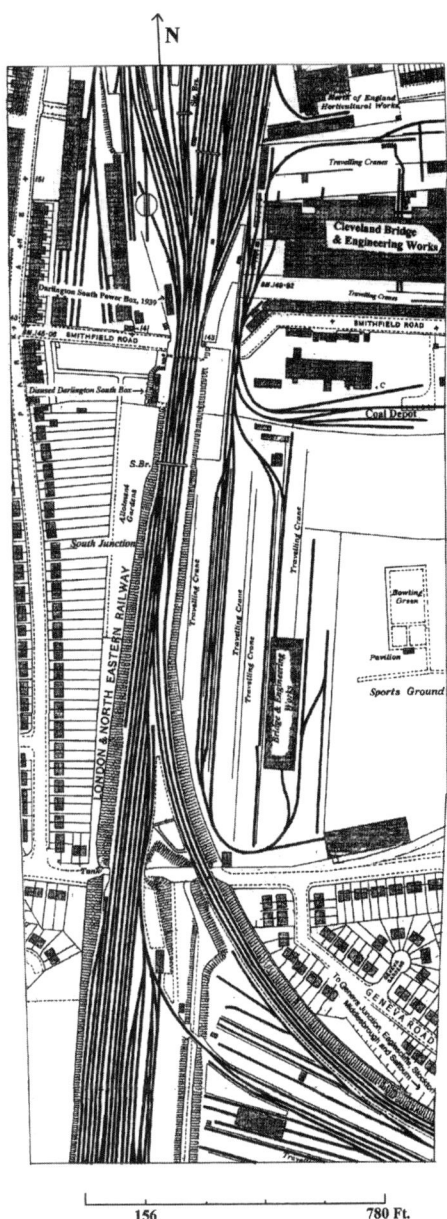

Above left: Croft Yard, Darlington, 1939.

Above right: The lines south of Darlington with the junction for Stockton and connections to various engineering firms.

Durham coast. The tracks here went SE to Geneva Junction on the Saltburn line and formed a 'modern' (1887) diversion from Oak Tree Junction on the Stockton & Darlington Railway, which originally ran across to Darlington North Road via Fighting Cocks and crossed the ECML on the level a mile north of Bank Top station at S&D Crossing box.

The main line station at Bank Top had one huge island platform protected by two roofs in three spans (each 60 feet high by 1,000 feet long) reaching across from a central rank of cast-iron columns and archways, partly closed at each end by glazed screens. The main Down side of the island was platform 4 and the Up side platform 1. Platforms 2 and 3 were the two bays at the south end and platforms 5 and 6 the two at the north end, where there was also a dock road; there were two middle roads between bay platforms 2 and 4. Starting outside the station on the west side was the Down Duplicate line, which ran through to Parkgate Junction, where a loop diverged; the former line was extended during the war into a second Down Goods line through to Darlington North. These lines gave access to and from a turntable and seven more siding roads, some of which served the horse dock and loading docks associated with the Civil Engineer's shops.

On the east side inside the station sidewall, there was an Up Duplicate line, connected with the Up platform line by a scissors crossover, as was the corresponding Down line and an Up and Down Siding. Outside the station on the east side were five through lines: Down main, Up main, independent lines and No. 1 Up Siding, which, as well as connecting with the Up Independent at Darlington South, joined a No. 2 Siding to become the Down Siding round to Geneva Junction. Also on the Up side opposite the South box was a cattle dock and the Cleveland Bridge and Engineering Works and other factories, and then a group of seven Up sidings known as the 'GN Yard'. To the east of the Up Independent lines was Darlington Bank Top Goods Depot with a marshalling yard (eight through roads) and another cattle dock.

North of Bank Top station as far as Parkgate Junction were other yards. On the Down side were the carriage sidings, Northgate Coal Yard and power station sidings (with coal cells and eight southward roads), and further on were ten northward roads and access to the Henry Williams Railway Works. On the Up side was a yard known as Haughton Bridge Up Sidings (11 southward roads), together with the main Darlington locomotive shed. A loop ran round the eastern side of Haughton Sidings, first serving a loading dock and spawning three northward roads before giving access to the south end of the locomotive yard and its large coaling stage. On the western side next to the main line were three through reception lines and a fourth line that connected with the engine roads at each end of the depot. Before 1939, the shed only had four through engine lines, but at the beginning of the war, extensive improvements had been made to the layout as well as expansion of Haughton Bridge Sidings.

Darlington South box was located on the Down side at the south end of Bank Top and controlled all the lines south as far as Eryholme Junction including Croft Yard. North box was a large manual one with 150 levers, situated almost opposite the locomotive depot and controlling all the lines at the north end of the station. On the Up side, North box handled the sets of crossovers on the through lines and the several connections into the locomotive and goods yards, while on the Down side, it managed the coal yard and other sidings. In May 1939, control of the scissors crossovers midway along the Up and Down (platforms 1 and 4) lines, previously worked by the small East and West boxes situated in the main station buildings, was taken over by North and South boxes respectively.

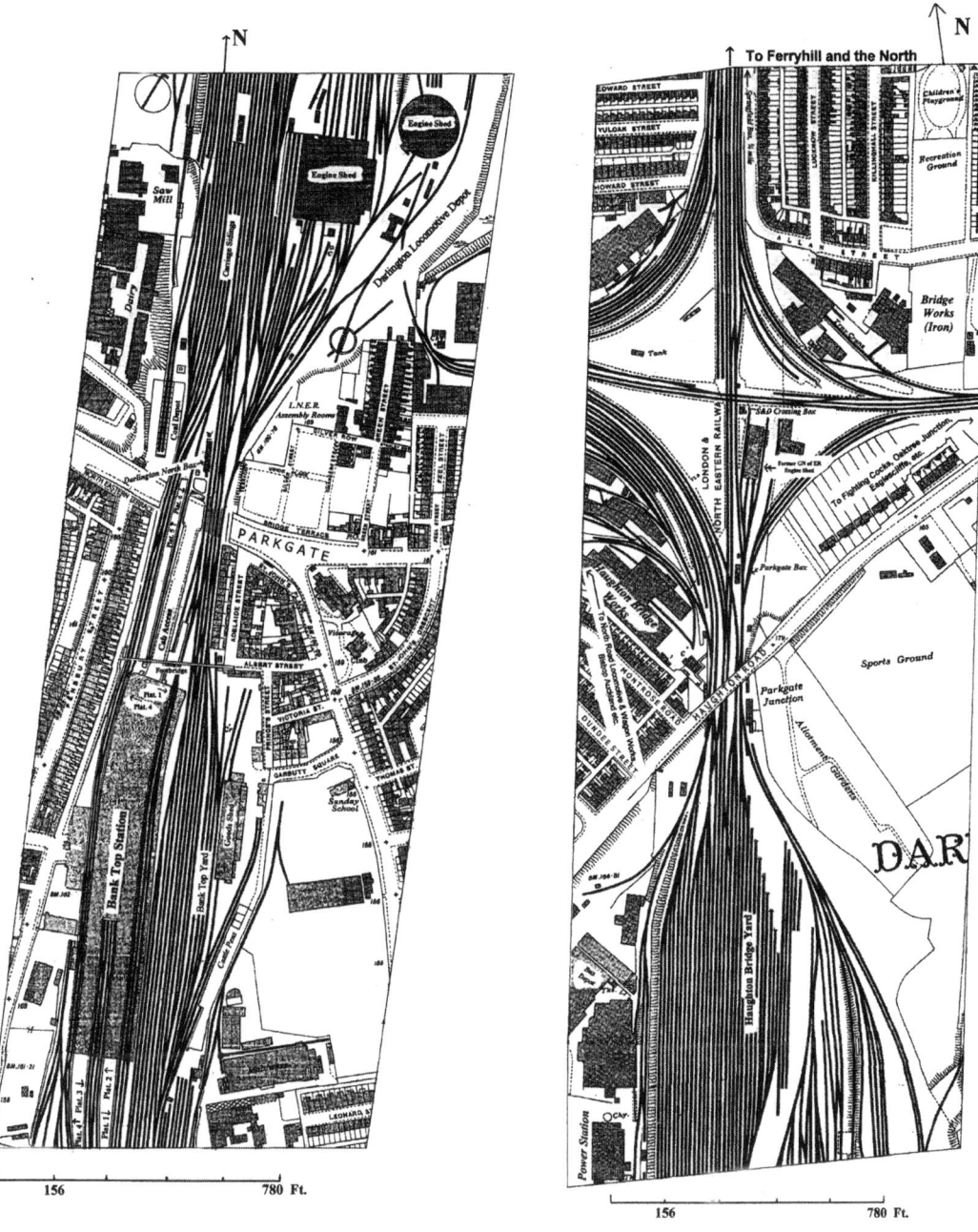

Above left: Darlington Bank Top station with the Carriage Sidings and locomotive shed to the north.

Above right: Haughton Bridge Yard, Darlington, and the junctions with the old Stockton & Darlington line.

Apart from the heavy passenger and freight traffic on the ECML, and the busy and thriving service of Teesside local trains to Middlesbrough, Redcar and Saltburn, there were quite frequent local trains from Bank Top to Bishop Auckland and on to Crook with a few extended to Tow Law, or to Wearhead in the depths of West Durham. The Wearhead passenger trains (four in the end, weekdays only) were taken off in June 1953, and those to Tow Law were cut back to Crook in June 1956. Usage was much enhanced by diesel cars, but services were cut back to Bishop Auckland in March 1965. Freight continued on the Wearhead branch, but was cut back in stages in the 1960s to Eastgate Cement Works. A service of six weekday trains also ran from Bank Top to Middleton-in-Teesdale via Barnard Castle until the line was closed in November 1964 (April 1965 for freight). Finally, there was the cross-Pennine line via Barnard Castle over Stainmore to Kirkby Stephen, Penrith and Tebay. This was eventually closed completely in January 1962, after a passenger service of four or five trains (and one on Sundays) had survived to run from Darlington to Penrith, with connections (until December 1952) at Kirkby Stephen to Tebay. This infamous line, with weak viaducts and propensity to snowdrifts, had to be worked with smaller engines, which were often paired. The NER J21 0-6-0s were the most popular, but also GER E4 2-4-0s worked the line until 1942. After Nationalisation, LMSR 2MT 2-6-0s took over, followed by the BR Standard 2MT and 3MT Classes. Locomotives working over Stainmore were mainly allocated to West Auckland and Kirkby Stephen sheds.

Some of the lighter branch services in the Darlington District were entrusted to G5 0-4-4Ts and before 1940 to steam railcars based at West Auckland. The important feeder services from Richmond, Teesside and Bishop Auckland were hauled by A5 and A8 Class 4-6-2Ts, also by V1 and V2 2-6-2Ts and in the 1950s by L1 and LMSR 2-6-4Ts. These locomotives were from Darlington shed or Middlesbrough, Saltburn, Stockton or West Auckland sheds. In 1957, a substantial five-road depot was constructed at Darlington for a large allocation of DMUs, which were kept in the former Carriage Sidings on the Down side opposite the steam shed; from summer 1957, they took over virtually all the local services from Darlington, usually running at more frequent intervals than previously.

Many of the main line freight trains in the Down direction at Darlington originated at Croft Yard, though on the Up, they were largely through from Tyneside Yards to York and beyond. They would have similar motive power to that seen in and around York, but there were numerous local workings that would provide the sight of NER types more characteristic of the pre-Grouping company: Q5 and Q6 0-8-0s and 0-6-0s.

Darlington to Newcastle

The North Road complex of major locomotive and wagon works, and ancillary workshops, together with Hope Town Goods Depot and the various privately owned engineering works at Albert Hill, was not visible from the ECML, being up the former S&DR line to Bishop Auckland, Barnard Castle, etc. This line branched off—with three tracks on the Down side—at Parkgate Junction, one mile north of Bank Top. The large 90-lever Parkgate signal box controlled the northern end of the Haughton Bridge Up Sidings, as well as the branch connections and the West Sidings on the far side of them. It also controlled the northern exits from Bank Top Locomotive Yard, the entries to the Carriage Sidings and the sidings associated with the old East Curve.

The ECML then passed—on the Up side—the former Great North of England Railway engine shed building and crossed the original S&DR double-track line at S&D Crossing box. This box controlled only the S&DR route and for the ECML movements was overruled by Parkgate box. Interestingly, only the south to west curve between the ECML and the S&DR routes was used for through traffic, in spite of maps generally tending to suggest otherwise. There were remnants of three other loops as follows: a west to north curve from Albert Hill was formed by a siding that splayed out into six siding loops mainly concerned with the adjoining Albert Hill Foundry and Darlington Forge Works; north to east loop sidings, mainly facing north but one running through; and a single east to south loop from the Fighting Cocks direction, flanked by two south-facing sidings within the triangle of which were the Oil Gas Works and five further south-facing roads.

Beyond S&D Crossing box, the main line ran, supplemented by the Up Independent line for nearly a mile and over the River Skerne, to Springfield box. Along here on the Down side were more Works and sidings of the Darlington Forge Co. and also (from 1940) an extra Down Goods loop, which was out of use by 1952. Traffic fed into the Up lines from Darlington Wire Mills, Nestfield Works of Rolling Stock and Engineering Ltd and Skerne Ironworks; further on were the Harrowgate Hill Locomotive Works of Robert Stephenson and Hawthorns. Springfield box was abolished in 1954 and its functions incorporated into those of Parkgate box.

Over the 36½ miles down the ECML across County Durham to Newcastle, the main line traffic was heavy, but the line was still double-track for most of the way. There were crossovers only at Parkgate Junction and Springfield box, and then at Aycliffe and at Bradbury. New Down and Up loops had to be put in during the war on this stretch at Preston-le-Skerne. Between Darlington and Ferryhill (13 miles), the ECML followed the valley of the River Skerne and crossed the river no fewer than six times. Aycliffe station was a wayside station with a small goods yard on the Up side and branches on the Down side serving a quarry. West of there, during the war, a vast Royal Ordnance Factory stretched for miles, but was connected to the Darlington–Bishop Auckland and Shildon–Teesside lines not the ECML. After Aycliffe, the ECML ran under the mineral-only Simpasture section between Shildon and Stillington of the Shildon–Newport line. This line was so heavily used it was electrified in 1915, although only until 1934, after which it reverted to steam operation.

Here, on the Up side, could be seen the disused Aycliffe electrical substation, which was particularly large because it had been built in expectation of the electrification of the York–Newcastle main line, a plan projected by the NER after the First World War but forsaken at Grouping. There followed Preston-le-Skerne box, then a little station at Bradbury with goods yard on the Down side. A mile further on, the Chilton Mineral branch passed overhead from the west towards Sedgefield on the Ferryhill–Stockton line, then the main line curved northwards to be joined by the Stockton line just north of its connection with Mainsforth colliery at Ferryhill No. 3 box.

Ferryhill did not serve a place of any size, but was a meeting-point of many lines. It lay at the intersection of the ECML with the important line that carried mineral and freight traffic from North and West Durham to Teesside via Stockton, and just north of Ferryhill the original main line of 1844 ran on to Gateshead via Leamside, Washington and Pelaw. Avoiding Durham, this Leamside line lost its local passenger service (four trains a day) south of Leamside in July 1941, but was used a great deal for freight and at times as a diversionary route for expresses. Also, early each Sunday morning, a through train ran over it from York to Newcastle—before the war with a restaurant car, and in the 1950s, an Up early morning newspaper train ran that way on weekdays.

The service on the Leamside lines sank after the war to just one train between Washington and Newcastle, but this lasted until September 1963. From Ferryhill, branches ran to Bishop Auckland in the west and Hartlepool in the east. Each had flourishing services before the war, which were cut back to near extinction (one or two trains per day) after the war, to be closed for passengers in March 1951 (Spennymoor and Stockton) and in June 1952 (West Hartlepool). The local services were worked chiefly be G5s and before the war by steam railcars from Sunderland, West Auckland, West Hartlepool, Stockton and Middlesbrough sheds. Freight on the lines around Ferryhill was much more important and lasted much longer.

Ferryhill was therefore a busy junction with a maze of lines and interconnections, while its yards and the engine shed were of modest size. The small Ferryhill shed had been closed in November 1938, so in the war was used to shelter some of the locomotives and rolling stock from the LNER York Museum. The station resembled Darlington Bank Top, having a wide island platform (No. 1 Down, No. 4 Up) with canopies, offset on the Up side from the through lines and provided with two bays at each end for the branch trains: Nos 2 and 3 at the north end, Nos 5 and 6 at the south end.

Ferryhill Yard, south of the station, comprised two groups of northward dead-end sidings (six and seven roads) and an Up group of about 15 southward roads, all on the Up (east) side of the main and Station lines. Between the Down Yards and the station—in addition to the Down and Up through platform lines—ran an Up (Leamside) Slow line and two Down and two Up Goods lines, all of which interconnected with the ECML and the Stockton line at No. 3 box (101 levers). On the west side of the station ran the Down and Up main passenger lines, with a Down Slow line and carriage siding separating them from the Down platform line. West of the main lines was another substantial goods yard, a branch to Chilton Quarry (Pease & Partners) and the yard of the disused engine shed.

Ferryhill No. 2 box (55 levers, rebuilt in December 1953) was at the south end of the station. No. 1 box (104 levers) was on a gantry beyond the north end, spanning the main and station lines. Until December 1954, there was in addition Ferryhill Sidings box (27 levers), located on the Up side adjacent to the south end of the station. This box was principally engaged in the control of the north end of Ferryhill Yard and the branch to the Lime Works on the far east side. No. 1 box controlled a complex of interconnections between these lines and with the Goods lines on the east side; it also regulated movements in and out of the Down side goods yard and engine yard.

Opposite the north end of the station, the branch from Thrislington Colliery and Mainsforth Lime Works formed the most easterly Up line. Then between No. 1 box and Coxhoe Junction, there were no fewer than eight running lines (from east to west): Up and Down Hartlepool lines, Up and Down Leamside Slow lines, Up and Down main lines, and the Down goods independent line. For much of the way, there was an extra Down Goods

The East Coast Main Line's Principal Points

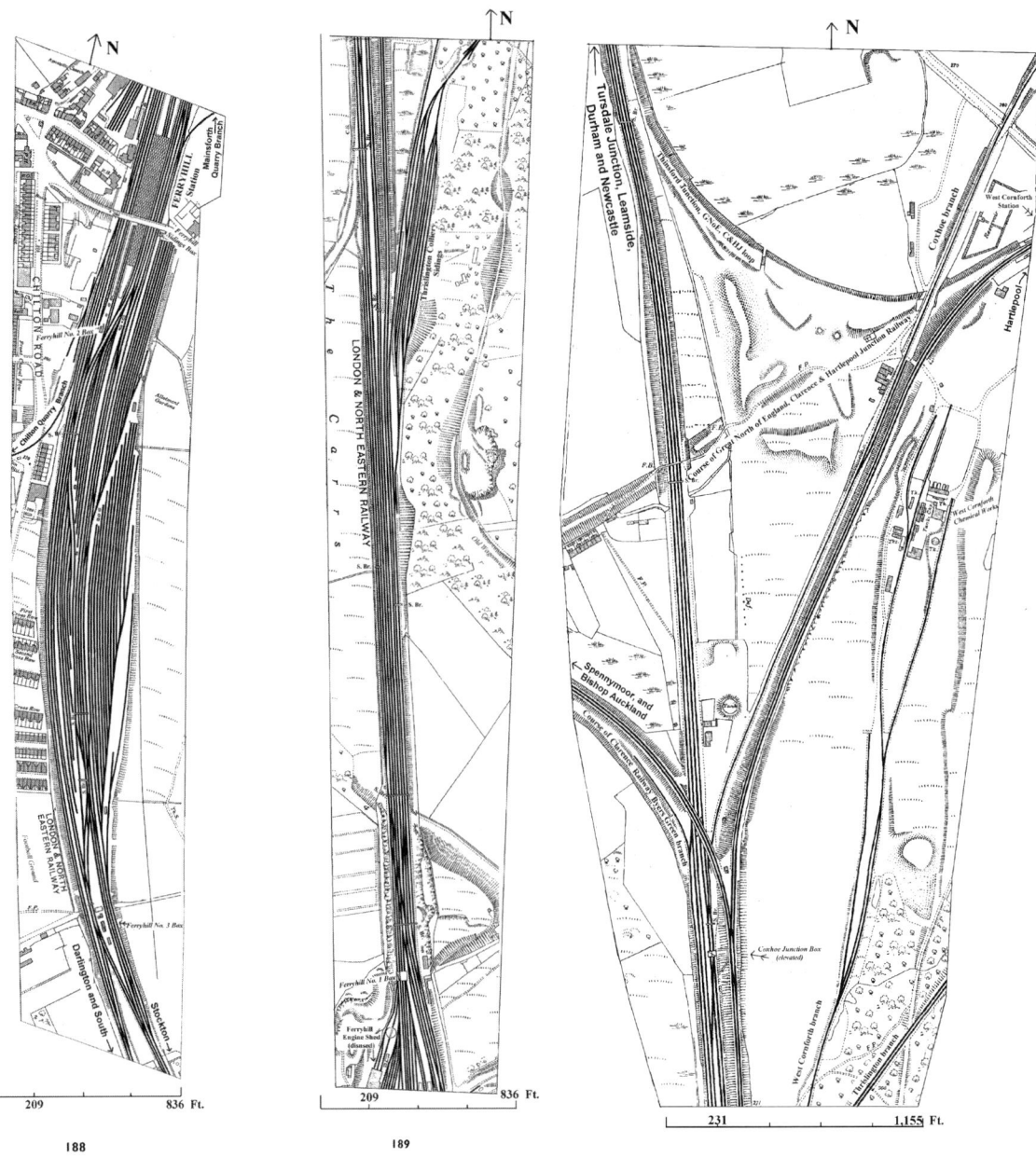

Above left: Sidings at Ferryhill to the south of the station.

Above middle: Lines to the north of Ferryhill station and sidings for Thrislington Colliery.

Above right: Coxhoe Junction to the north of Ferryhill, 1939.

siding, and on the Up side, an incline (with eight associated sidings) came down from Thrislington Colliery and West Cornforth Chemical Works and joined at Ferryhill No. 1.

A mile from Ferryhill came Coxhoe Junction. Here, there were multiple crossovers as the Hartlepool branch turned away to the right. The Bishop Auckland branch had already begun to climb left over the main lines on a flyover and curve away to the west, so the Coxhoe signal box (55 levers) was built on a gantry over the Leamside (Slow) lines at the level of the other branch; both branches were double-track. Also at Coxhoe Junction, two tracks turned off right from the Slow lines to combine into the single-track goods-only Coxhoe branch (closed in 1966). Down the main line, the cutting of the abandoned link between the Bishop Auckland and Hartlepool branches was crossed next. A mile further on at Tursdale Junction, there was a double crossover and the main line swerved away west from the direct Leamside line. Shortly before Tursdale box were two sidings for Thinsford (Tursdale) Colliery on the Up side, with a ground frame controlled from Tursdale box. South of their stops, the formation remained of the abandoned north to east loop to the Hartlepool branch.

The rather switch-back and winding seven miles of the main line on to Durham, through a succession of wooded cuttings and embankments, cut across the grain of the country, crossing the Wear on a high viaduct at Croxdale and further on the Dearness[33] and Browney rivers, to approach Durham from the south-west. This length was split up into block sections controlled by boxes at Hett Mill, Browney, Littleburn (until December 1956), Bridge House, and Relly Mill. The longest section (2.56 miles) was between Hett Mill and Browney boxes, between which was the remains of the station at Croxdale, closed in September 1938; Hett Mill box was at a level crossing—the only one between York and Newcastle. There was a relief siding on the Down at Browney (made a loop during the war) and on the Up side at Littleburn was a group of sidings serving a colliery branch, again with one line made into a loop in the war; there were crossovers at Browney, Littleburn and Relly Mill.

At Bridge House Junction, a double-track loop slipped off on the Down side to connect with the Durham–Consett branch at Baxter Wood No. 2 box. As the loop turned away from the main line, it went under the important line coming from Bishop Auckland to join first the Consett line and then the ECML about half a mile away from Relly Mill. Meanwhile, perched high on a bank to the left was Dearness Valley box, regulating the junctions of the Bishop Auckland line with that from Waterhouses to the west and of the loop northwards to Baxter Wood No. 1 on the Durham–Consett line, which in turn converged at Relly Mill.

The Waterhouses branch only had two passenger trains (and one, through from South Shields, on Sundays) even in 1939, reduced to just one in the war and withdrawn in October 1951; freight on the branch continued until April 1965. Although the line up the Lanchester Valley to Consett had already closed to passengers in May 1939, it continued to have excursion traffic and freight, closing completely in July 1965. The Bishop Auckland line was kept open to main-line standards until August 1968 for diverted ECML trains and for freight traffic as a relief to the main line to Darlington, although local passenger services (five or six trains to the end) ceased in May 1964.

A minor summit was reached at Relly Mill, then the ECML fell steeply through Durham, approaching the station on an 11-arch viaduct high above the western side of the city. Durham station was probably designed by G. T. Andrews and had stone buildings of Tudor style with generous and striking glazed canopies that roofed the bays overall. There were long Down and Up platforms (Nos 3 and 4[34]), each on loops off the through lines and there were bays at each end for local trains (Nos 1 and 2 at the north end of the Down platform and Nos 6 and 7 at the south end of the Up platform).

There was also a short single loading-dock at the north end that curved round to the far side of the station buildings on the Down side, another curved bay (platform 5) behind the north end of the Up platform and a dock at its south end. The North and South boxes controlled their respective ends of the station: the North box the yard of the small two-road engine shed (with a separate turntable line) on the Down side and a siding on the Up side. An unusual feature was the absence of a Goods station; Durham's facilities were at Gilesgate, which had been the original terminus of the line from Sunderland, on a short branch off the Leamside line.

Many of the ECML expresses stopped at Durham. Up expresses that paused were usually banked out of the station over the viaduct towards Relly Mill by an A8 or G5 tank engine. On account of the sharp curve off the viaduct into the station, there was a severe speed restriction for Down trains, and a special detector rang an alarm in Durham South box if any exceeded the speed limit. Quite frequently, local trains ran south-west to Bishop Auckland and north-east to Sunderland, many being through to one or the other and the odd one through to Newcastle. They were worked by A8s or V1s, most often from Sunderland or West Auckland sheds. Durham shed was closed in December 1958 when DMUs were introduced, but these only ran until the closure of the branches in May 1964. Apart from these normal services, passing through Durham on summer Saturdays were through trains between Newcastle and Blackpool via the Stainmore line, also various excursions and specials, such as the convalescent miners' train that ran fortnightly to Grange-over-Sands.

The last 14 miles on to Newcastle from Durham roughly followed the valley of the Wear; it crossed viaducts over its tributary streams at Plawsworth, Chester Moor and just north of Chester-le-Street station. About 300 yards from Durham North box was a ground frame under its aegis at Crook Hall, for the siding for Aykleyheads (Grange) Colliery on the Down side. At Newton Hall box, two miles from Durham, the four tracks from Durham ended and a branch to Sunderland curved off to the east to join the old main line at Leamside. The ECML then became double-track again as far as Ouston Junction, falling gradually from Durham into the Team Valley with a long ruling gradient of 1:150; there were crossovers at most stations and junctions and at Kimblesworth, Chester Moor and Birtley North boxes.

The sidings for the Kimblesworth Colliery branch were passed on the Down side and then about 2½ miles after Newton Hall came Plawsworth station with a small goods yard. Chester South Moor Colliery with its several sidings was passed next on the left and then the relatively prosperous Chester-le-Street station, which had a sizeable goods yard and sidings for coke ovens. There were now four tracks, with the Slow lines on the west side, from Ouston Junction. There the branch from Blackhill and Consett via Stanley (closed to passengers in May 1955) came in on the Down side, immediately after the ECML had passed underneath the Pontop & South Shields line at South Pelaw. This latter pioneering railway was built to bring limestone and coal from West Durham to the coal staithes and ironworks on the south bank of the Tyne. The more easterly half from Tyne Dock (South Shields) to Consett remained in use on a modified course, taking ore in the opposite direction, until 1980 when Consett Ironworks closed.

Private mineral wagonways abounded in County Durham and South Northumberland. One was the Beamish Wagonway, which crossed over the ECML directly after Ouston Junction and before the wagonway joined the Pontop & South Shields. Another came shortly before Birtley station, where the ECML crossed the branch of the Pelaw Main Wagonway from Ouston and Urpeth Pits, the other branch—from Ravensworth Colliery—crossing the ECML at Lamesley. In between Birtley and Lamesley—where Tyne Marshalling Yard was later built—the ECML crossed the Bowes Railway (Pontop & Jarrow until 1932). These privately-owned colliery railways were worked by their own locomotives, but handed over to the National Coal Board (NCB) from January 1947.

In the Team Valley, past the stations at Birtley, Lamesley, Low Fell and Bensham, there was a good deal of industry with many sidings. At Birtley, there was a substantial group on the Up side serving the goods yard, the neighbouring Ironworks, Henley's Telegraph Works and Union Brickworks sidings (with ground frame), on the Down, and the Birtley North Sidings for Birtley ROF (built in the First World War). Lamesley, which closed to passengers in 1945, also had a goods yard on the Down side. Just south of Low Fell, a branch trailed in on the Down side from the Team Valley Trading Estate, which had an extensive internal railway system; as well there was a carriage siding on the opposite side. Just north of Low Fell station was the junction of busy Goods lines that diverged left for Low Fell Down and Up Sidings and Engineers' yard and went on to Norwood Yard, Dunston Staithes, Blaydon and the Newcastle–Carlisle line. This route was taken both by trains coming from Forth Goods using the loop at Norwood, and also by trains from the Gateshead direction, which needed to call at Low Fell Sidings and came from King Edward Bridge Junction via Bensham Curve. The stiff climb on to the main line out of Low Fell Sidings often needed the services of a banker.

On entering Gateshead came Bensham station, then a short distance further on a Goods line—used by passenger trains in an emergency, from Blaydon via Dunston passed under the ECML and then rose alongside it in a deep cutting to run parallel as far as King Edward Bridge Junction. After connecting there, its four tracks ran straight on to form a through route on the Gateshead side of the River Tyne, connecting with the lines from Newcastle to Pelaw and thence to South Shields and Sunderland and on which freight trains went principally to Park Lane Yard. Two triangular junctions enabled trains to enter/or leave Newcastle Central, i.e. in either direction by means of the King Edward Bridge or the High Level Bridge. The two Gateshead stations adjoined each other immediately to the south of the junction of the lines approaching the High Level Bridge: Gateshead West on the line from King Edward Bridge Junction and East on the line from Felling, Pelaw, Sunderland, etc. Thus, ECML trains from the Durham direction and calling at Gateshead West (and some not calling) used the High Level Bridge and passed Gateshead shed.

The connections with the four-track curve on to King Edward Bridge and the double-track curve from the bridge joining the route along the Gateshead side of the river were all worked by one signal box—King Edward Bridge Junction. This box also controlled the double crossovers and the exit line of the Redheugh Colliery Sidings, which joined on the Down side short of the main junction. In contrast, the more easterly triangle at the south side of the High Level Bridge was controlled by two boxes—Greensfield and High Street. Greensfield box particularly dealt with the movements of locomotives from Gateshead shed and Works, which flanked the line from King Edward Bridge Junction on the north side, as well as empty

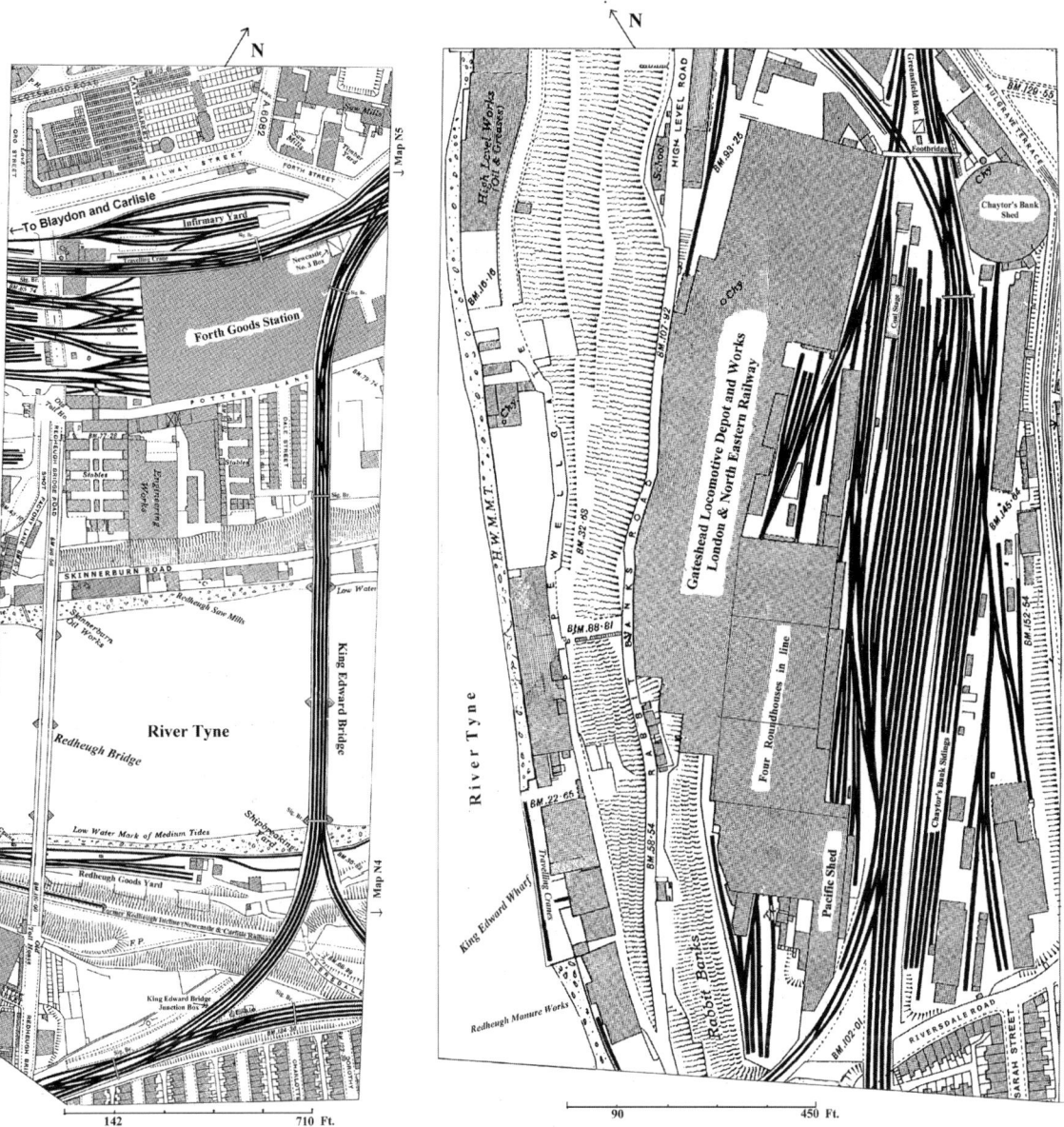

Above left: King Edward Bridge Junction and Forth Goods station, Newcastle, 1939.

Above right: Gateshead Works and locomotive shed were perched on land above the River Tyne.

stock from Chayters Bank Sidings situated on the south side. All these signal boxes, together with the three boxes at Newcastle Central station, and those at Forth Goods, Park Lane and Manors Junction, were equipped with electro-pneumatic frames installed for the NER in 1906–10, most remaining in use until 1959 and in some cases later.

Newcastle

Newcastle Central station had three main platforms (Nos 8, 9 and 10, No. 8 being 1,389 feet long), with eight bay platforms (Nos 1–7 and a double-line fish dock) at the east end; at the west end were five bay platforms (Nos 11–15) and double milk docks, which later served as the Motorail Terminal in the 1950s. Platform lines Nos 8 and 9 were available in either direction and also interconnected by scissors crossings with two sidings (A and B) that ran between them. The bays at the east end were used principally by the North and South Tyneside Electric services, but as well by eastbound local steam trains. Bays at the west end were used by the Carlisle Line trains and by locals westbound and some southbound. Freight trains used the four avoiding lines outside the station on the south side: two on the approaches, dividing into four as they passed the station, with the outermost (Up) line having eastward sidings off it at the west end. More sidings connected to the adjoining factories—principally the Forth Bank Works of Hawthorn Leslie & Co.

There were three arched roofs over Central station, each 61 feet wide, the centre one being lower than those flanking it and the one nearest the Tyne spanning only platform 10 and a carriage yard of four through sidings. Beyond the roofs, wide canopies extended to near the ends of the platforms and a wide range of traverse roofs protected the east end and the relatively separate group of terminal platform Nos 1–7. The main entrance to Newcastle Central was by an arcaded portico on the north side on Neville Street. Most of the public facilities were grouped around the large circulating area that adjoined platform 8 and separated the eastern from the western bays. The main Up platforms (Nos 9 and 10) were reached over a large footbridge, while bay platforms 1–3 had their own concourse.

The Newcastle District offices were grouped in and around the Central station. Offices belonging to the operating superintendent, the district control, the motive power superintendent, and the passenger superintendent were all housed in the main station building. A goods superintendent's office was located at Irving House by the east end of the station; at the west end was a large building housing the revenue accountant's office, also the registered offices of the Easingwold and North Sunderland Railways.

Of the two main railway bridges over the river, the High Level (1,372 feet long with six spans) at the east end was the oldest, being completed in 1849. Under its three railway tracks (Down Fast, Slow and Up), it carried a roadway on the lower level, leading from the centre of the city down St Nicholas Street over to Gateshead. At the west end was the newer King Edward Bridge of 1906 (1,150 feet long with four spans), having four railway tracks only (Down and Up South, Down and Up East). With triangular junctions at the Gateshead end of each bridge, it was possible for trains for any destinations south of the Tyne to leave Newcastle from either end of the Central station. At the west end, trains from King Edward Bridge could enter platforms 8 to 14 only; platform 15 and the docks and sidings were accessed only from the Scotswood

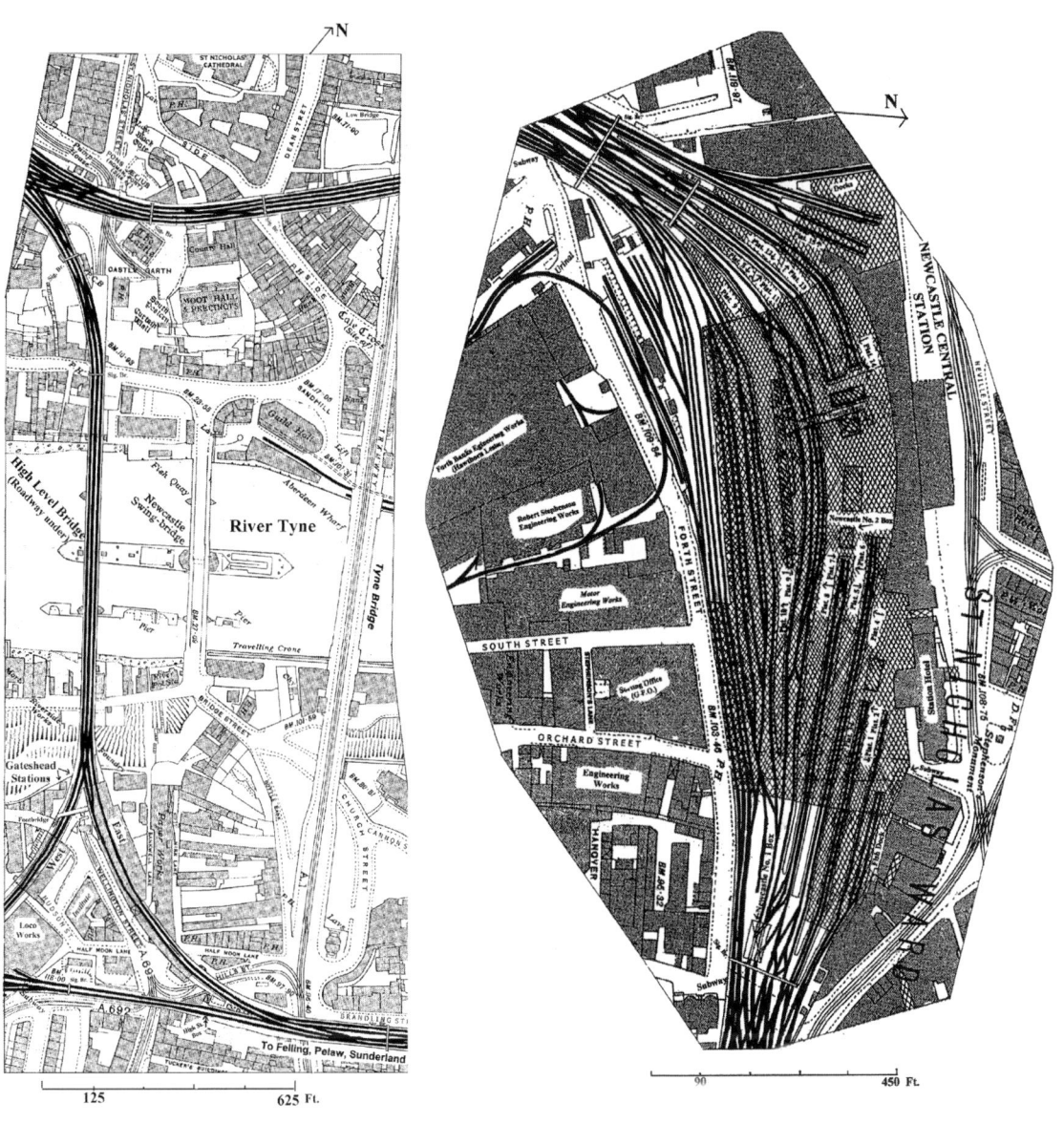

Above left: Route from Gateshead (East and West) across the High Level Bridge to the east end of Newcastle Central station.

Above right: Newcastle Central station, 1940, with platform numbers added.

line. At the east end, trains could go over the High Level Bridge only from platforms 3–10 and not from platforms 1 and 2 or the fish dock. The Goods lines had access from both bridges.

Until the 1950s, when colour-light signals replaced them, enormous gantries of NER signals spanned the lines at each end of the station, under the command of Newcastle Nos 1, 2 and 3 boxes; the gantry at the west end, with its 25 dolls and 57 arms, was the largest in the country. All the signalling was electro-pneumatic, the signalman watching illuminated track diagrams and operating miniature levers. No. 1 box (268 levers and a staff of five men and two lads) was on a substantial bridge of girders spanning the two main through lines at the east end. It controlled all movements at that end, including those across the famous diamond crossing (of no less than 77 intersections), also double crossovers on the North and Tynemouth lines and on the High Level Bridge.

No. 2 box (67 levers) controlled movements in the station and was situated in the centre of platform 8. No. 3 box (211 levers), standing at right angles to the station between the lines west through Scotswood and those over the King Edward Bridge, had control over double crossovers on the four tracks on the bridge and on the five of the Scotswood line, as well as the junction and the station at its west end. All three Newcastle Central boxes, along with Manors Junction box, were superseded in April 1959 when, after the whole area had been radically resignalled in stages, a single all-electric panel signal box with 641 switches took over. Newcastle Central was one of the busiest provincial stations in the country, handling in mid-December 1959 1,652 train movements, 684 in the Manors direction.

Main line services at Newcastle Central principally comprised expresses from King's Cross to Edinburgh and other Scottish destinations, which normally entered from the south over the King Edward Bridge, and those originating from Newcastle. The latter were those to King's Cross, Leeds, Manchester and Liverpool, Birmingham, Bristol and South Wales, also to Bournemouth and Colchester. Most of the London services went straight up on the main line through Durham, while a few expresses ran via Sunderland, West Hartlepool, Stockton and Northallerton; some of the Leeds trains went via Harrogate instead of York. Trains taking the coast line via Sunderland included an overnight Sleeper to King's Cross, two daytime trains to Liverpool and (after the war) one to Colchester. There was also a morning train from Sunderland to King's Cross, which ran empty stock from Heaton to Sunderland and attached a portion from Saltburn at Stockton.[35]

A train from Bristol after the war ran that way only in the Down direction, but neither the London sleeper nor the Colchester service ran via the coast in the Down direction. Trains that were routed through Sunderland normally left Newcastle by the High Level Bridge, although the loops in Gateshead made it possible for them to leave by the King Edward Bridge, and this route was used by the 10 a.m. and 4 p.m. trains from Newcastle to Liverpool. This arrangement of routes was particularly convenient for turning whole trains round, which was necessary when the sequence of vehicles needed to be maintained—for example, trains conveying travelling post offices (TPOs), and it was not unknown at busy times for trains to be sent all the way round the bridges until one of the three platforms was available. An annual event at Newcastle Central was the rush on Friday evening and Saturday at the start of the Tyneside and Wearside 'Shipyard' Holidays at the end of July–beginning of August. Then, a large number of additional and relief trains were run from Newcastle and Sunderland to destinations all over the country and special reservation arrangements were made for loading the trains.

Locomotives for these main line expresses usually included a Pacific or V2, though before and during the war, 4-4-0s (D20s and D49s) in pairs were commonly employed on the expresses to Leeds. Before the hostilities, NER Atlantics still played their part, and after 1945, B1s took a hand with some of the lighter trains. The Pacifics and V2s were provided by both of the main Tyneside sheds at Gateshead and Heaton, otherwise by Haymarket for trains from Edinburgh and York, Neville Hill, Doncaster, Grantham, New England and King's Cross for trains from the South. The majority of Anglo-Scottish expresses changed engines at Newcastle, and if northbound, the fresh locomotive from Gateshead would wait on the High Level Bridge before backing in to take over. The tough starts on the curves over either of the bridges, especially that onto the King Edward Bridge, meant banking assistance had to be given in starting heavy trains and to assist drivers of the banking and train engines, electric bells and repeater lights were installed at each end of platforms 8–10—as they were at several other main ECML stations that were on curves. Moreover, the regular provision of banking assistance at Newcastle, as well as in the Down direction at York and at Darlington, was instituted in the war when ECML expresses became so lengthy.

In the 1940s, stopping trains on the main line, principally to Alnwick, were worked by NER Atlantics or by NER D17s or D20s, in the 1950s by B1s and to some extent by LMSR or BR 2-6-0s.[36] There were quite frequent semi-fast services from Newcastle via Sunderland around the coast line to Middlesbrough and via Hexham to Carlisle, as well as stopping services on these routes; except through to Carlisle, these services were run on an hourly basis. The most usual motive power for the smartly-timed secondary services to Middlesbrough, which were made up of corridor stock, were the Gresley 2-6-2Ts (mainly V3s) from Gateshead and Middlesbrough sheds. Comparable trains ran on the Carlisle line with V3s from Blaydon or Gateshead, or D49s from Gateshead and Carlisle Canal sheds. Pacifics and V2s also worked on these lines, as from 1944 did B1s, and occasionally Canal shed sent over NBR 4-4-0s or (after Nationalisation) LMSR Class Fives. Also by way of Hexham ran the three or so slow trains to Riccarton Junction and on to Hawick, until the Border Counties line closed in October 1956. As a former NVR service, this was worked by NBR 4-4-0s (from Blaydon or Hawick sheds), and in the 1950s, by D49s or K1s, or by LMSR Ivatt and BR Standard 2-6-0s, provided by Blaydon or Gateshead.

There were many local trains from Newcastle Central to Durham, Sunderland, North Wylam, Hexham and Blackhill. Before the war, there was quite a good service to Durham via Leamside and a few on to Ferryhill, but in the war (July 1941), they were cut back to Leamside—afterwards to just one train to and from Washington in the morning. In pre-war days, the trains by the two routes to Blackhill were quite numerous with even some on Sundays, many running through as a circle service. The Sunday trains were taken off during the war, and after it, the service was progressively cut back to skeletal proportions before ceasing altogether—via Scotswood in February 1954 and via Birtley in May 1955.

The same happened to the North Wylam service, although the latter dragged on until March 1968, being provided in the 1960s by DMUs that worked through to Hexham. Before and early in the war, steam railcars, shedded at Heaton, Tyne Dock, Middlesbrough or Stockton, were commonly employed on these local trains. Subsequently, a G5 (or N8 or N10) on three NER coaches formed the trains; in rush hours, a longer train and an A8 or V1/V3 would be needed. In the mid-1950s, LMSR-type 2-6-4Ts worked on Newcastle locals to a certain extent. The DMUs, maintained at the EMU Depot at South Gosforth, which was enlarged to accommodate them, took over many of the Sunderland and Middlesbrough service because the Metro-Cammell four-car units employed lacked sufficient power. Before the war, it was normal for trains on both services to include a buffet car, but even when 'modernised' with DMUs in the late 1950s, a refreshment trolley only was provided on just two Carlisle trains and a 'mini' buffet only on the summer Sunday service to Keswick via Carlisle.

A major element of the traffic at Newcastle Central was the Electric (600-volt third-rail) suburban trains. These dated from 1904 in the case of the North Tyneside service, only since March 1938 for South Tyneside, when the whole system was modernised and new stock provided for the North Tyneside trains. Services to Tynemouth (using platforms 1–4) took one of three routes. Basically, a train left every 20 minutes for Tynemouth and went either via Jesmond, Benton, Backworth and Monkseaton, returning via Wallsend and Heaton or *vice versa* around the loop. In addition, one train per hour went to Tynemouth via the Riverside line calling at all stations and returned as an express, fast to Manors North from West Monkseaton via Benton, and *vice versa*; this was confined to rush hours only in the 1950s. There were extra trains at rush hours, a few running fast from Manors East by the main line and Benton South-East Curve.

A total of 158 trains per weekday left Newcastle Central for Tynemouth and 74 on Sundays. These Electric services were supplemented by an hourly steam service from Manors North, fast via Jesmond to Backworth then on to Newbiggin. On summer Sundays and Bank Holidays, a particularly intensive service was provided to the coast. Several of the trains then included either Electric Parcels cars or 'pram vans' (converted from old Electric coaches with most of the seats removed) to cater for families with small children. Normally, the Electric parcels cars, often hauling fish vans, were employed on independently scheduled stopping Parcels services north and south of the Tyne, while at these holiday times, two of them also hauled a push-pull set of six ex-NER coaches. The South Tyneside service used platforms 5 and 6 at Newcastle Central and went over the High Level Bridge to call at all stations to South Shields. Rush hour services were not particularly popular and no special arrangements were made for them. There was also a 20-minute steam service from South Shields to Sunderland.

Through parcels trains were handled at No. 8 platform whenever possible, to avoid having to use lifts and the subway from platforms 9 and 10. Vans were also placed in No. 7 platform and the east-end dock, which was also used by the electric parcels vans. For southbound traffic, vans were placed in the west-end docks for loading during the day. There were long runs with trains of barrows between the various platforms and the parcels office at the east end of the station. During the peak period before Christmas, some parcels traffic and parcels post was diverted to Newcastle Forth station, in order to relieve the Central station when it was liable to become overwhelmed. The parcels office was at street level in Lower Neville Street, and there was a covered area off the road for parcels vans to load and unload, but the delivery bays and sorting areas were in several arches under the east end of the station, which were connected by a lift to a covered sorting area behind the east-end dock.

The freight and mineral traffic passing through Newcastle Central was heavy, and in wartime virtually continuous with trains constantly queuing on the Goods lines. Many unbraked freight trains continued to run on the main line through the 1950s, albeit in lesser numbers. As much of the freight and mineral trains originated and terminated locally

View from the Castle Keep as J27 No. 65781 passes by No. 1 box (on gantry) with a train of empties bound for the Tynemouth line on 12 June 1954. North Tyneside EMUs can be seen in platforms 5 and 6, while to the right are the District Offices between platform 1 and Westgate Road. *Photograph: B. W. L. Brooksbank*

or had been remarshalled in Tyneside Yards, there was a preponderance, at least during daytime, of relatively short trains between the yards. They were hauled by the smaller locomotive types, most except the J39 0-6-0s being of NER classes, until the 1950s when there were LMSR-type 2-6-0s as well as many Austerity 2-8-0s around.

The long-distance workings, some coming through from Scotland, but many originating from Heaton Yard and destined for various yards in the South, were hauled by Pacifics, V2s, K3s, B16s, the various 2-8-0s and Q6 0-8-0s. Surprisingly, until some went to Thornaby shed in March 1959, BR 9F 2-10-0s were never allocated to NE Region sheds, other than Tyne Dock for the special workings of iron-ore trains up to Consett. Consequently, the relatively few seen at Newcastle Central were from Doncaster or from sheds further south. Eventually, as elsewhere in the country, the 9Fs were seen on expresses at busy times, yet it was not until August 1955 that one worked down to Edinburgh and that was on a parcels train. During the war, the main line freight and coal trains might be hauled by almost any of the passenger and freight tender engines from anywhere on the LNER. Certainly, the home sheds of freight engines included not only the five Tyneside Depots, but virtually all those in the NE Area and from further afield. From October 1942 to July 1943, even 'King Arthur' 4-6-0s had to be borrowed from the SR for freight work, until the USA, WD and LMSR 2-8-0s came successively to redress the shortage of motive power.

In 1953, on a peak summer Saturday Newcastle Central dealt with 420 steam and 350 Electric loaded trains per day, with corresponding numerous empty stock and light engine movements; in winter, up to 200 freight trains passed in a weekday. The only traffic that did not pass through Central station comprised the Blyth and Newbiggin locals from Manors North and the freight that passed through Gateshead from Blaydon via Dunston and Greensfield to Park Lane Yard, etc. During the war and in the period when most expresses changed engines at Grantham or Peterborough, King's Cross engines appeared rather infrequently. Still, with Carlisle Canal shed's locomotives coming in (not to mention Scottish Pacifics and V2s), all of the Gresley 'Big Engines' could be seen at Newcastle.

Newcastle to Edinburgh

On leaving Newcastle Central towards Edinburgh, the ECML curved left past the Castle as the lines to the High Level Bridge swerved off to the right over the famous crossing. Four running lines were provided as far as Heaton South Junction, the Fast lines being on the left (Down) side and the electrified local lines on the right; after Heaton South, there were mainly only two through lines. In under half a mile from Newcastle Central came Manors Junction, where there were double crossovers and the electrified lines (signalled from Newcastle Central for reversible working) to the coast via Jesmond turned off on the Down side immediately before Manors East station. Thus, the combined Manors station had its East platforms on each of the four lines towards Heaton—the Up Tynemouth line platform being considerably shorter, while the North platforms were almost at right angles to the aforementioned. All these platforms had generous, high-pitched canopies.

At Argyle Street Junction, a north to east single-line curve came in from Trafalgar North Yard and New Bridge Street Goods station on the Jesmond loop and split into two lines, one of which connected directly with all the through lines and the other forming a Down loop that joined the Down lines 200 yards further on.

Opposite Argyle Street box on the far side was the electrified Trafalgar South Yard, the exit from which was by the Up Granary line that joined the Up Tynemouth line just north of the

Looking north from the Castle Keep on 12 June 1954. Manors station is in the distance (centre), an EMU has been stopped by a signal and D20 No. 62375 approaches with a train from Alnmouth. *Photograph: B. W. L. Brooksbank*

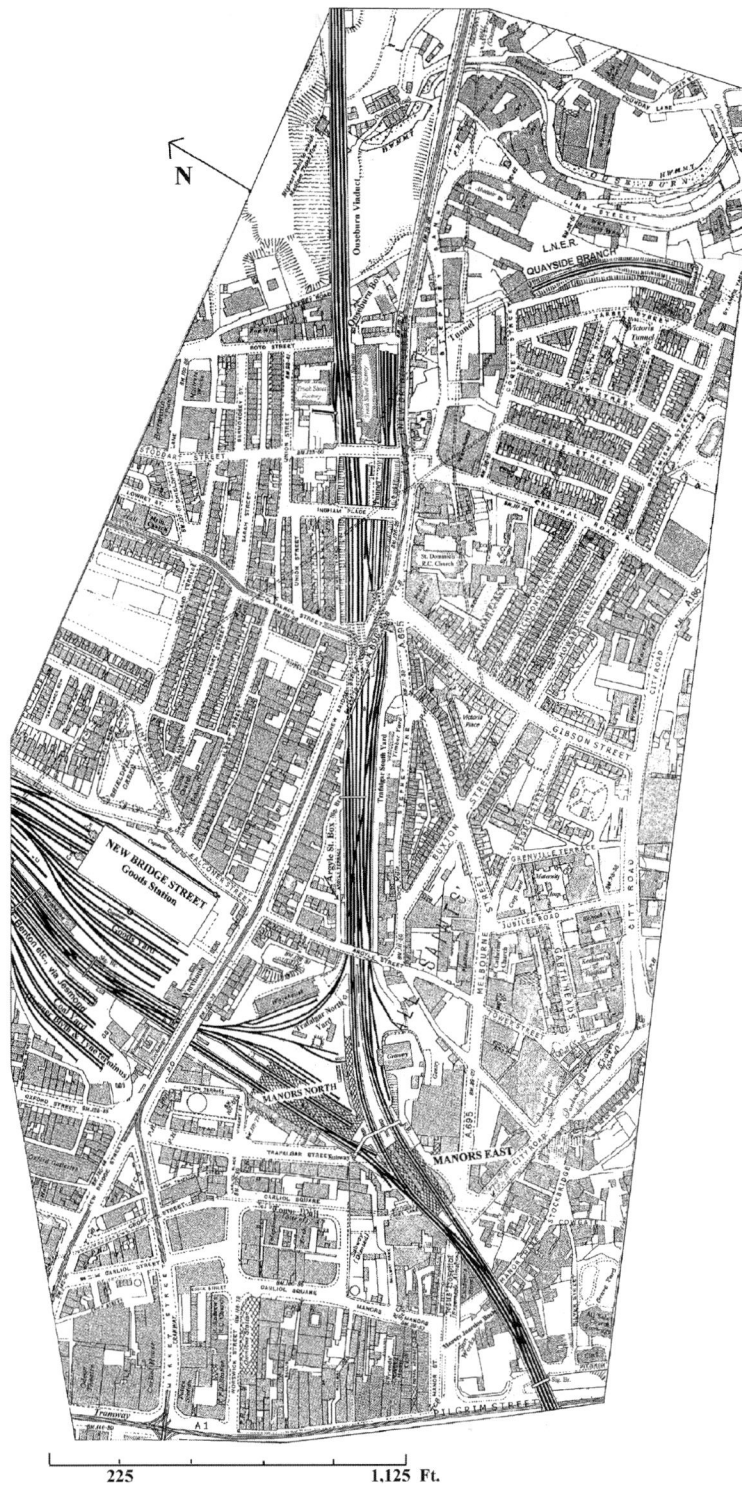

Lines to the north of Newcastle Central station with the two Manors stations, Trafalgar North Yard and New Bridge Street Goods station, 1942.

platform at Manors East and from which the branches led to the Granary and Newcastle Corporation Generating Station. The yard comprised three through roads and four short westwards dead-ends. Alongside the far road was a loading dock, while the other two roads connected with the Quayside branch, which rose up through the tunnels and under the other sidings very steeply (1:30) from the Quayside. Busy with important import/export traffic, this unusual branch had been electrified by the NER, with third-rail supply but overhead supply in the Quayside Yard and in the Trafalgar Yard beside the ECML. Two dual-fitted Electric locomotives had been purpose-built for working the branch.

Shortly after Trafalgar Yard, the main line crossed the three-arch Ouseburn Viaduct. Ouseburn box (on the Up side) controlled more crossovers and some small sidings on each side. Then, at Riverside Junction, the electrified Riverside branch curved off the Tynemouth lines sharply to the south, to serve eventually most of the North Tyneside shipyards and engineering works before rejoining the Tynemouth lines at Percy Main. Here, a connection was made with the mineral lines of the Blyth and Tyne system, which ran from the many Northumberland collieries to the north down to the extensive yard and quays of the Tyne Improvement Commission and to Tyne Commission Quay. However, the connection was northwards and the Scandinavian Boat Trains from King's Cross and Newcastle, having followed the easier and more direct route via Wallsend from Newcastle, had to turn north at Percy Main and then reverse down under the Electric line and past Percy Main shed to reach the Quay.

At 1½ miles from Newcastle Central was Heaton station, which had two island platforms, accessed from the main station buildings on the Heaton Road overbridge at the east end. About a third of a mile further on was Heaton South Junction, where—preceded by double crossovers—the electrified Tynemouth lines branched off and immediately gave access to the Heaton Works of Parson's Ltd (Electrical engineering) and other factories situated on the south side of the line.

The ECML, still electrified as far as the Benton Quarry Junctions, curved left at Heaton South. It was flanked by an independent and two reception lines on the Down side, and on the Up side by three Independent and three reception lines, all serving the yards on each side that extended for about ¾ mile from Heaton South box to beyond Benton Bank box, these signal boxes controlling respectively the Yards' southern and northern exits.

On the Down side was Heaton Down Yard, with one group of 23 northward roads with their stops adjacent to Heaton South box, then a cattle dock and beyond it another set of 11 dead-end northward roads and the eight dock roads of the permanent way stores yard. These were controlled by Heaton Down Yard box, where there was access to the main line but the multiple reception lines constricted to just one line, until the trackwork was modestly improved during the war. Northward of that cabin were again two Down reception lines and also the New Yard—little used until the war—of six dead-end northward roads, all joining the main line at Benton Bank box. Beyond the yards on the Down side were sidings serving industrial premises, which after the war included a large WD&HO Wills cigarette factory. The Up Yard had 19 sidings all of which were through roads, the entry and exit of them, along with the reception lines, being handled by Benton Bank and Heaton South boxes only, although the southern shunting neck was by the locomotive shed and some way short of the latter box. During the war, a new group of five Up reception sidings was built a short way north of Benton Bank box at Little Benton.

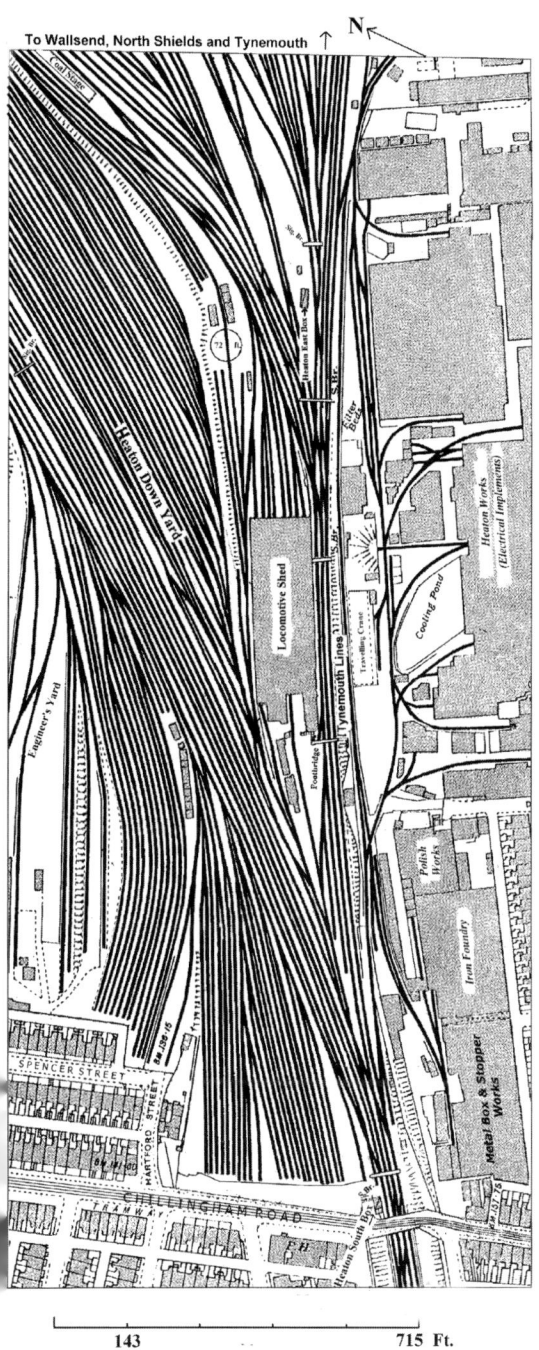 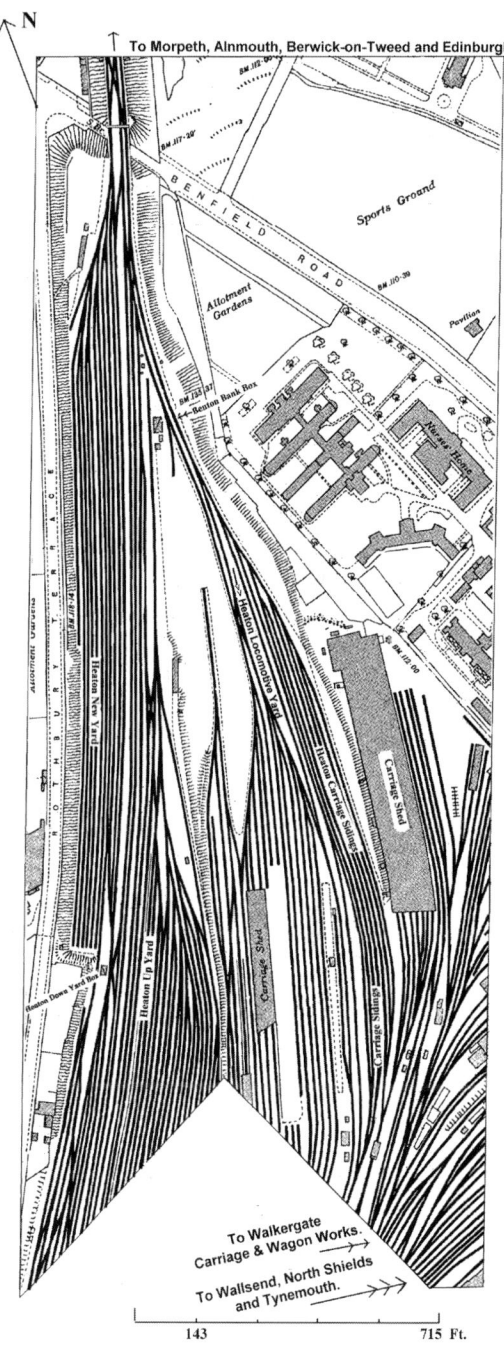

Above left: Heaton Down Yard and locomotive shed before the wartime alterations.

Above right: Heaton Carriage Sidings and Shed with the Up and New Yards, 1940.

Heaton shed was located on the Up side at the south end of the complex, with the locomotive yard extending back some way towards Benton Bank box, where the principal access was situated. Before the war, locomotives had to share this with empty stock trains coming in and out of the Carriage Yard, otherwise they only had an awkward access from Heaton South. During the war, an independent engine line was inserted directly from Benton Bank with connecting lines also from the reception roads of Heaton Up Yard. This work was done when major improvements were made to the locomotive depot itself, which included making through lines to allow easy access also from the south end.

As well as the Up Yard, beyond the locomotive yard on the Up side there were the Carriage Sidings, Wagon Shop and Carriage & Wagon Works. The Carriage Yard was partly electrified and all lines eventually fed into the Up Tynemouth line at Heaton East Junction. There were some 15 through carriage roads, and it was possible for Electric trains to run Up from Benton Bank on the main line to Heaton East Junction on the Tynemouth lines through the carriage sidings, but the facility was little used. Dead-end sidings in the complex amounted to 45 roads, including seven in the carriage-washing shed, about five in the wagon shop, which was transformed into another carriage shed during the war, and 16 next to the Tynemouth lines in the Carriage & Wagon Works. At the Benton Bank end double lines served as the entry and exit route to the carriage and locomotive yards and joined the ECML just north of the box, which was on the Up side. The exits from Heaton Down Yards were 100 yards further on, while the entries to the Up Yards were 150 yards southwards from the box.

In 1939, about 20 scheduled freight trains ran each way on weekdays between Newcastle, Berwick and Edinburgh, although this number doubled during the war and was dealt with in the reactivated Heaton New Yard and the new Up reception Sidings built just to the north at Little Benton. An indication of the traffic handled at Heaton is that even in 1954, Heaton Down Yards dispatched 35 daily scheduled freight trains northwards and the Up Yards a similar number southwards.

Going past these yards, the line climbed for nearly two miles at 1:200 from Heaton South Junction. On to Morpeth (16½ miles from Newcastle), there were local stations at Forest Hall, Killingworth, Annitsford, Cramlington, Plessey and Stannington. At Benton Quarry Junction, shortly before Forest Hall, double-track electrified lines turned off on each side, the first west to Benton and South Gosforth and the other east to Backworth and Monkseaton; a direct east–west chord crossed over the ECML just north of the junctions. Another curve was put in early during the war, going west to north from Benton on the Jesmond Loop to the new Benton North box on the ECML.

After Heaton, nearly all wayside stations to Berwick-upon-Tweed had relatively simple layouts with Up and Down platforms conventionally arranged. Many of the stations were built of stone in a Tudor style, being only single-storey buildings with veranda-type waiting rooms giving on to the platforms. Most had the usual goods facilities, including NER coal-drops. The stations at Morpeth and Alnmouth were rather larger. Killingworth station had seven sidings (three with platforms) half a mile south on the down side, which were used only for race meetings at the nearby Gosforth Park Racecourse, their access (from the south only) being controlled by Killingworth Sidings box. During the war, these platforms were used by the army for storage and the Sidings box was rarely opened, although it did remain in use until at least 1957. At Cramlington on the Up side was a large airship shed sited on Cramlington aerodrome, to which there was a short branch off the Up goods yard. Built in the First World War, this was the civil airport for Newcastle, but it was not used during the Second World War and was superseded afterwards by the present Newcastle airport at Woolsington on the Ponteland branch.

In spite of numerous collieries in the area, there was not a great deal of local freight or mineral activity to be seen on the stretch of the ECML to Morpeth because most of the collieries were served by the Blyth and Tyne system and tended to feed the coal towards the seaports. During and after the war, much of the output of this major mining area[37] found its way onto the ECML through Morpeth or Newcastle and locally to the two large Stella power stations west of Newcastle; also during the war as 'convoy' coal trains to much further afield. There were several mineral branches joining the ECML but owned by the colliery companies, later the NCB. At Killingworth, there were sidings on the Up side for handling the Hartley Main Coal Co's traffic. Their engines brought coal from Weetslade, Dinnington, Seaton Burn, Hazelrigg and Burradon Collieries and (from March 1950) Havanneh Drift, either from the east along the West Moor (or Seaton Burn) wagonway, or by their branch that ran from the Up side at Killingworth parallel to the main line for a mile before turning west, across the ECML, to join the company's line from Holywell and Backworth collieries and down which most of the output was sent to staithes on the Tyne at Percy Main. A mile on from Killingworth, at Dudley box near Annitsford station, there were sidings on the Up side serving Dudley Colliery and also the Hartley Main's branch that extended from the former B&T system at Seghill.

The ECML between Benton Bank and Berwick was mainly double-track, with additional running lines (in each direction) only between: Dudley and Dam Dykes boxes just before Cramlington, Stannington and Clifton Crossing box, Wooden Gate box and Alnmouth, Little Mill and Stamford Crossing box, Belford and Crag Mill box[38], Beal and Goswick. Otherwise, there were only refuge sidings. Those at Morpeth (Temples Siding, Up) and Chevington (Down and Up) were converted into loops during the war[39], and crossovers were provided at most of the stations, also at some other points such as Benton Quarry and Dudley. A feature of this stretch was the dearth of road bridges in flat localities and correspondingly a large number of public level crossings—13 in the 35 miles between Alnmouth and Berwick, out of 44 on the whole ECML (1947). Most of the public crossings were manned under the control of crossing boxes or of adjoining signal boxes.

On the approach to Morpeth from Newcastle, there was a sharp right-hand curve, demanding a severe speed restriction as this had also been the scene of several derailments of expresses going too fast. Shortly before the station, the former NBR Wansbeck branch from Scotsgap to Rothbury joined on the Down side, the branch locals being accommodated at the outer face of the Down island platform. The main station buildings were on the Up side, and on the east side of the Up platform, there was a bay platform and a dock, which was the original separate terminus of the B&T for its trains from Bedlington. The goods yard was also on the Up side, and on the north side of the Bedlington line, there was a yard of three through and seven eastward sidings and a shunting neck. On the Down side at Morpeth, the facilities for the Wansbeck line included three docks and a turntable.

In 1939, there were four trains on weekdays from Morpeth to Rothbury (two being through from Newcastle) with connections at Scotsgap to Reedsmouth. These lines were closed to passengers in September 1952, after the service had been reduced to two trains each way on weekdays, but goods traffic continued as far as Woodburn on the Reedsmouth branch until October 1966. A passenger service also ran from the Up bay at Morpeth to Bedlington. This was worked by a Sentinel steam railcar from South Blyth shed before the demise of these vehicles in the 1940s. While the service was relatively frequent before the war, it was cut back drastically during the conflict and ended up as just one morning train from Blyth—and none out, before the trains vanished in April 1950. The Bedlington line carried a heavy coal traffic from the B&T collieries to Scotland and the trains had to reverse at Morpeth until an east to north curve was added in the 1960s.

Northwards from Morpeth on the 18¼ miles to Alnmouth, the signs of industry disappeared. Stannington Vale viaduct crossed the River Blyth between Plessey and Stannington stations, another a mile north of Morpeth traversed the Wansbeck Valley, the River Lyne was spanned at Ulgham near Widdrington, and later, a viaduct crossed high over the Coquet Valley north of Acklington. Small intermediate stations on this stretch of the ECML were at Pegswood, Longhirst, Widdrington, Chevington, Acklington and Warkworth. There were goods facilities at each, those at Longhirst and Warkworth being more extensive and situated on both sides of the main line, while at Acklington and Belford, there were weekly cattle markets to provide considerable livestock traffic.

At Pegswood, there was a colliery on the Down side, and between Pegswood and Longhirst, a mineral line owned by the Ashington Coal Co. had run eastwards from a former Ashington Junction to Ashington and other Collieries. Although the junction had been severed by the LNER in March 1939, the line was restored at the outbreak of war for possible use in an emergency. In the event, from the Ashington end, it was used only for bringing timber evacuated from Hartlepool and taking it away later; post-war, it was used for wagon storage.

Just beyond Widdrington was Stobswood Colliery on the Up side, with sidings and access to the Up main line. After the war, a large open-cast site was established and to serve it a set of sidings was built on the Up side of the ECML together with an extra signal box (Widdrington North). From Southside box, between Acklington and Warkworth, a lengthy branch owned by the co-operative wholesale society went west to their Whittle Colliery. Also a shorter branch, again westward, went from Shilbottle box (south of Alnmouth) to their New Shilbottle Colliery, and sidings were provided for each branch beside the main line. Finally, a mile north of Chevington at Amble Junction a branch, which had a passenger service until July 1930, turned away to the east to the little seaport of Amble. Although most of the coal (from Broomhill and other collieries connected to the branch) was shipped from staithes at Amble, freight survived until October 1969.

Alnmouth station had a loop and island platform on the Down side for the branch trains, a sizable goods yard on the Up side south of the station and, beside the station and between it and the engine shed on the Down side, was a yard of three through sidings and one dead-end. There were two signal boxes (south and north), both on the Up side near each end of the Up platform. Served by its own line, the locomotive turntable was nearly half a mile north of the shed in the vee where the double-track Alnwick Branch, having left the main line at the north box, turned off to the north-west.

As the junction for Alnwick, Alnmouth station was of some importance. Before the war, 16 trains on weekdays and 11 on Sundays travelled through to Alnwick, many being from Newcastle, and 14 (eight on Sundays) during the war. There were again 17 weekday and nine Sunday trains in 1948, but the service was soon cut back; there were no Sunday trains from 1951, and in spite of dieselisation the service was withdrawn altogether in January 1968 (October for freight). Until September 1930, branch trains used to go on from Alnwick through Wooler to Coldstream, though subsequently this line was freight only. After the August 1948 floods severed the main line between Ilderton and Wooler, it was worked as two separate branches until closed; Alnwick–Ilderton in March 1953, Coldstream–Wooler in March 1965.

North of Alnmouth, the main line crossed the River Aln by a substantial viaduct, climbed the Aln Valley for five miles at 1:170 on Longhoughton Bank, then fell again on a similar grade to Chathill, but nevertheless, the 32¼ miles to Berwick would be covered by expresses at a high average speed. At Longhoughton, there was a whinstone quarry branch on the Down side and a sizeable goods yard on the Up. There was also a quarry on the Up side at Howick Heugh (before Little Mill) with a signal box to control its branch, which had no connection with the Down line. At Little Mill itself, there were short branches to another stone quarry on the Up side and to a lime works on the Down, with associated sidings. The independent North Sunderland Railway trailed in on the Up side at Chathill station from the fishing port of Seahouses. This line was quite busy, with five or so trains—several of them mixed—each day, including Sundays. During the war, only the Sunday trains were lost, and a good service was maintained until closure in October 1951. Until 1949, this independent line had its own Manning-Wardle 0-6-0T locomotive (*Bamburgh* of 1898) and also ran an 0-4-0 diesel (*Lady Armstrong*, built by Armstrong-Whitworth in 1933[40]), but in its last days, the branch was worked by a tank engine hired from BR, which, owing to a very weak bridge, had to be one of the Y7 0-4-0Ts. Chathill Station had a bay on the Up side for the North Sunderland trains, but otherwise, there were very limited facilities for handling them.

The other wayside stations between Alnmouth and Berwick were: Longhoughton, Little Mill, Christon Bank, Newham, Lucker, Belford, Beal, Goswick, Scremerston and Tweedmouth. Each small station had a goods yard, except Newham, Lucker, Goswick and Scremerston; these were quite well-endowed and the facilities at Belford were substantial on either side of the line. Even before the war, many wayside stations between Alnmouth and Berwick were served by only four passenger trains each way per day on weekdays and two on Sundays. Much the same prevailed between Berwick and Dunbar, with only two all-station trains on weekdays and one on Sundays, even in August 1939.

Permanent closures began in 1950, and with all but a handful left open by 1958, by the mid-1950s, there were only two trains on weekdays calling at all stations and none on Sundays. Meanwhile, between May 1941 and October 1946, all the intermediate stations between Alnmouth and Tweedmouth, except Chathill, Beal and Belford, were temporarily closed. Apart from these public facilities, about a mile north of Christon Bank, there were the remains of the former private station at Falloden[41], and between Crag Mill box and Beal was Smeafield, which although closed in May 1930, also continued in use as a private station.

The stations along this section of the line were good examples of Benjamin Green architecture. Belford (serving Bamburgh) and Beal (for Holy Island) survived until January 1968. Belford had a vintage NER gantry signal box, while Goswick differed in having staggered platforms—the Down being to the south of the crossing. The ECML ran close to the sea from Goswick to Tweedmouth, and after Scremerston, a branch trailed in on the Down side at Billingdean from Scremerston Colliery on the Great North Road.

On approaching Tweedmouth, on the Up side, there were three through cattle wagon sidings and a 'cattle-washing platform'. Then came Tweedmouth shed, situated on the Down side before the station and accompanied by a complex of sidings of six northward roads and three southward dock roads. Opposite on the Up side was Tweedmouth Marshalling Yard. This had 17 west-facing roads and others serving the Goods station on its further side. From there, a branch went to the tweed dock, a two-stage steep trip entailing a reversal at Spital. Tweedmouth station—a typical example of Benjamin Green—had a two-platform arrangement with an additional Down Through line. Next to this was a run-round road for trains from the Coldstream branch, which had to reverse to reach Berwick. There were also three Up reception lines for the Yard, running round behind the north-east side of the station. The Tweedmouth area was under the control of two signal boxes, both on the Up side: south, controlling entry to the locomotive and marshalling yards, and north, managing the other end of the yard and the junction of the Kelso branch.

The branch from Coldstream, Kelso and St Boswells, which attained temporary main line status after the August 1948 floods, turned off left from the Down loop just beyond Tweedmouth station. Before the war, there were six trains to Kelso and even more from there to St Boswells, yet by the end of the 1950s, there were only two and they ceased in June 1964; freight to Kelso lasted until March 1965. Although some services to Kelso were operated with a steam railcar until March 1941, they were worked mainly by NBR 4-4-0s or 4-4-2Ts from Hawick shed or by NER 0-4-4Ts from Tweedmouth shed, later by BR Standard 2-6-0s from Tweedmouth or Hawick. The service ran from Berwick (reversing at Tweedmouth), as did most of the trains from the north off the Burnmouth–Eyemouth and Reston–Duns branches.

Less than a mile beyond Tweedmouth station, the ECML crossed the River Tweed on the Royal Border Bridge—2,160 feet long with 28 arches and up to 126 feet above the river—immediately before it entered Berwick-upon-Tweed station. Berwick was relatively modern, the former NBR station having been rebuilt in 1927. It comprised one wide island platform, with a large gabled canopy stretching most of its length. The main station building adjoined the castle on the Up side and was constructed in stone but of a restrained Georgian style with a balustrade and central clock-face.

To reach their train, passengers had to cross a footbridge at the south end, where there were prominent lift towers. The structure contained remains of the old stonework from the former Berwick Castle, out of which the original 1846 station had been constructed. On the south-west side of Berwick station, there was a Down Goods loop, which divided into two west of the station, and beyond the station there was also an Up Goods loop. The signal box was situated between the Down Goods and Down platform lines, opposite the centre of the station. The goods shed and coal yard were on the Up side (facing Down), and there was also a southward fish dock on the Up side and a Down Yard with four sidings beside the station, followed by nine northward dead-ends.

The border into Scotland was two miles further on, at Marshall Meadows (Lamberton Toll on the main road), but from the railway point of view, the boundary was at Berwick station and was where NER metals ended and NBR lines began. At Marshall Meadows, there were Down and Up loops, where often freight trains would stop and the Heaton

Looking north from the crossing at Belford station on 11 May 1965. The signal box was new at the time and contrasts sharply with the station's architecture. *Photograph: B. W. L. Brooksbank*

To the north of Belford, Beal station—seen looking south—still retains the original signal box, which sits more harmoniously in its surroundings, 11 May 1965. *Photograph: B. W. L. Brooksbank*

crews on trains from Newcastle would change over with St Margaret's or Tweedmouth crews; during the war, a mess room was provided there for them. A measure of the change in traffic flow brought about by the war on this part of the ECML is the fact that whereas in September 1939, about 15 main-line freights were scheduled each way through Berwick on weekdays, this number was twice that in 1955.

From Berwick, the line climbed for five miles at 1:190 to 200 feet above sea level at Burnmouth. The erosion of the cliffs in this area had necessitated the diversion of the track inland in the past and signs of the old formation could still be discerned. Again, further north, for a mile beyond Cockburnspath, the line was quite close to the sea and offered quite impressive views.

The first 25 of the 57½ miles between Berwick and Edinburgh Waverley were the hilliest of the whole ECML. After the climb to Burnmouth, there was a respite of four miles past Ayton, then 7½ miles of more climbing, mostly at 1:200 winding up the narrow valley of the Eye Water—crossed seven times—to the summit of 385 feet, the highest point on the ECML, just beyond Grantshouse. After that, the line fell for 4¾ miles at 1:96 through Penmanshiel Tunnel and down the valley of the Pease Burn to Cockburnspath, to the County Boundary at the high Dunglass Viaduct over the Burn, thereafter easing to 1:200 to Innerwick. Cockburnspath Bank was—for southbound trains—the most formidable incline on the whole run from Edinburgh to King's Cross. Many Up trains were banked out of Dunbar, and the incline was exceeded only by the brief mile at 1:78 between Piershill and Abbeyhill Junctions for northbound trains on the last two miles into Edinburgh Waverley station.

Between Berwick and Dunbar (28¼ miles), there were stations at Burnmouth, Ayton, Reston (for Coldingham and St Abbs), Grantshouse, Cockburnspath, and Innerwick, each with goods facilities. At Burnmouth, a short branch (closed between August 1948 and June

Thompson A2/3 Pacific No. 518 *Tehran* crosses the border with an express in the summer before Nationalisation.

1949 by the floods and finally in February 1962) dropped down directly after the station to the sea at Eyemouth. At Reston, a country branch to Duns and St Boswells left the station immediately on the Down side. Here, facing the branch direction, there was a group of cattle sidings as well as general goods sidings on each side of the main line. The branch was closed completely between Duns and Greenlaw in August 1948 after the floods, finally to passengers from Reston to Duns in September 1951, for freight November 1966. The Eyemouth branch had a quite frequent service prior to the war and before closure still had four trains; strangely these trains were worked by GER 2-4-0s early in the conflict. The Duns branch had a service of six trains in 1950, operated by D17/2 4-4-0s sub-shedded there from Tweedmouth.

Dunbar was a relatively important station with an imposing two-storey stone-built structure and a fine station garden on the Up side. Its two platforms, with canopies joined by girders across the tracks, were on a loop, bypassed on the south side by the Down and Up Independent through lines. After Dunbar, there were stations on the final stretch at East Linton, East Fortune, Drem, Longniddry, Prestonpans, Inveresk, New Hailes, Joppa and Portobello. The wayside stations each had small goods yards; at Dunbar, East Fortune, Drem and Longniddry, there were separate sidings on the Down and Up sides, while at Longniddry, the goods shed was on the Up side and the Down sidings served a 'dung lye' for horse manure from Edinburgh and a lime works. Between Innerwick and Dunbar, there were several sidings on each side serving the large cement works at Oxwellmains; there were also goods sidings on the Up side at West Barns and Beltonford west of Dunbar, at Ballencrieff (until January 1959, west of Drem) and also at Wallyford (Down side) and Morrison's Haven (mainly Up side) west of Prestonpans.

All the stations between Berwick and Edinburgh were of the usual two-track layout; Portobello was the only island platform station, with separate entrance and main buildings. Reston and Longniddry had island platforms on the Down side to accommodate branch trains, while Burnmouth had an Up bay for its branch services. Before the war, the ECML was double-track all the way from Berwick to Portobello East Junction, except that there were independent running lines in each direction at Marshall Meadows box and at Dunbar, with otherwise only refuge sidings for freight, although this was generously remedied in the war. There were crossovers at each intermediate station and also at the boxes at Marshall Meadows, Beltonford, Seton, Morrison's Haven and Monktonhall Junction.

From Dunbar, there was a branch from North Berwick, joining the ECML on the Up side half a mile east of the station and from which there were many local trains for Edinburgh. At Aberlady Junction (1½ miles before Longniddry), the remains of a branch from Gullane joined on the Up side; this was closed to passengers in September 1932, although used by excursion trains well into the 1950s and kept its freight until June 1964. At Longniddry, the branch from Haddington, after running parallel for ¼ mile, joined the main line just west of the station and its trains used the outer face of the Down island platform. This branch was closed to passengers in December 1949, in spite of a frequent service, and freight remained until April 1968. Longniddry also dealt with Gullane branch traffic. Prestonpans was the station for the short Tranent Colliery branch, closed in August 1958. It joined the ECML on the Down side, while on the Up side were small shunting yards used to serve branch traffic from Preston Links and Northfield Collieries.

Dunbar station in the 1930s.

There was a small two-road engine shed at Dunbar, used for the 4-4-0s (fitted with slip-couplings), which worked a few stopping trains to Waverley but were employed mainly as local pilots and as bankers on the climb to Cockburnspath. A similar shed at Longniddry beside the Haddington branch housed, as well as the branch engine—normally a C16 4-4-2T—the Prestonpans 0-6-0 pilot, which also ran trips on the Gullane and Tranent Branches. Both of the sheds were sub-sheds of St Margaret's.

At Monktonhall Junction, shortly after Inveresk station, a branch came in on the Down side variously from Smeaton, Ormiston, Gifford and Macmerry. These all lost their passenger services between July 1925 and April 1933, while coal traffic was heavy and the branches still served the various collieries until closed in stages between January 1959 and December 1980; the section from Monktonhall Junction to Seton survived the rest by over 15 years to serve the Meadowmill washing-plant. There was a separate pair of goods lines that paralleled the ECML and connected with it at Monktonhall Junction. These comprised one branch of the Lothian Lines system, coming off the Smeaton branch. At Monktonhall Junction, a facing connection also turned away on the Down side to join this Lothian Lines branch and go west to cross the old Edinburgh and Dalkeith line (the commencement of the Waverley Route) and diverge at Wanton Walls, one branch going ahead to join up with the Edinburgh Southside Suburban line and the other to go towards Portobello and South Leith; these lines survived until 1963–67. Monktonhall Junction box had 58 levers to work all these switches and crossovers and also sidings on each side of the ECML.

The Southside Suburban line was a major route to Haymarket West Junction, bypassing Waverley station. At its eastern end, it diverged from the Waverley route at Niddrie North Junction and had a loop southwards to the Waverley route at Niddrie South Junction. At its western end, by virtue of the connection from Gorgie Junction to Haymarket Central Junction, a Circle service of local trains was run to and from Leith Central through Waverley, and the triangular junction at Gorgie was useful for turning round complete trains or vehicles. Niddrie West Yard was located on the Suburban line west of Niddrie West Junction. Niddrie, along with several other yards, was subsequently superseded (May 1963) by the new Millerhill Marshalling Yard, built astride the Waverley Route and connected to the ECML by a loop from near Monktonhall Junction. Next after Monktonhall Junction came New Hailes station and Junction, where there was a Down Goods loop, duplicated in the war. Here, the short double-track branches from Musselburgh and from Fisherrow Goods joined on the Up side. Fisherrow Goods branch closed in November 1961 and the Musselburgh branch in September 1964 (to passengers, to goods in July 1971). The main line then curved nearer the sea and passed Joppa station.

Immediately after the Edinburgh end of the Up platform at Joppa, the Portobello Yard complex began. A Down Goods line diverged on the Up side and gave off two further lines, the South Leith Down Goods, which continued only for the ¼-mile to Portobello East Junction, and the Joppa Straight line. This led to and from the direction of Meadows Yard and South Leith and from which a group of five eastward roads branched off on the south side. On the north side was the Portobello goods and coal yard with some 10 roads devoted to various facilities including timber storage—all preceding Portobello Marshalling Yard itself. Just west of Joppa station, the Lothian Lines single goods-only line crossed overhead on its way from South Leith to Niddrie Junctions and the Lothian collieries.

At Portobello East Junction, there was considerable rearrangement of the tracks of the ECML as it was joined by the Waverley Route lines coming from Galashiels, Hawick and Carlisle. The Down Fast divided into a Down Fast and a Down Slow, the former now being on the outside and the latter forming the Down platform line of the island at Portobello station; the same arrangement of the Up lines occurred in reverse from Portobello West Junction, the Up Fast being on the north side outside the Up Slow serving the island platform. The Down Goods line divided at Portobello East to form Nos 1 and 2 reception roads of Portobello Yard. From Portobello West Junction, the Down and Up Goods lines ran through to Piershill Junction, having become Slow lines from Craigentinny box and Branch lines at Piershill Junction.

At Portobello East, the South Leith Down Goods from Joppa was in effect continued as the South Leith Lye, leading to South Leith Junction. In parallel, the Joppa Straight, together with connections from the Down Goods and the South Leith Down Goods lines, led into the Down and Up South Leith through lines, which serviced the Portobello North Yard and Exchange Sidings before continuing to Meadows Yard, South Leith, etc. Portobello East Junction box also controlled the connections with the Waverley Route. They comprised, in order: a Down Fast connecting with the ECML Down Fast, a Down Connecting link leading from the Waverley Route Up Fast into the ECML Down Slow, and an Up Fast off the main Up Fast and crossing the ECML Down Fast. The Goods connections to and from the Waverley Route connected to and from the Down reception lines and the South Leith Lye, across the two ECML Fast lines to join the Up and Down Waverley Route main lines. All this made Portobello East box (94 levers) a key box. It was unusual in that the NBR had placed the box on a gantry spanning the through lines and accompanied by a public footbridge as well.

South Leith Junction box (86 levers), situated beside Portobello station, controlled the west end of Portobello Yard and its connections with the South Leith lines. It had no part to play on the main line, other than working with Portobello West box (78 levers) in passing

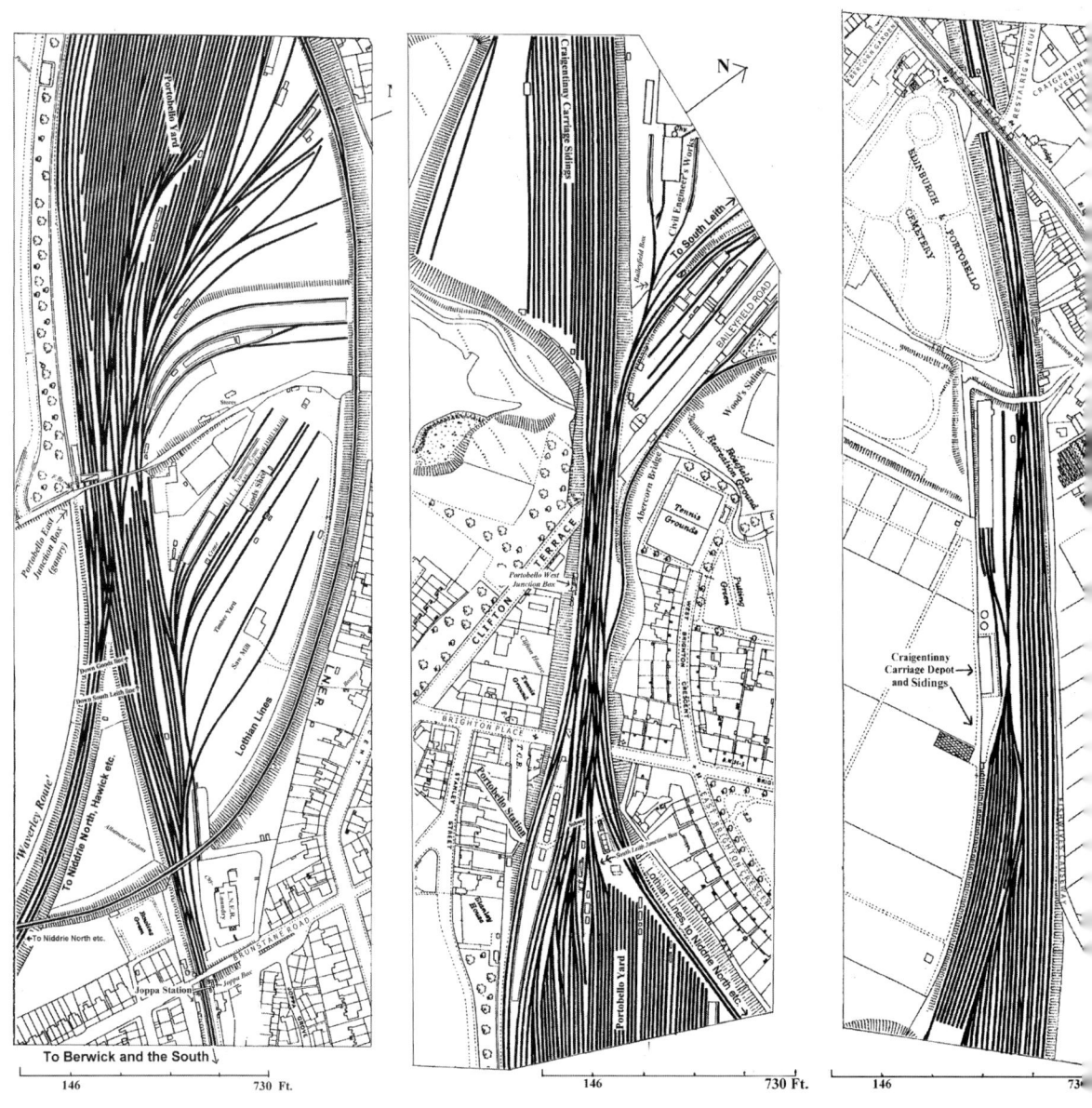

Above left: Eastern half of Portobello Yard and the junction for the Waverley Route.

Above middle: Western half of Portobello Yard and Craigentinny Carriage Sidings.

Above right: Craigentinny Carriage Sidings and Depot, 1932.

traffic on and off it. The box also controlled Wood's Siding, which served several industrial premises in Portobello, but a major function was to regulate the traffic of the Lothian Lines to South Leith. The heavily-graded single line from the Niddrie direction swept round the north side of Portobello Yard and before the junction divided into four tracks. Two of these connected with the Nos 1 and 2 Up and the Down Goods lines of the ECML, while the other two became the Down and Up lines to and from the heavily industrialised South Leith and Leith Dock areas and curved away on the Up side beyond Portobello West box.

Portobello Yard dealt with 50 to 55 main line freight trains in or out in each direction every weekday, 15 to 20 of which ran on the ECML or Waverley Route, and in addition with an untold number of local workings. It extended to the north of the station all along the half-mile between the East and West boxes. First, on the north of the South Leith Goods lines, there was the North Yard, comprising two through reception lines and four groups of eastwards dead-end sidings (eight roads each) and on the far side various ancillary roads and buildings; all converged at Portobello East into the South Leith Goods lines. Then, branching off the South Leith Down Goods west of Portobello East and north of the South Leith Lye were the three through Exchange Sidings. South of the South Leith Lye and passing on the station side of South Leith Junction box were two Down reception lines, serving a Down Yard of eight westward stop roads.

West from Portobello West Junction as far as Craigentinny box, there was an extra Down loop line and a locomotive line (both outside the Down Fast), as well as the extra No. 2 Up goods independent line to South Leith Junction. For most of this two-thirds of a mile, the ECML passed the large Craigentinny Carriage Sidings on the Down side and on the opposite side there was an Engineer's depot. Craigentinny Sidings had about 20 roads—mainly westward and a few under cover—and was the main ECML Carriage Depot in Edinburgh. Empty stock trains, often with engines at each end, ran frequently from there to and from Waverley. Craigentinny box was situated at the west end of the yard on the Up side, and controlling the double-line entry and exits and the associated crossovers, where the tracks were rearranged to give Down and Up Fast on the south side and Down and Up Slow on the north.

There followed in under half a mile Piershill Junction, where there were double crossovers and on the right, an important double-track line went ahead to Lochend Junction, North Leith, Leith Central and Granton, also to Leith Walk Goods station. As well as for much freight, the route was used by the local trains serving Piershill and Abbeyhill stations before rejoining via London Road Junction the main line at Abbeyhill Junction, less than half a mile from Waverley. Also, some local trains went straight from Waverly to Leith Central after having gone all the way round Edinburgh by the Southside Suburban line. Owing to competing local tram services, Leith Central never flourished and lost its trains in April 1952. Also, except for the Granton line and the loops from London Road Junction, the other Branches disappeared even for goods traffic by the end of February 1968.

The main line swung left at Piershill Junction and then, flanked by one or two sidings on each side, just two through lines ran past St Margaret's shed. This major depot was situated—inconveniently—on both sides of the main line, access being controlled by St Margaret's box. Just beyond the Up side of the Depot were the small Meadowbank Sidings, followed by Rose Lane Goods Yard (10 roads) short of Abbeyhill Junction. The Junction

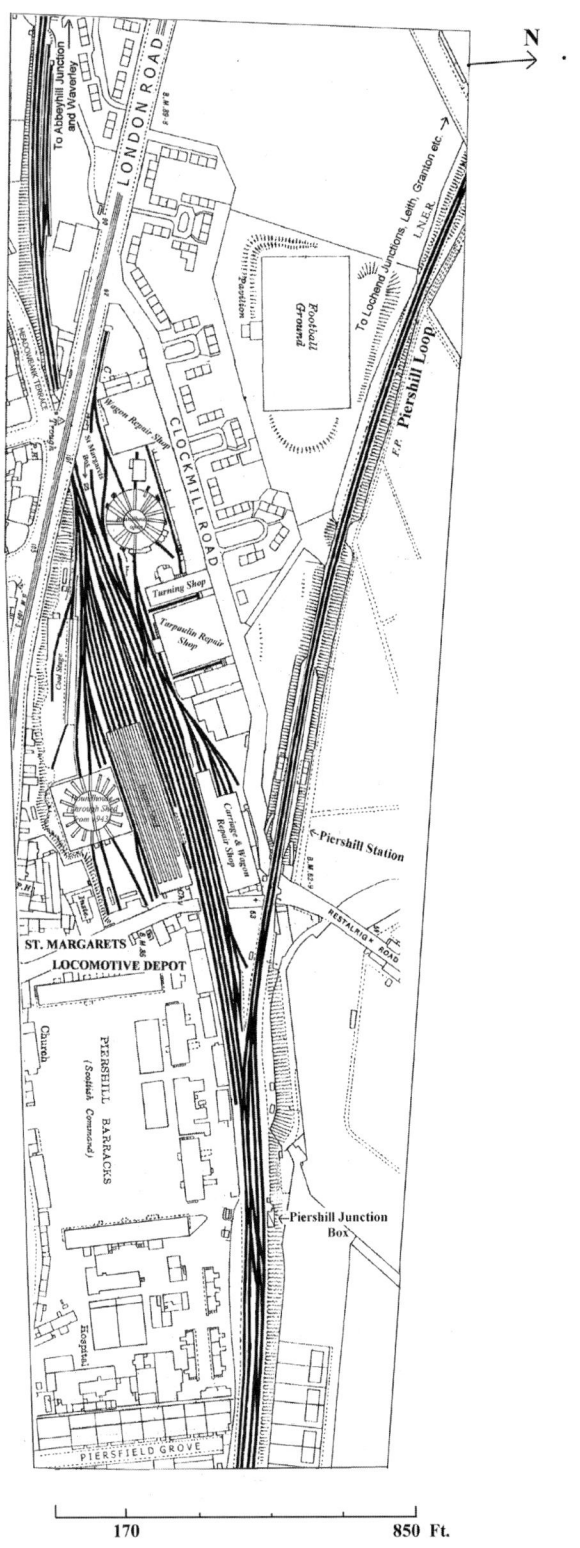

St Margaret's locomotive shed and Piershill Junction, 1932.

box at Abbeyhill controlled this goods yard and was in a prominent position between the main line and the loop line that rejoined beside it from Piershill Junction. The latter came round past Piershill and Abbeyhill stations and at London Road Junction had in turn been joined by the lines from Granton, North Leith and Leith Central to Waverley.

Edinburgh Waverley

Waverley was one of Britain's largest and most imposing stations, with 21 platforms covering 23 acres. As much as half of this area was underneath the glazed roofs, which contained 47,000 square yards of glass, and in 1939, 645 trains passed through in one day. Waverley station was situated on Princes Street in the very centre of Edinburgh and was in the valley between the Old and New Towns. In spite of its size, the station had just two main through platforms (of 1,608 feet each), both being able to accommodate two full-length trains and was signalled for reversible working, there being central double-crossovers connecting with flanking loop lines.

The through platforms were numbered 1/19 on the north side and 10/11 on the south side. They enclosed a very large island into which were inserted 15 bay platforms, roughly evenly divided between the East end (platforms 2 to 9) and the West end (12–18—platform line 18 being double faced); there were middle roads between platforms 2 and 3, 14 and 15, 16 and 17. South of the main station, separated by a granite wall, the south loop and a siding, was an additional island (suburban platforms 20 and 21). Beyond that was the Down Goods Loop and the yard of the goods station (15 roads, with three under cover) situated at the east end and the fruit market siding to which there was access from both east and west. North of the main station was the north loop and two carriage sidings, one of which served two through Independent lines, also sidings serving the Waverley Market and the General Post Office.

Signalling at Waverley had been modernised and electrified in 1936–1938, the station thereafter being worked from two all-electric boxes—Waverley East (207 levers) and Waverley West (227 levers). The east box, situated on the south side opposite the station throat and adjacent to the loading bank and goods station, controlled all lines as far as St Margaret's (exclusive) including Abbeyhill Junction and leaving only London Road Junction as a mechanical box. West box was on the south side opposite the ends of the platforms and by the eastern mouth of the Mound Tunnel; it controlled as far as Haymarket (exclusive) and also the reversible workings on the through platform lines, their scissor crossings and the north and south loops. Colour-lights were mainly three- or four-aspect, although a few were just two-aspect, and there were roller-blind route indicators and banner signals for calling-on. There were plentiful crossovers, and at the east end, they allowed movements in or out of any of the through platform lines to either of the Calton Tunnels, which each had an Up and Down line, while at Abbeyhill Junction, there was a double crossover allowing interchange again between the Tunnel lines before the divergence. At Waverley West, there were similar crossover arrangements, but owing to limited space—even with a crossover inside the Mound Tunnel—trains to and from the southernmost lines could not reach the northern Mound Tunnel nor *vice versa*, although interchange between the four main lines was made possible by a double crossover in Princes Street Gardens.

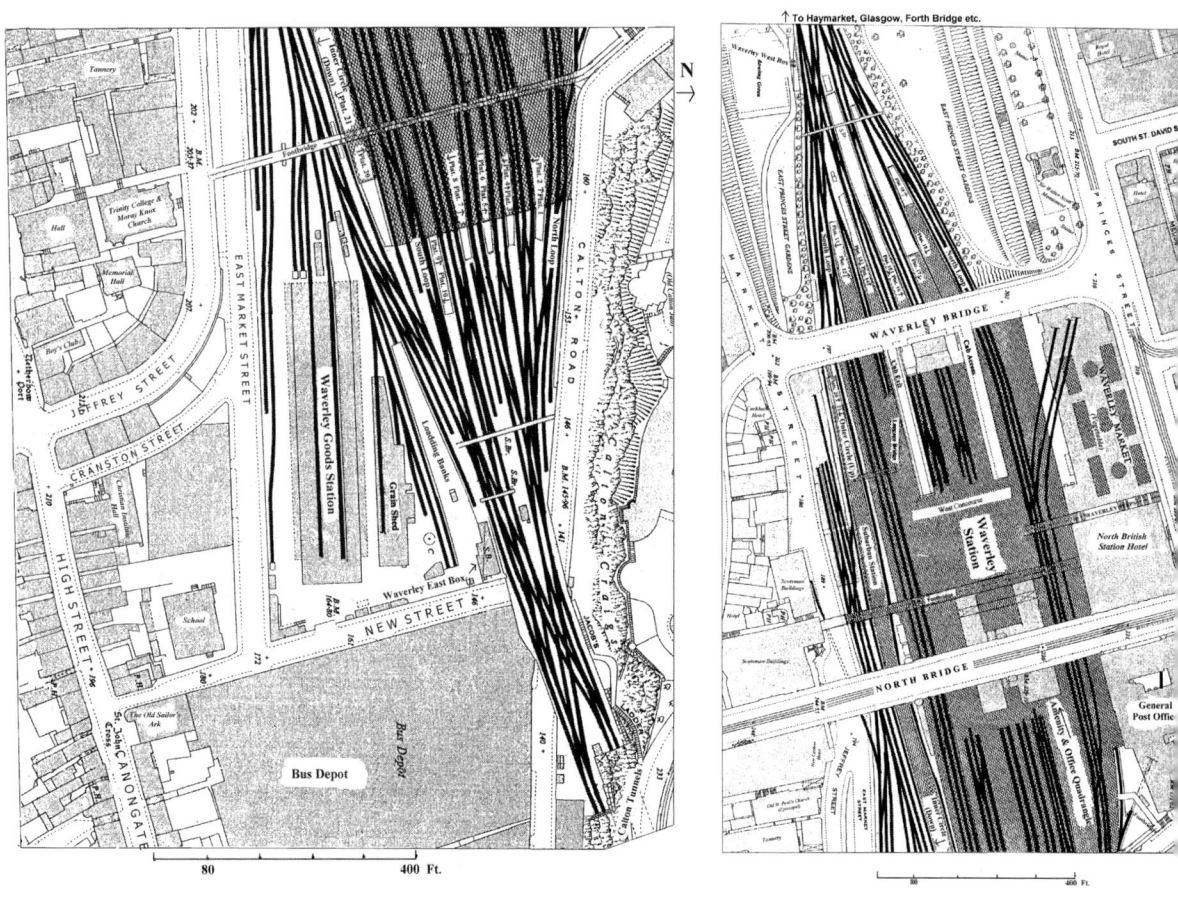

Above left: The eastern end of Edinburgh Waverley station and the goods station, 1947.

Above right: The central and western sections of Edinburgh Waverley station, 1947.

The west end of Waverley station seen from the Mound. The North British Hotel is prominent on the left and Waverley West box is in the right corner.

Inside the modernised Waverley East signal box.

In the 1940s and 1950s, the train services at Waverley, apart from those on the ECML, included: expresses and stopping trains to Dundee and Aberdeen, Perth and Inverness via the Forth Bridge, and to Glasgow Queen Street; expresses and stopping trains to Berwick and on the Waverley Route to Galashiels, Hawick and Carlisle; stopping services to Dunfermline, Larbert, Stirling, Perth and the Fife coast.

Westwards, local services went to Corstorphine (until January 1968), Bathgate and via Airdrie on to Glasgow Queen Street (Low Level) and beyond. Eastwards, trains went to Dalkeith (only until January 1942), North Leith (until June 1947), Leith Central (until April 1952) and—by the loop serving Abbeyhill and Piershill—to Musselburgh (until September 1964), Polton (until September 1951) and Penicuik (cut back to Rosewell & Hawthornden in September 1951 and withdrawn entirely in February 1962), Galashiels via Peebles (until September 1962), lastly to North Berwick and Dunbar. Finally, the Southside Suburban circular service ran westwards via Duddingston & Craigmillar to Portobello or Leith Central (Inner Circle) or *vice versa* (Outer Circle); after Leith Central closed, the service ran round from Waverley to Waverley, until ceasing entirely in September 1962. These Edinburgh Suburban trains were frequent—even intense as Musselburgh had 33 a day—and most survived until the mid-1960s when all but the North Berwick and Dunbar services were abruptly terminated. The very short-distance services succumbed to bus and tram competition soon after the war; that to Leith Central, which amounted to 26 per day in 1939, was cut to 10 in the war and was not revived afterwards. Branch freight services lasted longer: Polton until May 1964, Penicuik to March 1967 and Musselburgh until September 1971.

Principal expresses were hauled by Pacifics and V2s, while after the war, B1s worked many but the most arduous duties. Apart from the two Edinburgh sheds (Haymarket and St Margaret's), these express locomotives came from various other major Scottish Depots: Eastfield (Glasgow), Dundee, Perth and Aberdeen Ferryhill provided much of the motive power from west and north of Edinburgh, while locomotives from Carlisle Canal came in by the Waverley Route. Perhaps the most impressive engines were the Gresley P2 2-8-2s, built for the Edinburgh–Aberdeen expresses, and a common sight at Waverley.

Secondary services were operated mainly by 4-4-0s of various NBR Classes, the GCR-design D11/2s, some GNR D1s and Gresley D49s, K2s and K3s, but all were supplanted to some extent after the war by Thompson B1s. These locomotives hailed from St Margaret's shed as well as from Haymarket, Hawick, Eastfield, Stirling, Dunfermline, Thornton Junction, Dundee and Perth. Locomotives from the Northern (Great North of Scotland Railway) Section of the Scottish Area did not appear in Edinburgh, except when some B12/1s and the odd D41 were transferred to St Margaret's and/or Haymarket and Eastfield for a year or two in the middle of the war. In 1939, there had been the odd LMSR working into Waverley from Larbert, but after Nationalisation, ex-LMSR engines worked in regularly, particularly from Perth, while from mid-1951 BR Class 5 4-6-0s also came from Perth and Eastfield.

Local services were usually worked by NBR 4-4-2Ts and Gresley 2-6-2Ts, although not infrequently by NBR 0-6-0s, from St Margaret's and Haymarket, also Dunfermline and Stirling sheds. While the Gresley V1s remained the principal motive power for Suburban trains until the advent of DMUs, in 1939, there were NBR G9 0-4-4Ts and steam railcars operating the short runs to North Leith and Leith Central and on the Musselburgh branch.

Empty stock for the main line expresses worked from Craigentinny Carriage Sidings to Waverley, usually behind V1s. Stock stabled at the subsidiary Sidings at Corstorphine, if that of a Haymarket working, was often used as a local passenger service to Corstorphine.

DMUs were used temporarily on the Peebles line locals as early as June 1956, but it was June 1958 after a depot was built for them at the old Leith Central station, when local services from Waverley were completely turned over from steam. In the meantime, Swindon-built six-car Inter-City DMUs with buffet cars were put to work, initially in January 1957 and fully from June 1958, on the main line between Waverley and Glasgow Queen Street, giving an improved regular-interval service. Main line diesels came to Edinburgh in April 1959, with the start of a major allocation of Birmingham Type 2 Bo-Bos (later Class 26) to Haymarket, beginning a long association between this class and the Scottish Region. They began working the Edinburgh-Aberdeen expresses in August 1959 and were observed working down to Newcastle in October. Then, at the end of 1959, the English Electric Type 4s (later Class 40) allocated to Gateshead began to head expresses from Newcastle.

Freight trains on the ECML from Newcastle and the south were worked largely by St Margaret's numerous 2-6-0s and 2-8-0s, but they also brought Pacifics, V2s, K3s and 2-8-0s of various kinds from Heaton, Gateshead, York and sometimes from further south. In October 1951, Carlisle Canal shed was transferred from the LMR to the Scottish Region (ScR) and duly acquired LMSR Class 5s and 8Fs, working through to Waverley along with their ex-LNER shed-mates. The normal practice was for engines to be changed at Niddrie on through freights. These included the fish and meat trains from Aberdeen to London and the numerous, but seasonal, seed-potato trains from Eastern Scotland to Eastern England. This practice also encompassed mixed freights working through from such Yards as Craiginches (Aberdeen), Dundee, Thornton, and Glasgow High Street, to Heaton and further south. Thus freight locomotives came to Edinburgh from many other former NBR sheds, principally Eastfield and Parkhead in Glasgow, Polmont, Stirling, Perth, Thornton Junction, Dunfermline, Dundee and Aberdeen Ferryhill.

2
Alterations to the Way and Structures (1939–1959)

Pre-1939

Throughout the 1930s, the LNER struggled to earn revenue because of the global trade depression, which affected many of the industries the company served. With the railway having no funds for key maintenance and improvement projects, the government stepped in and created the Railway Finance Corporation, empowered to make low-interest (2.5 per cent) loans to the 'Big Four' Railways, for schemes that would keep the industry afloat and people in employment.

Spurred on by the availability of these loans, the LNER planned a number of improvement schemes. The largest of these were the Manchester to Sheffield and Wath main-line electrification and London Liverpool Street to Shenfield suburban electrifications. On the ECML there were station improvements and signalling upgrades at Doncaster and York, extension of the existing colour-light signalling from Northallerton to Darlington and—in collaboration with the LPTB—the electrification of the London suburban branches to High Barnet, Edgware and Alexandra Palace. All that was completed before the outbreak of war was the Northallerton–Darlington resignalling and the substitution of a number of intermediate manual signal boxes on the ECML by automatic colour-light signals. There were several other schemes, but they were never started and were abandoned after the war.

The electrification in North London was completed early in the war, albeit in a modified form. The lines between Finsbury Park, Highgate and Alexandra Palace were not electrified, although the conductor rail was laid up the branch; the planned connection with the LPTB Northern City line at Finsbury Park was not carried through. The Edgware branch was electrified only as far as Mill Hill East, primarily to serve the barracks there. Physical remnants of parts of this scheme remained for many years. The girders of a new bridge over the Seven Sisters Road at Finsbury Park, for the connection with the Northern City line at Drayton Park, were removed elsewhere during the war. As well, Finsbury Park was left with a temporary entrance on the Up side under girders of this connection until the Great Northern Line Electrification of 1976. On the relinquished LPTB Northern

Line Extension from Edgware to Bushey Heath, there remained for many years the Depot built at Aldenham, which was converted during the war into an aircraft factory and used afterwards as a London Transport bus depot.

Work on the other projects was in abeyance during the conflict, and in some instances was not finished until the 1950s—if at all. Doncaster was left half-finished until 1949 and at York the full resignalling had to wait until 1951, although the provision of extra platforms and track rearrangements had been almost completed in 1939.

Wartime New Works

In the run-up to war, £4 million was spent on air raid precautions (ARP) to protect the railways, and by the end of 1944, a further £7.6 million had been added to this figure; the ongoing maintenance and servicing of ARP cost £10.1 million. The principal precautionary measures had been for: the protection of staff, administrative centres and vital points[1] on the line; provision of stocks of materials for emergency repairs; and provision of additional equipment and materials for enforcement of light restrictions. During the war, the main categories of expenditure were for: protective equipment for staff; air raid spotters; cleansing and other squads; fire-fighting; removal or protection of glass; movement of trains through gassed areas (rehearsals); alternative electricity supplies; railway power station protection; breakdown cranes; and other plant.

As part of the contingency plans made in the year before war broke out, the Railway Executive Committee on behalf of the minister of transport set rules for extra traffic and emergency routes; these were put into action when the time came. The extent of the measures that could be taken to increase line capacity was limited, and less than ideal as major works would take a year or more to carry out. Before the war, the railways were working below capacity and in most cases sufficient extra line capacity for freight could be achieved by making refuge sidings into loops and dividing the block sections by means of automatic intermediate signals. However, this had the drawback of passenger services being severely restricted. Nevertheless, after the first year of the conflict, the output of the war factories, the needs of the forces, the dislocations due to enemy bombing and the transfer of much of the overseas traffic to the west coast ports, which was occasioned by the enemy's threats to the east and south coast sea traffic, led to such a great increase in rail traffic that it became essential to carry out major new works.

Provision of extra running lines and extensive new yards was required to relieve freight traffic bottlenecks, which in 1940–41 threatened to strangle the railway system, as well entirely new trunk telephone systems were established for centralised traffic control. Other large projects were undertaken, largely in anticipation of more serious destruction of the docks and depots at places such as Liverpool and Glasgow than in the event occurred. These included: the construction of two entirely new ports in Scotland, at Faslane and Cairnryan; six large new inland goods depots adjacent to the major west coast ports, also several emergency goods depots in the London suburbs—which were actually little used.[2] While the LMSR and GWR were more directly involved with the emergency facilities, the LNER had to deal with as much extra freight traffic as any of the other companies, partly because of the role it played in relieving the LMSR and GWR of the enormous north–south flow of traffic. By the end of 1944, the new works to improve operating arrangements had cost the exchequer £13,467,000, £3,571,000 of this being on the LNER. At the same time, the railways spent £3,730,000 on way and works for the government (£1,031,000 by the LNER).

Works were carried out at government expense on the understanding that, in the case of new works of long-term benefit to the railway companies and which they wished to retain after the war, suitable financial terms would be agreed when the time came. On the LNER, new works required after the war included virtually all of those which facilitated the flow of traffic and the servicing of locomotives, but excluded those involving new connections with other companies' systems, although the retention of Connington and Addison (Blaydon) Marshalling Yards and the loop at Harringay with the LMSR were originally deemed of doubtful long-term value. The cost of the new works that directly involved the ECML was no less than £1.045 million.

Major New Works

Coal for London and the South-East

There was concern that severe bombing of London would disrupt the vital movement of the large tonnages of coal passing across the Thames Bridges, and particularly that the dip of the widened lines under the Metropolitan Line between King's Cross and Farringdon would flood, due to the fracture of massive sewers and water mains. In December 1939, nearly 2,000 wagons were passing per day across Blackfriars Bridge—two-thirds from the GN Section of the LNER and one-third from the LMSR Midland Division. At the outset, to facilitate cross-London traffic over Blackfriars Bridge, new connections were put in during November 1939 (at a cost of £9,000) between the widened lines and the Metropolitan lines at King's Cross, to allow the traffic to be diverted in an emergency to the East London line.[3]

In addition, a new crossover was inserted at Ludgate Hill, to enable either half of Blackfriars Bridge to be used (costing £2,000 in May 1940). In the Blitz, the route over Blackfriars Bridge was thought to be very vulnerable, on account of the destruction of other bridges on the elevated sections of the SR. With the frequent interruptions of traffic across the Thames Bridge from September 1940, it was realised that new links were needed for the diversion of cross-London traffic for the south. The East London line was vulnerable and had very limited capacity. The first viable alternative route for this traffic made use of the loop, built during the First World War and reinstated in March 1940 (at a cost of £4,700), from Harringay on to the LMSR&LNER Joint Tottenham and Hampstead line and via another loop (restored in March 1940, for £6,000) at Gospel Oak to the North London line.

For traffic from the north to the southern counties, diversion away from London was deemed preferable. Routes were planned based on the existing and new junctions of the LMSR Cambridge–Bletchley–Oxford lines and the GWR from Oxford through Reading. Meanwhile, a new link was installed between the GWR and SR at Staines; this was opened in June 1940 but was not used until September 1940. It enabled traffic from the GWR—and indirectly from the LNER via Banbury or Sandy—to reach the SR by its Windsor line; in practice, however, the route was awkward and was relatively little used—the majority of diverted traffic was run over the line between September 1940 and May 1941.[4]

On the Cambridge–Oxford line, a north to west loop was opened in September 1940 for £19,000, connecting from Blunham to the ECML 1.4 miles north of Sandy. Also, an east to south loop (opened in July 1940 at a cost of £18,000) from the LMSR line west of Claydon to the ex-GCR main line at Calvert[5], new loops and signal boxes on the LMSR line, a new connection between the LMSR and the GWR at Oxford (opened 1940, £10,000), and enhancement of line capacity between Oxford, Didcot, Reading and Basingstoke. The Sandy link enabled new routes for traffic from the LNER to the south. Reopening of the connections near Peterborough, between Fletton Junction and Longville Junction on the LMSR was considered but rejected.

The ex-GCR route was followed from Calvert: either to Northolt Junction, thence on to the GWR via Greenford, West Drayton and Staines on to the SR, or via Neasden and the LMSR North & Southern Western Junction line to the SR at Kew Bridge. Traffic for the important Solent area and round to the LB&SCR section of the SR via Chichester could run onto the GWR at Oxford via Reading West and Basingstoke. The heavy flow of traffic heading eastwards from Reading on to the SR was facilitated by a new main line connection (opened in March–May 1941, £91,000) east of Reading. Paths were scheduled in the winter of 1940–41 for 12 freight trains daily each way between Sandy or Cambridge and Northolt Junction via the Calvert Loop (four to reach the SR via the Staines Loop), plus six via Oxford to Basingstoke and beyond.

No more than six trains ran per day by the Staines route during the Blitz period (with Peterborough New England O1s and O2s working through to Northolt Junction), and thereafter the preferred route was through Oxford. The overriding requirement was to keep the traffic moving, and for this, an extra 100 miles of journey was unimportant—at least for coal, providing the wagons were not tied up or the sidings choked. Nevertheless, the situation in October 1940 was so serious that ideas were put forward for really major new works. These included widening and connecting the Branches to Uxbridge from Denham and West Drayton, building a marshalling yard and locomotive depot at Colnbrook, or alternatively upgrading the GWR High Wycombe–Maidenhead Branch and building a new line from Cookham to Bracknell, or even building a new line all the way from Princes Risborough to Wokingham.

However, the abrupt cessation of severe enemy air raids after May 1941 rendered unnecessary such drastic construction projects. Early in the war, it was recognised that the former GCR 'London Extension' route would have to bear a much greater proportion of the north–south traffic than hitherto, to relieve the other trunk lines. Consequently, a major investment of £300,000 was committed as early as March 1940 into the construction of a Down Yard and enlargement of the Up Yard at Woodford, enlargement of Annesley Yard and provision of new loops at Woodford, Charwelton, Rugby Central, Ashby Magna, Swithland, Loughborough Central, Ruddington and Hucknall. Later, further enhancements were made to the yards at Woodford (also Banbury on the GWR) and Annesley, and five new loops built on the GWR&GCR Joint line.

York–Northallerton Bottleneck

At an early stage, the vital need for a major increase in the capacity of the ECML, particularly between York and Northallerton, was recognised, in part because of the massive increase in coal traffic along the main line. In March 1941, an average of 114 freight trains ran each way daily on this stretch of track, which was a 56 per cent increase on the pre-war figure. Even in September 1939, there was a 15 per cent rise over the corresponding weeks in 1938 in forwarding from NE Area stations—even more from the Darlington and Middlesbrough Districts. As a result, Thirsk and Stockton Yards were recommissioned very soon after the war started. Additions were made to Thirsk Up Yard in August 1942 and it continued to be used extensively for some years after the war, additional connections being put in as late as February 1952.

Major new works were soon undertaken and more followed later. First, work was done to facilitate the running of freight traffic, especially convoy coal trains, through York without remarshalling. Some expansion of York Up Yards was undertaken in February 1941 (£5,500), and in June 1941, a new electro-mechanical signal box (75 levers) was brought into use at Skelton Junction, and from there the signalling through to Clifton, as well as to York Yard North, became all-electric. In August 1941, a new Up Independent Goods line was brought into use before Skelton and Clifton at a cost of £14,800, to allow more freight to pass through York station and to enable through trains to be examined and locomotives and crews to be changed at a point conveniently near their depot. Also new connections from the Up main line were installed at Dringhouses in June 1942 (£2,000); this in turn necessitated the handling of some York traffic back at Thirsk Yard, which was already becoming overburdened with traffic from Teesside and the North.

Subsequently, in December 1942, £82,000 was spent on a substantial new yard north of Skelton Junction. This consisted of six Down and six Up through roads, with a shunting neck at the north end. Down and Up engine lines were provided between the two groups of sidings, off which were facilities that included a 70-foot turntable for servicing locomotives, so minimising movements to and from the main depot at York. The Down Independent was taken round the new yard and continued over the River Ouse on a new bridge and was ready in October 1942 (£24,000). However, a badly needed flyover for Up freight trains was not built. Such trains entering Skelton New Yard continued to approach on the solitary Up line over the river and conflict with trains on the Down Fast; this occurred at the manual but remotely controlled (partly by telephone) Skelton Bridge crossovers.

Although the signalling was modernised, with a number of intermediate automatic signals, at the outbreak of the war the ECML between York and Northallerton was quadruple only from north of Skelton Bridge to short of Alne station and north of Thirsk station to Northallerton—just 16 of the 30 miles of this heavily occupied stretch. There was an extra Down line for five miles through Alne to short of Pilmoor station, but two-track bottlenecks still existed over Skelton Bridge and from short of Pilmoor to Green Lane before Thirsk. Apart from building the new Down Goods line over the Ouse at Skelton, it was deemed essential to undertake further widening where it could be done fairly easily.

Costing a total of £383,070 and completed in May 1943, the widening was carried out over the ensuing years between Pilmoor and Thirsk. The existing Down Slow line was extended (as a Goods line) from Sessay Wood (south of Pilmoor) to connect with the existing loop at Green Lane, and an Up Goods line was built from Green Lane south to Pilmoor North. The work also entailed the remodelling of junctions and partial rebuilding of certain stations. Sessay was completely rebuilt, with a platform in the Down direction only on the new Goods line but with an island created on the Up side. Pilmoor station was also rebuilt on the Down side. Thirsk

The new bridge over the River Ouse at Skelton is erected early in the war.

station was rebuilt with island platforms accommodating both the Down and Up Slow lines, public access was moved from the Down side to a new forecourt on the Up side, and new connections were inserted with the Melmerby line and with the Down and Up Thirsk Yards.

Except at Thirsk, the block sections of the new lines were not at first signalled with colour-lights to conform with existing modernised signalling north of Skelton Junction, but were operated by Permissive Block, an extra block section being inserted between Pilmoor and Thirsk by the building of a new signal box at Sessay. On account of engineering difficulties, the five miles of Up line between Pilmoor and Alne were not duplicated until June 1960, while the signalling of the new Goods lines between Pilmoor and Thirsk remained by Permissive Block until modernised in 1959.

Northallerton Avoiding Line

Northallerton, being a focal point on the ECML at an exposed high level with three rail-over-rail bridges and especially vulnerable to interruption by enemy action, had a new loop commissioned as a matter of urgency in July 1940, and this was completed in June 1941 (officially December) for £21,170. The line ran to the northward ECML at Castle Hills from Romanby Gate box on the existing Low Level avoiding line connecting the Leeds Northern and the ECML from York with the line to Teesside at Northallerton East. It allowed traffic to Darlington and the north to be independent of the High Level route through Northallerton station, and an emergency station of wooden platforms was erected on the Low Level line just south of Romanby Gate.

The new loop had the unique feature of a low bridge just a few feet high, carrying the conflicting south curve of the Wensleydale Branch over it. This bridge could be removed on

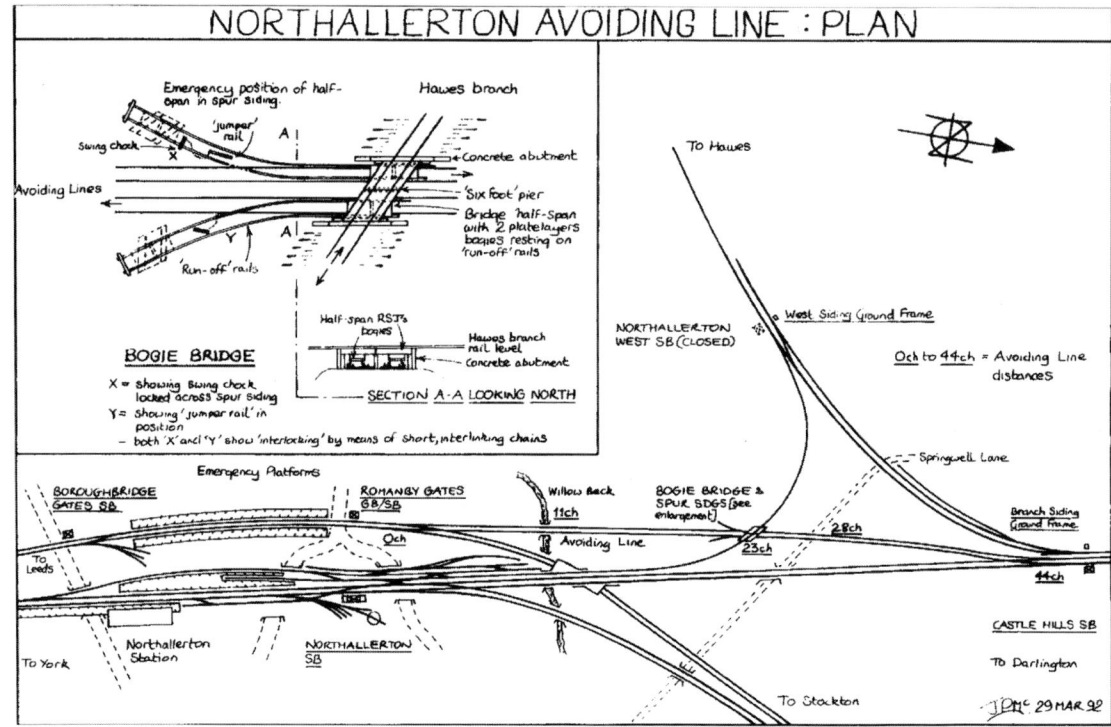

Plan of the Low Level avoiding lines and station at Northallerton.

bogies if the avoiding line was needed, but apart from occasional tests, the loop was never used, and it was taken up in 1947. Signalling alterations included a renewed and lengthened frame at Romanby Gate, covered frames at Castle Hills (for controlling the lines towards the station and the Hawes Branch north curve), at Wiske Moor and at Danby Wiske. Each of these boxes was to be designated as a block post and the emergency mechanical signalling, with oil-lit semaphores, was capable of substituting in case of power failure on the recently electrified installation. All of this was ready in June 1941.[6]

Other Enhancements of Line Capacity

North to South

All the extra Scottish traffic on the ECML could not be accommodated in Edinburgh by Niddrie West Yard, therefore in 1940, Meadows Yard was reopened and in February 1943 was provided with new locomotive watering facilities (£2,300). By November 1940, Meadows Yard alone was dealing with over 700 ECML trains per month, in and out. Even so, the facilities at Niddrie had to be expanded by the provision of two extra Up loop lines (April 1942, £16,840), and in November 1943, new coal storage sidings were brought into use off the South Leith goods line near Portobello.

New goods loops were installed at most of the intermediate stations between Edinburgh and Berwick, partly by making refuge sidings into loops, but in most cases by installing entirely new down loops on both the Up and the Down sides. The following improvements were made: Newhailes, the Down loop was extended to take 80 wagons and another added; at Prestonpans, the Up refuge siding was converted to a Goods loop, with a new connection to the Preston Links Colliery Branch (March 1943, £8,850); at Drem, a Down refuge was converted to a loop (May 1943, £2,160); at East Linton, the Up Goods loop was extended and a new Down loop was made by extending a shunting neck westwards and a new subway was also built (August 1942, £9,530); at Dunbar, the Up and Down platform loops were extended westward and the West box was replaced on a new site (March 1942, £12,170); at Innerwick, an Up refuge was converted to a Goods loop and the Down loop extended west (December 1941–March 1942, £7,000); at Grantshouse, the Up and Down refuges were extended to loops and new water columns installed (June 1943, £19,040); at Reston, a new Up loop was installed east of the junction and a new Down loop created by extending the Branch platform line to form a loop (April 1943, £17,250); and at Ayton, new Up and Down loops were installed west and east of the station respectively (April 1943, £18,190).

In addition, intermediate automatic colour-light signals were installed at several locations on the stretch between Berwick and Grantshouse (December 1942 to March 1943, £10,150), also on the Edinburgh South Suburban line between Blackford Hill and Duddingston (September 1942, £4,180).

The Royal Border Bridge was a significant target for the Luftwaffe and consequently improvements were carried out on the partly single-track Kelso Branch, which were sufficient to allow its use for the diversion of trains from the ECML at Tweedmouth to the Waverley Route at St Boswells. The work entailed extending running loops at Kelso and at Roxburgh Junction, the insertion of a loop at Maxton and a short extension of the double-track at Kelso Junction, St Boswells (1942, £9,270). The work proved valuable in the post-war years when the floods of 1948 washed-out much of the ECML in the area.

Between Berwick and Newcastle, a new Down loop was made at Chevington and a very long Up loop was formed from the former Amble branch line, which was connected with the main line at Amble Junction (March 1943, £13,675); an extra water column was provided at Alnmouth in July 1944, and a new Up Independent line was inserted at Morpeth in August 1944 for £5,050.

In the Newcastle area, a north to west connection between the ECML and the Blyth and Tyne line at Benton had been installed in September 1940 (£9,120), mainly to allow the main-line traffic to be diverted via the Jesmond loop in case of enemy destruction of bridges on the main line; a new signal box—Little Benton North —was erected at its junction with the ECML. In September 1941 (£58,900), a substantial marshalling yard was constructed at Addison, west of Blaydon, for handling the greatly increased traffic over the line to Carlisle.

On the ECML at Heaton, rearmament traffic had led to the reactivating of the New Down Yard in March 1939. The traffic on the Down ECML had doubled, and it was found that the arrangement of yards on the Down side was very unsatisfactory. This was because one of the North Yard reception sidings had to be reserved for trains entering the New Yard from the south, and the Down Independent had to be kept clear for trains departing from the North Yard. The resulting delay saw trains having to be stored at other places up the line until they could be brought back to Heaton.

In May 1941, changes costing £3,100 were made that allowed trains to go in and out of each yard independently, being controlled by a reconstructed yard box that was operated as a ground frame released by Heaton South box. Later, new independent connections were installed between the North and New Yards and the main line (August 1942, £3,140). However, the number of freight trains running through Newcastle to Scotland without remarshalling was increasing, but these trains had to be stopped for examination, reduced for the heavier grades, or re-engined, and it was found that they often blocked the Down reception lines at Heaton. Accordingly, two sidings of the Engineer's yard were taken over to accommodate these trains (June 1943, £900). Meanwhile, five new Up reception sidings were positioned just to the north of the Heaton Yards, between Little Benton North and a new Little Benton South box, which was erected in place of 'C' Pit box (December 1942, £21,060). At the same time, improvements were made at Heaton locomotive shed.

South of Newcastle, new loops were made for both directions at Preston-le-Skerne between Bradbury and Aycliffe (October–December 1942, £31,860), together with new intermediate colour-light signals between Aycliffe and Preston-le-Skerne. At Darlington, where up to 1943 traffic through the several yards had increased by 36 per cent, the capacity of Haughton Bridge Yard was enhanced initially by 37 per cent in late 1939 (£14,015), the two reception roads being doubled to four and two extra sidings being installed and others lengthened. A new Down loop was laid in August 1940 at a cost of £3,200 and further sidings added in June 1944 amounted to £2,000. Also, in November 1942, a siding on the Down side of Bank Top station was converted into a second Down Independent line (£7,260).

In addition to the widening of the main line, many more loops were built on the Leeds Northern route through Ripon, Harrogate, Tadcaster and Church Fenton to help relieve the route through York. These cost £76,000 and included a new Down Independent line no less than 1¾ miles long between Sherburn-in-Elmet and Church Fenton (August 1942, £22,915). South of York on the ECML, long new loops were provided on both the Down and Up sides between Escrick and Riccall and additional signal boxes (Escrick South and Riccall North) were constructed to work them (February 1942, £16,115).

Elsewhere in the NE area, at the yards at Newport (Middlesbrough), the inwards yard was overloaded by 1943 as it struggled to deal with 27,000 wagons a week (33 per cent up on pre war) and was eventually enlarged by June 1944 at a cost of £12,940. At Shildon, a further £3,580 was spent on reopening and extending the marshalling yard, which was ready for use in September 1944. On the Richmond Branch, the Light Railway from Catterick Bridge to Catterick Camp Centre was upgraded in October 1943 (£3,570), to deal with the swelling local and special traffic. Also the disused station on the branch at Eryholme was restored in September 1944 (£3,540), with a new island platform on the Up side, being primarily for RAF men based at Croft Airfield.

By November 1941, the bottleneck facing Up trains at Doncaster from the Marshgate Junctions had been relieved by a new Up Independent line over the river bridges, forming the Up Passenger Independent No. 2 line (serving the new platform 1) and was extended through in December 1941 (£2,200). In July 1942, to relieve the pressure on the Down side, and pending the completion of major improvements of all track and signalling, new connections were made between the ex-GCR lines and the ex-GNR Goods line between that and the South Yorkshire Goods line. Finally, in October 1944, temporary connections were installed in order to make use of the new Down Passenger Independent line already installed before the war. This required extensions to be made to the frame in Frenchgate box, although it was destined to be abolished.

Before the extra freight traffic seriously taxed the yards at Doncaster, major work was begun in 1941 and speeded up under the *Bolero* programme in 1942, being costed at nearly £80,000. On the Up side, the Old and New Decoy Yards were separate and single-ended, with only one reception road between the boxes at Carr and Decoy No. 2. This meant that often the Up Goods and even the Up Fast lines had to be used as receptions roads, so causing serious delays to the flow of through traffic. Accordingly, four new reception lines were installed, together with an extra engine line and shunting neck, while the capacity of the Up Yard was expanded to handle 36 per cent more wagons by combining and extending the former two groups of sidings, and a new points box was constructed to control them all. This was a large project, entailing the displacement of the extensive stacking area for sleepers and rails; it cost £73,000 and took until February 1943 to complete. During the war, more freight trains ran through Doncaster—from York, Peterborough and elsewhere—without remarshalling and trains were longer, so they often fouled the connections off the reception lines, while the locomotive went off to get water or to be replaced. For this reason, new water columns were provided (late in 1944) adjacent to the Up slow and fast goods lines.

At Decoy Down Yard, there was a similar problem with accepting trains, and so a fourth reception line was provided, and some alterations made to the signalling (January 1942, £10,940). Finally, in October 1944, the layout was rearranged so that an extra Down Goods line ran through much of the Decoy complex (£4,530).

The capacity of the ECML between Doncaster and Grantham was enhanced in 1941–43 by the provision of additional sidings and goods loops. At Retford, the existing Down loops were extended and duplicated, as were those between Dukeries Junction and Tuxford North Junction, also new Down and Up loops were installed between Egmanton box and Dukeries Junction. A Down loop was inserted north of Crow Park, Up and Down loops were added at Carlton-on-Trent and Up loops were put in at Claypole, in all costing around £75,000. At Barnby box (south of Newark), additional sidings were installed in June 1943 (£2,000).

The layout at Grantham station was unsuitable for dealing with the increased traffic off the Nottingham line, which had to cross the Down ECML and pass through on the single Up main line. Therefore, to allow Nottingham line passenger trains to arrive as well as depart from the Down side of the station, the tracks and signalling were rearranged, with reversible signalling of the Down Western platform (No. 5) and Down Goods lines (May 1943, £7,900). The Up main platform was also too short for the long wartime trains. Eventually in March 1945, the Up platform was extended northwards by 400 feet, with alteration of the connections to the Up Bay and provision of two new sidings outside it.

South of Grantham, the Down ECML between Stoke and Grantham South boxes had a long stretch of five miles with no relief line, often causing delays by slow moving freights. Accordingly, a new Down Goods loop (for 100 wagons), with points and signals controlled electrically from Grantham South box, was installed at Saltersford in December 1943 (£14,900).

With the opening of a new Mine at Colsterworth, ironstone traffic off the Stainby branch at Highdyke had risen in 1941 to 1.9 million tons from 733,000 tons in 1938. Additional sidings, extensions and new connections were installed at Highdyke, in two separate enlargements (August–November 1940 and November 1941, £11,660), which included the provision of sidings and a new signal box at Colsterworth North.

The cramped facilities and lack of relief platforms at Peterborough led to the practice of Down troop trains making a 20-minute refreshment stop at Essendine instead. Until a facing connection was inserted in late 1943 (£2,277) between the Down main and Goods lines there, these trains had to be put in the Stamford Branch platform and then backed out onto the Down main before proceeding. In addition, all the traffic for nearby airfields and military depots necessitated the construction of a small Down Yard at Essendine with new through connections, completed in January 1944.

At Peterborough, long overdue relief of a Down side bottleneck was achieved by converting one of the sidings of the Nene Carriage Yard at Crescent Junction into a running line, so forming an uninterrupted Down Goods line past the north station (March 1942, £7,420).

At New England, several quite minor alterations permitted a freer flow of traffic. Before the new Down Yard at Connington was available to ease the handling of Down empties traffic, shortage of reception lines for the empties yards was a problem; trains had to be dealt with at North New England, using the Down Goods line as a reception line and so blocking it. Consequently, the two westernmost sidings of the old empties yard were connected by a facing lead to the Down Goods line at New England South, and an extra reception line was added to the west empties yard. At the same time, to avoid a circuitous route for transfers between the west coal and Spital Yards, one of the sidings of the latter was connected with the easternmost line of the former; in compensation, two sidings in Spital Yard were extended. All this work was completed in October–December 1941 at a cost of £13,590.

By October 1943, the GN&GE Joint line and other routes into East Anglia were overloaded. Therefore, much southward traffic for East Anglia was diverted into London through Peterborough and the ECML, but the Up side at New England was unable to cope. Some further rearrangement of the yards at Peterborough was needed. It was not practical in the short term to do anything radical, but the commissioning of the new yard at Connington lightened the burden on the Down side at New England. It was possible then to switch one of the Down Yards, the Down West Empties Yard, to the handling of Up traffic.

For this changeover, the following alterations were made at a total cost of £14,100 in September 1944. The layout at Spital Junction was changed to enable one of the Engineer's sidings to become an Up departure line on to the main line, making it possible for an Up train to leave the West Yard at the same time as an Up coal train was leaving East Yard. An additional connection was made at West Empties Yard: the facing connection at New England South (provided in 1941) leading from the Down Goods line to the Old Down Empties Yard was moved. Also a new water column was provided at North New England, to allow engines to take water without detaching and going to the shed.

The handling of the extra traffic through Peterborough in the Down direction was facilitated principally by major new work at Connington (between Abbots Ripton and Holme). There, a new Down Yard, with 12 through roads, a shunting neck at each end and a hump, was opened in October 1942 (£68,800). A new Connington North box was provided to control the northern exit, the southern end being controlled by the existing

Connington box (renamed Connington South). The Yard was used mainly for sorting empties, relieving the Down Yard at Ferme Park; it remained in use until at least 1948.

At St Neots in 1940, the siding on the east side of the Up island platform was converted into an Up Slow line. At Sandy, apart from the new north to west loop at Sandy North to the LMSR line, the very heavy interchange traffic, especially of petrol to and from the large RAF Fuel Reserve Depot at Sandy Heath on the LMSR line towards Potton, and of bombs to the large Depot further on at Lords Bridge. This led belatedly to the provision of new connections between the parallel LNER and LMSR in the goods yard south of the station (April 1944, £640).

At Hitchin, Cambridge line traffic presented problems. Much of this was from the north and had to be crossed over to the Down Yard. Traffic from the Cambridge direction increased later in the war, when relief to the overburdened ex-GER line to London was given by routing some local coal trains from Whitemoor along the ex-GNR line from Cambridge and from Langley Junction on to the Hertford Loop. The problems were eventually eased, between December 1944 and December 1945 by installing new facing connections between the main Goods lines at Cambridge Junction (£11,920). Also, a direct connection was inserted from the Cambridge branch into the Up yard, with alteration of sidings in the latter and extension of the signal box frame.

At Hertford, new sidings had been installed in January 1942 (£940) beside the River Lea on the line connecting the North to the East station, where coal was transferred to barges for onward passage to public utilities down the Lea Valley. A more effective connection between the Hertford Loop and the Eastern Section existed potentially at Palace Gates (Wood Green). There, just 20 wagons at a time could be fed through a siding between Bounds Green and Palace Gates boxes, and in September 1943, the LNER proposed a scheme to make the connection capable of carrying full-size main line trains on the New England–Temple Mills route. A revised scheme costing £8,900 was approved in January 1944 and brought into operation in July, but it consisted merely of a reversibly worked single-track link, which eventually cost £14,400. The link provided a relief route for freight to/from the ECML via Seven Sisters and South Tottenham for Temple Mills Yard and the Docks. It later proved very useful for diversions, for example when the ex-GER Cambridge line was flooded in March 1947, or when total possession of the ECML was required on Sundays during the Potters Bar widening work. It was also used well into the 1950s for excursions, such as from Hertford North to Southend or Clacton.

At Hatfield, wartime freight traffic for the St Albans, Luton/Dunstable, and Hertford branches was double the peacetime level by 1941 and increased another 25 per cent in 1942. It became too great to be dealt with in the Up and Down Yards at Hatfield, with up to 16 special trains being run in a day on the Dunstable branch alone. In the first instance, the sidings on the Down side and their connections were rearranged to provide a through Down Goods line as well as a through/reversible line on the western face of the Down platform. It was then possible for Down local passenger trains to remain clear of Down fast trains and for local and branch trains to reverse or detach/attach independently of the working of Down freight trains.

Traffic in the Up direction could not reach the branches to Dunstable and Hertford at Welwyn Garden City and had to go on to Hatfield, where much inconvenience arose from its sorting and transfer from the Up to the Down side in the restricted layout, before it was worked back to Welwyn Garden City. Space was lacking at Hatfield for any major work on the Up side, but eventually after much discussion and revision, in September 1944, matters were eased by the installation of new facing leads between the Up main and slow lines and the former Hertford branch single line, which was converted into an Up Goods line. After that, the connection with the Dunstable and Hertford branches was at Welwyn Garden City.

Alternatives, such as building a connection between the LMSR and LNER at Luton (with exchanger sidings) or a direct Up loop line from Welwyn Garden City to Luton were rejected in favour of building a new marshalling yard at Welwyn Garden City. This had five new through roads and two new dead-end roads, and the existing goods yard and its covered accommodation were enlarged. An engine pit, water columns and a new siding to hold Branch passenger trains were provided, all spanned by a long new footbridge; the work was completed in September 1944 at a cost of £71,200.

Enhancements for Bolero

Most of the aforementioned improvements were dictated by the need to increase line capacity for general wartime needs. However, in 1942, an additional programme of New Works had to be drawn up to cope with the further burdens to be imposed on the railways by the American armed forces. Following the strategic decision to plan for a second front in Europe mounted from Britain, the *Bolero* plan was devised to accommodate in this country vast army and air forces and their equipment and supplies brought over from the United States. Necessarily, the extra burden would be felt virtually nationwide, although the greatest effect was expected to be felt by the GWR and SR. The execution of these new works was urgent and given high priority at a time when demands on labour and materials were at their highest and needed careful regulation. As far as the ECML and associated lines were concerned, the planned expenditure amounted to £848,000.

By the second half of 1942, the US Forces were flooding in, but through the ports on the west coast. It was hard to find any more room for Anglo-Scottish traffic through the bottleneck at Carlisle, so the capacity of the ECML had to be further enhanced. The ECML through Berwick, Newcastle and Ferryhill was already saturated—the count of freight trains at these three points in April 1942 was 30, 70 and 57 respectively each way per day, and delays of up to 12 hours were being suffered through lack of loop lines and reception sidings. Yet, for the *Bolero* traffic, an additional increase of 30 per cent had been anticipated. Therefore, freight train loading limits were raised, while a steadily increasing number of military 2-8-0 locomotives became available at the right time, being allocated to the LNER in particular at York, Neville Hill, Heaton and St Margaret's sheds.

In the *Bolero* plan, the LNER's ex-GCR lines were assigned a major role, and the line capacity on the Sheffield–Woodford stretch was further augmented after major enhancements had already been carried out. Likewise, the extra load envisaged on the ECML was planned to be mitigated by routing military traffic over the joint line through Lincolnshire and in the NE area by the Leamside and Stillington lines in County Durham and via Harrogate and Church Fenton in Yorkshire. The capacity of the Waverley Route was increased by providing new loops at several places, but these measures only exacerbated the situation at Carlisle. The principal alternative was the ECML through Berwick, although to relieve this main line it was even decided to run some extra troop trains from Scottish ports over the Border Counties line, which was already carrying some Anglo-Scottish freight. For this, the bridge over the North Tyne near Hexham was strengthened to allow K3 2-6-0s to haul specials (1942, £960) and the signalling between Hexham and Riccarton Junction was improved to facilitate night-time working.

For *Bolero*, the east coast ports also came back to prominence, and an interesting scheme had been mooted earlier, but was not undertaken although it would have been very useful. This was for a connecting line with associated yards, for handling heavy war supplies which would have been landed at Newcastle Quay. The existing steeply-graded single line up through the tunnels to Argyle Street was quite unsuitable, and the Newcastle Corporation offered, in May 1941, to join the LNER in building a better line eastwards to join the Riverside Branch at St Peters. The military and port authorities (movement control and port and transit control) were in favour, but the LNER steadfastly refused on the grounds of expense and disruption with poor prospects for traffic after the war, so the idea was dropped in March 1943.

Other Wartime New Works

Locomotive Depots

Improved facilities were provided during the war at many locomotive depots on the ECML, with several receiving very substantial investment. At St Margaret's, the site was very cramped, and consideration was given to building an entirely new depot in the Edinburgh suburbs, but time and resources were too scarce and improvements had to be confined to the existing site (£39,820, May 1941–March 1943). Also in September 1944, the disused LMSR shed at Seafield was reopened by the LNER as a relief depot for St Margaret's to handle 17 locomotives with a staff of 100 and it was renovated at Government expense (£8,980).

At Heaton, locomotive utilisation almost doubled by 1941, but the depot was essentially single-ended with awkward access. Therefore, major work had to be undertaken to convert it to a through shed, easily accessible from either direction, and with improved connections into the locomotive yard at the north end (£28,800, August 1943).

Extensive rebuilding began before the war at Darlington shed and was taken to completion in October 1940 at a total outlay of £69,500; further improvements were carried out later in the war (£12,010, December 1942–January 1945).

York shed also had a massive increase in utilisation and required major work to improve the turn-around of locomotives, in spite of the provision of extensive servicing facilities at Skelton Sidings. Also, after heavy damage sustained in an air raid in April 1942, Nos 1 and 2 roundhouses had to be rebuilt.

Important, if lesser, investment was made in locomotive depots at the following: New England (March 1944, including the provision of a 'light-tunnel' for the examination of locomotives at night, £1,860); Grantham (January 1944, £3,000); Selby (April 1943, £2,510); Gateshead (March 1943, £4,260); and Haymarket (November 1945, £5,670). Depots closely associated with ECML traffic that received substantial improvements included: Blaydon (November 1942, £3,500); Newport (December 1942, £20,000); and Stockton (July 1943, £3,400).

Government Sidings

At numerous places up and down the country, new sidings and associated signalling were installed to handle the traffic of government depots connected to the railway system. Those serving food stores were particularly extensive; for example (on the ECML), the sidings provided for the cold store at Northallerton (opened in October 1941) cost £6,930.

At the Royal Ordnance Factories across the country, not only extensive sidings but new Branches and stations had to be provided. Two ROFs off the ECML—Thorpe Arch and Aycliffe—had dedicated passenger-carrying railways with several halts built. A halt was built in April 1941 for the Vickers Armstrong Works between Elswick and Scotswood, just outside Newcastle Central on the Carlisle line, and in August 1942, £1,350 was spent on one for the de Havilland Aircraft Factory near Hatfield at Lemsford Road on the St Albans Branch. A halt for the standard telephone works near New Southgate was mooted but on account of 'engineering difficulties' was not built.

For Ranskill ROF, which was directly on the ECML, a triangular connection was built on the Up side south of Ranskill station—costed at £24,960 when approved in April 1941. The southward loop to the ECML was double-track, but with one line (worked reversibly) used for passenger trains to the terminal station in the factory, the other line being used for goods traffic. Before the station was built inside the factory, a platform was provided on the Up loop from August 1941 until May 1942; a waiting shelter was also erected on the Down platform at Ranskill station. Northwards from the factory there was only a single line connecting with the Ranskill Up loop, the southward goods line joining the loop near its exit. The southward passenger line joined the main line just south of the exit of the loop, where there was a crossover. A novelty was that the single lines were operated not by token, but electrically by the track circuits, with 'acceptance plungers' in Ranskill box. A factory box controlled the junction of the north and south loops, also the sidings and station in the factory. When the ROF ceased production in the 1950s, the site was used for dismantling condemned rolling stock, shunted by a Y3 Class Sentinel from Doncaster Works.

Telecommunications

Before the war, the 'real time' regulation of trains was, to a large extent, simply under the control of the signalmen, especially those at junction signal boxes, and except on the LMSR, there was little in the way of centralised traffic control. Moreover, many signalmen had no more than the block telegraph by which they could communicate with other boxes. They had no telephone links, or else in some cases, communication between signal boxes or between stations or depots could only be made by means of the national Post Office telephone network, which formed an important part of the long-distance links between railway installations.

While railways did have exchanges and trunk lines of their own, the latter were by no means complete throughout the railway system. This situation was very unsatisfactory in war conditions, when a much wider and more flexible system of control was essential, especially when enemy action interfered with the network. District Control Offices supervised traffic continuously in their area by telephone links to key stations, yards and signal boxes. This work was vital for dealing with any out-of-course or special traffic, the handling of problems with motive power, rosters and so on, but in war, their functions were vulnerable. During the war, a great deal of money (in the order of £100,000) was spent and labour engaged[7], on the provision of wide and more complete telephone links, also of emergency reserve systems that were dedicated to the railway and independent of the Post Office network.[8]

Much of this work was undertaken following the problems of communication encountered during the Blitz, and in particular by November 1941, telephone circuits had been established, enabling a daily 'teleconference' to be held between the chief operating officers of the 'Big Four' together with their counterparts in the Railway Executive Committee, in order to respond to operating problems and allow for the smooth co-operation vital for the proper functioning of the railways in wartime.

On the ECML, extensive additional and/or emergency telephone circuits were set up; also shortwave radio links were established between key control offices and the LNER Traffic Control at Gerrards Cross. Some of the new telephone circuits were brought into use quite early in the war, such as between Knebworth and Gerrards Cross Controls, between GWR and SR Control Offices for handling traffic across and around London, also Doncaster–York, York–Hull and York–Spofforth and Scholes, along the M&GN routes. Lastly, in February 1941 one was made between Cambridge, Sandy, Calvert and Oxford.

However, it was well into the war and after the Blitz when many of the links were installed. In February 1942, a Newcastle–Carlisle Control circuit was set up, and in June 1942, a circuit was in place to connect the Control Offices of the LNER at York and the LMSR at Leeds. By July 1942, a dedicated line circuit was available between the Southern Area (Western section) Control Office at Gerrards Cross and the LNER's own exchange at King's Cross. In December 1942, a Control circuit was provided between Cambridge and Knebworth, also between the Control Offices at Knebworth, East Leake, Bawtry and Blankney. A circuit was completed between Peterborough and the LMSR at Leicester and Bletchley in June 1943, but not until October 1944 was one established between Bawtry and Mexborough.

A wartime innovation within the domain of the signal and telegraph engineers was the installation of communication between airfield control towers and signal boxes, in situations where runways of nearby airfields were very close to the railway. The matter was first raised in September 1942 and accepted for action in May 1943. The LNER's chief general manager (Sir Charles Newton) was the prime mover, on account of the situation at Burn Airfield beside the busy ECML at Henwick Hall near Selby.

Burn had two runways, which were roughly on a west–east orientation, with the east end a few yards from the railway line. It was a heavy bomber base and planes normally took off and landed straight over the railway; crashes on the railway had already occurred. The plan devised for Burn, and eventually brought into operation in 1944 (£1,750), entailed the burying of telephone wires and the running of tripwires on light poles eight feet above the track, over a stretch of 2,044 yards encompassing the two runway 'funnels'. A good distance from the runways, emergency colour-light distant and stop signals were installed for Down and Up lines. These would be illuminated in the event of an aircraft cutting the tripwires, also an audible and visual warning would be induced in Henwick Hall signal box, with which telephone links were set up to the airfield control tower. The stop lights were fitted with telephones for the benefit of train crews. Subsequently, similar protective installations were set up at 37 airfields nationwide, although several comprised merely the telephone links with control towers. The other Airfields which adjoined the ECML and were so equipped were: Tempsford (Everton box), Tholthorpe (Alne), Croft (Eryholme box) and Acklington.

Miscellaneous

Apart from the works aimed at increasing line capacity, securing telecommunications and so on, there was much expenditure on the repair of air raid damage. For example, £16,100 was spent on temporary repairs at York station and £29,600 in October 1942 on a new office block for the Hull District at Ferriby. Especially, provision of alternative facilities had to be made as insurance against the effects of further damage, these being part of the large programme of ARP works. Generators and emergency electrical and hydraulic supplies were installed at King's Cross in April 1943 (£4,000) and in June 1943 at Edinburgh Waverley (£1,900).

The extra traffic in heavy items, such as aircraft engines, being handled at many goods depots necessitated the provision of new and stronger cranes. It was found that fixed cranes at goods depots were a hindrance because wagons had to be placed beside them to be unloaded, so inhibiting free movement in yards and increasing the amount of shunting necessary. Therefore, it was usually mobile cranes that were needed, and these had the further advantage of being capable of working at outstations when the need arose, for example during the construction of airfields.

On the ECML, mobile cranes—usually of 6-ton capacity, each costing in excess of £2,000—were eventually supplied in the last year of the war or soon after, on hire from the Ministry of War Transport, at: New Southgate, Hitchin, Peterborough North, Grantham, Newark, Retford (Babworth), Doncaster, York, Darlington and East Fortune. Several mobile cranes were provided at various other places on the LNER, but some requests were not in fact satisfied.

At principal stations, refreshment facilities were enhanced, especially with mobile buffets for the benefit of servicemen. Also, fluorescent lighting was substituted for ordinary gas and electric lights, and loudspeakers were installed to help all the crowds of passengers. Wartime conditions forced the railways to build canteens at most of their major depots, for round-the-clock provision of meals; one at King's Cross cost £7,800 and had to cater for 3,200 workers in the goods yard and locomotive shed, another at Newcastle cost £9,450, Grantham £5,460, etc.

The LNER alone spent no less than £287,500 on these and other accommodation in the category of 'Non-Technical New Works'. Such provision ranged from the big staff canteens through improved ventilation in workshops (where staff were using lead instead of white metal alloys), to bicycle sheds. Also, between 1944 and 1946, accommodation for female staff was built at various depots and stations at government expense. Many of the improvements were not even started, let alone completed, until just after the end of the war, but the circumstances then made them more than ever necessary.

Post-War Improvements

Introduction

A post-war development committee was founded as early as May 1943—when it first reported, and the LNER had a comprehensive plan for new projects. These encompassed the rebuilding of King's Cross, electrification to Welwyn Garden City, a new joint station at Peterborough, quadrupling between New Barnet and Potters Bar, and improvements at York and Newcastle. New marshalling yards planned included a very large one at York, based on the wartime Skelton New Sidings, and one in Edinburgh between Niddrie and

Duddingston. A plan was also drawn up for the substitution of diesel locomotives for steam on ECML express services. Many other improvements were suggested, notably in the Scottish Area. However, circumstances just after the war were inappropriate for such projects, and the majority were postponed until the 1950s.

Doncaster Resignalling

The remodelling at Doncaster had begun before the war, with the rebuilding of the station and widening at the north end; the new Doncaster South signal box had been constructed in 1939 but not commissioned. Although the essential new Up Passenger Independent line was completed and connected in November 1941, the actual resignalling part of this work, in which the station area was to be under the control of two power boxes, was not taken up again until a few years after the war and was completed in 1949.

Off the south end of the Down platforms, the new south box (opened in January 1949) controlled the points and signals formerly under the mechanical boxes at South Yorkshire Junction and Doncaster South. The new north box (opened February 1949) was off the north end of the Down platforms and took over the functions of 'A', 'B', Frenchgate and Marshgate Junction boxes.[9] The new boxes had panels with illuminated diagrams, but there was no route-relay interlocking. Hand switches changed points and signals, and the interlocking was by a new 'sequence switch interlocking' system[10], the first of its kind in the world. Signals were three- or four-aspect colour-lights, with position lights at junctions and some theatre-type route indicators. The Block system was not employed between the north and south boxes, because movements were all controlled by means of train-describers and bell codes. Some

Interior of the new Doncaster North signal box.

Gresley A3 Pacific No. 60053 *Sansovino* heads south at Doncaster with an express for King's Cross. The new Doncaster South signal box is on the left, level with the last carriage of the train.

relatively minor track alterations were made when the new signalling was brought into use. Later (December 1952), as a result of the serious accidents at Bridge Junction in 1947 and 1951, the track layout there was modified and the signalling modernised.

York Resignalling

Major alterations to the station and the track were undertaken in 1938–39, but this large project was also interrupted by the war. Resumed in 1946, it was not entirely completed until May 1951. The work was carried out while normal traffic continued to pass, except in the very last critical stages of the changeover when major weekend line occupations with hand-signalling were necessary.

The first stage after the war entailed conversion to power-operation of all points in the York area. This encompassed Naburn and Copmanthorpe in the south and west to Skelton in the north—where connection was made with the existing colour-light signalling to Darlington—and to Burton Lane (Down) and to Bootham (Up) on the lines to Scarborough and Hull. The points remained connected to the existing manual boxes at York. Certain permanent way alterations were made, including new connections between Down and Up lines south of Holgate Bridge, a connection of Up and Down lines between Clifton and Waterworks, and—after locomotive yard box was dismantled—new connections between the Down and Up Leeds lines and the platform 15, 16 and engine lines.

Meanwhile, the large new panel signal box was built (over platform 13 and the north end of platform 14), and in stages, the semaphore signals were replaced by three- or four-aspect colour-lights, position light signals, and (where necessary) theatre-type route indicators. In the control room, there were four panels, each with a console, illuminated route diagram and train describers for the four main approaches to the York area; each was operated by one man at a time. Trains entering the confines of the area were described by the signalman at the nearest adjoining box by means of coded impulses that activated the appropriate display in York box. A route was then set through York by one of the four operators, employing one of the route-setting switches on the York console; the switch had set in

D20 Class 4-4-0 No. 2021 heads south out of York station under Holgate Road Bridge and an impressive array of signals, *c.* 1930.

motion a sequence of checking for conflicting movements, checking the track circuits, and the activation of the appropriate point-motors and colour-lights for the route. All this was carried out by electrical latching relays in no more than nine seconds. Capable of setting up 828 routes through a layout covering 18 miles of running, loop, and platform lines (33 track miles), the installation was the largest route-relay, 'one control switch' system in the world and cost £562,000. Requiring a staff of only 27 men—against 70 in the old manual signal boxes —the new system allowed freight to pass through the station 20 per cent more quickly than before, although the avoiding lines were not included in the scheme and remained controlled by York Yard north and south boxes for many years subsequently.

Newcastle Resignalling

The area of Newcastle Central, including the King Edward and High Level Bridges and Manors Junction and station, was taken over in April 1959 by a large panel box similar to the installation at York. From 1936, the electro-pneumatic semaphore signals in the area had been gradually replaced by three- and four-aspect colour-lights, position lights and theatre-type route indicators. The panels of the new box, situated in the middle of Central station between platforms 9 and 10, were divided into four sections as at York, and were operated by a similar 'one-control switch' system of route-relay interlocking, with 641 switches. The panels controlled 131 sets of points (13 switch diamonds), 94 main colour-lights (84 with subsidiary position lights, 61 with theatre-type indicators) and 86 independent two-aspect position lights. The new box superseded Newcastle Nos 1, 2 and 3 and Manors boxes and was worked by a total of 23 men in shifts, compared with 62 in the aforementioned boxes.

New Barnet-Potters Bar Widening

The need to relieve the traffic bottlenecks on the ECML near London had been felt for decades. The LNER long had the necessary parliamentary powers and even acquired some land, but could not afford the expense of providing new bores for up to five tunnels, let alone the reconstruction of Welwyn Viaduct.

After the war, the rapid expansion of population in the outer suburbs of London, including the establishment of a new town at Stevenage, compelled action. This was given its initial impetus by the strong recommendation of Sir Alan Mount, the ministry chief inspector, after the serious accident at Potters Bar on 10 February 1945. He advised that the convergence of the Up Slow into the Up Fast at the approach to Potters Bar station be altered to a convergence to the south of the station. Plans were drawn up in 1948 by the REC and accepted by the new British Transport Commission, first for a full widening and reconstruction at Potters Bar as far as the tunnel, then for a scheme restricted to the Up side only. However, the treasury would not allow any expenditure until April 1953, by which time further and more comprehensive plans drawn up by the railway executive were authorised. This embraced the whole scheme for widening through from Greenwood box, with the Potters Bar station scheme as Stage 1, and was costed at £1.82 million.

Work was begun in September 1953, but it was not until May 1959 that it was all completed. Four through lines were then provided for three miles from Greenwood box through the two Hadley Tunnels and Hadley Wood station, then through Potters Bar Tunnel and Potters Bar station. The first stages of the project comprised the reconstruction of Potters Bar station to a modern design with two island platforms and a subway in place of the footbridge, widening of the cutting on the London side, the provision of Up and Down Slow lines for the mile from the northern portal of Potters Bar Tunnel, and the rebuilding of the major underline bridge over Darkes Lane with two single-line and one double-line spans.

In addition, the new goods yard on the Up side at the north end was rearranged and enlarged; also a number of crossovers were installed to interconnect the new four-track

Hadley Wood station after reconstruction in the late 1950s, when new running lines were added.

arrangement through the station and for nearly a mile to the south. This work was completed in March 1955, along with the commissioning of an entirely new power box, situated at the north end of the station to the east of the Up Slow line. The power box had a novel form of entrance-exit route-relay interlocking; all the signalling was converted to colour-lights and the points to power operation.

The rest of the widening scheme was then taken in hand, with the boring of new twin-track tunnels on the west side of the existing three tunnels and the reconstruction of Hadley Wood station to a three-island plan. The tunnelling through the clay was not easy; special tunnelling shields were used and the circular bores were lined with pre-cast concrete segments rather than bricks. Only the longest of the three tunnels was provided with ventilators. At the south and north ends of the tunnels a great deal of excavation also had to be done to widen the deep cuttings. All the work had to be carried out with the normal ECML traffic passing, except for the final conversion from two tracks to four, which was executed during five weekend possessions in April and May 1959. Greenwood box was then eliminated and with automatic intermediate colour-light signals the remodelled stretch was thereafter under the control of an extended New Barnet North box and the new Potters Bar panel box. The completed project was formally opened on 20 May 1959 by Sir Brian Robertson, who unveiled a commemorative plaque on Hadley Wood station.

Alne–Pilmoor Widening

Planned in 1947, but not completed until June 1960, but without the planned fly-under and new Up line bridge over the river at Skelton, this project was the fulfilment of the last

BR Type Four, later Class 40, diesel electric locomotive No. D276 passes the new signal box at Tollerton during the early 1960s.

of the York–Northallerton quadrupling, which is the installation of an Up Slow line from just north of Pilmoor to and through Alne. This involved the demolition of the previously closed stations at Alne, Raskelf and Pilmoor. A new all-electric signal box was built at Tollerton and the boxes at Alne and Pilmoor North were abandoned.

Other Works

There were several modest schemes carried out on the ECML. The considerable expansion of open-cast mining, which was begun in the latter part of the war and shortly after it, resulted in new traffic flows and the building of new sidings and loops. Most new sites were in the North Midlands, their traffic affecting the ECML only indirectly through Colwick Yard. On the ECML itself, they were established at Meadowmills (just east of Prestonpans), also—as late as 1952—at Widdrington; from the latter site six trains departed northwards daily in 1952, and a long section was relieved by a new signal box at Widdrington North.

At the Scottish end of the ECML, there was considerable expansion of the Lothian Coalfield after the war, which provided the impetus for the construction of a large new marshalling yard at Millerhill, connected to the ECML by a new loop from Monktonhall Junction. The plans for the yard at Millerhill were drawn up in 1952. Just south of Niddrie on the Waverley Route, this was the only accessible site large enough for handling the 5,500 wagons per day being dealt with in Edinburgh, mainly at Niddrie, Portobello and Meadows Yards. The Scottish Division of the National Coal Board wanted to sink a new mine at Millerhill and the Scottish Region did not want their new hump yard under constant threat of subsiding. The dispute took a year to resolve and the two parties only just averted a legal battle in the High Court, but the yard was subsequently a victim of 'lack of funds' and did not get authorised until 1963 and then the need had dissipated.

Generally, improvements in the 1950s involved either the modernisation of passenger and goods station facilities or the improvement of permanent way. In the first category were preliminaries to the complete remodelling of Peterborough North: a new central stores depot, together with a new staff hostel, were completed in April 1954. Then a new goods station, and road motor depot were commissioned in July 1959 on the Up side between Spital and Westwood Junctions. In addition, the goods stations at Darlington and York were modernised in the 1950s. Mainly to save on scarce and expensive labour, the modern depots all featured mechanical handling equipment, such as slat-conveyors, pallets and fork-lift trucks. Also, horses were progressively replaced by motor vehicles for cartage work, and a new depot for 400 motors was built at King's Cross goods station in 1957. Modernisation of passenger stations entailed the complete renovation of waiting and refreshment rooms with cafeterias, coffee machines and other labour-saving devices. Many more stations were fitted with fluorescent lights in place of gas.

Introducing DMUs and diesel locomotives in the second half of the 1950s necessitated the construction of several new maintenance depots, as well as the provision of facilities for fuelling and servicing diesel locomotives at existing steam depots. The only diesel depot actually adjacent to the ECML and opened in this period was Darlington. There,

Horse-drawn cart used by King's Cross Goods Depot in the early 1930s.

an entirely new through shed, with three running and two repair roads, each capable of accommodating a four-car DMU set, was built in 1957, along with a two-way washing-plant and ancillary services. The Newcastle District DMUs (134 cars in all) were accommodated at South Gosforth Depot, where new facilities were provided, augmenting those already there for the Tyneside EMUs. In the meantime, several steam locomotive sheds on the Eastern and North Eastern Regions were in a state of disrepair. While roofs, etc., were rebuilt, the opportunity was taken to carry out other improvements, especially at Doncaster, York and Gateshead. Also, the carriage-cleaning facilities at York (Clifton), Darlington, Heaton and Craigentinny were extensively modernised.

Work on the permanent way of the ECML entailed the essential and costly replacement of various underline bridges, culverts and embankments washed away in the 1948 floods on the Berwick-Dunbar section. Also, some other bridge renewals, included the Ouse Bridge near Huntingdon, Muskham Viaduct near Newark and Coquet Viaduct near Acklington. Other improvements were the installation of a new Down crossover at Copenhagen Junction and on the Up side at East Goods Yard. In 1958, the curve at Shaftholme Junction was eased, involving the reconstruction of the bridge carrying the West Riding and Grimsby line over the ECML and the resiting and replacement of the signal box, with provision of jacking placed to take into account future mining subsidence in the area. In the late 1950s, as a preliminary to alterations at Peterborough, the ECML was straightened at Werrington Junction, and connections were remodelled and upgraded to allow a 60-mph turn-out from the Spalding line.

At this time, it became possible to take advantage of new technical innovations to reconstitute the track formation, improve drainage where the underlying ground was wet or unstable, and generally take some of the hard work out of the ganger's job. 'Track blanketing' was undertaken at a number of places. In connection with this work, the bridge at Huntingdon over the River Ouse was reconstructed in 1958–59. This entailed extensive temporary rearrangements: the Down goods independent line past Huntingdon station was upgraded to become the Down main and a temporary platform was installed, while the Down Slow was converted to become the Up main with Up trains being accommodated at the former Down Slow platform. At the Ouse Bridge, a temporary signal box was erected, to control the new connections with the Goods lines now ending there from the southerly direction. An opportunity was also taken to extend the Up Goods line from Stukeley box—where the Leys turn-out was removed—as far at Huntingdon No. 2, also to build a new signal box at Wood Walton between Abbots Ripton and Connington South. In 1959, the track-bed all the way from Wood Green to Hertford North was reformed, allowing the speed limit to be raised to 70 mph for the new DMU service and for the better employment of the Hertford Loop for diversions.

Wiske Moor troughs, which had been damaged by frost, were renewed in early 1950 with a system of supply that ensured much quicker re-filling. Flat-bottomed rails were first installed between Darlington and Aycliffe in July 1943, and their use gradually spread after the successful installation of a complete junction of this type at Benton Quarry in 1947. Also, many stretches were relaid with heavier 109 lb/foot rail. This was first installed between Tollerton and Alne in June 1949, and the diamond-crossing at Waterworks Junction (York) was relaid with it soon after. Then came the invention of long-welded rail (300 feet), which on the ECML was first installed near Carlton-on-Trent in September 1957. All these improvements formed the basis of the accelerations of services achieved from the 1960s.

Apart from the major signalling modernisations, various improvements in telecommunications were made elsewhere in the period. They included the installation in March 1959 of a 'flying-spot' radio communication system between key signal boxes down the line and the yardmaster's and station announcer's offices at King's Cross, as well as a large new private telephone exchange at York.

The standard automatic warning system (AWS), adopted eventually by BR, was developed from the Hudd electro-magnetic design already used on the London, Tilbury and Southend section, and tested by the LNER just before the war on the Edinburgh–Glasgow main line. After the war in 1946, experimental equipment devised by Westinghouse, giving repetition of the four-aspect colour-light signals, also audible warning of caution signals, was tried between Greenwood and Potters Bar with C1 No. 3293 so fitted, but it was not adopted. Instead, a modified Hudd system was developed and given extensive trials on the ECML between New Barnet and Huntingdon from July 1950 after 54 locomotives had been fitted. The rest of the ECML from London to Edinburgh was then equipped in stages from April 1956, the ER Section in late 1958 and the NER Section (as far as Darlington) in 1959.

Some schemes not carried out included: the widening of the line to four tracks through Arlesey station; abolition of bottlenecks between Huntingdon and Yaxley; an Up Relief line on the east side of Peterborough North station; quadrupling of Stoke Tunnel; opening out of Askham Tunnel, to allow the construction of loops in both directions between Lincoln Road box and Retford; Down loop at Great Ponton; and Down and Up loops south of Peascliffe Tunnel.

3
Locomotives of the ECML (1939–1959)

Stock Changes: Wartime (1939–45)

At the end of 1938, the LNER possessed a capital stock of 6,518 steam locomotives, also 80 steam and four oil-electric railcars and 13 Electric locomotives (all stored out of use, except for two shunting engines). In service stock, the company had 18 steam locomotives and three petrol railcars. The LNER was the least profitable of the 'Big Four', and probably had the greater proportion of superannuated steam locomotives than any of the other three groups; the average age of the LNER locomotive stock had risen from 22.4 years in 1924 to 27.7 in 1939, and reached 31.6 years in 1944.

During the 1930s, Gresley's construction of new locomotives had tended to concentrate more on the large Pacifics and V2 2-6-2s, needed for speeding up the long-distance passenger and freight services—including the new prestige services, to the relative exclusion of motive power for the more 'humdrum' services. Otherwise, capital was just not available for building new locomotives. Instead, the company could only modernise its motive power by modifying its existing units—and charging the cost to revenue account. Unlike the SR, there was no extensive electrification programme, at least until just before the war and then not on main routes: unlike the LMSR and GWR, only a certain degree of standardisation of steam locomotive types had been achieved on the LNER.

At the outbreak of war, the LNER—along with the other three companies—was forced by the circumstances not only to halt the scrapping of older steam engines, but also to reinstate large numbers of those which had been recently withdrawn from service. In late 1939 and early 1940, 45 of 143 locomotives withdrawn earlier in 1939, were reinstated. A substantial proportion of these were ex-NER 0-6-0s because the government had requisitioned 108 Dean Goods 0-6-0s from the GWR for service with the army, the GWR being partially compensated by the transfer of 40 ex-NER J25 0-6-0s from the LNER. Ten of the J25s were returned to the LNER in March 1943, but the rest stayed until November–December 1946.

Nevertheless, the LNER did continue to scrap a certain number of engines during the war. There were 30 withdrawn in 1940, 7 in 1941, 23 in 1942, 118 in 1943, 63 in 1944, and 69 in 1945. Prominent among these scrappings were the greater part of the stock (mainly of MR design) obtained in October 1936 as part of the acquisition of the M&GN Joint Railway. Also, in the last three years of war, substantial inroads were made into the older express engines of the former GNR and NER Companies, for example the Atlantics and D17/1 Class 4-4-0s. The only classes that disappeared during the war and before the end of 1945 were: C2 (GNR); C9 (NER); C11 (NBR); C17 (M&GN); D7 (GCR); D13 (GER); D17/1 (NER); D36 (NBR); M&GN 4-4-0s Classes A, D52, D53 and D54; G9 (NBR); M&GN 0-6-0 Classes J40 and J41; O5 (GCR—rebuilt to O4); and P2 (rebuilt to A2, later A2/2).

The scrapping of the old LNER motive power did not really alter the locomotive scene during the war, except that the demise of the M&GN classes noticeably changed that at Peterborough North. Also, the substantial stock of Sentinel steam railcars, employed on lightly loaded branch services all over the system especially in the NE area, was decimated during the war years, there being only 26 left at the end of the conflict. Their demise was no doubt due to their inflexibility—being able to haul no more than a four-wheel van—and to difficulties in maintenance during wartime.

Only four LNER locomotives were scrapped as a result of damage in enemy air raids. Two—A4 No. 4469 *Sir Ralph Wedgwood* and B16/1 No. 925—succumbed as the result of a direct hit while both were inside York North shed on the night of 28–29 April 1942. Another casualty was M&GN 4-4-0 No. 047, which was hit (and buried) at Norwich on the very next night (29–30 April 1942). The last was J17 No. 8200 after a 'V2' rocket explosion near Stratford on 15 November 1944. A measure of the relative inefficiency of the Luftwaffe—compared with the vast damage the Allied Air Forces inflicted on railways on the continent—is provided by the fact that altogether a mere seven locomotives were damaged beyond repair by the enemy in Britain during the war, although a large number were damaged but repaired to return to service.

Construction of new locomotives by the LNER during the first two years of the war was limited (36 in 1940 and 1941) and confined to established Gresley classes, principally V2s, V3s and J39s. The CME (Gresley) died in office in April 1941, just after the appearance of his latest design, the V4 2-6-2, of which only two were ultimately built. Gresley was succeeded by Edward Thompson, who had major plans to standardise the LNER's fleet.

Thompson was not slow to produce these, although wartime exigencies prevented him from initiating them quickly. His first standard locomotive—B1 No. 8301 *Springbok*—was not completed at Darlington Works until December 1942 and was only followed by the second in June 1943; just another 10 would be erected during the war. After initial running-in from Darlington shed, the first ten B1s were distributed widely over the LNER system, but by December 1944, six were settled in the overstrained GE section. New construction of LNER locomotives in 1942 (53) and 1943 (22) were otherwise of Gresley V2s and O2s, although Thompson did introduce the first of his new designs, several of which were rebuilds of existing locomotives. The very first was the Q1 0-8-0T for heavy shunting work and these were rebuilds of GCR Q4 0-8-0s, 13 being completed between May 1942 and September 1945. Thompson's first experiment in rebuilding Gresley three-cylinder types was his redesign of D49/2 No. 365, which was rebuilt as a two-cylinder locomotive in December 1942. This Class 'D' 4-4-0 was the only D49 to be rebuilt in this way and continued to work with the other D49s in the NE Area until scrapped due to an accident in November 1952.

In January 1943, Thompson turned out the first P2 2-8-2 rebuilds to a Pacific (4-6-2) wheel arrangement, in addition to three separate sets of valve gear to operate the three cylinders, which had previously been operated by Gresley's patent '2 to 1 lever' system. The whole class of six was dealt with by December 1944. In October 1943, Thompson completely rebuilt No. 6166 of the GCR B3 Class 4-6-0s as a two-cylinder locomotive, which except for the larger diameter wheels was very much like his B1.

The LNER Workshops built only 18 new steam locomotives for the company's own stock in 1944, but this number included some of Thompson's new designs. The NER B16s had been involved with a rebuilding programme begun by Gresley, but the new CME amended this to dispense with the Gresley motion and use three independent sets instead. Between 1944 and 1949, 17 B16/1s were altered becoming B16/3s; the Gresley rebuilds were classified B16/2. Following the B1 Class, in February 1944, the new standard 2-8-0 was introduced, being a GCR O4 rebuilt to use a standard boiler and cylinders and a total of 58 would be completed up to 1949. Later in April 1944, the first of four V2s on order that had been converted to Pacifics emerged from Darlington to offer a comparison between the A2 and V2 boilers on a similar chassis.

In 1944, the LNER also began to experiment with a shunter possessing a diesel engine. The company acquired four 350-hp 0-6-0s from English Electric, and these were later supplemented by one from Brush Electrical Engineering Co. (later Brush Traction) in 1949. These were similar to the examples already working for the other railway companies and were the forerunners to the innumerable locomotives later built by BR.

During February 1945, K3 No. 206 was rebuilt as a two-cylinder locomotive and reclassified K5. This remained the sole example and Gresley K4 No. 3445 proved to be the prototype for the Peppercorn K1s when rebuilt at the end of the year. Both rebuilds spent long periods allocated to New England, Peterborough, and were often seen on ECML freight workings.

A total of seventeen B16s were rebuilt between 1944 and 1949 to plans produced by Thompson. No. 922 (built at Darlington in November 1920, later BR No. 61418) was the first in mid-1944 and poses here for the official photograph.

Thompson's most controversial rebuild was that of Gresley A1 No. 4470 *Great Northern,* which was to serve as a basis for the LNER's new express locomotive, but in the event, the engine remained the only example of its kind. Before the war was over, Thompson presented his standard 2-6-4T, the L1. No. 9000 was completed in May 1945, preceding the remainder of the large class by two years; the L1s later played a prominent role at King's Cross. Finally, in August 1945, the first Class B2 Thompson rebuild with two cylinders of a B17 pattern appeared and a further nine would be so treated up to 1949. One, No. 2871 *Royal Sovereign,* became the 'Royal Engine' and could be seen at King's Cross and the southern part of the ECML working the Royal Train.

In the middle of the war, priority for new construction was given to heavy freight locomotives and between 1943 and 1945 both Doncaster and Darlington Works built the standard Stanier 8F 2-8-0s of the LMSR. The first 60 8Fs built by the LNER were numbered in the LMSR range 8500-8559 and were treated as being on loan to the LNER. A further 25 8Fs were built by the SR at Brighton Works and taken into LNER stock as Class O6 Nos 7651–7675. These latter were renumbered by the LNER in 1946 to Nos 3100–24 and further additions were made to the stock in 1945–46 with Nos 3125–67. These O6 Class engines were handed over to the LMSR in 1947 along with those on loan, all being renumbered in the 87XX series. On the LNER, the 8Fs operated from many of the principal depots concerned with the heavy loose-coupled freight and mineral traffic on the main lines. The notable exception to this was Peterborough New England, which took a number of USA and Austerity 2-8-0s, before and after they served on the Continent.

Locomotives Lent to and from the LNER During the War

In spite of the increase in freight traffic from the beginning of the war, the LNER was initially able to spare the aforementioned 40 J25s. However, subsequently, the company suffered a dire shortage of freight locomotives, especially after 30 O4 2-8-0s were loaned to the similarly pressed GWR, and also when the Government (War Department) requisitioned 92 of the same class. Those on the GWR were soon returned (August 1942–February 1943), but the others were sent to the Middle East and did not return, many working for a number of years after the war for the Egyptian and Iraqi Railways, an outcome similar to that of the many Stanier 8F 2-8-0s sent overseas by the WD. The LNER received £5,700 for each O4 after overhaul, having acquired many from the Government dumps after the First World War, making a profit in the transaction.

Along with the other railway companies, the LNER lent several engines (0-6-0Ts and short-wheelbase 0-4-0Ts) to the Ministry of Supply for shunting in military depots and at ROFs. As well, the LNER continued to lend shunting engines to collieries and other industrial concerns, in addition to providing small tank engines to the hard-pressed Easingwold and North Sunderland Railways. The LNER handed over at least one locomotive—a life-expired D21—for the RAF and USAAF to use as target practice.

At the beginning of the war, 26 2-4-2Ts of Classes F4 and F5 were set aside to haul trains on the LPTB's Metropolitan and District lines in case of interruption to the electricity supply by air raids. Fortunately, these locomotives remained unemployed, as did the

15 F4s and F5s that were fitted with armour-plating and employed in 12 self-sufficient armoured trains, which were hastily established after the fall of France in 1940. These trains comprised a truck and two armoured wagons equipped with anti-tank guns, with the locomotive sandwiched in the middle.

Based at relatively isolated sites, although not too far from locomotive servicing facilities, each train patrolled considerable lengths of railway relatively close to the threatened shores round the south and east coasts of England and the east coast of Scotland. As much as possible, they were kept off the busy lines, but some parts of the ECML did come under their jurisdiction: Train 'K' (with engine No. 7573) was based at Longniddry and patrolled the ECML and branches between Edinburgh and Berwick; Train 'B' (No. 7072) was based at Alnmouth or at Morpeth and ran between Newcastle and Berwick also most of the branches off it; Train 'H' (engine No. 7071) patrolled the East Riding from Market Weighton to York, but was removed to Kent in 1940; Train 'M' (No. 7784) visited Peterborough North when based at Spalding; and Train 'F' (No. 7177), while at Hitchin for a short period went down the ECML to Sandy as well as the Branches on the way.

Early in the war, the SR was the only one of the 'Big Four' with locomotives to spare and lent them to the other three Companies. The LNER took two LB&SCR B4 4-4-0s (Nos 2051 and 2068) from November 1941 until December 1944, during which time they were worked hard from Neville Hill and York sheds (also Bridlington for a time), even being called upon as pilots for main line expresses at times. Ten Urie N15 'King Arthurs' (Nos 739/40/2/4/7-51/4) were lent between October 1942 and July 1943. These were all allocated to Heaton and worked the main line freights to Edinburgh—at least once on to Glasgow—and down to York. They were also used on passenger workings, for example No. 751 (piloted by D21 No. 1243) worked the Newcastle–Liverpool express to Leeds and back on 31 January 1943. One was noted on a freight at Retford and even on an empty stock train at Stoke Summit; another was reported to have taken over a 20-coach train from Berwick to Newcastle.

The LNER's need for heavy freight engines was met in the latter part of the war mainly by the loan of a very large number of the new War Department 'Austerity' 2-8-0s, supplemented in the first months of 1944 by the 2-10-0 version of the design. Also, the S160 2-8-0s of the US Army, strange-looking American engines, became a familiar sight in many parts of Britain during 1943 and 1944. Although having great pulling strength, they suffered from a lack of braking power and were prone to breakdown—also, three of them suffered in traffic disastrous collapse of the firebox crown. The class began to work on the LNER from St Margaret's shed and eventually 168 were running on LNER lines. They were common on the ECML, mainly north of York—north of Peterborough at least. Allocations were: Neville Hill (25), Heaton (25), St Margaret's (22), March (50), Stratford (21) and Woodford (25). A substantial number of 0-6-0T shunters were also shipped over by the US Army and put to work in Britain—sometimes with American crews—mainly at military depots, one close to the ECML being at Boughton on the LD&EC line near Tuxford.

Starting in February 1943, the LNER had use of no less than 350 'Austerity' 2-8-0s, becoming a very familiar site along the length of the ECML. The earliest were sent to New England, which acquired 35, and these took over from LNER 2-6-0s and 2-8-0s on many of the mineral workings between Peterborough and Ferme Park Yard. 'Call-up' of these 'Austerities' followed the dispatch of the USA 2-8-0s to Europe in the autumn of 1944,

Above: F4 Class 2-4-2T No. 7071 armour-plated during the war and assigned to train 'H', which was based at Canterbury.

Below: No. 90540 (WD No. 7071) was constructed by Vulcan Foundry in mid-1943 and was taken on loan by the LNER between July and December 1944, when transferred to the SR. The locomotive returned to work for the company in September 1947 at March shed, and from 1951 until withdrawal was based at Frodingham. No. 90540 is seen at Grantham station on 2 May 1955 with a coal train. *Picture: Bill Reed*

others were redistributed in England, mainly to the GWR, but many others still worked on the ECML, including up North from Heaton. Ten 2-10-0s were allocated to New England in the first half of 1944 and Peterborough saw many more working through from the LMSR. As the 'Austerities' were mainly intended for use in Europe, to replace the many destroyed locomotives on the continental railways, after victory in Normandy in 1944, they were all collected and shipped across the channel.

Locomotives Working on the ECML During the War

The motive power of the diminished passenger services remained very largely unchanged from that in peacetime. The one major difference was in the widespread use of V2s on expresses and special passenger trains, rather than on fast freight trains, which were discontinued for the duration. Large numbers of new V2s were turned out from Doncaster and Darlington Works, and they proliferated from 71 at the outbreak of the war to 184 in July 1944.

Under pressure from the Unions, lodging-turns were eliminated, although management pressed for their retention because they represented a saving of scarce manpower. Through locomotive workings to King's Cross from Newcastle and Edinburgh, and eventually from Leeds, became much less common, as did the appearance of Pacifics from London in Edinburgh. The principal changes in distribution of Gresley Pacifics during the war included the return of A1/A3s from the GCR line to King's Cross and Grantham sheds, as well as New England and Copley Hill.

On the numerous wartime specials, the Pacifics played an important part. Equally, the V2s played a significant and unsung role, vying with the Stanier Class Five for the title of 'the Engines that Won the War'. The V2s had the advantage over the Pacifics in being able to work over the whole length of the GN&GE Joint line, although 2-6-0s and 4-6-0s were often preferred on this route. The principal relief route for the ECML was the GCR main line, carrying numerous military specials, including troop trains, primarily from the north to the south and south-west. Locomotives usually worked through from York to Leicester via the Darnall Curve. This route was also followed by the timetabled Ashford–Newcastle through train, which reversed at Sheffield Victoria and was taken on by two NE area 4-4-0s.

By mid-1939, the GNR Atlantics had virtually ceased to work main line expresses, except sometimes those from King's Cross to Cleethorpes. Occasionally, a C1 Class locomotive had to take over a heavy wartime express from a Pacific or V2; in 1942–43, a Doncaster C1 worked the 22.25 Down Leeds express after working up to King's Cross with a stopping train. By this time, the C1s were largely relegated to secondary duties, such as the London Outer Suburban services, those on the Lincolnshire lines and between Doncaster, Leeds and Hull. In the 1930s, there were still a few allocated to York, and early in the war, C1s quite often worked northward as pilots for big engines on very heavy expresses. Occasionally, one even reached Perth by way of Edinburgh and Glasgow. They were frequently used on ECML goods trains, as were some of the NER Atlantics that had survived scrapping before the conflict began.

Motive power on local trains continued as before the war, although owing to heavier demands the steam railcars often had to be replaced by locomotive-hauled trains, also the intense traffic of munitions workers to the ROFs required a number of transfers. A8s and

V1s were drafted to West Auckland and West Hartlepool for the Aycliffe ROF workings and to Neville Hill, Starbeck and Selby for the Thorp Arch trains. For the Ranskill ROF workings from West Yorkshire, A5s were transferred to Ardsley to supplement its C14s, while GCR 4-4-0s transferred to Langwith brought workers from the Mansfield direction.

The changes in motive power on the freight side during the war were altogether more noticeable. The vastly increased traffic, the running of all the coal trains up the ECML from the Northumberland and Durham pits and the iron-ore trains down the ECML from the Midland ironstone fields necessitated the almost indiscriminate use on freight work of all adequately powerful passenger locomotives of all types. While this was also the case on the other railways, it was perhaps only on the LNER that the largest and fastest express locomotives were pressed into service on unbraked coal trains. For the first three months after the outbreak of war, some of the A4s were 'in store', but they soon returned to traffic and some were even recorded passing over the Woodhead route into Manchester.

The ECML suffered particularly in the first three years of the war from lack of sufficient heavy freight locomotives. Conflicting needs for locomotives on different parts of the ECML and its feeder lines caused dissension between the operating superintendents of the three areas regarding the relative distribution of the generally useful engines, such as the K3s, V2s and J39s. A particularly difficult time was in the crisis winter of 1940–41. The NE area had to relinquish a number of its K3s to the southern area and make do more than ever with passenger engines for coal trains. Consequently, as well as employing passenger locomotives for freight work, the LNER had to send its smaller 0-6-0 engines on much longer journeys than they would ever make in peacetime. A common-user policy led to the through working of locomotives away from their normal areas becoming much more commonplace. The working of LMSR locomotives along any reasonable distance of the ECML was extremely rare before Nationalisation, but during the war, some did, especially at times of emergency, such as the evacuation specials of 1940 when Class Fives and 4Fs were noted at Retford station.

That the altered pattern and intensity of freight traffic during the war did not lead to more changes in the allocation of locomotives than it did is surprising. Nevertheless, there were a number of re-allocations of motive power on the LNER. The introduction of Convoy coal trains early in 1940, and of the iron-ore trains to Scotland, was accompanied by the transfer of a number of O4s to Heaton, Tyne Dock and West Hartlepool, along with a few to York; many of these had been on the Hull and Barnsley section for the traffic in export coal to Hull.

With their semi-autonomous organisation, the three LNER areas had in peacetime interchanged a minimum of their locomotives. Such transfers of pre-Grouping locomotive types to other 'foreign' areas as had been made before the war were often reversed during the conflict. For example, at the start, the aforementioned dispatch of 40 J25s to the GWR ultimately led to the recall of a number of J27s that had earlier been on loan to the GE section; they spent periods shedded at Grantham or Retford when returning. Again, some J24s were returned to the Scottish area from the north-east; most of the GNR 4-4-0s that had worked for many years in Scotland moved south, while the GER E4s working over Stainmore from Darlington were returned to East Anglia, but not before a spell in the Borders.

There were examples of the opposite move occurring, including: NBR J36s to Blaydon, Borough Gardens and Malton; J37s to Heaton; GNR J3s to Malton; GNR J6s to York; and GER J15s to Doncaster, Barnsley and Mexborough. In the 1930s, several J21s had wandered away from their native NE area, and throughout the war, the odd class member or two remained south at Doncaster, Retford, Langwith, Boston and New England, in some cases staying until the 1950s. The minimisation of complexities and difficulties in undertaking repair work was the most likely reason for more widespread transfers taking place. Indeed, in the middle of the war, a policy was followed of concentrating certain locomotive classes at specific depots. This also coincided with the influx of 'Austerity' 2-8-0s.

The more obvious manifestations were the accumulation in 1943 of the whole of the NER B16 4-6-0s at York and the J26 0-6-0s at the Teesside sheds; new V2s were concentrated in large numbers at Doncaster, York and Gateshead, K3s at Heaton and J39s at Darlington, Heaton and Blaydon. At the southern end of the line, the 'Austerities' ousted the O2s and older O1s (later O3s) from New England, which went from there mainly to Doncaster with a few going to Grantham. In January 1944, Colwick acquired no less than 44 O2s, mainly from Doncaster in exchange for O4s, to help along the other O4s and numerous 'Austerities' there and at Annesley, to move the immense traffic for *Overlord* up the GCR main line. In 1945, many of these O2s moved back to New England or Grantham where they displaced O1s (O3s).

On the section from Peterborough southwards, wartime freight working brought to London a constant stream of New England's allocation, while there were also visitors from sheds north of Peterborough, especially from Colwick and Doncaster, as well as from Retford, Ardsley, Immingham, Frodingham, Sheffield, Gorton and various NE area depots. Consequently, the normal procession of Gresley 2-6-0s and 2-8-0s and 'Austerity' 2-8-0s was varied by the appearance of such Classes as B7, B16, J6, J11, J39, O4 and even occasionally Q4 and Q6. This occurred particularly in 1945 after the military locomotives were called abroad and before they returned; in the interim the Stanier 8Fs (Class O6) were used. Appearing at Ferme Park Yard were J17s, J19s, J20s, and J39s from March, Cambridge or Stratford; from mid-1944, these classes worked to Temple Mills Yard over the Hertford Loop and the new connection from Bowes Park.

At Doncaster, far more locomotives appeared from the NE area sheds than had in peacetime, including most NER tender classes as well as Gresley types. At York, those from the principal GNR sheds, and far more GCR tender engines of all types, turned up on heavy freight trains. On the other hand, York locomotives—B16s, Pacifics, V2s, K3s, etc.—regularly worked on special troop and freight trains up the GCR main line via Nottingham and Banbury to London, as well as up the ECML through Doncaster to Peterborough. Often, some southern area locomotives went as far north as Tyneside, Teesside and even Scotland.

March shed sent GER 0-6-0s via the GN&GE Joint lines far north as York. Northallerton saw all manner of types, the heavy gradients of the Leeds Northern route often necessitating the use of assisting engines. Combinations of all kinds were used and often unsuitable types were enlisted as bankers. Many mineral and other lateral workings at the busy centres of Darlington, Ferryhill and Newcastle produced countless ex-NER 0-6-0s and 0-8-0s.

There was a remarkably sharp rise in freight traffic on the ECML between Newcastle and Edinburgh. To handle this, Heaton shed was allocated many additional heavy freight locomotives (mainly O4s), but often there were not enough. As a result, Heaton dispatched NER Atlantics and J27 0-6-0s to Scotland, as well as 0-6-0s and 0-8-0s from other depots in the area; later, the SR 'King Arthur' 4-6-0s were employed. From Edinburgh, St

Margaret's shed often rostered Gresley J38s and NBR J37 0-6-0s down to Newcastle and sometimes these found their way to York and Doncaster. To a small extent, the Border Counties line was used as a relief line to the ECML, although it had a decidedly limited capacity and J39s were the heaviest locomotives allowed across the North Tyne Bridge at Humshaugh, until it was strengthened to take K3s in November 1942. In contrast, the Newcastle–Carlisle line could take any locomotive and was very heavily used, the motive power being mainly K3s and J39s from Blaydon.

Stock Changes in the Post-War Years

Due to economic difficulties and the high level of freight traffic, continuing for several years after the war, the scrapping of older LNER classes proceeded relatively slowly at first, yet gathered momentum later. At Nationalisation, the LNER still had 4,085 pre-Grouping locomotives (55 per cent of all the pre-Grouping stock taken over by BR). The total number of LNER locomotives withdrawn from 1946 to 1957 was 2,441 (188 a year on average), but as the Modernisation Plan was enacted, 512 were withdrawn in 1958 and 678 in 1959. At the end of 1959, there were still 3,569 LNER locomotives at work, of which 199 were Pacifics, 184 V2s and 1,275 pre-Grouping types. Probably the most conspicuous classes to disappear first were the passenger tender engines that had been employed on the principal expresses when new and had fallen down the 'pecking order' as they aged. While the Atlantics of GNR and NER varieties lasted until 1950 and 1948 respectively, the GCR, GER, NER and NBR 4-4-0s continued for some time afterwards, along with the principal pre-Grouping freight and shunting classes.

After the war, arrears of maintenance and the fact that many old locomotives that would have otherwise been scrapped were kept at work, resulted in a dramatic rise in the incidence of engine failures to double that of 1938. Construction of new locomotives therefore had to be taken in hand on a large scale; also a large number of WD locomotives surplus from the Armed Forces were also borrowed or purchased outright. At first, Thompson concentrated on ordering more B1s and many were built by outside Contractors, eventually totalling 409. The B1s were spread all over the LNER system from King's Cross to Aberdeen, the initial new arrivals after the war being taken on at King's Cross and Hitchin, hastening the demise of the C1s.

The Ministry of Supply (WD) locomotives began to be shipped back to England from the Continent in November 1945. Usually in batches of four, on their way to LNER sheds, the 'Austerities' took the Dunkirk–Dover train-ferry and the SR, then on to the ECML by the North London line and Canonbury. The company purchased 200 locomotives for £4,500 each. These were classified O7 and numbered 3000–3199, subsequently to be followed by another 278. In addition, the LNER had 20 'Austerity' 2-10-0s on loan between June 1945 and November 1946, and these had never been overseas. By the end of 1948, BR had no less than 733 'Austerity' 2-8-0s, 470 of which worked from ex-LNER sheds. The 'Austerities' were employed, largely on heavy mineral and unbraked freight trains, for the next 20 years. They were based mainly at sheds in areas close to heavy industry or marshalling yards, such as New England, Colwick, Mexborough, March, Neville Hill, Heaton and St Margaret's.

Another transaction between the LNER and the Ministry of Supply concerned 75 'Austerity' 0-6-0 saddle-tank locomotives built between 1944 and 1946. The LNER classified the locomotives J94 and allocated them to a number of sheds, so they became a common sight in the yards along the ECML.

Thompson retired in June 1946, just after the appearance of his first standard 6-foot 2-inch Pacific—No. 500 *Edward Thompson*. A further 14 to this design were completed at Doncaster Works, but his successor A. H. Peppercorn amended the design, mainly the position of the bogie; 15 in total were built between December 1947 and August 1948. Peppercorn also discarded Thompson's A1 design and instead modified the A2 design. This principally entailed increasing the coupled wheel diameter to 6 feet 8 inches and using a Kylchap double blastpipe and chimney. Between August 1948 and December 1949, 49 Peppercorn A1 Pacifics were erected, with Darlington completing 23 and Doncaster 26. While these engines took over many of the principal expresses from the Gresley A3s and V2s, they could not overthrow the A4s on the non-stops due to the lack of a corridor tender.

The orders for 99 L1s remained in place after Thompson stepped down, and these appeared between 1948 and 1950. At first, these were not very numerous on the ECML until later in the 1950s. Seventy Peppercorn K1s were also built just after Nationalisation, their design being based on the Thompson K4 rebuild. The L1s were mainly centred around the north-east, with Darlington initially receiving 30 and Blaydon 10. The K1s worked not just freight, but in the summer months, they were often used to work excursions and specials.

Before the introduction of the BR Standard Classes, the authorities decided to use other modern LMSR designs to replace antiquated pre-Grouping locomotives across the various regions. Between July 1950 and September 1952, 112 of the LMSR Ivatt Class 4MT 2-6-0s were built at Doncaster and Darlington, and 102 of these (Nos 43050-99, 43100-11/22-61) were sent new to the Eastern Region, North-Eastern Region and Scottish Region. New England shed received 24, South Lynn 17, Yarmouth Beach 5 and Melton Constable 11, this influx replacing the majority of the locomotive stock working on the M&GN Section. In the NE region, 11 went to Darlington, 1 to Scarborough, 16 to Dairycoates, 2 to Heaton, 5 to Selby, and 1 to Neville Hill; in the Scottish Region, 6 went to Eastfield, 1 to Carlisle Canal and 2 to Polmont. Subsequently, a number of these 2-6-0s were transferred to Colwick and Boston.

Some of the smaller LMSR Fairburn/Ivatt Class 2MT 2-6-0s were also sent to former LNER depots; in June 1950, three went to St Margaret's and two to Dundee, and between June and October 1951, three were allocated to Cambridge, two to Colchester, four to Darlington, four to West Auckland and five to Kirkby Stephen. Those at St Margaret's were mainly put on local trains to Galashiels via Peebles, while the Cambridge engines appeared at Huntingdon, Peterborough and occasionally at Hitchin; the others were more commonly seen at Darlington. In March 1952, three LMSR Fairburn Class 4MT 2-6-4Ts were drafted from the SR to the NER and worked from Darlington to Saltburn and from Whitby. Later in the 1950s, a modest further number of 2-6-4Ts were transferred to the NE region sheds on the ECML, such as York, Darlington, Gateshead and Heaton.

In the early 1950s, the motive power in use for shunting in yards up and down the ECML was just beginning a transformation. By 1955, 36 of the LMSR-type 250-hp English Electric 0-6-0 shunters (BR Class 11) were in use, along with 49 of the BR Standard design.

Also, 33 200-hp English-Electric diesel mechanical 0-6-0s and 7 204-hp diesel-hydraulic 0-4-0s had been delivered. The old J50s, J52s, J71s, J72s, J77s, J83s and J88s continued to perform the shunting duties and to work short-distance freight.

In the first ten years after Nationalisation, former LNER sheds received only 1,250 new steam locomotives (including the 545 acquired from the Ministry of Supply), which was proportionally less than at depots on other parts of the BR system. Despite the announcement of the Modernisation Plan in 1955, at the end of the decade, there were still 14,452 steam locomotives at work, and several years would elapse before a noticeable decline of steam engine use would occur on the ECML.

Nationalisation and Inter-Regional Redistributions

When BR divided the country up into various regions, only in the LNER's Scottish area, which became part of the Scottish region, was there any significant incorporation of LMSR lines or depots. A minor addition to the eastern region was the former LMSR shed at Peterborough Spital Bridge, and on the ex-M&GN system.

In 1956, there were boundary changes that radically affected the distribution of locomotives, when a number of former LMSR sheds in West Yorkshire were brought into the north-eastern region, together with the Ardsley District from the Eastern Region. Subsequently, in February 1958, the ex-GCR depots on the London Extension and in the Manchester area were transferred to the London Midland Region. At the same time, ex-LMSR depots in the Sheffield District were acquired by the ER, while Kirkby Stephen was transferred to the LMR. These redistributions resulted in a net gain to the NER of approximately 400 ex-LMSR and 120 BR (including WD) locomotives; the ER gained 160 ex-LMSR locomotives but lost 190 ex-LNER and 55 BR steam engines.

After Nationalisation, the appearance of ex-LMSR engines at Edinburgh became much more frequent, as Stanier Class Fives—even occasionally Caledonian Railway 4-4-0s—arrived from Perth and sometimes from Dundee via Leuchars Junction. Perth LNER shed was closed in 1950, and its duties were incorporated into those of the ex-LMSR shed. In Edinburgh, St Margaret's acquired a small number of ex-LMSR engines, as did others including Eastfield, Thornton Junction and Dundee. LMSR Class Fives and 8Fs also worked into Edinburgh freight yards from Carlisle by the Waverley Route.

York and Leeds were very much frontiers between the LMSR and LNER, but after Nationalisation, it became commonplace for former LMSR locomotives from both Midland and Central Division sheds of the LMR to work past Leeds City station to York and on to Scarborough. In the late 1940s, ex-LMSR engines also travelled north from Leeds up the Leeds Northern line to Northallerton and beyond. At first, this happened on freight, Pigeon specials and excursions, yet by the mid-1950s, there were some regular LMR workings to Northallerton, West Hartlepool and Newcastle. Football excursions in particular brought Class Fives and 'Jubilees' very frequently to Sunderland and Newcastle.

Further south, in the 1950s LMSR 2-8-0s came to work on the ECML between Newark and Doncaster on regular iron-ore trains from Welham Sidings on the ex-GN&LNW Joint line. Finally, as time went on ex-LMSR engines were allocated singly or in small batches to various ECML sheds for no obvious reason. For example, 0-6-0Ts to Doncaster and York, Stanier and Fairburn LMSR 2-6-4Ts to York, etc. There were also occasions when following major blockages of the West Coast Main Line—such as the Harrow disaster of 8 October 1952, during repairs to Kilsby Tunnel in September–October 1953, and after the Watford Junction accident of 3 February 1954—numerous WCML trains with their LMSR motive power were diverted onto the ECML, either at Grantham (via Uttoxeter, Egginton Junction and Nottingham Victoria) or at Peterborough (via Northampton).

Instances of LNER locomotives working onto former LMSR lines were most prevalent in the ScR, but also occurred on such routes as Leeds to Manchester, and from Lincoln and Sheffield to Birmingham. Down at Peterborough, the acquisition by the ER of Peterborough Spital Bridge shed was soon followed by the transfer of several J39s and J52s for freight work, and later D16/3s and B12/3s, which worked passenger trains on the former MR line to Leicester.

BR Standard Locomotives on the ECML

At Nationalisation, BR's locomotive department, headed by R. A. Riddles, began work on designs to meet the traffic needs of the time and those expected in the future. An event was made of the 1948 locomotive exchanges, conducted between the principal types produced by the 'Big Four', although in reality the information gathered did not particularly inform the designs for the standard classes. Riddles, along with key members of his team, had a background with the LMSR and so the standardisation employed by Stanier was keenly embraced. Also, labour-saving features were adopted in response to the negative image of locomotive maintenance following the war.

The years 1951–55 saw the introduction of eleven Standard Classes, although these did not make too great an impact on the ECML. The first class to be introduced was the 'Britannia' Pacific, but none appeared often until 1961. That year, there were several working from Immingham shed and were used on the Cleethorpes–King's Cross expresses, joining the ECML at Werrington Junction. Also built in the early 1950s were the 'Clan' Pacifics and Class 5MT 4-6-0s; later in the decade, both classes could be seen in the north-east, as the former were allocated to Haymarket and 10 of the latter were sent new to York.

In December 1952, the first of the Class 4MT 2-6-0s appeared, and between then and September 1956, ten of these were sent new in ones and twos to NE region sheds at York, Darlington, Gateshead, Dairycoates and Sunderland. A number were also based at Neasden shed, but also appeared on suburban and freight trains in the King's Cross area. Nine of the smaller Class 2MT 2-6-0s were sent new in December 1953–March 1954 to West Auckland shed to work the Stainmore line. Therefore, they could be seen at Darlington and later at Northallerton, where a number were stationed to work the Wensleydale line. During 1954, ten of the twenty Class 3 2-6-0s were sent new to Darlington and spent their brief lives in the NE region.

Four Class 3 2-6-2Ts were allocated new to depots in the Darlington District in late 1954 and five Class 4 2-6-4Ts went to York and Whitby in 1955, but these remained the only examples of their classes to work on the ECML.

BR 9F Class 2-10-0 No. 92193 takes a through line on the eastern side of Darlington Bank Top station during April 1961 with a steel-empties train consisting of four trestle wagons and others.
Photograph: B. W. L. Brooksbank

Indeed, the only Standard Class to work on the ECML in any numbers was the 9F 2-10-0. In late 1954–early 1955, 14 were sent to New England shed and later these were supplemented by a further 21 from mid-1957 to early 1958. These went to work on the coal trains to Ferme Park, becoming the mainstay of this important traffic. Doncaster received 10 new 9Fs between December 1955 and March 1956, followed by eight between August 1956 and February 1957, and 21 more were received in the 12 months from December 1957. Twenty from Doncaster were later dispatched to new pastures, while the remainder stayed working heavy coal and unbraked freight trains up, down and off the ECML. Their duties also included the Newcastle-Holloway empty stock train and the new fast fish train, the 'Blue Spot' from Aberdeen to King's Cross.

Diesel Multiple Units

Towards the end of the 1950s, the secondary passenger and branch line services began to be transformed with the introduction of diesel multiple units, which accelerated the scrapping of old pre-Grouping locomotives. For operators and passengers, the DMUs were clean, comfortable and—in general—robust and reliable. The introduction of the DMUs was piecemeal, to allow for the training of crews, the provision of suitable maintenance depots and the solution of technical and operating teething troubles. However, unlike locomotive-hauled trains, the DMUs could not be easily adapted to large variations in demand. For this reason, steam locomotives were used at peak hours on suburban services, also at holiday times on trains to seaside resorts, so the life of many otherwise redundant engines proved to be extended.

Diesel Locomotives

Under the Modernisation Plan, 174 main-line diesel locomotives were bought from several contractors, for evaluation before large orders for a range of standard types were placed. The aforementioned number consisted of Type 1, 2 and 4 power categories, covering both diesel-electric and diesel-hydraulic engines and transmission combinations. The British Transport Commission—under pressure from the government—rushed too quickly into this task, giving insufficient time for evaluation or for the creation of the workforce and facilities to deal with their maintenance. Indeed, the original plan of allowing a three-year period of testing before wholesale substitution of steam locomotives by diesels was abandoned as early as February 1957, and large orders were placed for locomotives with little operational data behind them. The result, which particularly affected the eastern region at the London end of the ECML, was the waste of a great deal of time and money, trying to operate important business services with unreliable locomotives having basic design faults.

In January 1959, the prototype English-Electric 3,300-hp 'Deltic' came to work on the ECML after unsuccessful trials on the LM region. At the time, this locomotive was the most powerful single-unit diesel. However, it was out-of-gauge except on the former GNR lines, therefore considerable alterations had to be made when the order for 22 locomotives was placed later. The prototype did work to Newcastle once or twice under special restrictions and on a test run managed to beat the pre-war 'Silver Jubilee' express time by 15 minutes. From June 1959, 'Deltic' worked a regular King's Cross–Doncaster diagram and was so employed until the production examples began to arrive in 1961.

Until January 1958, when a new agreement was negotiated with the Unions, a saving of labour costs by the switchover from steam to diesel was not very much, except on shunting engines. At the aforementioned date, BR was allowed to benefit a little from single-manning of Diesel or Electric locomotives on passenger trains, also DMUs and EMUs. However, this applied only when a run was for less than two hours, non-stop under 100 miles and not between 1 and 5 a.m. On freight trains, the corresponding limits were 75 miles and two hours non-stop. In consequence, in 1959, whereas footplate wages cost 10 p per total engine-mile for steam, they were only 5.75 p for diesel and 3.6 p for Electric traction.

New depots for DMUs working onto the ECML were completed at Lincoln, Cambridge, Leeds Neville Hill, Darlington and Leith Central. Hull Botanic Gardens and Bradford Hammerton Street depots were turned over entirely to DMU maintenance and the EMU depot at South Gosforth was enlarged and adapted for them. Later in the 1950s, facilities were built for the servicing and maintenance of main line diesel locomotives at many of the existing steam depots. In London, a new depot dedicated to diesel traction was built at Clarence Yard, Finsbury Park. When it opened in March 1960, the diesels from Hornsey and the shunters from King's Cross were moved there.

The acquisition of new diesel locomotives by former steam depots in the ER and NER accelerated in 1956–59. Many of those allocated to the GE section, especially at March shed, came to be seen regularly at ECML centres such as Peterborough and Doncaster. With the Hornsey Type 4s working on their new intensive diagrams in September 1958, the 'Deltic' running down to Doncaster and Type 4s working from York, there were around 20

At Harringay West station while on trial in early April 1959 is the prototype Deltic locomotive. *Photograph: B. W. L. Brooksbank*

diesels working on the ECML. In addition, there were the Type 2s at the London end, off the GE section, in the north-east and at Edinburgh, working secondary passenger services and freight onto the ECML at all the major centres.

Nevertheless, the Pacific locomotives of Gresley, Thompson and Peppercorn design continued to work the principal expresses through to the end of the 1950s. Even with the introduction of diesels, the general consensus at the time was that the steam locomotive was still capable of being worked hard reliably. The Gresley Pacifics in particular were revived by the fitting of Kylchap double blastpipes and chimneys in the late 1950s; this was a modification planned by Gresley before his death but subsequently delayed. Pacifics often substituted for failed Type 4 diesels during this period and were able to do so with distinction, often keeping to—and bettering—the accelerated schedules.

4

ECML Locomotive Depots, their Allocations and Workings

King's Cross District

The most renowned ECML shed was located amid the yards of King's Cross goods and coal depots, on the spur that joined the main line from King's Cross station between Gas Works and Copenhagen Tunnels. It was out of sight of the main line, but the rear of the shed buildings was visible from the main line out of St Pancras, and the yard could be seen from the North London line, which crossed high above it to the north. The depot's location certainly contributed to the general problems of operating trains in the King's Cross area as there was mutual conflict of movements in and out of the locomotive yard and the goods yards because the latter were sited on both sides of the former.

Although there were Down and Up engine lines out of the depot, the movements of locomotives between it and the passenger station entailed double reversals to get off the main lines at Belle Isle on to the Goods lines and into the locomotive yard, involving the co-operation of four signal boxes—King's Cross, Belle Isle Up, Copenhagen Junction and Goods and Mineral Junction. It was no wonder that many engines stayed in the yard at the station for coaling and turning and that at busy times there were queues waiting to go in or out of 'Top' Shed. Not that it was easy to get into the station's locomotive yard from the arrival platforms at King's Cross, for at least a double reversal was necessary. Delays at King's Cross Depot resulted from inadequate entry and exit lines, even after an extra line was laid in 1953. All locomotives necessarily had to leave the depot 30 minutes before required at King's Cross.

The depot was divided into main-line and local sections, both buildings being of the straight dead-end type. The main-line section had eight roads, most of which extended into the crescent-shaped repair shop behind, while the 'Met' (local) section had seven roads. In addition, there was a range of seven other through roads provided with inspection pits in the open air. The Depot was extensively reconstructed in 1931–33 and at this time was equipped with a 70-foot turntable, 500-ton mechanical coaling plant and water-softening tank, along with other ancillary apparatus needed for servicing the 170 or so locomotives based there. The repair shop, with two electrically-operated wheel drops and a 30-ton travelling crane, was capable of undertaking quite heavy repairs, as well as regular thorough examinations. In 1945, a special white-tiled and fluorescence-lit inspection pit was installed in the repair shop. When diesel shunters first came to be used in 1952, two roads in the 'Met' shed were partitioned off for diesel maintenance and repairs.

The King's Cross District motive power superintendent, whose office was at Great Northern House in Euston Road, was in overall charge, and his assistant lived—until driven out by the Blitz—in a house near the depot, quite marooned from any other dwellings. The DMPS was responsible to the district traffic manager (King's Cross), or to the line manager after the reorganisation when the GN Lines Section of the ER was set up. Day-to-day running of King's Cross shed was in the hands of the shedmaster, who had a staff of about 1,200. Operations were controlled by a Running Foreman on each of the three shifts; in addition, a running foreman ran affairs at the locomotive yard at the station.

King's Cross shed provided Pacifics, C1 Atlantics, V2 2-6-2s, K2 and K3 2-6-0s and—after the war—B1 4-6-0s, for main line expresses, fast freight, parcels and newspaper trains. With the Pacifics—to a small extent also the Atlantics and V2s—the depot covered more than half of the expresses from the terminus in the summer of 1939. This proportion remained the norm, with the important difference that during the war and for a period in the 1950s, the express diagrams were arranged for shorter distances and the majority of expresses were re-engined at Peterborough or Grantham. On the other hand, unlike in 1939, with the reintroduction of longer-distance diagrams in the 1950s, Leeds Copley Hill had a number of through workings to King's Cross. Before the war, the V2s and 2-6-0s were employed primarily on parcels and fast freight duties, although the 2-6-0s also did some Outer Suburban passenger work. During the war, the 2-6-0s were soon transferred away, while a steadily growing number of new locomotives were acquired and the V2s were put to work on expresses. By 1939, the Ivatt Atlantics were coming to the end of their careers and they were largely confined to the Outer Suburban services until replaced by B1s after 1945.

Express locomotives were operated on the ECML at high speeds over long distances. Diagrams often entailed running successive trips amounting to 500 to 800 miles in 24 hours or so, without layover other than for coaling and watering. Although before the war locomotives were normally manned by men from the same depot, the crews worked at most about 350 miles in a shift, or 200 miles without a break, working out-and-home or lodging. Consequently, the highest standards of examination, repair and preparation had to be maintained at the principal ECML sheds concerned, most of all with engines working the non-stop between London and Edinburgh. The standard was indeed high before the war and the 'Streamliners' were given special treatment. At King's Cross shed, Top Link drivers were assigned an assistant fitter to help them with their routine preparation of locomotives for high-speed runs. Then on their return, these engines were routinely examined by a senior fitter after every run, whether or not any problems were reported by the driver. Particular care was taken at King's Cross—and Haymarket —that sufficient coal was taken on for the non-stop and at least nine tons was carefully stacked and packed in by hand.

During the war, all this care was not possible and a degree of 'common user' (sharing rosters between depots) arose for the locomotives. After the war, standards of workmanship fell because of the difficulty in recruiting both skilled and unskilled staff, on account of the arduous, dirty work and 'unsocial' hours. Other more congenial and better-paid work

There were many drivers and firemen at King's Cross shed that became famous to enthusiasts throughout the steam era. In the 1950s, driver B. Hoole and fireman A. Leech were noted for the hard running they did with A4 Pacifics, notably No. 60007 *Sir Nigel Gresley*, but in this instance, they are seen with No. 60032 *Gannet*.

was available elsewhere, far more attractive than shovelling out hot ashes or washing out the boiler. Consequently, turn-around times became longer, and fewer locomotives were available for traffic. The problems were particularly acute at King's Cross, where many Polish and Commonwealth immigrants had to be taken on.

Of its quota of about 20 A4s, nine were assigned in May 1956 on a regular basis to two drivers each. To a certain extent, this was a return to the system employed before the war and in the pre-Grouping period. The nine engines and their eighteen drivers worked a well-organised rolling roster, part of which involved overnight lodging at Leeds or Newcastle, although one job entailed a run to Leeds and back the same day. A year or so later, King's Cross acquired a dozen of the extremely reliable and economical A1s for the through runs to Leeds and Newcastle. The A4s achieved average weekly mileages of 4,800, but with the A1s the figure was 6,400; one A1 (of the five with roller-bearings on the axleboxes) covered a record of 197,000 miles between general repairs.

The acquisition of A1s at King's Cross and at other ECML depots freed V2s for their duties on fast fitted freights for which they were really intended. Nevertheless, the A1s, which had a reputation for unsteadiness at speed, were not as popular with the footplate men as the A4s and regular Top Link drivers stuck with their A4s. By the winter of 1957, King's Cross also had A3s again and achieved a maximum allocation of 42 Pacifics with 17 locomotives in the roster with a regular driver. Many more men were now having to lodge overnight at Newcastle, the most difficult duty being the seven-hour stint on the Down 'Scotch Goods', which left at 15.05 from King's Cross Goods for Niddrie Yard. This heavy train was the freight equivalent of the *Flying Scotsman* and its crews used to compete to see who could get the farthest before being overtaken by the Down 'Afternoon Talisman', which left King's Cross at 4 p.m.; the record was Retford, 138 miles away.

The local section at King's Cross shed provided the power for most of the local passenger services in the London area, it comprised around 60 N2s, with occasionally an N1 being used. Hornsey and Hatfield sheds were assigned the remainder of the Inner Suburban duties and normally employed the condensing members of their small N2 allocations, or at times Hatfield would send up one of its N7s. On the GN line locals, the N2s were worked with as much briskness as did the N7s on the trains from Liverpool Street; moreover, they were occupied intensively, achieving up to nine trips in and out of London in 19 hours of continuous duty. The system of sharing one particular engine between two drivers was applied to the N2s on the suburban duties, and some men stayed with the same engine for years.

Locomotives working down the Metropolitan Widened Lines were supposed to condense their smoke in the tunnels. In 1939, most of the members of Classes N1 and N2 and some J52s were fitted with condensing-apparatus. However, often the equipment was not used because the flap-valve in the blastpipe tended to clog up; from 1951, the condensers were removed from the N1s. Many of them were then sent to work in West Yorkshire, as was the case with a few of the N2s. Moreover, the J50s put to work on the freights to the Met lines and over Blackfriars Bridge did so without condensing gear. The N2s working on to the Underground (Metropolitan, or Northern Line beyond Highgate after 1940) also had trip-cock gear fitted, as used on all Underground trains to cause automatic brake application should a driver pass a signal at danger.

The King's Cross empty stock workings were undertaken by King's Cross and Hornsey sheds. Either the older Ivatt N1 or the Gresley N2 0-6-2Ts did the work, until 1950 when the L1s and J50s were employed. The L1s were assigned to take out the very heavy sleeping car sets in the morning, but often shamed themselves on the steep flyover on the Down side at Wood Green and double-heading had to be resorted to.

Hornsey

Built at the turn of the century to deal with burgeoning coal traffic at Ferme Park, Hornsey shed had a straight, dead-end building with eight roads. It was located on the Up side of the main line, facing London and parallel with Hornsey station on the east side of the Up Yard and freight reception lines. A footbridge connected the station with the shed, but this was severed by a bomb in October 1940 and not rebuilt until several years after the war. There were the usual servicing facilities, including a 52-foot turntable and mechanical coaling plant, which dispensed 1,115 tons per day in February 1940.

The allocation of about 70 locomotives at Hornsey comprised almost entirely tank engines, chiefly Classes N1, N2 and J52 in 1939. At this time, a C12 was also on the stock and was engaged on shunting duties in the LNER Carriage Sidings at Highgate. For many years, a C12 was also employed to provide steam for the heating system in sleeping cars at the coronation shed, located south of Bounds Green depot. After initial trials—including on transfer goods to Hither Green and empty stock work, with No. 15004 of the small

Type Twos and J50s outside Hornsey shed in the 1950s.

LNER batch—a few 350-hp diesel shunters of the LMSR/English-Electric variety began working in Ferme Park Yard from July 1952. However, it was not until 1959 that the BR Standard type arrived in any numbers. Meanwhile, 20 to 25 350-hp shunters had gone new to King's Cross shed, taking over its shunting duties and also the Snow Hill banking duty.

A radical change occurred at Hornsey in 1958 when facilities for routine fuelling and servicing of main line diesel locomotives were built, pending the construction of the diesel maintenance depot at Clarence Yard (Finsbury Park), which was opened in early 1960. Hornsey then acquired an allocation of five English-Electric Type 4s from April 1958; these were made fully operational in the autumn of 1958 on intensive and accelerated main line diagrams—notably the 'Master Cutler' to Sheffield. In January 1959, the prototype 'Deltic' came to Hornsey to work prolonged trials on ECML expresses.

A quick transition was made to diesels with the acquisition of Type 2s from several makers for the Outer Suburban services and empty stock workings. Between July 1958 and March 1959, 20 new Birmingham Railway Carriage & Wagon Co. Type 2s arrived at Hornsey, and another six were on loan for a while. Then, between December 1958 and March 1959, 10 new North British Locomotive Co. Type 2s and, in May and June 1959, 10 English-Electric/Napier 'Baby Deltic' Type 2s were allocated to Hornsey shed. Unfortunately, none of these units were reliable and they lasted little more than a year at work in the area. Brush Type 2s, which first appeared in December 1959, fared better and were at work in London long after the demise of steam.

King's Cross and Hornsey sheds were the source of all the motive power for the local freight and shunting duties, which in 1939 were undertaken by J52s, N1s and N2s and in the 1950s by J50s and J94s. In addition, there always had to be a Banking Pilot on duty at Farringdon, to assist southbound trains up the 1:45 through Snow Hill Tunnel on to Blackfriars Bridge. Until about 1950, it was provided by King's Cross and after that by Hornsey; normally, an N1 was employed until superseded by an 0-6-0 diesel.

There was a small batch of tender 0-6-0s at Hornsey of Class J6, supplemented in the war by GER J17s and by J20s in 1951–53. These worked local goods on the main line, but also on the steeply graded loop off the LMSR Tottenham and Hampstead line at Harringay with transfer freights between Ferme Park and the yards belonging to the LMSR, GWR and SR on the west side of London. Although Hornsey men worked to New England, no Hornsey locomotives were involved in long-distance workings, passenger or freight. Nevertheless, the depot played an important part in fuelling, watering and turning many of the heavy freight locomotives that worked from Peterborough.

Pilots in the London Area

Most of the pilot duties were from 6 a.m. Monday to 6 a.m. Sunday continuously. A few did continue through Sunday, especially in the war, but some were day shifts only and others night shifts only. In 1948, King's Cross shed provided on weekdays three shunting and five or six empty stock pilots at King's Cross station. On weekdays, it also catered for ten booked shunting pilots in the goods yard complex and the adjoining Caledonian Yard, plus one for trips on the North London Link, two for East Goods Yard, one each for Clarence, Highbury Vale and Ashburton Grove Yards, and one to shunt at Edgware.

Two passenger shunting pilots were sent to Holloway Carriage Sidings and there were 12 travelling goods pilot duties from King's Cross shed for trip and run-round work. Hornsey shed supplied a passenger pilot each at Hornsey, Waterworks and New Southgate Carriage Sidings and four shunting pilots to work at Ferme Park Yard, one at Hornsey Goods and one (two part-time) at New Southgate. As well, both sheds furnished numerous pilots for the cross-London runs. The types of pilots remained unaltered until July 1952, when a few 350-hp diesel shunters were brought in and the N1s and J52s were substituted by J50s and in the late 1950s by ex-WD J94s, which latter could not work down on to the Widened Lines.

Before the war, the regular goods and coal workings from Ferme Park to the SR via the City Widened Lines went via Loughborough Junction to Battersea Yard or Herne Hill Sorting Sidings, also to Brentford Central or Feltham Yard (via Factory Junction and Clapham Junction), or to Hither Green Sidings. Also via London Bridge, to Bricklayers Arms, New Cross Gate or Hither Green Yards. In East London, trips from Ferme Park or East Goods Yard went via Canonbury Junction, to Kingsland, Poplar, Victoria Dock, Hackney Wick or Royal Mint Street North. All being vacuum-fitted, the N1s were preferred for trips with vans or fish wagons, while the J52s were employed on the mineral trips. N1s were also worked through the tunnels on Sunday excursions. In addition, there were a number of trips between the yards at Ferme Park, Clarence, East Goods and King's Cross Goods, also some to Farringdon Goods; lastly, from King's Cross Goods round the loop to St Pancras Junction on the North London line. Except during the war, none of these trains were scheduled to run during the passenger rush hours, by either of the three main routes; any goods trains that did so ran only by special arrangement. Each route had its own distinguishing lamp code.

The SR did not send any of its standard types to Ferme Park, yet SR engines were commonplace at Temple Mills, Brent, Sudbury and Acton Yards. There were severe restrictions of both train length and engine size over the misleadingly named 'Widened Lines' under St Pancras and King's Cross stations, but this does not explain why SR—or even LMSR—locomotives never went to Ferme Park via the Tottenham and Hampstead connection until 1958. Diesels were not employed on the local freights until the 1960s; even then, on account of weight restrictions, they were banned from the workings 'down the hole' on to the Southern Electric. Thus, steam tank engines continued to be used until the route over Blackfriars Bridge was closed altogether in 1985. The few GWR locomotive types that were not out-of-gauge for one reason or another on the LNER never came anyway, perhaps because they had to disable their Automatic Train Control apparatus.

In the GNR suburban area, there were trips (all from Highbury Vale Yard) to Mill Hill Gas Works, Edgware, High Barnet and Alexandra Palace; N2s were normally employed on these workings. Finally, there were several local main line goods trains down to Hatfield and Hitchin, and around the Hertford Loop.

Hatfield

This small depot was situated next to the station on the Down side. There was a small two-road building (one road being through), a small turntable, coaling hoist and other facilities. Most of Hatfield's small stud of 25 to 30 were tank engines, and the depot was mainly concerned with the workings on the branches, especially the busy one to Luton and Dunstable. It had some N2s, and until early 1941, there were two ex-GCR N5s, but the majority were N7s.

In the 1930s, when they worked to Moorgate, these N7s were fitted with condensers, and in the 1950s, they occasionally worked up to King's Cross. The N2s were banned early in the 1950s from the Dunstable line on account of their instability on sharp curves—a restriction that also kept the N2s off West Riding Branches. Just before the war, Hatfield had J6s, which were employed on the Dunstable–King's Cross through trains. For shunting, Hatfield used ex-GER 0-6-0Ts, although in the early 1950s, it did have J52s. During the war, there were some Y3 Sentinels for the industrial sidings at Luton. Diesel shunters were acquired at the end of 1957. Hatfield's scheduled shunting pilots were: one each in Hatfield Down and Up Yards; at Welwyn City Yard; Hertford North; and Luton (another one part time). Until the branches closed, Hatfield had small sub-sheds at St Albans and Luton, where some of the branch-line engines were serviced.

Hitchin

Hitchin was another small depot devoted to local work, although unlike those at Hatfield, its 25 to 30 locomotives worked up the main line to King's Cross and down the line to Cambridge on the slower trains of the Outer Suburban services. The depot was alongside the station on the Up side and was a dead-end straight shed of two roads, with one or two more in the open and the usual servicing facilities, including a coal-hoist and 60-foot turntable. Cramped between the main line and a prominent chalk cliff, the locomotive yard was unusually stretched out. Moreover, not only did most of Hitchin's allocation stand in the open, but on account of its position between King's Cross and Peterborough and on the junction for the Cambridge and Bedford lines, the yard always contained one or more 'failed' express or freight locomotives.

Hitchin was also a resort for former express locomotives superannuated from their previous main line work. In 1939 and throughout the war, these were chiefly Ivatt C1 Atlantics and Ivatt D2 and D3 4-4-0s. Some of the C1s were already being scrapped from 1943. After the war, their demise was accelerated and their duties taken over by B1s. Later in the 1950s, Hitchin also employed L1 2-6-4Ts, but they were not a success and had to be relegated to lighter duties. Two LMSR Fowler 2-6-4Ts, tested for 18 months from January 1955, were not popular either. The few 0-6-0s (J1, J3 and J6) worked local freights and Engineers' trains. During and after the war, 0-6-0s worked also a regular Services' Leave train from Henlow Camp on the MR Bedford Branch, then in the 1950s by E4 2-4-0s, which Hitchin had for a time or by one of its J15s.

A steam railcar—*Royal Forester*—remained active until August 1943 as a staff train mainly to the new Connington Yard after the suspension of the passenger service on the loop line to Hertford North in September 1939 on which it operated through to Baldock. During the war, locomotives from many places off the ECML appeared at Hitchin. The shed was also the base for an armoured train, hauled by an ex-GER 2-4-2T. There were usually one or two N2s at Hitchin used on local workings, while for shunting ex-GER 0-6-0Ts were employed until 204-hp 0-6-0 diesel shunters came in December 1957.

The scheduled shunting pilot duties were: one each in the Up and Down Yards at Hitchin; two at Letchworth; one at Royston; and one each (part time) at Biggleswade, Sandy and St Neots.

New England, Peterborough

The large and important shed at New England, 1.3 miles north of Peterborough North station, was in the middle of the yard complex. The depot was the base of a district locomotive superintendent until the district was abolished and passed into King's Cross district in February 1958. New England comprised a very large through shed with nine roads and a dead-end shed with five roads, which was rebuilt in the late 1950s to accommodate diesels with a substantial new repair shop. The extensive locomotive yard stretched in both directions and there were two further groups of sidings for coal supplies east of the coal stage. The depot could be entered from either end, with New England south and north boxes in control of them respectively. The expansive site allowed the provision of a triangle on the south side joining up with each end, so a turntable was not needed.

The depot had been extensively modernised in the 1930s, with the construction of a massive mechanical coaler, the existing coaling stage being retained in reserve. There were wet ash pits, a rotary sand drier and an unusual watering gantry across all the through roads. The water, which had passed through a softening plant at the nearby Werrington Troughs, was stored in a large water tower. The circumstances of war led to further improvements being made, notably the provision in March 1944 of a covered inspection-pit, lit by fluorescent lights and quite separate from the main shed. This installation was unique at the time and eased the tasks of fitters; it led to similar provision very soon after the war at Doncaster, March and Darnall depots.

There were nearly 200 rostered duties—apart from shunting pilots—out of New England and the 200 or so locomotives allocated there spanned the whole range of types from no less than 20 different classes. Main line duties on the ECML, the loop and elsewhere took express passenger, mixed traffic and heavy freight locomotives with their crews to a remarkable range and variety of destinations, including along the ECML from London to Newcastle.

Just before the war, there were few main line express diagrams and no Pacifics on allocation, but already a number of V2s were at New England for working fitted freights and there were still more than 20 Ivatt Atlantics there. The latter occasionally deputised for Pacifics from elsewhere, but worked mainly the secondary services, especially those on the Lincolnshire lines to Boston, Grimsby, etc. The Atlantics were assisted to some extent by a number of 4-4-0s, including ex-GCR D9s, which also worked the M&GN line from Peterborough North. In 1940–42, New England briefly had a couple of B17 Class 4-6-0s, and these worked to London as well as on the Grimsby line. After the war, new B1s took over most of the secondary duties and were also employed on fast freights.

The light tunnel installed at Peterborough New England shed to help fitters carry out maintenance work during the wartime blackouts.

With the abolition of lodging turns on the ECML at the outbreak of war, there began a complete change of ECML express locomotive diagrams, with much engine-changing at Peterborough, and therefore New England acquired an allocation of Pacifics—11 A3s in mid-1944 at the height of the *Overlord* traffic, and in 1955, it still had four Class A diagrams. Moreover, the proliferation of V2s during the war resulted in large numbers of these engines being allocated to New England. They were put to work principally on regular and special passenger work on the ECML, but also on every kind of freight train—including heavy loose-coupled coal trains. Thereafter, New England maintained a large collection of these versatile engines, using them after the war on the many fast freight workings that were then reintroduced and multiplied. A main line express standby pilot—normally, a V2, though usually an Atlantic pre-war—was routinely provided by New England. It stood outside the former engine shed that was situated on the Up side at Peterborough North station.

Before and throughout the war, there were also at New England a very large number of the other principal mixed traffic type—the K3 2-6-0s, along with some K2s. These engines were employed on fast freight trains before the war and to some extent later, having the advantage over the V2 of not being too heavy to run on the loop line to Grimsby, Immingham, etc. During the conflict, they worked side-by-side with New England's large stud of 2-8-0s on the innumerable unbraked coal, brick and general merchandise trains running in both directions in and out of the New England yards. The 2-6-0s worked to Colwick, Doncaster and various destinations northwards rather more than to London, in which direction the 2-8-0s tended to predominate on the 20 or so daily trains to Ferme Park.

New England's 2-8-0s were of the Gresley two-cylinder O1 (later O3) and three-cylinder O2 Classes before the war. The O1s were subsequently moved north to Doncaster and replaced by a multitude of O2s and K3s, until early 1943 when 'Austerity' 2-8-0s were acquired in considerable numbers. When these WD engines went to Europe, even more K3s and also a few O4s were drafted to New England, while the 'Austerity' 2-8-0s soon came back there in droves after the war, now permanently. From 1954, the BR 9Fs arrived to take over the coal trains (up to 100-wagon) to Ferme Park and remained on this work until the end of steam.

With the numerous yards and branches in the Peterborough area, not least the brickworks sidings, and the many freight workings on the M&GN Section for which New England was responsible, the depot had a large number of 0-6-0s (about 50 tender and 20 tank engines) on its allocation. The depot was also responsible for the yards at Spalding, so a number of 0-6-0s were out-stationed at the sub-shed there. Former GNR Classes, especially J6s and J52s, predominated, but there were some ex-GER 0-6-0s just before and during the war, these having recently been transferred from the former GER shed at Peterborough East, which closed in April 1939 but was still used for short-term standage. There were also some ex-NER J21s, J11s and Q4s of the GCR, also there was a small squad of ex-GER 0-6-0Ts.

When the LNER took over the operation of the M&GN in 1936, some of the M&GN 4-4-0s and 0-6-0s had been transferred to New England, but these did not last long and the majority had been scrapped by 1945. Ivatt 4-4-0s and 0-6-0s took their place, although modern ex-GCR types were preferred and D9 4-4-0s came to the M&GN sheds and to New England for passenger work and J11 0-6-0s for freight. In the 1950s, no fewer than 24 of the LMSR-type Ivatt 4MT 2-6-0s were allocated to New England, mainly for the

M&GN duties and also on the less arduous freight work on other lines, including the ECML.

In 1939, New England shed provided five travelling-pilot engines, and the following shunting pilots: four (sometimes seven) for Fletton and Yaxley; one each for the New England East and Old Coal Yards and the West and Old Empties Yards; one each for the North Cripple, Westwood, and South Goods Yards; and two for Spital Yard. The pilot jobs were considerably expanded during the war and after, not least with one or two 0-6-0s working at the new Connington Yard.

Until the advent of diesel shunters in July 1954, New England employed almost entirely J52s for shunting, although it did have the last two J55s in 1943–44 and a handful of ex-GER 0-6-0Ts. For the travelling pilots and for local goods work, mainly J6s were employed, but also a remarkable variety of other 0-6-0s—J3, J4, J11, J15, J17, J19 and J21. Additionally, in 1956–58, the depot had two or three LMSR Standard 3F 0-6-0Ts.

New England also had to furnish two passenger pilots for Nene Carriage Sidings, also one extra for north station which was employed as the banker that assisted the restarting of heavy Down expresses. These pilots were the old Ivatt C12 4-4-2Ts, until the late 1950s when N5 and then N2 0-6-2Ts were employed. Before the 1950s, the branches from Essendine to Bourne and to Stamford were worked by New England C12s and J6s, branch engines being out-stationed at Bourne (closed June 1953) and at Stamford (closed June 1959).

Peterborough Spital Bridge

The LMSR locomotive depot at Spital Bridge, although not on the ECML, deserves to be mentioned because its operations interacted with those of New England. With its exit, locomotive yard and coaler situated just across the ECML relief and LMSR lines to the west of the north station at its north end, Spital Bridge comprised a typical MR roundhouse. With an allocation of about 50, it was brought into the Eastern Region in August 1950. Spital Bridge was in the Peterborough District until the latter's abolition in February 1958; the depot then passed into the Cambridge District for the final two years before it was closed in February 1960.

The LMSR engines at Spital Bridge were mainly MR-type 4-4-0s, 0-6-0s and 0-6-0Ts, and its 'youngest' engines were Hughes 2-6-0s. During the war, the depot also had three ex-SE&CR F1 Class 4-4-0s on loan from the SR, substituted in 1944 by ex-L&SWR S11 4-4-0s. Moreover, as Nottingham (LMSR) also had three ex-L&SWR K10 Class 4-4-0s on loan, the Southern Railway was well-represented at Peterborough during the war. In October 1952, Spital Bridge—now in the Eastern Region—acquired a number of D16/3s and J39s, and in December 1955, it also gained some B12/3s. These LNER types ran to Leicester, Rugby and Northampton. Owing to the 'cyclic' diagrams of the LMSR/LMR, visiting locomotives at Spital Bridge came from a wide variety of depots on the Midland and Western Divisions. Finally, early in the 1950s, Spital Bridge had some C12s, then in 1958–59, some ex-LT&SR (Tilbury Line) 4-4-2Ts came to work the Seaton–Uppingham Branch.

Pilots shunted the LMSR Yards (Wisbech Sidings opposite the New England Yards, Crescent Sidings next to north station) as well as working transfer trips between these sidings and Peterborough East Sidings and the ex-GER Bridge and Stanground Sidings. The shunting pilots were normally 3F 0-6-0Ts, but in the 1940s, former MR 1F 0-6-0Ts were also used and in the 1950s J52s; trips were worked by 3F or 4F 0-6-0s.

Grantham

Situated opposite the station on the west side beyond the goods lines, Grantham shed, with an allocation of about 60 locomotives, was of moderate size, in line with its function primarily as a staging point for many ECML expresses. It had two four-road dead-end sheds sited quite separately, known as the old and new sheds, even if 'new' meant 1897. The basic facilities of the depot, which were modernised in the 1930s, included a mechanical coaler and 52-foot and 70-foot turntables. These both had serious problems; in September 1951, a turning triangle had to be resorted to, which was unique in having its apical lines crossing each other in scissors form. The main way out of the depot was onto the Down lines at Grantham North box, but there was also access at the south end by the goods yard.

Grantham had Gresley Pacifics almost from their introduction, which was in keeping with the Depot's important duties on the ECML expresses. When engines were changed at Grantham in the war and in the mid-1950s, the depot had a number of Pacifics on its books, many of them A4s. On the other hand, there were few if any V2s allocated to Grantham. The Pacifics were for the heavy ECML expresses, and it was not normal for them to work on to the Nottingham line, although in the war, A3s did get to Derby. In 1939, Grantham's 12 C1s were responsible for secondary—and occasionally principal—passenger trains; one regularly brought the important nightly Staffordshire Milk train up non-stop from Netherfield and Colwick to Finsbury Park. The C1s worked many of the trains to Lincoln, Boston and Skegness, on which also ran the Grantham's Ivatt 4-4-0s, but after the war, the Atlantic duties were taken over by B12/3s. D3 No. 2000 was also based at Grantham for working officers' specials and was specially turned out for this duty.

Grantham had a stud of eight-coupled engines (O4s and Q4s, later Gresley O1s and O2s, and briefly in the late 1940s, one or two 'Austerities'), for working the Highdyke iron-ore trains, of which there were up to 12 daily, mainly to Frodingham in partnership with the same types shedded at the latter. For local goods and some of the branch passenger trains, there were 15 to 20 0-6-0s (J2, J3, J4, J6 and J39). Grantham had only about five shunting engines (J52 and J69) and a C12. The last mentioned was employed as passenger pilot for the normal duties and for assisting Down expresses on their start from the station. Goods pilots were diagrammed (one each) at South Yard and Ambergate Yard off the Nottingham line beyond Barrowby Road.

Half a dozen locomotives were sub-shedded by Grantham at Newark until Nationalisation, after which these came from Retford. The Newark locomotives were J3 or J6 0-6-0s and N5s at Retford. At Newark, the pilots worked four duties, one each in the Down and Up Yards, one to work trips to Bowbridge Siding and to Muskham and one for various transfer trips, including the LMSR line as well as private sidings. After Southwell, ex-MR shed (sub to Mansfield) was closed in January 1955; a MR 0-6-0T and two MR 0-4-4Ts were also accommodated at Newark shed. The 0-4-4Ts worked the Southwell Branch from

Rolleston Junction on the LMSR Nottingham–Lincoln line, until it closed to passengers in June 1959. Diesel shunters came to Newark in July 1958, but the shed closed in January 1959.

Retford

Retford was unique in that it consisted of two separate depots: ex-GNR and ex-GCR, nearly half a mile apart but under one administration since Grouping. The former GNR Depot was situated to the west of the ECML near the station, largely hidden from it by the intervening sidings, while the GCR depot was on the GCR line a short distance east of the flat crossing and not visible from the ECML. The GNR depot had a dead-end straight shed with four roads. It suffered from the inconvenience of its exit crossing the Sheffield line on the level before joining the Down main line north of Retford North box.

Each Retford depot had about 30 locomotives of similar, predominantly pre-Grouping type; half the combined allocation in the 1940s being J11s and some Q4s, together with a few ex-GNR 0-6-0s and J39s; also two ex-NER J27s until about 1942, followed shortly after by three J21s. The 0-6-0s worked most of the short distance freight duties, including trips on the ECML from Harworth Colliery and Scrooby Sidings, but also several of the pilot duties. There were few tank engines at Retford—usually a small number of N5s, as well as a J52 in the early 1950s. The J39s and Q4s, along with a stud of a dozen or so O4s, later Gresley O1s and O2s, worked various long-distance mineral duties, including down the ECML to Doncaster or up to New England and to Whitemoor, as well as on the GCR Sheffield–Lincoln axis.

The two Retford depots had at least 10 pilot duties, five of which were for Worksop, Gainsborough and Kirton Lindsey, the other five being: one each for shunting at Low Yard and Whisker Hill, two at Babworth, and one for banking eastwards on the GCR line as far as Clarborough Junction. The Sentinel Y3 at Retford was usually engaged at Gainsborough. Retford men had signing-on points at Gainsborough and Kirton Lindsey.

Few passenger trains originated at Retford. The passenger engines allocated to either shed included ex-GCR Atlantics and 4-4-0s; in the war, ex-GNR 4-4-0s and C2 Atlantics were employed on stopping trains. These were mainly on the GCR line, but included also the munitions workers' trains for Ranskill ROF from Mansfield.

Doncaster

Doncaster shed was necessarily large, being in a vital position on the ECML as a staging point and for the GCR (Manchester, Sheffield and Lincolnshire) main lines. The duties worked were therefore very varied. The district motive power superintendent at Doncaster also had to supervise the locomotives for traffic in the great local yards, which alone amounted to 40,000 wagons per week. The area embraced numerous collieries, dispatching between them 2,000 wagons of coal per day. The number of locomotives allocated to Doncaster shed was about 180 and the working timetable (WTT) for winter

1945 shows 118 engines were booked to leave the depot each weekday; to these would be added an unknown number of unscheduled workings. The routing of engines coming off shed was so varied and complex that a describing apparatus was set up near Carr box, with illuminated numbers and plungers. Enginemen had to use this to inform the signalman where they were going.

Doncaster depot comprised a 12-road through shed, modernised before and during the war, with extensive repair shops, massive coaling plant and with other associated facilities. For turning locomotives, there were 45-foot and 65-foot turntables, but early in the 1940s, the larger one became life-expired. Then a turning triangle was provided instead, the land for this on the east side of the site being transferred from the Civil Engineer's department. In the 1960s, a new 70-foot turntable was constructed at the depot. Egress was possible from either end of the locomotive yard, at Carr box into Decoy Up Yard or at Bridge Junction in the direction of the station.

Doncaster was responsible for a great deal of engine-changing on ECML expresses, more particularly because Pacifics and V2s could not go on to Hull. Consequently, its allocation included 10 to 15 Pacifics, also eventually 20 to 25 V2s for main line passenger, special and freight workings. In the war, these 'Big Engines' were employed extensively on loose-coupled freight work. The more senior Doncaster men needed to have an exceptional range of route knowledge.

Doncaster V2s not only ran the length of the ECML—and in Scotland, often beyond Edinburgh—but also on the GCR lines to Banbury and London Marylebone, and to Manchester—even to Liverpool for the numerous troop specials run to and from that port. As well, the large number of K3s at Doncaster were fully engaged in this type of traffic, especially down the GN&GE Joint line. Until after the war, many of the secondary passenger services radiating from Doncaster were dealt with by the numerous Ivatt Atlantics on the allocation. During the first half of the 1940s, eight or so B17s were so employed, together with some ex-GCR B4s and D10s—also on the important Ranskill munitions workers' trains. Post-war, B1s took over many of the secondary duties.

The local tripping of the immense coal traffic at Doncaster was catered for by the 30–40 0-6-0s: J6, J11 and J39 principally. There was at least one J21, used for moving coaching stock because Westinghouse-fitted, also J15s during the war. On longer distances, the coal trains were hauled by Doncaster's 50 or so 2-8-0s, which at first were Gresley O1s and ex-GCR O4s, later 'Austerities' and O2s. Although nearby Mexborough was supplied with countless 8Fs and 'Austerity' 2-8-0s, which worked into and through Doncaster during and after the war, Doncaster itself did not acquire these classes permanently, and it used the seven USA 2-8-0s commissioned at the works for no more than three months in mid-1943. Later, it did acquire a large stud of 9F 2-10-0s. The long-distance duties performed by Doncaster freight engines ranged on the ECML from New England, Whitemoor, Colwick and Banbury southwards, to Hull, Ardsley, York and Heaton northwards and on the GCR lines from New Clee and Frodingham in the east to Wath and Mottram in the west.

Like most major LNER depots, Doncaster acquired various 'oddities' from time to time. These included ex-NER A7s for heavy yard shunting, the last two GNR J55s and one of the last ex-H&BR 0-6-0Ts, some N2s in the war and one or two N5s. Also, the S1 0-8-4Ts spent their last days there in the 1950s, although mainly engaged merely in shunting at the

Doncaster Carr locomotive shed's north side in the early 1950s with a wide variety of types seen from the top of the mechanical coaler.

shed. In December 1955, an ex-MR 1F 0-6-0T was acquired, which stayed for 18 months before it was scrapped.

Doncaster shed, with 30–40 0-6-0Ts on its books, supplied a large number of regular shunting and trip pilots, including: Down Decoy north and south ends; Old Up Decoy; New Up Decoy; Down Empties Yard; Up Mineral Yard; Belmont Yard; South Yard and transfers; Hexthorpe Down and Up Yards; Hexthorpe Junction; Cherry Tree Yard; Marshgate; Stainforth (two); Thorne Junction; and Warmsworth South. The last J55 saddle tank ended its days as Carr Wagon Works pilot, while virtually all other pilots were J50s or J52s and diesels did not begin to be employed even for shunting until early 1958 when 0-6-0 diesel-electrics appeared. Main line standby pilots were supplied for both Down and Up expresses; in the 1940s, these were usually a C1 at the north end and a Pacific at the south. There were three passenger station pilots: one for the Down side, one for the Up and one for the Old Yard and Cattle Dock; the old J52s were on these duties until the mid-1950s.

Besides its normal allocation, Doncaster enjoyed the use—for a few weeks at least—the first of every new class emanating from the plant, also for a few days every locomotive repaired there. Apart from the shunting engines, Doncaster did not acquire diesels until towards the end of the 1950s. However, as the mechanical inspectors at Doncaster Works were responsible for accepting and testing most of the main-line diesels for the ER and NER, these machines would be seen at Doncaster on acceptance trials, up the ECML to New England or up the Joint line to Spalding.

Selby

Selby shed was located a short distance south of the station, on the north side of the main lines from Leeds just before they were joined by the Down Leeds Goods line. Therefore, it only had access onto the Leeds line and had its back to the ECML. It comprised two roundhouses (with 42- and 50-foot turntables) and modern facilities including a mechanical coaling plant. During July 1943, an extra access line was installed, together with a new ash-pit and sidings with improved watering facilities.

Selby's allocation of 50 locomotives was concerned mainly with traffic on the lines from Leeds to Hull and Bridlington, with only a few duties on the ECML itself. It had a number of D20s (D49s in the 1950s) for stopping trains on the lateral lines, and G5s and steam-railcars for the Goole branch. However, most of the engines at Selby were engaged in the working of coal trains from pits served by Gascoigne Wood Yard, also local goods on the Goole and Cawood branches. The freight engines were principally NER 0-6-0s and 0-8-0s, supplanted to some extent in the 1950s by Standard 2-6-0s of LMSR and BR design.

Selby shed had a number of shunting pilots, locally and at the large Yard at Gascoigne Wood; there its heavy T1 4-8-0Ts, or for a while Q1 0-8-Ts, were employed. It had a variety of 0-6-0Ts, including J73s, J77s, J94s after the war and in 1958–59 an LMSR 0-6-0T. There were also three Sentinel 0-4-0Ts, the work of which included shunting the sidings at the large British Oil and Cake Mills. The shed was closed in September 1959 when Gascoigne Wood Yard was closed.

York

Dating from pre-Grouping days when six different companies worked to York, the south shed comprised two separate roundhouses and a three-road straight shed. The roundhouses were used only by shunting pilots or for non-locomotive purposes; the straight shed was for the servicing of LMSR locomotives working from the south and as a signing-on point for footplatemen. Until the war, it was a minor satellite of the Sheffield District of the LMSR Midland Division and coded 19F, but by 1939, it had only one solitary 'Black Five' on its allocation. From the outbreak of war, there was no permanent allocation at all at York South, yet it remained active for stand-over and servicing.

In the 1950s and later, the crumbling sheds were mainly used for storing surplus engines and other equipment. Opposite, on the Up side of the main line, there was another former engine shed, Queen Street, which by 1939 was also used only for turning and watering locomotives. For a time in the 1950s, it housed York's initial allocation of 350-hp 0-6-0 diesel-electric locomotives.

York North shed was on the Down side of the main line on the Clifton Curve and was the main Depot of the York District. Access to it for locomotives was either from the Down and Up main lines at Clifton box, or from the engine line that ran past York station on its western side. The covered accommodation at the depot consisted of four roundhouses, with turntables of 70 feet (from 1942) in No. 4, 60 feet in No. 3, 50 feet in No. 2 and 45 feet in No. 1; at the far end of the yard, there was another 70-foot turntable.

There were extensive repair facilities, including a wheel drop and a very large mechanical coaler. During the war, four extended wet ash pits, served by a steam grab crane, were installed, along with new or extended examination pits, a new standby coaling stage and new water hydrants; also alterations were made to the layout to ease movement of engines. During the same period, a good deal of work had to be carried out to repair the roundhouses which were badly damaged in the air raid of 28–29 April 1942. In 1957–58, No. 4 roundhouse was reconstructed along with No. 3 under one roof, Nos 1 and 2 being demolished and replaced by a straight shed. The extensive locomotive yard was not only right beside the main line, but also a public road passed alongside it, allowing those interested to see what was 'on shed'.

York was one of the major depots on the ECML and had 170 locomotives. All manner of duties were catered for because many of the ECML expresses and most of the freight trains changed engines at York. After the war, there were about 10 regular Pacific diagrams in both directions on the main line—not all 'Top Class', but after York acquired a very large stud of V2s during the war, these were employed on at least five further express diagrams. The majority of expresses were re-manned at York and crews had to both work the incoming locomotives from other ECML depots and to have a very extensive route knowledge. For secondary passenger work, York had a large number of NER Atlantics, a squad of D49/2s and a few other assorted 4-4-0s.

During the war, it retained several Ivatt Atlantics and these worked regularly on secondary services in all directions as well as on freight, to which the Raven three-cylinder C7 Class Atlantics were usually relegated. The Worsdell two-cylinder counterparts (Class C6) were used mainly on the Scarborough and Bridlington services. After the war, all the Atlantics quickly disappeared, and York acquired a number of B1s. The end of the 1950s saw the arrival of a batch of BR Standard Class 5 4-6-0s, in addition to the Type 4 diesels.

York V2s worked special and freight trains during the war, from Aberdeen in the north to King's Cross in the south and up the GCR lines to Marylebone or to Manchester. The K3 and K1 2-6-0s ranged more widely than the V2s, as they were allowed up the GN&GE Joint line to Whitemoor. As well, the very large number of freight duties covered by York engines were filled by the depot's large battalion of B16s—the whole 69 being based there from 1943 until around Nationalisation.

The B16s also worked on the GN&GE Joint and on the GCR lines; they also came up to New England and sometimes London; in summers, they were prominent on excursion, relief and Saturday trains.

York rarely had any eight-coupled locomotives allocated, although many were serviced, until the 'Austerities' arrived on loan in the war. Afterwards, some Stanier 8Fs and the odd 'Austerity' kept the wheel arrangement represented. For short-distance freight workings, York had only 15 to 20 0-6-0s, mainly ex-NER Classes, although early in the 1940s, it had ex-GNR J6s. In the 1950s, the 0-6-0s were substituted by a number of LMSR-type 4MT 2-6-0s. After an interim period when LMSR 2-6-4Ts were used, by late 1959, York engaged LMSR-type 2-6-0s on Scarborough line passenger and freight workings, on which otherwise an assortment of mainly ex-NER engines of all sizes, types and classes were employed.

York shed had to provide passenger pilots at the station and at Clifton Carriage Sidings, the former requiring the constant attention of two shunting pilots. Main line standby pilots—

View east from York North shed's coaler during a strike in 1949; there are over 50 locomotives present.

Thompson O1 Class 2-8-0 rebuild No. 63773 based at Staveley shed is serviced at the west end of York North locomotive yard and seen from Leeman Road on 20 April 1961. *Photograph: B. W. L. Brooksbank*

usually V2s—were provided at each end of the station. For freight work, up to 25 pilots were needed (1952): eight (nine at night) in York yards on shunting and transfer trips; one in Branches Yard; two in Goods Shed Yard; two in Dringhouses Up Yard; one in Dringhouses Down Yard; three on transfers between Dringhouses Yard and York yards; three for relieving engines off inwards traffic; two each at York Wagon and Carriage Works; in the beet season, one at the sugar factory. Although York had several A7 4-6-2Ts for heavy yard work, before and during the war, most of these pilot duties were worked by J71 and J72 0-6-0Ts, but after 1945, ex-WD J94 0-6-0STs were used for many of the transfer jobs, along with J25 0-6-0s. Later in the 1950s, several LMSR 3F 0-6-0Ts were acquired and employed on pilot jobs.

Northallerton

A small depot, Northallerton shed was situated adjacent to the station on the Down side next to the Low Level line. It comprised a two-road straight building with minimal facilities. Its allocation of ten rather elderly ex-NER locomotives was employed on local passenger services, including those on the branch to Hawes. In the 1950s, the more modern J39s and K1s were acquired for the freight work. Northallerton shed provided a pilot for Low Yard and also one for Thirsk Yard and the goods station at Thirsk Town. Its Sentinel was employed at Leyburn, where there was a sub-shed until May 1954.

Darlington

One of the ECML's large depots, Darlington Bank Top shed dealt more with traffic on the former S&DR system than the main line. It also had an important role handling the new and repaired locomotives from Darlington Works. The shed was located on the Up side, half a mile north of Bank Top station and on the east side of Bank Top marshalling yard. It had been extensively rebuilt and modernised in the late 1930s, the work being completed by October 1940.

At the north end were new wet ash pits with a grab crane, also the layout had been altered. The main through shed had been rebuilt and extended, but in such a way as to allow the extension of Haughton Bridge Up Yard. A new vacuum-operated 70-foot turntable had been built at the south end, where the tracks were rearranged to make easier access to Bank Top station. Repair facilities had been extended and new wheel drops provided, while other new buildings included a shed for the breakdown set, mess room, store house and office building. The depot then comprised, in addition to the original roundhouse, a seven-road straight shed of the through type and a three-road repair shop. A large mechanical coaler had been erected in an unusual design, which was suited to the softer coal of the north-east pits and only perpetuated at Thornaby shed in 1958. With engine utilisation above the peacetime level by a third, further improvements were essential by the middle of the war. In October 1942, four extra inspection pits were provided in existing roads at the south end; track rearrangement at the north end was completed in August 1944, and in January 1945, a new water tank and supply system were installed.

View west from Haughton Bridge Sidings to the locomotive shed and Power Station. Several classes are visible on 20 April 1961, including Q6, K1, A3 and B1. *Picture: B. W. L. Brooksbank*

The allocation at Darlington ranged from 100 to 120 engines and always included a large complement of ex-NER classes. Gresley types were in the minority and they were mainly J39s, of which there were 40 in the late 1940s. As Darlington was not a staging point on the ECML, there were few Gresley 'Big Engines' allocated there, only a couple of Pacifics being acquired from 1948 in place of scrapped C7s for the main line standby duties. The main line passenger work passed from the Atlantics to the B1s, but nearly all the depot's passenger services ran on branch lines, notably those to Richmond, Saltburn and Bishop Auckland, etc. in West Durham; a few locomotives were out-shedded at Middleton-in-Teesdale until September 1957.

For these local duties, Darlington employed a fleet of 13 GCR-design A5/2s built in the 1920s, supplanted in the 1950s by L1s and LMSR 2-6-4Ts. Darlington shed was responsible for most of the workings via Barnard Castle and over Stainmore to Kirkby Stephen, Tebay and Penrith. Main line freight duties, mainly from Croft Yard, were entrusted principally to Darlington's B16s, Q6s, J39s and K1s. For the many shorter-distance goods workings, there were a considerable number of 0-8-0s (Q5, Q6 and Q7) and 0-6-0s (J21, J25, J27 and J39), even (in 1956) ex-GCR J10s.

The pilot assignments were undertaken by N9s and 0-6-0Ts of NER Classes J71, J72 and J77, along with J94s after the war. Duties included: two for passenger station; one at each end of Croft Yard; Bank Top Goods; Haughton Bridge Up Sidings; West Yard; Albert Hill; Northgate; and Nestfield Sidings. Four pilots were provided at North Road Works and one pilot each at Shoppers, Faverdale and Stooperdale Sidings and the paint shop.

Gateshead and Heaton

These two main sheds together catered for the traffic through the Newcastle area on the ECML, with Gateshead responsible more for main line passenger work and Heaton for freight.

The locomotives from other Tyneside sheds (Blaydon, Borough Gardens, Tyne Dock and Percy Main) were involved with local and lateral traffic on Tyneside rather with that on the ECML.

Gateshead was the primary depot of the Newcastle District, but was situated on a rather restricted site between the River Tyne and the loop between King Edward Bridge East Junction and Greensfield Junction. The site was also occupied by Gateshead Works, which was reopened for repair work at the beginning of the war and continued to be so engaged until March 1959. The locomotive accommodation at Gateshead comprised four roundhouses: three with 60 feet and one with 48-foot 5-inch turntables.

Pacifics, which were too long to fit in any of the roundhouses, were accommodated in a very cramped two-road straight shed of their own. They could be turned only on one of the triangles of running lines to the east and west, until 1956 when two of the roundhouses were dispensed with and the easternmost one rebuilt with a 70-foot turntable. There was no room for a modern coaling plant and a large stage had to suffice, while some improvement was carried out to the coaling and watering, also repair facilities at the depot in June 1943. Likewise, there was little stabling room for locomotives in the yard and, even after wartime improvements, access from the running lines was not easy, especially from the west. Despite the problems, 100 locomotives were housed on the site.

Gateshead's very extensive main line express duties necessitated the allocation of 25 to 35 Pacifics (eight being A4s) together with a large number of V2s (25 by the end of the war). The diagrams worked by the Gateshead Pacifics in the later 1950s were as arduous as any on the ECML, entailing travelling up to 800 miles in little over 24 hours. The V2s, together with a squad of K3s, were engaged during the war a great deal on special troop trains as well as freight trains of all kinds on the ECML. After the war, along with some 6-foot 2-inch Pacifics and later with a batch of K1 2-6-0s, they worked the abundant fast freight services.

As at York and Darlington, there was a sizeable allocation of ex-NER Atlantics at Gateshead in the early and mid-1940s, and there were also a few at Heaton. They had played a major role on the ECML expresses in the past, including working through to Edinburgh, where some were allocated to Haymarket. However, in the war, they were reduced to working stopping trains and unbraked goods, especially to Edinburgh. Gateshead also had a number of D49s, which were employed in pairs on second-rank but important expresses, such as the Newcastle–Liverpool services, as well as singly on the Carlisle line. After the war, the place of the Atlantics was taken by B1s, of which Gateshead had a fair quota. Its batch of V3 2-6-2Ts was employed largely on the smartly timed passenger services to Middlesbrough via Sunderland and West Hartlepool.

Heaton shed was located in the 'V' between the main line and the Tynemouth line just beyond Heaton South Junction. The depot was larger and more extensive than Gateshead, with one main straight shed of eight roads facing northwards and only one of which went through the end wall. Principal access was from Benton Bank box, nearly a mile to the north and over a line shared with empty stock trains. The congestion this caused during the war necessitated extensive improvements, not completed until August 1943: three more roads were made through to the south end of the shed building, giving easy access to Heaton South Junction. In September 1944, a new Independent engine line was laid from Benton Bank box with connections from Heaton Up Yard reception lines, together with three additional sidings for coal. Before the war, repair facilities were basic, with only sheer-legs for lifting engines off their wheels, so a new machine shop with wheel drop and wheel lathe was built during the wartime alterations. There was a 70-foot turntable, but no mechanical coaling plant, the provision of fuel continuing to be carried out from hand-barrows on a typical NER stage; wet ash-pits were also installed in 1942.

Heaton locomotive yard extended for some way beside the ECML on its east side. The allocation was about 100 locomotives before the war and in the 1950s, but rose to nearly 150 during the war. It was responsible for a number of main line express duties in both directions on the ECML, although not normally south of Peterborough, and in peacetime for many braked freight workings. Heaton had a substantial stud of K3s, some Pacifics and a number of V2s, although during the war, the latter were concentrated for a time at Gateshead.

The normal duties of Heaton's Pacifics and V2s took them to Edinburgh and to York, Leeds and Grantham, with few turns to Peterborough and King's Cross. Heaton men normally went no further than Grantham, whereas Gateshead men regularly worked to London, except in the years when there was no lodging. It was normal practice for Heaton engines working trains south to take their empty stock from the adjoining Carriage Sidings into Newcastle Central station. In the war, Heaton's complement of 35 to 40 2-8-0s were employed on the heavy freight traffic on the ECML. At the beginning, O4s were acquired as these were surplus on the H&BR lines. However, there were not enough 2-8-0s, until the American S160s arrived in 1943, so in the meantime 'King Arthur' Class 4-6-0s were used, on loan from the SR. When the American locomotives went to Europe, their place was taken by WD 'Austerities' for a while, then LNER-built Stanier 8Fs.

Northwards, Heaton locomotives worked to Edinburgh and sometimes beyond, but the men worked only to Marshall Meadows, Tweedmouth or Berwick, where they exchanged with Edinburgh crews. Southwards, Heaton's locomotives and men worked to many destinations, including Tyne Dock, Sunderland, Consett, West Hartlepool, Stockton,

The north end of the straight shed at Heaton.

Newport, Croft, York, Hull, Leeds, Normanton and Doncaster. While Heaton possessed no Q6 0-8-0s, many of these appeared from other NE area sheds on workings from the south.

In the early 1950s, when the number of unbraked freight trains down the ECML fell while braked trains proliferated, Heaton no longer needed eight-coupled engines. Instead, it acquired a large batch of V2s and some B16s, for the fast freight duties. This was part of a general reshuffle, with 2-8-0s leaving the NE Region for the Eastern Region in exchange for 2-6-2s and 2-6-0s. The stud of 0-6-0s at Heaton consisted of J27s and some J39s, along with an assortment of ex-NER and ex-NBR classes, all being used on local coal and freight duties.

The many Gresley 2-6-2Ts on Heaton's allocation were employed principally on empty stock workings to and from Newcastle Central, but also along with G5s on the Blyth and Tyne local trains. The N8s and N10s helped with carriage yard and empty stock working. Heaton's G5s had more rural duties, on the branch trains from Morpeth, working from Reedsmouth and Rothbury sub-sheds. There were six steam railcars at Heaton in 1939, and before they were progressively scrapped during the war, they assisted on many of the local services from Newcastle, albeit few on a regular basis on account of their unreliability.

There were of course numerous shunting and trip pilots at work in the Tyneside area. Shunting was done by J71s and J72s, but Blaydon and Borough Gardens also employed J77s. Heaton had a J73 for New Bridge Street Goods station, and Gateshead had Y3 Sentinels for work at Dunston. Heaton also had its two unique centre-cab Electric locomotives for the Quayside branch. The 350-hp diesels did not begin to take over on Tyneside until 1956, when they were first allocated to and serviced at Percy Main until facilities were provided for them at Heaton, Gateshead and Blaydon.

Gateshead's freight pilots were as follows (1954): one 0-6-0T each for Forth Goods and Infirmary Yard; Dunston Staithes (Old and New sides); Redheugh Bank Foot and Team Valley factories; Greensfield (Chaytors Bank); Gateshead fitters' pilot; two at Gateshead Works; one Sentinel each for Dunston Staithes (Old and New sides); one 0-6-2T each for Redheugh Bank Foot, Lobley Hill Flats and Low Fell Yard; and a J39 was Gateshead shed-pilot. In addition, two of Gateshead's 0-6-2Ts were kept at its sub-shed at Bowes Bridge on the Bowes Railway.

Heaton's freight pilots were: one 0-6-0T each for Heaton Down Yard, Down Yard West Sidings, Up Yard east and west ends and New Yard; Walkergate Wagon Shops; New Bridge Street Goods; Trafalgar South Yard; Newcastle Quay; shed pilot and shed fitters' pilot; one Electric locomotive for Trafalgar South Yard and the Quayside Yard. Two passenger pilots (J71s or J72s) were in attendance continuously at Newcastle Central, one at the west end being provided by Gateshead and at the east end one by Heaton, the latter having at times to give brief rear-end assistance to heavy expresses starting out over King Edward Bridge. Soon after Nationalisation, these pilots, like those at York and Edinburgh Waverley, were painted bright-green and kept well-burnished.

Alnmouth

The two-road shed at Alnmouth was next to the station on the Down side. It had an allocation of 10 engines, many of which in the late 1940s and 1950s were superannuated 4-4-0s employed on stopping services between Alnwick and Newcastle. Its small stud of

0-6-0s worked the mineral lines in the neighbourhood and the goods to Coldstream—to Ilderton after August 1948. A famous member of Alnmouth's stud in the early 1940s was D17/1 No. 1621, which on withdrawal in July 1945 was preserved in the York Railway Museum, on account of its record-breaking exploits in the 'Races to the North' of 1895.

Tweedmouth

The depot at Tweedmouth comprised both a roundhouse with a 45-foot turntable and a four-road dead-end straight shed, some other roads and a 60-foot turntable. In the summer of 1939, the accommodation was much more than required because the nearby Berwick Marshalling Yard had been closed earlier in the year, following the institution of through working of almost all freight trains between Newcastle and Edinburgh. The roundhouse was used during the war, and for some years afterwards, for sheltering preserved locomotives from York Museum. However, this did not prove to be a safe location because it was bombed during the conflict but without any damage to the stock.

Tweedmouth's allocation of 30 to 40 locomotives included a few ex-NER Atlantics, which were mostly engaged as 'standbys' for failed Pacifics before the war, then inevitably relegated to freight and stopping trains. In the 1950s, the changing of engines at Tweedmouth was reintroduced on some ECML freight services and the depot regained importance, acquiring a number of V2s, K3s and J39s. There were several ex-NER 4-4-0s, including elderly D17s, for stopping trains on the main line, most being kept at the sub-shed at Alnmouth; some were employed on the branches to St Boswells, via Kelso or via Reston and Duns. In the war, Tweedmouth also had ex-GER E4 2-4-0s. The mixed collection of 0-6-0s at Tweedmouth were employed on local and branch freight duties, also for working passenger trains on the steeply graded Eyemouth branch. Shunting tanks (former NER 0-6-2Ts and 0-6-0Ts) had pilot duties at Tweedmouth Yard, Tweed Dock, Berwick and Kelso.

St Margaret's

The ECML sheds in Edinburgh complemented each other, as Heaton and Gateshead did on Tyneside. St Margaret's—named after an ancient well underneath the site—was the main freight engine depot, although it also had a substantial number of passenger locomotives on its allocation. For a shed of its importance and with well over 200 locomotives, St Margaret's was cramped and badly sited. There were proposals in the 1940s to replace it entirely, possibly at Millerhill. However, the will to move the project forward was not there, and in the 1950s, neither was the finance.

The depot, located just west of Piershill Junction and adjacent to Piershill station on the loop, was in two halves separated by the main line. Staff had to be constantly crossing the ECML, and with no through tracks, the shunting of engines entailed many awkward movements, often out on to the main line. Moreover, there was no footbridge, so leaving the men exposed—and sometimes succumbing—to the dangers of unseen trains on the main line. On the south side there was a roundhouse and a six-road dead-end shed, several open-air sidings, some of which had inspection pits, and a large but primitive manual coaling stage. On the north side also, there was a roundhouse, but lacking a roof since a fire in the 1930s. This was owned by the NER, with their running powers into Edinburgh.

The preparation, handling and repair of locomotives at St Margaret's was difficult, dirty and dangerous for its 1,500 staff. Some of the allocation was kept at sub-sheds: South Leith, Seafield, Galashiels, North Berwick, Peebles, Dunbar, Longniddry, Penicuik and Polton. Nevertheless, on Sundays, long lines of St Margaret's goods engines had to stand on the Up loop line at Craigentinny. During the first part of the war, congestion—with consequent waste of engine hours—became so bad that some locomotives (including 2-8-0s) were transferred temporarily to Haymarket, where a main line goods link was established.

Meanwhile at St Margaret's, major improvements were hurriedly undertaken, including the demolition of the roundhouse on the south side and its substitution by a further five servicing roads. As an interim measure, the 60-foot turntable was brought over from Seafield sub-shed and extended to 65 feet, being installed before a new 70-foot turntable was constructed. Other improvements included the extension of the coal stage by 50 feet, the building of a new machine-shop with wheel drop, oil store and sand drier and the alteration of the siding layout, along with repositioning of the water column.

The traffic worked by St Margaret's was of all kinds. Just before the war, it had a few Pacifics, the last NBR Atlantic and one or two NER Atlantics. It also had a few V2s and some K2s and K3s. After the war, more V2s and many more K3s were added to the allocation, along with the new B1s.

During the war, St Margaret's shed shared with Heaton the working of the expanded freight traffic on the ECML to and from Newcastle. Like Heaton, from at least 1943 onwards, it took on many 2-8-0s when they became available. Earlier in the war, St Margaret's was forced to use various passenger engines on freight services and the variety of these was perhaps unsurpassed anywhere. For example, as well as the ex-NBR classes and the ex-NER types, the depot had ex-GER B12/1s and ex-GNSR D40s loaned for a while from Aberdeen Kittybrewster.

After Nationalisation, St Margaret's was early in acquiring former LMSR types, ex-Caledonian 4-6-0s, Stanier Class Fives and Hughes 2-6-0s, and later some BR Standard 4-6-0s. In December 1959, four BR Standard 'Clan' Pacifics were acquired from Haymarket. These were put to work mainly on freight duties on the ECML and Waverley Line, as well as the extensive freight duties north of Edinburgh. Other oddities at St Margaret's included some ancient GER Class F7 2-4-2Ts, which were used on the Fountainhall–Lauder branch, and in the 1950s, an LMSR 2F Dock 0-6-0T.

Secondary and local passenger working were a very important part of St Margaret's duties. These were mostly from Waverley's east end and they included the majority of the Edinburgh suburban services, for which V1s were provided in the main, supplemented by some NBR 4-4-2Ts. Before their demise, there were also steam-railcars working from St Margaret's until 1947. A particularly important local service was that to North Berwick, which was an 'upmarket' outer suburb of Edinburgh, rating the newest sets of coaches and the North Berwick V1s dedicated to these workings were kept in immaculate condition.

There were 20 4-4-0s at St Margaret's, including D49s, D11s and NBR classes, as well as ex-NER D17s, GNSR D41s in the war; also, an LMSR 2P was also tested briefly in 1948.

Gresley A1 Pacific No. 2574 *St Frusquin* heads north between the two sides of St Margaret's shed.

Y9 Class 0-4-0T No. 8122 stands with other small tank engines around the exposed roundhouse turntable at St Margaret's shed on 13 August 1948. *Photograph: B. W. L. Brooksbank*

The NBR 4-4-0s were used indiscriminately, not only for secondary passenger work, but also for assisting expresses and on freight and pilot duties; D34s were put on fast braked freight trains also. By the 1950s, St Margaret's employed some of its smaller LMSR-type and BR Standard 2-6-0s on local trains, in addition to the tank engine equivalents.

St Margaret's, together with Seafield, provided the motive power for a very large number of local freight duties, principally the movement of coal from the many pits in the Lothian Coalfield to the docks at Leith and Granton, also to Portobello, Niddrie and Meadows Yards for movement to yards west and north of Edinburgh. For this work, there were no fewer than 60 0-6-0s allocated to St Margaret's. The majority of these were ex-NBR Classes J35, J36 and J37 or Gresley J38s. There were also ex-NER J24s for the Gifford and other 'delicate' branches, substituted in the 1950s by Standard Class 2MT 2-6-0s. There were a few J39s for main line work, which was also undertaken by J37s and J38s at night-time after they had worked much of the day on local trips.

St Margaret's had to provide numerous shunting pilots. Two passenger pilots worked at Waverley (east end) and two at Craigentinny Carriage Sidings; one worked at Dunbar as the Cockburnspath banker. Goods pilots were employed as follows (1947): one each at Waverley Goods, Bonnington, Granton station (and West Beach), Granton Docks, Heriothill, Lochend, North Leith station, Prestonpans (two in the war), Rose Lane, St Leonards, St Margaret's Meadows, and North Leith Docks; at least three at Duddingston; four at Hardengreen and Niddrie West; six at South Leith Docks (three in the Docks); and seven at Portobello.

In addition to the shunting duties, there were no fewer than 24 trip workings from Portobello (by three engines), also three from Niddrie West, five from South Leith, two from Meadows and one from Millerhill; all these were normally provided by St Margaret's or its sub-sheds. For many of these duties, N15s were provided, of which 15 to 20 were on the allocation, and there was a marked tendency for a particular engine to be kept on the same job year after year. There were also a variety of 0-6-0Ts of NBR Classes J83 and J88, also soon after the war a few J50s, and for awkward sidings, GER J67s or NER J72s. Pilots at Heriothill and St Leonards were J88s, as were some on the Docks, along with Y9 'Pugs' which also worked to Bonnington. Signing-on points for St Margaret's men were at: Hardengreen, Portobello, Niddrie, Granton, Waverley East, North Leith, South Leith, Duddingston, Craigentinny, Heriothill and Leith Walk.

Diesel shunters first came to St Margaret's in September 1955, with many more in 1958, while it was mid-1959 before the Waverley pilot duties were taken over by the 350-hp diesel-electrics. Meanwhile, a number of smaller 200-hp locomotives began work in 1955 at Leith and elsewhere.

Haymarket

Although not on the ECML, Haymarket cannot be left out as it supplied much of the motive power for expresses leaving the Scottish capital. The depot was situated on the north side of the main line to Glasgow and the North, opposite Haymarket Central Junction. The accommodation comprised an eight-road through shed, with up-to-date servicing facilities, including a 70-foot turntable and large mechanical coaling plant. In May 1944, approval was given for the extension of the repair facilities, including the installation of a wheel drop taken from Rugby Testing Station (a project halted by the war), also the provision of two 75-foot ash pits at the west end. The work was not completed until November 1945.

In the summer of 1939, Haymarket had 55 locomotives allocated and of these 12 were Pacifics (seven A3s and five A4s) and two Gresley P2 2-8-2s. For the Pacifics, two sets of Top Link crews were allocated to each engine, particularly for the workings on the non-stop *Flying Scotsman* and *Coronation* services. In 1939, the depot had no V2s, but they were soon acquired and put to work on the main line expresses. The allocation during the war markedly increased to 80 because many locomotives were needed for the inflated freight traffic on the ECML.

The Pacific stud swelled to 26, partly by transfers from Aberdeen and Dundee, with the introduction of through working from Edinburgh to Aberdeen, also after the war by the acquisition of Thompson Pacifics. Haymarket's express locomotives had many diagrams up the line to Newcastle, but few went beyond. The 6-foot 2-inch Pacifics were usually put on the No. 1 braked fish and freight trains. Haymarket had five BR 'Clan' Pacifics for a year or two from October 1957: these were mainly used on the Waverley Route, as well as running to Glasgow and Aberdeen or up the ECML to Newcastle and even York.

Much more than those at St Margaret's, Haymarket's allocation of 4-4-0s were engaged on secondary duties, largely west and north of Edinburgh, although they were also employed piloting heavy southbound ECML expresses. No heavy freight locomotives were allocated, except four 'Austerities' in December 1943 for about two months. The small contingent of 0-6-0s and shunting tanks was used on the limited range of local goods and pilot duties. Regular trip and shunting duties provided by Haymarket were: two passenger pilots at Waverley (west end); two or three goods pilots at Gorgie; and one each for Haymarket, Ratho and Broxburn. Lastly, the South Queensferry goods branch was worked by Haymarket's J36 (No. 9673 *Maude*, BR No. 65243). Haymarket men had a signing-on point at Waverley West.

5
Passenger Rolling Stock on the ECML

Coaching Stock

In 1939, apart from the 'Streamline' trains and the Pullman cars on the *Yorkshire Pullman* and *Queen of Scots Pullman*, the most luxurious carriages on the ECML were the sets built just a year earlier for the *Flying Scotsman*. Like the 'Streamliner' sets, these coaches had Stone's pressure ventilation and heating system, operated electrically from dynamos, and double glazing; in first class, there were cushions and foot-rests. Although compartment or semi-compartment coaches, they had picture windows, while the interior coverings were of Rexine and the fittings were of chromium plate. The sets had a triplet articulated unit of first- and third-class restaurant cars, flanking an anthracite/electric kitchen car. Also, there was a separate buffet lounge carriage, fitted with equipment for preparing hot snacks on demand, which comprised a segregated saloon with loose chairs for 20 people and a ladies' retiring room—complete with attendant maid. During and just after the war, these sets were run without the restaurant and buffet cars, but did continue to run as part of the *Flying Scotsman* until late 1948, at which time the set was disbanded.

The coaching stock used for all other expresses was of Gresley's earlier standard designs. These included the special East Coast Joint Stock (ECJS) sets built for the London-Edinburgh traffic. These were owned and operated jointly by the GNR, NER and NBR before Grouping, but continued as a separate pool by the LNER afterwards. There was a similar arrangement for the stock travelling between King's Cross and Newcastle. Each batch of sets tended to be downgraded to slightly less prestigious services and not usually split up, but rather kept intact for particularly important services.

In 1939, there were still a number of Gresley's pre-Grouping corridor coaches in use on ECML express trains, including the ECJS. Coaches not designed by Gresley for the GNR but by the engineers of other constituents of the LNER, were still much in evidence on the less prestigious services. The ex-GNR and the ECJS displayed all the Gresley hallmarks: teak bodies, high-pitched elliptical roofs with rounded ends, double-bolster bogies and buckeye couplers. Windows had square corners, which were predisposed to decay, and the lighting was electrical. Construction had been mainly of side-corridor coaches, with external doors to each compartment, Pullman-type vestibules and picture windows only on the corridor side, while there were also some open saloon coaches. The several different destinations served by many of the ECML expresses from King's Cross made it necessary to have a high proportion of brake-composite and brake-third vehicles, in each of which the guard was provided with a cabin. The first Gresley sets were the 'Sheffield stock' dating from 1906, although very many coaches of similar design were built in the next 30 years or so.

Much of the ECML express stock of the 1930s and 1940s comprised coaches built in the early 1920s, differing little in design from the pre-Grouping stock except for having retractable buffers. However, in the 1930s, there had been considerable new construction of express trains. A shift was made, from the traditional compartment types with individual external doors to the compartments, to compartment coaches with external doors only at the ends and leading into spacious end-vestibules. This change enabled picture windows to be fitted on both sides, greatly improving the view out. In the war, the vestibules, along with the side-corridor, provided room for a large number of standing passengers and the bulky baggage of servicemen. Pre-Grouping stock, as well as LNER stock of this type, ran on ECML expresses well into the 1950s. Unlike the LMSR, and SR in particular, the LNER was slow to build saloon coaches, and in the 1930s and war years, these were relatively rare on the ECML expresses. Gresley main line compartment coaches were by 1939 almost all two-a-side for first class and three-a-side for third class, with retractable arm rests, which when raised allowed one extra seat each side.

The LNER was slow, compared to the other three companies, to change over from coaching stock with wooden panelling to the inherently safer all-steel coach. Reasons for this included the adherence to external compartment doors, the corrosiveness of steel and running noise. Yet, from the late 1920s, Gresley began building a small number of all-steel coaches, albeit still painted to look like teak and with tumblehome sides, while construction of all-steel stock in the 1930s was mainly confined to non- and semi-corridor vehicles for short-distance working, but including the King's Cross–Cleethorpes trains. Additionally, the tourist stock was built in some numbers, with its 'Jazz-style' design and bucket seats, emulating the competing road motor-coaches. With the abolition of excursions during the war, these coaches were run indiscriminately on main ECML services. For short-distance trains, especially in the NE area, semi-corridor vehicles, providing access only to lavatories and with no gangways, were the norm. The NER was a line using Westinghouse brakes, and all coaches built before the late 1920s had to be dual-fitted with both vacuum and air brakes.

Even before the end of the war, prototypes of a new design of standard coaches were exhibited by the LNER and were introduced on the ECML as early as March 1946. They were employed on the principal ECML services, along with the Gresley coaches, although displacing most of the latter by 1948. The *Flying Scotsman* was the first train to be fully modernised in this way and the new kitchen and restaurant cars were included in its sets. On these coaches, steel panelling on teak frames was used, with deeper and wider windows, the painting remaining imitation teak. The view out was much improved by having corridor windows in line with those in the compartments.

There were also two transverse passages with external doors midway on each coach, but perhaps the most characteristic feature of these Thompson carriages was the oval window of the lavatories. The *Flying Scotsman* vehicles had pressure ventilation and double glazing. These sets were transferred in 1952 to the 'Capitals Limited' and then to the 'Elizabethan' briefly, until superseded by standard BR stock. From the beginning of 1949, the stock of the principal expresses was running in the new livery of crimson lake and cream (popularly referred to as 'blood and custard'), the former Streamliner carriages also being painted in this way. This livery was in turn superseded by maroon for locomotive-hauled coaching stock and green for DMUs and EMUs. On the ECML, the first all-maroon train was *The Talisman*, introduced in October 1956 with an articulated first-class saloon twin set.

In the 1930s and 1940s, the expresses off the other railways, most of which came on to the ECML at York, brought stock from the LMSR especially, but also from the GWR and SR, while LNER stock worked balancing services on to those lines; for example, to Liverpool, Bristol, Swansea, Bournemouth and even Penzance. This interchange was managed by the use of gangway adapters, although the Gresley buckeye couplers were on their own superfluous when working with other companies' stock.

Before the war, local services used Gresley standard non-corridor compartment coaches built in the 1920s, or superannuated pre-Grouping non-corridor stock and even some six-wheelers. Many of these trains were used until the introduction of DMUs in the late 1950s. The non-corridor coaches were shorter (51 feet over the headstocks) than the corridor coaches (60 feet), with relatively spacious compartments (6 feet 1 inch for third class).

For intermediate distances, there were comfortable non-gangwayed vehicles with side-corridors giving access to two lavatories in the middle. A number of non-gangwayed vehicles, with and without lavatories, were built in the Thompson era just after the war. The important exception was the London area, where Gresley articulated sets were used. These were mainly quadruplets—also known as 'quadarts', having four bodies articulated on five bogies—while there were also a number of twins, triplets, and quintuplets. Most of these were built in the 1920s and were not popular with passengers; the padding of the upholstery was thin and uncomfortable and the compartments were narrow in order to provide the maximum number of seats in the small space.

The post-war LNER stock ceased to be manufactured by 1950, when it began to be superseded by the new BR standard designs. The BR Mark 1 stock was built for the use all over the system and was based on two underframe lengths: 63 feet 5 inches for gangwayed and 56 feet 11 inches for non-gangwayed coaches. Large numbers of these various types of vehicles were constructed in the following 20 years.

The Mark 1 carriages were of all-steel construction, with buckeye couplers, Pullman-type vestibules and central doors with transverse passageways—all used by LNER stock. The compartment coaches sat three-a-side and had arm rests, with seven compartments per coach for first class and eight in third class (second class from June 1956). The saloons with centre gangways had two seats on one side of the gangway and one on the other in first class, two and two in third, while the restaurant cars had moveable chairs. In 1955, a modified saloon-third was introduced with offset central gangway, giving three seats on one side and two on the other. Kitchen cars were fitted with anthracite stoves and electric grills. The guard's accommodation was also improved.

Prototypes of the first new BR coaches were on show in September 1950 and complete sets of new stock began to run in time for the Festival of Britain in the summer of 1951—those on the ECML running on the *Heart of Midlothian* service. The *Flying Scotsman* was made up of new stock from summer 1952; for much of the early post-war period, it continued to include a buffet lounge with ladies' retiring room, as did the 'Capitals Limited' and then the 'Elizabethan'.

Thereafter, the BR standard coaches were made up into many of the ECML express sets, although until March 1953 certain civil engineering restrictions in the West Riding limited their use there. By June 1955, there were numerous BR standard coaches allocated to depots on the ECML, and in the 1950s, many of these sets were branded with the particular designation of the service on which they normally ran.

Standard BR non-gangwayed stock appeared on the ECML at King's Cross in December 1952, and it was well on the way to ousting LNER stock on local services by January 1955. During the early BR period, replacement by new BR stock on local services proceeded in the Edinburgh area and to some extent in the NE region, sooner than in the London area. In 1955, a large number of semi-corridor, non-gangwayed lavatory coaches were built for London Outer Suburban and Edinburgh District medium-distance services and to a considerable extent replaced non-corridor vehicles.

On the King's Cross Inner Suburban services, the 'quadarts' continued to dominate the scene until the late 1950s. Elsewhere, pre-Grouping coaches gradually disappeared from local trains and were displaced by later standard Gresley and Thompson coaches. Finally, in early 1955, BR standard non-corridor thirds, brake-thirds and composites were used on these services.

Electric Multiple Units

At the end of 1938, the LNER had 109 EMU vehicles. The North Tyneside Electric services were operated with sets that in 1939 looked strikingly modern, having been built in 1937 and resembling the LNER tourist stock. Trains were made up of articulated twin units with integral all-steel bodies and underframes, one unit being either a motor-third or luggage-motor-third and the other either a driving-trailer-first, a third, or trailer third. All coaches were open saloons with 'bucket' seats and the external livery was cream and red, though altered to Quaker grey and Marlborough blue from 1941 and green under BR. There were also trailer cars converted from older stock into Britain's only 'perambulator vans', for accommodating children in prams when their mothers took them to the seaside. The depot for these trains was at South Gosforth, and they lasted until the North Tyneside Electric services were abandoned in 1967, to be superseded by DMUs and eventually in part by the new Tyneside Metro.

The appearance of the North Tyneside trains was in contrast with the other local trains at Newcastle. The South Shields Electric service was operated by the ex-NER stock built for the North Tyneside services originally in Edwardian times, but mainly comprising stock modified in 1920–22 from that damaged in a fire at Heaton Carriage Depot in 1918. These were refurbished and passed to the South Tyneside line when it was electrified in

1938. The original stock was built at York as two-car units (driving-motor and driving-trailer), with several variations. The roofs of the 1920–22 stock being semi-elliptical in contrast to the original clerestory. This stock lasted until early 1955 when displaced by new two-car units of the Southern Electric all-steel 2-EPB design built at Eastleigh, comprising motor-brake-thirds and driving-trailer-composites. To allow coupling to other coaches, drop-head automatic buckeye couplers and retractable buffers were fitted at the outer ends of these vehicles.

Diesel Multiple Units

After first being introduced in 1954 on the Leeds Central–Bradford Exchange services, in the first stage of the Modernisation Plan, it was planned to build in 1955–56 488 motor cars, 143 control-trailers and 213 trailer vehicles, to be made up into two- and four-car DMU sets, each vehicle being 57 feet 6 inches long. The lines associated with the ECML on which these first DMUs were to run were: the Lincolnshire lines, Leeds–Harrogate–York, York–Hull, York–Scarborough, Leeds–Selby–Hull, Newcastle–Carlisle, Newcastle–Sunderland–Middlesbrough and Edinburgh–Glasgow.

BR works at Derby, Swindon and Eastleigh were already busy building DMU sets, and vehicles were also erected by contractors, each of which produced their own distinctive variety. Sets constructed in 1956 at Swindon were employed on an accelerated service between Edinburgh and Glasgow, made up of three cars; a further two sets could be added to this. Therefore, these sets had to be fitted with a gangway and one driving end had to have a half-width driving compartment. There were first-class coaches with compartments and a buffet, and second class was open saloons. Vehicles were based on the BR standard 63-foot 5-inch frame, suitably modified to take the under-floor engines, etc.

These sets were not normally seen on the ECML down to Newcastle, except on excursion workings. In 1957–58, a number of three-car sets were produced by Metro-Cammell and put to work on the NER and ScR. They included ten three-car sets for the NER, with more powerful Rolls-Royce engines and a buffet in the trailer. In addition, Cravens built for the ER and ScR further two-car sets comprising motor-brake open-second and driving-trailer open-composite. Further three-car sets in 1958–59 were built for use in the NER and ScR appeared from the Birmingham Railway Carriage and Wagon Co. and from Metro-Cammell, made up from motor-brake open-second, motor open-composite and trailer open-second.

6
Management and Staff of the ECML

Management of the LNER

In 1939, the ECML was just a part of the operations of the LNER, a statutory company owned by its stockholders and run by a board of directors. Under the chairmanship of Sir Ronald Matthews, who had recently taken over from William Whitelaw following his retirement the previous year after heading the LNER since Grouping, the board made their decisions by consensus. This was done in light of recommendations made by the various directors' committees, including the three area boards, and the advice of the chief officers. Directors brought to the board a wide range of experience in industry, banking, engineering and other spheres of endeavour, although until Sir Charles Newton was appointed in 1947, only Oliver Bury of their number was a professional railwayman.

Under the direction of the board, the top level of management at the company's headquarter offices (divided between King's Cross and Marylebone), comprised a chief general manager (Sir Charles Newton), an assistant general manager (Robert Bell), AGM (Staff), AGM (Parliamentary and Industrial) and the secretary, chief accountant, chief mechanical engineer, chief legal advisor and advertising manager. The continental traffic manager was at Liverpool Street, and at York, the freight rolling stock controller.

Before Bell retired in May 1943, Newton had two specialised AGMs but afterwards he had five, the extra three being AGM (Works and General), AGM (Traffic and Statistics), and AGM (Public Liaison). The upper echelons of management also included the divisional general managers (DGM) in charge of the three areas of the LNER: the DGM southern area had his offices at Liverpool Street, the NE area DGM presided at York and the Scottish area DGM at Edinburgh. However, the management of the LNER was to a great extent decentralised and each DGM had under him in his area: a divisional operating superintendent (DOS), goods manager, passenger manager, locomotive running superintendent (LRS), civil engineer, estates and rating surveyor, chief of police and hotels superintendent; in the southern area, there was also a mineral manager.

Most of the superintendent officers therefore reported to the divisional chief officers and not directly to the men at HQ; for example, the LRSs came under the DGMs and not the CME. Moreover, before the war, the southern area was divided into two separate sections (western and eastern), each with their own OS. Likewise, the Scottish area was divided for certain purposes into southern and northern sections, corresponding to the pre-Grouping NBR and GNSR.

At the outbreak of war, the DGM southern area was H. H. Mauldin, who had succeeded Charles Newton earlier in 1939 and was in turn succeeded in 1941 by G. Mills until 1945, when the post fell to V. M. Barrington-Ward. At the HQ at York, the north-eastern area was managed by C. M. Jenkin Jones and the Scottish area by G. Mills until 1941, then D. J. M. Inglis until 1944 and finally T. F. Cameron. Under Mauldin, the divided southern area was recombined under one OS (V. M. Barrington-Ward at Liverpool Street), who had one assistant OS for the western section (J. Lees, succeeded in 1941 at Gerrards Cross by E. Rostern), another for the eastern section (J. E. Sharpe at Shenfield).

At York, S. T. Burgoyne was the OS until 1940 when he became passenger manager, changing places with E. M. Rutter, and at Edinburgh under Mills was R. Gardiner. During the war, there remained two divisional LRSs in the southern area, G. Musgrave being the western section officer and C. H. M. Elwell (succeeded by L. P. Parker in 1941) in charge of the eastern section, both sections being run from Liverpool Street.

In the NE area, the LRS was C. M. Stedman, and in the Scottish area, E. D. Trask occupied the post, both these men remaining throughout the war and until Nationalisation. Barrington-Ward was appointed chairman of the Operating Committee of the Railway Executive Committee at the outbreak of war, and when in July 1942 an all-line Central Traffic Office for the LNER was established (at Marylebone), he was appointed to run this also, with the title of AGM (Operating). In September 1945, Barrington-Ward became British member of the European Central Inland Transport Organisation, set up to organise the restoration of railways in the liberated countries of Western Europe, while at the same time he carried the burden of DGM southern area.

On the commercial side, in 1939, the goods manager southern area was G. Marshall, in 1945 succeeded by C. K. Bird; his colleague in the NE area was P. Gibb and in the Scottish area (at Glasgow) was A. E. Sewell (succeeded in 1946 by F. W. I. Arkle). The mineral manager at Doncaster was O. C. Gatenby, succeeded by J. E. Kitching in 1941. The passenger manager southern area was C. J. Selway (succeeded by A. L. Gibson in 1941 and by C. G. G. Dandridge in 1944), with E. M. Rutter in the same post at York until 1940 when he was promoted to DOS in place of S. T. Burgoyne; at Edinburgh, the passenger manager southern Scottish area was G. S. Begg, succeeded in 1944 by M. A. Cameron, then by L. E. Marr in 1946.

Notable among the chief officers at headquarters was the chief mechanical engineer. All workshops and depots for locomotives, rolling stock, road motors, dock machinery and other outdoor machinery were the ultimate responsibility of the CME, although LRSs came under the direction of their DGM. Sir Nigel Gresley held the office until he died in April 1941, when Edward Thompson succeeded him, the latter on retirement being followed in June 1946 by A. H. Peppercorn.

In 1939, Gresley had D. R. Edge as his assistant CME, while Thompson was mechanical engineer (ME) at Doncaster, Peppercorn was ME at Darlington, F. W. Carr ME at Stratford and T. E. Heywood ME at Cowlairs. Meanwhile, a post of ME (Outdoor) had been created,

A group of the leading men at the LNER take time to relax at Eden Grove Sports Club, Doncaster, during the 1920s. Back row (left to right): R. A. Thom, A. H. Peppercorn, unidentified, Colonel Firth, and F. H. Eggleshaw. Front row (left to right): H.N. Gresley (later Sir), W. Whitelaw, F. Wintour, and Sir Ralph Wedgwood.

being filled first by C. H. M. Elwell, who was succeeded by J. Blair. An ME was created for Gorton, and this position was held by J. F. Harrison until he went to Cowlairs in 1945 and was succeeded by G. C. Gold; Harrison later became assistant CME under Peppercorn. The latter took Thompson's place at Doncaster in 1941, being succeeded at Darlington by R. A. Smeddle, and in 1942, Heywood was succeeded at Cowlairs by L. Reeves.

When Thompson retired in 1946 and succeeded by Peppercorn, the latter's place at Doncaster was taken by R. S. E. B. Hart-Davies. After Gresley's death, a separate appointment was made of a chief electrical engineer (CEE), with an assistant and three area EEs; H. W. H. Richards occupied the post of CEE until the demise of the LNER.

Until 1942, all civil engineering work was the responsibility of the three divisional engineers (R. J. M. Inglis at King's Cross for the southern area, F. E. Harrison at York for the NE area and J. C. F. Train at Edinburgh for the Scottish area). However, in the middle of the war, the work of the engineers needed to be directed on an all-line basis, in order to meet the pressing needs of wartime and make the best use of limited resources. The chief civil engineer (CCE) appointed was Train, who became accountable for all permanent way and structures on the LNER, with G. B. Barton as his assistant CCE. T.H. Seaton as ACE (Bridges), while A. E. Tattersall was signal and telecommunications engineer.

Subsequent changes during the war included the appointment in 1943 of F. E. Harrison as assistant to the CCE, Barton becoming engineer London; an extra ACE (Development), R. C. Rattray was appointed in 1943, and finally in 1946, an ACE (Architectural) was created, the post being filled by J. M. Harrison. The posts of divisional engineer remained, with changes incumbent when Train and F. E. Harrison were promoted to head office.

The ECML passed through the King's Cross, Doncaster, York, Darlington, Sunderland, Newcastle and Edinburgh Districts. Impinging on it were the Cambridge, Nottingham, Lincoln, Manchester, Leeds, Hull, Glasgow and Burntisland districts; there was also a Peterborough district, but it was not an operating district. The divisional operating superintendents commanded the district operating superintendents (DOS), to whom the stationmasters and yardmasters reported.

For the purposes of traffic operation, each DOS had his control office, which was manned on each turn of duty by a deputy chief controller, a controller for trains, one for traffic and one for trainmen relief, with assistant controllers. The divisional LRSs (later Motive Power) superintendents supervised the district LRS (DLRS, later DMPS) and to them the shedmasters reported. The divisional goods manager (later commercial manager) was responsible for the district goods and docks managers, who in turn had authority over the various goods agents and docks superintendents. These officers ran the main goods stations and docks, and managed all the commercial business with freight customers.

The district passenger managers (DPM) directed the ticket, information and parcels offices and parcels cartage, as well as all commercial contact with travel agents, passengers and parcels customers. This administrative hierarchy was perpetuated after Nationalisation under the regional organisation of BR, although there were some differences.

Wartime

During the war, the board of directors and the management of the LNER continued in harness, but with the government in overall control through the minister of transport, with its railway executive committee. This REC, had as Chairman Sir Ralph Wedgwood, who had recently retired as chief general manager of the LNER.

In view of its vital functions, as soon as the war started, the REC occupied a special suite of bomb-proof offices, which in the preceding months had been built in the Piccadilly Line tunnel on the site of the closed Down Street station, and the Executive worked in this environment for the duration. Before the war, the REC operated from the Railway Companies' Association offices at Fielden House, Great College Street, London SW1, and returned there after the war until it was disbanded in December 1947. At the same time, most railway headquarters and District Control Offices in major cities were moved to 'safer' sites. The headquarters of the LMSR moved to the Grove near Watford, that of the GWR to Beenham Grange near Aldermaston and the SR transferred to the Deepdene Hotel at Dorking.

The LNER departments were more widely dispersed. The CGM and a number of his headquarter departments, along with the King's Cross DOS' office, went from King's Cross station to the Hoo, a mansion of Lord Hampden's at Whitwell near Knebworth, this establishment later being designated 'HQ 1'. There, the central office was manned continuously, with two officers in charge of Intelligence on each shift, one liaising with the REC and one for ARP matters; the departments returned to London (Dorset Square) in November 1945.

Other HQ offices moved to different locations out of London, for example: the CME's Office first moved to Gresley's house at Watton-at-Stone ('HQ 2'), later to Bush Hill Park, with the main department at Doncaster and entirely so when Thompson was CME. Important departments such as the all-line traffic and rolling stock controls moved to York; other departments were housed in minor stations such as Oakleigh Park or Hadley Wood and even in saloon coaches there. The southern area DGM went to Gerrards Cross, where a western section control office was set up, while the eastern section control office was relocated to Shenfield.

King's Cross District Control was located in a reinforced brick and concrete building at Knebworth station; F. W. Warriner was DOS there in 1939 and until 1941, when W. E. Green took over for the rest of the war; the DLRS was J. F. Sparke, succeeded in 1941 by J. A. Frampton; W. Emerson was DLRS Peterborough throughout. Doncaster district superintendent's office and control were moved to new reinforced buildings adjoining Bawtry station; the DOS in 1939 was F. J. Trotter, succeeded in 1943 by E. J. Stephens, and the DLRS was G. Oakes throughout the war.

At York, the NE area headquarters and District Control Offices went to emergency quarters built under the city walls. L. Sproat was DOS throughout the war until the position was taken over by H. F. Pallant in 1944; the DLRS, who also ran the Hull locomotive district until 1945, was J. J. Lovatt. Darlington District was run by T. B. Hare until 1944, then J. E. M. Roberts, with O. P. Hutchinson as DLRS until 1940, followed by R. Thompson until 1943, then I. V. Longley. For the Newcastle District Control, a concrete bunker was built at Stocksfield, but it was perhaps never used. The DOS was W. A. Fiddian until 1942, then A. E. H. Brown for about two years, then L. Sproat and the DLRS was R. G. Kirkup until 1943, then R. Thompson.

The Scottish area headquarters were re-housed in the disused Scotland Street Tunnel in Edinburgh, district control being moved there from Coatbridge in November 1941. The Edinburgh DOS in 1939 was A. Hill, until 1942 when it was G. M. Johnston; the DLRS southern Scottish area (southern district) was E. H. Ker, followed in 1942 by R. P. Critchley and in 1943 by B. P. Blackburn.

To deal with emergencies, as at HQ 1, the central intelligence offices at York and Edinburgh functioned night and day, as did district intelligence committees. Communication between these control offices, indirectly concerned with the ECML, that were relocated to safety were: Nottingham to East Leake; Lincoln to Blankney; Manchester to Godley; and Leeds to Drighlington.

ECML Management After Nationalisation Until 1959

When the regions of BR were established under the control of the Railway Executive (RE) in 1948, chief regional officers (CRO) were appointed to run them. For the ECML: C. K. Bird was CRO for the eastern region (HQ at Liverpool Street) until 1957, then H.C. Johnson; North Eastern Region C. P. Hopkins (HQ at York) until January 1950, then R. A. Short; Scottish region (HQ at Glasgow) T. F. Cameron until 1955, then briefly A. H. Brown, followed by J. Ness.

The CRO (later regional general manager) headed the management structure of his regional organisation, with regional departmental officers for the following functions: accountant, carriage and wagon engineering, civil engineering, commercial, continental, estates and rating, marine, mechanical and electrical engineering, medical, motive power, operating, police, public relations and publicity, signal and telecommunications, staff, stores, and treasurer. Each region was administered for many of these functions by district, much as they had before Nationalisation. Indeed, to a large degree, the same management and staff continued to run the railway, while in due course, there was considerable cross-fertilisation by the pervasion of managers from other companies or regions and some of this was beneficial.

In practice, because the regional structure of BR fragmented the former LNER more than it did the other three groups, several ex-LNER departmental officers acted jointly for the ER and NER. Thus, the regional chief mechanical and electrical engineer for the ER and NER combined was A. H. Peppercorn until 1950, then J. F. Harrison, followed by K. J. Cook in 1952 until 1959, then T. C. B. Miller.

However, in 1959, a separate post was created on the NER and filled by M. C. Burrows. The Scottish region CM&EE was G. S. Bellamy until 1951, then M. S. Hatchell. The chief motive power officer on the ER was L. P. Parker until 1954 then E. D. Trask; on the NER, F. H. Petty held this position throughout the period, and on the ScR R. F. Harvey was in charge until 1950, E. D. Trask until 1954, then C. R. Campbell until 1957. The single chief carriage and wagon engineer for the ER and NER, A. E. Robson, was appointed in 1950; he was in charge until 1953 then the post was held by L. Reeves.

On the ScR, the corresponding appointment was filled by E. A. Milne in 1949, until 1952 when J. Blair took over. The chief civil engineer on the ER was J. I. Campbell until 1955, then A. K. Terris; on the NER, it was J. Taylor Thompson until 1951, then A. Dean. On the ScR, it was W. Y. Sandeman until 1952, I. R. Frazer until 1954, then M. G. Maycock. The chief signal engineers in the regions were: on the ER, A. M. Moss to 1956, then R. A. Green; on the NER, J. H. Fraser until 1952, then A. F. Wigram; and on the ScR, W. Bryson until 1955, then L. J. M. Knotts. The posts of the chief stores superintendent, of chief accountant and chief solicitor also remained combined for the ER and NER.

Although the ER and NER were not merged until 1968, from February 1949, the operating work of both regions was placed under the control of one chief operating superintendent (COS), E. W. Rostern in London, in effect partially restoring the arrangements pursued by the LNER before Nationalisation. Reporting to the COS were three divisional OS, *i.e.* two for the ER (eastern and western sections) at Liverpool Street and for the NER one at York; in addition the divisional OS of the ScR (eastern section) at Edinburgh also reported to Rostern. The ER (western section) officer was H. C. Johnson (who in January 1955 succeeded Rostern as COS), followed by G. M. Booth; A. P. Hunter was divisional OS at York until March 1957, when he was succeeded by L. Sproat; J. McCreadie, and later J. M. Fleming, was the officer at Edinburgh.

Each divisional OS had his own divisional control office and trains office, and under these superintendents came the district operating superintendents (DOS), with their district control organisations primarily concerned with freight and local passenger traffic, as well as their section of the ECML. District motive power superintendents (DMPS), in charge of not only locomotives and other rolling stock, but also the static machinery of various kinds (cranes, lifts, hoists, turntables, etc.), were responsible to the regional MPS. The district engineers, accountable to the regional civil engineer, dealt with matters of infrastructure: formation, permanent way, tunnels, bridges, and all the diverse railway buildings. Finally, under the regional signal engineer, district signal assistants controlled the telephone and signal networks, which from the 1950s included a microwave link between York, Darlington and Newcastle.

Later, a new line traffic organisation was devised for the ER by Sir Reginald Wilson (chairman of the interim eastern regional, later area board) and his assistant general manager (H. Johnson). From November 1957, the region was divided into sections more clearly related to the earlier systems. The new Great Northern Lines, run by G. Fiennes as line manager, to a considerable extent restored the administrative unity of the ECML. He combined on his line the former responsibilities of motive power, commercial and operating officers, in new offices at Great Northern House, Euston Road.

The GN Lines were divided into four traffic managers' areas or districts: King's Cross, with the control office still at Knebworth; Doncaster; Lincoln; and Sheffield. The ECML was covered by the King's Cross and Doncaster districts, the former including the main line as far as Grantham (inclusive) and the latter as far as the boundary with the NER at Shaftholme Junction. At King's Cross, a separate GN Line control office was also established, where a small staff was on duty continuously to regulate and coordinate between the district offices freight and passenger workings within the ER and between the ER and other regions.

The passenger service on the ECML itself was managed by the East Coast Committee, right through from LNER days until the sectorisation of the 1980s. The committee consisted of the chief operating and chief commercial officers of the three areas of the LNER and the regions after Nationalisation, with their train planning assistants and the regional restaurant car managers. At periodic meetings, they reviewed the service as a whole and considered proposed alterations for submission to general management for approval, but in practice, the committee possessed delegated powers to make most of the necessary decisions. The running of the ECML services was closely monitored daily and reviewed periodically. There was also a team of east coast inspectors, who travelled on all the important trains according to a planned schedule, to report on their punctuality, cleanliness, heating, lighting, loading, station working, mishaps, delays, etc., and generally looking after the passengers. While they were particularly valuable when anything went wrong, their daily reports were closely scrutinised even when things were normal.

The North Eastern Railway had been a pioneer in the organisation of train working from District Control Offices. This was perpetuated by the LNER after Grouping, so that by October 1939, all districts in the NE area operated the system. However, from 1922, overall control of the traffic on the ECML between Shaftholme Junction and Newcastle Central was sustained by York Main Line Control, using a novel diagram board on which representations of trains moved along clockwork-driven belts. There were nevertheless complications at York because traffic from the south via Church Fenton was under York district control, while that from Doncaster was under main line control.

Therefore, in late 1940, the day-to-day running of trains on the ECML from Shaftholme Junction to Northallerton was handed over to York district, along with the local controls at York and Gascoigne Wood Yards. This proved successful, and a year later, the stretch from Northallerton to Ferryhill was given to Darlington district and that from Ferryhill to Newcastle to Sunderland district. York Main Line Control thereafter exercised only a supervisory function.

There were detail differences between the three BR regions involved with the ECML, but the management arrangements for the NE region as outlined here were very similar on the two other regions. Managing ECML operations on the NE region in the 1950s, there were originally DOS with District Control Offices at York (Shaftholme Junction to south of Northallerton), Darlington (Northallerton to Bradbury), Sunderland (Ferryhill to Gateshead) and Newcastle (Newcastle to Marshall Meadows).

During the late 1950s, the York district was incorporated into the Leeds district, the Darlington district into the Middlesbrough district, and the Sunderland district into the Newcastle district. However, because of the cost of new telecommunications, the District Control Offices remained in the old locations well into the 1960s. Before these mergers, the two largest districts were Leeds and Newcastle, each having four district officers (i.e. district operating superintendent and district motive power superintendent) and district goods and passenger superintendents.

The two smaller districts (Darlington and Sunderland) had only a DOS and DPS, the commercial functions being undertaken by the district commercial superintendent (DCS) at Middlesbrough and by the DGS and DPS at Newcastle. York district only had a district traffic superintendent, who combined both operating and commercial functions, and a separate DMPS. When some districts were combined in the late 1950s, traffic managers were appointed at Newcastle, Middlesbrough, Leeds and Hull, to coordinate the work of the district officers.

As elsewhere, District Control Offices operated continuously, in three shifts, with a deputy DOS in charge. To maintain continuity and assist smooth operation, towards the end of each shift, the DDOS had a telephone conference with their respective colleagues, then in the morning the district chief controllers had teleconferences with area HQ. The district operating organisation at Newcastle, which controlled the ECML from Newcastle Central to Marshall Meadows in the 1950s, provides a typical example.

In addition to the district control office, there were separate sections for freight trains, passenger trains, accidents and signalling, staff (joint with the DMPS), minerals and wagons. In Newcastle district, the last operated as a separate mineral control for the supply of coal wagons and operation of the heavy coal traffic—most of it starting and terminating within the Newcastle and Sunderland districts, running from the Northumberland and Durham collieries to the ports, power stations and industrial plants.

The work of the control office was divided geographically, with separate desks for the North Main Line, the West Line and the Blyth and Tyne, as well as a motive power controller and a passenger controller for the district as a whole. Each controller was in constant touch with his yards, stations and signal boxes, to monitor, regulate and record the traffic in his section, so that with the current picture in front of him he could intervene immediately if any problems or mishaps arose. Extensive use was made of train graphs—again pioneered by the North Eastern Railway—to chart the progress of trains. Meanwhile, the district inspectors were the 'eyes and ears' of the DOS, investigating and dealing with matters as far as possible on the spot.

All yardmasters and stationmasters reported directly to the DOS, but some of the latter were also shedmasters (as at Durham) and had a dual responsibility to the DOS and DMPS. The stationmaster also answered to the DGS and DPS regarding goods and passenger commercial work as appropriate. Goods agents, who were in charge of the large goods stations, such as Newcastle Forth, Gateshead and Monkwearmouth, were responsible to the DGS for the terminal working, cartage and commercial work of the station, but also to the DOS for the yard working and wagon distribution.

At Newcastle itself, there were separate passenger and parcels agents answerable to the DPS, whereas at Sunderland, the passenger and parcels agent was combined in one post. Commercial contact with actual and potential customers was made directly by the DGS or DPS personally, one of their assistants, goods agents, passenger and parcels agents, stationmasters; a team of railway service representatives covered specific areas of the district or dealt with specific firms and traffics. Yardmasters were responsible to the DOS for the working of their respective traffic yards and coal staithes, as well as for the maintenance, cleaning and marshalling of rolling stock in their respective carriage sidings.

Almost every station had a resident stationmaster, and several of those at smaller stations were also local coal merchants, which was a long-standing practice introduced by the NER and perpetuated by the LNER, also for some time by BR. It often provided them with a better income than their official jobs. Many of them stayed on as coal merchants after their small stations had been closed, until the coal concentration depots eventually killed the already declining local traffic in domestic coal during the 1960s.

Staff, Pay and Disputes

In 1938, the LNER employed 177,200 staff (only 7,950 being women), comprising 6,600 in managerial positions, 21,900 clerical staff, 43,400 in the traffic department (including 21,600 drivers and firemen), 18,700 in the civil engineer's department, 31,700 in mechanical engineering, 37,700 workshop staff and 17,250 in ancillary services (docks, shipping, road motor operations, hotels, etc.). Perhaps a quarter of the total—45,000 were concerned with the ECML and its operations.

In 1947, there was a total of 195,100, with proportionately more in the traffic department. After Nationalisation, the total staff in the ER, NER and ScR was 238,900; in 1959, there were 219,200, and the three regions had respectively 39 per cent, 31 per cent and 30 per cent. By 1959, the proportion of women over BR as a whole was 5.9 per cent, but otherwise, the distribution between categories was little altered from pre-war.

The cost to the LNER of wages and salaries in 1938 was £32.1 million, and in 1947, £65.7 million; this representing as much as 67.5 per cent of the total expenditure in 1938, rising to 72 per cent in 1947. There was a trend in costs of running the railways, which was to continue after Nationalisation. As the cost of living had gone up between 1938 and 1947 by a factor of only 1.73, after the war railwaymen were already better off than before it. So were the colliery workers, as the LNER's coal bill in 1947 was 2.77 times that of 1938.

In the managerial posts, the chief general manager's annual salary was £8,000 (rising to £9,000 in 1940), that of his deputy a mere £4,000; the divisional general managers took home £3,500–£4,500, the company secretary received £3,000, a locomotive running superintendent £1,500–£2,000 and a works manager £900; the chief mechanical engineer received £5,000.

In the 'white collar' categories, annual salaries in 1939 ranged from £650 for a stationmaster or yardmaster at key stations such as King's Cross, or £350 for an ordinary stationmaster or a senior clerk, through £200 for lesser supervisory staff, to £35–55 for a junior clerk: female clerks got £80–180. In the 'conciliation' grades, weekly rates ranged between £3.50 and £3.75 for a yard foreman.[1] Other positions paid £2.40–2.85 for goods shed foremen, £2.50 rising to £3.25 after five years for guards, £3.60 rising after five years to £4.50 for drivers, £2.40–3.75 for signalmen, £2.15–2.25 for porters, £2.35–3.25 for permanent way gangers, £2.25–2.40 for labourers and so on.

These wage rates before the war accorded quite closely with the basic rates paid in industry and agriculture for comparable work, but the railwaymen had certain relative advantages. They benefited from more security in their job compared to many other industries, paid holidays, free or reduced-rate travel according to grade, and the salaried staff were all members of a contributory pensions scheme. The men usually had more opportunity for overtime work, on account of the 24-hour, 7-days-a-week duties, and for many there was a company house at quite a low rent. Rates for overtime (more than eight hours) were time-and-an-eighth in daytime, time-and-a-quarter at night, and time-and-a-third on Sundays. As well, for mobile grades such as footplatemen and guards, there was an alternative system: a trip of 140 miles was considered a basic eight-hour day's work, and every additional 15 miles counted as an extra hour's work.

Railwaymen were represented by the railway unions: National Union of Railwaymen (NUR), Associated Society of Locomotive Engineers and Firemen (ASLEF) and the Railway Clerks' Association (RCA), which became the Transport Salaried Staff Association (TSSA) from 1951. The men employed in the workshops belonged to a craft union.

After negotiations led by ASLEF, going back several years, in August 1939, the unions were about to strike over pay. The LNER was particularly singled out as the company that had not restored the whole of the 5 per cent cut from wages in 1931. The unions called off the threat and the Railway Staff's National Trust (RSNT) awarded in October 1939 an increase in the minimum wage of 5–10 per cent, with another 8 per cent to the drivers.

During the war, the unions pressed at least once a year for increases not only in line with the perceived cost of living, but also with respect to their indispensability and the exceptionally difficult conditions of work. Each claim had to be settled by arbitration with the RSNT and the March 1945 claim was only settled after the intervention of the minster of labour; the shopmen's claims were settled by the Railway Shopmen's National Council. As a result of more or less blanket 'war advances' most salaried staff, the 'conciliation' grades and the shopmen all gained substantial increases, and the minimum weekly rate rose from £2.35 in 1939 to £4.25 in 1947. In the six years of war until October 1945, the rates of pay of the lower-paid increased by up to 100 per cent, whereas the higher grades and more senior workers were getting perhaps only a third more. The cost-of-living index over the period rose by 44 per cent.

In the first half of the war, a large number of railwaymen volunteered for military service and a serious shortage of staff ensued. This made it necessary to employ relatively unskilled men and women in jobs hitherto the preserve of skilled men, with consequent union objections to the dilution. From time to time, considerable numbers of servicemen were drafted in to work on the railways, often on skilled work such as repair and extension of signalling and telecommunications facilities.[2]

However, after the first years of the war, key operating staff and train crews enjoyed the status of reserved occupation—they were spared military call-up, although they had to stick at their job. In spite of these advantages, railwaymen came out on strike 'unofficially' on various occasions at various places during the war. On the ECML, as early as September 1942, there were serious labour troubles at King's Cross goods and the enginemen came out on 24-hour stoppages at King's Cross in September 1943 and at Doncaster on a Sunday in April 1944.

Nevertheless, the management and staff of the railways took the full force of the extra burdens of wartime work and its perils. Staff of the LNER on duty suffered 303 deaths and 1,338 serious casualties due to enemy action. They earned 38 awards for gallantry (two George Crosses, two Members of the Order of the British Empire, nine George Medals and 25 British Empire Medals). Honours conferred on LNER staff for their outstanding railway work included: two Commanders of the Order of the British Empire, ten OBEs, 24 MBEs and 55 BEMs.

After their efforts during the war, a reaction of 'malaise' set in during 1944–45. Local disputes, especially those involving younger railwaymen, were more frequent; there were two separate 24-hour stoppages by enginemen at York in October 1945. Absenteeism became a serious problem, especially over Christmas and New Year; for example, it forced the imposition of extensive freight embargoes and even the cancellation of some passenger trains immediately after Christmas 1946 and over the New Year period.

During the war, there was a radical change in people's expectations. This was associated with the establishment of the 'Welfare State' and an accelerated trend towards the philosophies of egalitarianism and State involvement in a planned economy, as embraced by socialism. In parallel, the trade unions gained in status and confidence. The railway unions expected a lot more from Nationalisation, and demanded a 40-hour week (with extra pay for 'unsocial hours' and for Sundays), 12 days' paid holiday a year, a pension scheme, and the abolition of lodging turns. Moreover, they tended to pursue a policy of resisting technological advances that threatened job security, e.g. the fitting of steam shunting locomotives with mechanical stokers.

After Nationalisation, the railway unions, following the lead of the relatively high wages being paid in the other heavy industries (both public and private), pressed not only for frequent cost-of-living increases, but also for 'comparability'. Together with a 9 per cent increase on top of the cost-of-living increases awarded them during the war, they had achieved in December 1946 time-and-three-quarters for Sunday work and 12 days of paid holiday, and in July 1947, a further 9 per cent increase was awarded together with a reduction of the working week to 44 hours.

As they were with their charges, the railway companies were hamstrung by the insistence of the unions on uniform nationwide pay settlements, although they conceded that staff needed more pay in the London area. In the war, the NE area brought in complex, but successful bonus schemes for men working local mineral traffic quicker than the agreed norm. Moreover, the relaxation of the controls of engagement orders from 1949, by freeing skilled fitters to seek better work in private industry, contributed greatly to the falling off in standards of maintenance on the railways.

The appointment of two leading trade union officials to the British Transport Commission at Nationalisation seemed to make the railwaymen more intransigent. Furthermore, with the election of militant men as general secretaries, the BTC and the RE suffered more continual conflict with the unions than there had been before 1948, and in spite of the TUC usually supporting the management with its policy of wage restraint. The resentment of the men was fuelled by the government continuing with wartime compulsory arbitration until 1951, while at the same time there was a destructive lack of cooperation between the NUR and ASLEF, on account of the drivers' desire to maintain their higher status and differentials. These factors prevented the men from being able to force their demands by effective industrial action: strikes and working-to-rule were ineffective, sporadic and localised.

One set of incidents in particular affected the ECML, when locomotive men at depots in the NER and at Grantham stopped work on several Sundays in the summer of 1950, over a dispute about the reintroduction of the lodging-turns, which were resented by those men who did not qualify. At that time, there were 5,430 footplatemen working from the 12 principal ECML depots, of whom a mere 96 worked lodging-turns at an average of one night per week. For this, they received a lodging allowance of 5p per night plus 5p for each extra meal, on top of their mileage allowance, yet lodging could only be agreed on a purely voluntary basis.

The BTC was forced by the government to concede increases in pay of 7.5 per cent in January 1951; further increases were conceded again in September 1951, then again in November 1952, partly to prevent staff shortages. The raises were extracted through the RSNT from a BTC worried by their effect on BR's accumulating deficit, although aware of the men's desire to maintain their living standards. In 1953, average weekly earnings for 'conciliation' grades were up 28 per cent (£8.61) on 1948. Then railwaymen's earnings ranked tenth among the major industries, compared with sixth in 1948. Coal workers headed the list throughout, their wages being £10.23 (44 per cent above 1948).

With the return of a Conservative government, mounting hostility to the nationalised railways and their falling revenues, it was inevitable that railwaymen's pay would tend to fall behind, while the main concern of the BTC was to cut labour costs by inducing the unions to improve productivity, by cutting out endemic time-wasting and overmanning. Yet, productivity ('output' per head) rose by only 17 per cent between 1948 and 1959, when the number of staff was then still 83 per cent of the 1948 total.

During the 1950s, W. P. Allen (the ex-ASLEF member of the RE) had retained his role as chief negotiator with the unions when he was succeeded by A. R. Dunbar in 1958. On the union side, Figgins had been succeeded as NUR general secretary in March 1953 by J. S. Campbell, and Batty was followed at ASLEF from January 1956 by A. Hallworth. Disillusioned with the failure of public ownership to revolutionise their condition, railwaymen battled constantly with a BTC supported by the government and the nation as a whole.

As soon as they got their increase of 7 per cent in 1952, the unions applied pressure for more, which of course the BTC resisted. By February 1954, the commission had been forced by the cabinet to concede a further 6 per cent, for the government wanted to avoid a strike by the NUR at all costs. There followed a year of 'leap-frog' jockeying and ill-feeling between the NUR and ASLEF, and of political manoeuvring over the way the penniless BTC was to be subsidised by the state to finance the somewhat justified wage increases being demanded by all three railway unions.

This culminated in the Cameron Court of Inquiry judgment in January 1955 that: 'Having willed the end, the Nation must will the means, if fair and adequate wages are to be paid to railwaymen'. Basically, the court was expressing the obvious, that if the public wanted a good railway system, which at the time a substantial portion could not have cared less about, they must be prepared to pay for it out of taxes. Accepting the court's judgement, but only on the basis of the pious hope of better financial results in the future, the Conservative government allowed the BTC more borrowing power in the short term, and ordered the commission to concede almost all the 15 per cent demanded by the NUR, who called off the threatened strike.

The settlement with the NUR immediately provoked ASLEF into a demand for the restoration of their differentials, all efforts at mediation failed, and both Conservative and Labour sides became panicky because they were fighting a general election, which the Conservatives subsequently won. Yet the footplatemen went out on strike on 28 May 1955—the first major action in 29 years. However, the NUR and TSSA did not strike and there was little public sympathy for ASLEF. A service of sorts, amounting to a quarter of passenger and a third of freight trains, was kept running. The ECML was rather less affected than other parts of the country as a large proportion of footplatemen in the north-east belonged to the NUR.

After 17 days, the strike was called off on the suggestion of Sir Brian Robertson of putting the issue before an independent referee. The latter in fact came up with a compromise increase of drivers' pay that by no means restored the differential from guards and porters that footplatemen had enjoyed earlier and gave nothing to the firemen. Little was gained by anyone in this strike, least of all the railway industry itself.

In the second half of the 1950s, successive pay increases were extracted through the RSNT, mainly as cost-of-living increases: 7 per cent in January 1956, 3 per cent in December 1956 (ASLEF) and 5 per cent in March 1957 (NUR). In November 1957, Campbell was killed (by a lorry in Stalingrad), and Sidney Greene took over the position for the next 17 years. Greene achieved a reconciliation with ASLEF and between them a BTC suffering mounting deficits, and a government worried about wage-driven inflation, they succeeded before calling out a strike in getting another 3 per cent in June 1958, together with an undertaking by the government to carry out a 'comparability' study.

In the meantime, during January 1958, some progress was achieved in modernising the working practices of footplatemen to accompany the substitution of steam by diesel and electric traction, in that single-manning of the new non-steam cabs for very limited times and distances in daytime was agreed. The earnings of railwaymen, although keeping well ahead of inflation, had fallen back further compared to that of many other workers and in the end the Conservative government was forced to appoint in 1958 a major commission (headed by Prof. C. W. Guillebaud) to examine the comparability of railwaymen's pay with that in other industries. The commission, which did not report until March 1960, found that conciliation grade earnings had fallen since 1953 only slightly from 90 per cent of the manufacturing average to 88 per cent, while workshop men suffered a greater decline from 99 to 92 per cent, though the disparities were less tolerable than they seem because working conditions for railwaymen were poor compared with those of other industries. The index of retail prices had risen by only 20 per cent during that period.

In the meantime, rank-and-file railwaymen had become restive and, after prolonged unsuccessful negotiations almost leading to another strike, a 5 per cent interim increase was obtained in January 1959. By this time, the average weekly earnings of BR staff had risen to £11.95, 77.6 per cent above the 1948 figure, retail prices having increased by only 51 per cent in the interim, but this had been achieved after a great deal of conflict and one crippling strike.

When the Guillebaud Report came out, it recommended a 10 per cent increase for the more senior and responsible grades and 8 per cent for the rest (i.e. an extra 5 and 3 per cent respectively on top of the interim award), but it also castigated the BTC for the relatively poor working conditions of railwaymen and recommended a great simplification of the pay structure.

The Guillebaud awards brought railway pay close to the average for British industry as a whole and the unions were well pleased, while it cost the BTC £41.5 million and threatened to set a benchmark for future demands by the unions, whereas overmanning and restrictive practices remained rife in the industry. After Guillebaud, the average earnings of railwaymen were £14.25 per week, 105 per cent above 1948, the cost of living having risen 52.5 per cent in that time. Thus, the weekly pay of drivers (at three years) now became £13 per week (or £12.40 for drivers on shunting), firemen £11 (at three years), guards £10.50 (at three years), signalmen (Class 1) £12.15, shunters £9.70, and porters £8.40. The number of grades was much reduced and mileage allowances improved.

7
ECML Stations and Signal Boxes in 1939

Signal boxes under the supervision of the stationmaster or yardmaster at the locations here are shown in bold type. The intervals between successive boxes controlling main line trains are given in miles. Boxes not controlling trains actually on the main line are shown indented. On the other hand, boxes that were only open at certain times are included, therefore some Block sections were often longer than indicated by these distances. Ground frames and crossing boxes are not listed. Principal changes up to 1959 are recorded in the footnotes.

In 1939, there were electrically controlled colour-light signals and points at the turn-outs at Digswell, between Welwyn Garden City station and Welwyn North station boxes (controlled by the latter) and at Leys, between Stukeley and Abbots Ripton boxes (controlled by the former). There were also intermediate automatic or semi-automatic colour-lights in the southern area between the following boxes: Greenwood and Potters Bar station (at two sites: Ganwick, and north of Potters Bar Tunnel), Potters Bar station and Marshmoor (Hawkshead), Stevenage North and Hitchin South (Stilton Fen), Essendine North and Little Bytham station (Monkswood), Little Bytham station and Corby station (Counthorpe), north of—and worked by—Corby station box (Burton, Down only), Great Ponton station and Grantham South (Saltersford), Grantham North and Barkston South Junction (Peascliffe), Crow Park station and Egmanton (Weston Bank), Scrooby and Bawtry station (Down only), Bawtry station and Rossington station (Pipers Wood).

In the NE and Scottish areas, apart from the modernised York–Darlington stretch, there were intermediate colour-light signals between: Barlby North and Riccall South; near Naburn Bridge (Up line); Springfield and Aycliffe station (supplemented by additional ones in 1943); Aycliffe station and Preston-le-Skerne (Down line); near Ferryhill No. 3 (Up line); Low Fell station and King Edward Bridge; Berwick and Marshall Meadows (Down line); Marshall Meadows and Burnmouth station; Reston West and Grantshouse (Down line); Cockburnspath station and Grantshouse station (Up line).

King's Cross
Passenger	0.00
Belle Isle Up	0.51
Copenhagen Junction (Down)	0.09
Goods and Mineral Junction	

Holloway
Holloway South Down	0.60
Holloway South Up	0.01
Holloway Carriage Siding[1]	
Holloway North Up	0.30
Holloway North Down	0.08
East Goods Yard	
Finsbury Park No. 2	

Finsbury Park
Finsbury Park No. 4 (Up)	0.64
Finsbury Park No. 3 (Down)	0.01
Finsbury Park No. 6 (Up)	0.21
Finsbury Park No. 5 (Down)	0.03

Harringay
Station	0.70
Up Goods	
Ferme Park South Down	0.23
Ferme Park South Up	0.04
Ferme Park North Up	0.21
Ferme Park North Down	0.05

Hornsey
No. 1 (Down)	0.14
No. 2 (Up)	0.15
Up Goods	

Wood Green
No. 1 (Down)	0.68
No. 4 (Up)	0.10
No. 3 (Down)	0.09
No. 2 (Up)	0.09
Tunnel	0.31

New Southgate
Station	0.96
Cemetery	1.03

Oakleigh Park
Station	1.03

New Barnet
South	0.79
North	0.23
Greenwood	0.88

Potters Bar
Station[2]	2.65

Brookmans Park
Marshmoor	2.97
No. 1	1.04
No. 3 (Down side)	0.26
No. 2 (Up side)	0.04

Hatfield
Red Hall	0.76

Welwyn Garden City
Station	2.53

Welwyn North
Station	1.56

Knebworth
Woolmer Green	1.55
Station	1.59

Stevenage
Langley	0.95
South	1.27
North (Up side)	0.33

Hitchin
South	2.92
Yard	0.43
Cambridge Junction (Up side)	0.24
Cadwell	1.08

Three Counties
Station	2.32

Arlesey
Station   1.46

Langford Goods
Station   1.56

Biggleswade
South   1.32
North   0.25

Sandy
Station[3]   2.66
Everton   2.50

Tempsford
Station   1.10

St Neots
Station   4.00

Offord & Buckden
Paxton   2.32
Station   2.11

Huntingdon North
No. 1   2.82
No. 2   0.31
Stukeley   2.06

Abbots Ripton
Station[4]   2.40

Holme
Connington (South)[5]   3.88
Station   1.95

Yaxley & Farcet
Station   3.34

Peterborough North
Fletton Junction   2.32
Crescent Junction   1.23
North (Up side)   0.24

New England
Spital Junction (Down side)   0.18
Eastfield (Up side)
Westwood Junction   0.44
New England South (Up side)
New England East (Up side)
North New England (Up side)
Walton   1.61
Werrington Junction   0.82

Tallington
Helpston   2.38
Lolham   1.52
Station   1.40

Essendine
Greatford   2.31
South   1.42
North   0.21

Little Bytham
Station   3.54

Corby (Lincs.)
Station   4.86

Great Ponton
Stoke   2.96
Highdyke   1.20
Station[6]   0.79

Grantham
South   3.01
Yard   0.29
North   0.23

Barkston
South Junction   4.09
North Junction   0.45

Hougham
Station   1.38

Claypole
Westborough	2.19
Station	1.63
Balderton	1.53

Newark
Barnby	2.16
South	0.89
North	0.40
Midland Crossing	0.46
Trent	0.84
Bathley Lane	1.35

Carlton-on-Trent
Cromwell	1.72
Station	1.63

Crow Park
Station	1.12

Dukeries Junction
Egmanton	1.92
Station	0.81

Tuxford North
Junction	0.45
Station	0.28
Lincoln Road	1.11

Retford
Gamston	2.45
Grove Road	1.94
South	1.07
North	0.22
Babworth	0.44
Canal	0.42
Botany Bay	1.07

Barnby Moor & Sutton
Station	1.03

Ranskill
Station[7]	2.30

Bawtry
Scrooby	1.16
Station	2.60

Rossington
Station	3.61

Doncaster
Loversall Carr	1.02
Black Carr Junction	0.79
Childers Drain (Down side)	
Potteric Carr	0.43
Decoy No. 1 Down	0.19
Decoy No 2 Up	0.12
Red Bank (Down side)	0.28
Carr (Up side)	
Balby Junction	0.87
Sand Bank Junction (Up side)	
Bridge Junction	0.36
South Yorkshire Junction	0.23
South[8]	0.15
'C' (Down side)	
'A' (Up side)[9]	0.18
'B' (Down side)	0.03
Frenchgate	0.13
Marshgate Junction	0.11

Arksey
Station	1.71
Bentley Colliery	0.69
Shaftholme Junction	1.48

Moss
Station	1.97

Balne
Station	2.91

Heck
Station	1.34

Temple Hirst
Station	2.53

Selby
Henwick Hall	2.46
Brayton	0.77
Canal	0.59
South	0.54
North	0.24
Barlby	0.47
Barlby North	0.25

Riccall
Station[10]	3.33

Escrick
Station	2.63

Naburn
Bridge	3.18

York
Chaloner's Whin	1.91
South Points	1.12
Locomotive Yard	0.61
Platform	0.27
Waterworks	0.14
Leeman Road[11]	0.15
Clifton	0.25
Skelton	1.21

Beningbrough
Station	3.88

Tollerton
Station	3.91

Alne
Station	1.46

Raskelf
Station	2.20

Pilmoor
Sessay Wood[12]	2.01
Station	2.05

Thirsk
Station	5.96

Otterington
Station	4.10

Northallerton
Station	3.58

Cowton
Eryholme	8.45

Darlington
South	4.95
North	0.51
Parkgate	0.50
Springfield	0.96

Aycliffe
Station	3.78
Preston	2.41

Bradbury
Station	2.20

Ferryhill
No. 3	2.18
No. 2[13]	0.48
No. 1	0.28
Coxhoe	0.85
Tursdale	1.17

Durham
Browney	2.56
Littleburn	1.05
Bridge House	0.81
Relly Mill	0.48
South	0.95
North	0.19
Newton Hall	1.24

Plawsworth
Kimblesworth	1.81
Station	0.57

Chester-le-Street
Chester Moor	0.95
Station	0.57

Birtley
Ouston	1.41
Station	1.14
North	0.52

Lamesley
Station	1.27

Low Fell
Station	1.31

Gateshead
King Edward Bridge	1.98
Greensfield[14]	

Newcastle-upon-Tyne
No. 3[15]	0.41
No. 2	0.21
No. 1	0.14

Manors East
Manors	0.28
Argyle Street	0.26

Heaton
Ouseburn	0.33
Riverside	0.32
Station	0.23
South	0.38
Benton Bank	0.70
'C' Pit[16]	0.89

Forest Hall
Benton Quarry	0.74
Station[17]	0.67

Killingworth
Sidings	1.16
Station	0.23

Annitsford
Dudley	1.98
Dam Dykes	0.64

Cramlington
Station	1.23

Plessey
Station	1.68

Stannington
Station	2.25
Clifton Crossing	0.75

Morpeth
Station	2.09

Pegswood
Station	1.96

Longhirst
Station	1.48

Widdrington
Station[18]	3.06

Chevington
Station	2.32

Acklington
Station	2.85

Warkworth
Southside	2.29
Station	1.08

Alnmouth
Shilbottle	1.55
Wooden Gate	0.52

South[19] 0.87
North 0.18

Longhoughton
Station 2.49

Little Mill
Howick Heugh (Up only) 1.12
Station 0.86
Stamford Crossing 1.07

Christon Bank
Station 2.51

Chathill
Station 2.99

Lucker
Station 3.23

Belford
Station 2.36
Crag Mill 1.02
Smeafield 2.39

Beal
Station 3.66

Goswick
Station 2.19

Scremerston
Station 2.74

Tweedmouth
South 2.16
North 0.19

Berwick-upon-Tweed
Station 1.10
Marshall Meadows 0.99

Burnmouth
Station 3.90

Ayton
Station 1.62

Reston
Junction 3.76
West 0.25

Grantshouse
Station 4.95

Cockburnspath
Station 4.65

Innerwick
Station 2.74

Dunbar
Oxwellmains 2.48
East 2.07
West[20] 0.42
Beltonford 1.91

East Linton
Station 3.56

East Fortune
Station 2.40

Drem
Junction 3.11

Longniddry
Aberlady Junction 3.09
Junction 1.49

Prestonpans
Seaton Crossing 2.05
Station 1.70
Morrison's Haven 1.11

Inveresk
Wallyford 1.14
Monktonhall Junction 1.12

Newhailes
Junction   1.40

Joppa
Station   1.02

Portobello
East Junction   0.29
West Junction   0.50
Craigentinny   0.68

Abbeyhill
Piershill Junction   0.44
St Margaret's   0.32

Edinburgh Waverley
East   1.16
West   0.40

8
ECML Wayside Stations and Closure Dates

The local stations on the ECML, 82 of them north of Hitchin, had strong family resemblances depending on their pre-Grouping origin being GNR, NER or NBR. The GNR stations gave the impression of being severe and functional. They were usually of buff-coloured brick, which was often discoloured by smoke and age, and often on the ECML were of just one storey. Some were built of wood and looked little better than shacks—Abbots Ripton, Yaxley and Farcet, Crow Park and Dukeries Junction being examples.

Characteristic GNR architecture was Italianate with roofs of relatively low pitch and broad eaves edged with unembellished bargeboards; chimneys tended to be prominent, the single ones being tipped with a tall narrow pot. Similar roofs also characterised GNR signal boxes, although they had modestly decorated bargeboards. In the case of the buildings on the stations with island platforms, the roofs were flat and had very wide canopies with deep saw-toothed valances. Several GNR stations (on the ECML notably Hatfield and Doncaster) had the rather unusual feature of a canopy built over not only the platforms but also the platform lines, supported by a row of columns in the six-foot.

A regular feature of the smaller stations of the GNR on its four-track sections was their arrangement with two island platforms, main station buildings being separate and giving access to platforms by covered footbridges, although sometimes the entrances were on road overbridges. Therefore, stopping trains normally used the outer faces of the two islands, the fast lines being in the centre. This plan existed at Harringay and Hornsey, New Southgate, Oakleigh Park, New Barnet, Knebworth, Stevenage, Brookmans Park, Three Counties, Biggleswade, Tempsford, St Neots, Offord & Buckden, also at Huntingdon North on the Down side only.[1]

North of Peterborough, Little Bytham and Corby had two islands similarly arranged, while at Essendine only the Down platform was an island for on the Up side the goods shed was set in the middle of what would have otherwise been the 'Up Slow'. Indeed, only in this first 100 miles of the ECML were any wayside stations provided with four main line platforms. At Harringay and Hornsey, there was an additional Down main through the centre, allowing a Down express to pass a slower Down train at the main Down platform.

View south to Yaxley & Farcett station, 28 May 1956. *Photograph: R. Stephenson, B.W.L. Brooksbank collection*

Looking north at St Neots station, 17 May 1956. *Photograph: R. Stephenson, B.W.L. Brooksbank collection*

Independent through lines existed elsewhere, as at Hatfield, Welwyn Garden City, Hitchin, etc., to allow overtaking movements, but as a route noted for its high-speed trains the ECML was really singularly lacking in such facilities. North of Grantham, the GN Section of the ECML became double-track and GNR wayside stations were entirely of the conventional two-track pattern and of mean and undistinguished architecture—except perhaps at Arksey where the station was made to look 'half-timbered'.

North of Shaftholme Junction and as far as Berwick-upon-Tweed, it was NER territory, while at least as far as Morpeth, wayside stations on the main line continued to be almost entirely simple, unpretentious edifices. Nearly to Darlington, they were also built of brick, while further north were of stone. Perhaps more than those of most pre-Grouping companies, the smaller NER stations were almost instantly recognisable by several features characteristic of that railway. They were designed by gifted architects, including Andrews, Green, Prosser and Bell, the first of whom worked in the 1840s for companies that later merged into the NER. The Andrews stations, widely spread over the Yorkshire part of the NER, were built of brick to mildly Italianate design, similar to the GNR stations, though of more solid appearance and with characteristic NER bow windows in the station house, set low on the platform and often adjoining either glazed pavilions or shelters with sloping catslide roofs. Most intermediate stations and signal boxes between York and Northallerton were partially rebuilt in the 1930s by the LNER in brick and slate of a distinctly Teutonic style, with steep roofs.

Small local NER stations from North Yorkshire to the Tweed were built in a fashion similar to Andrews' but of stone and on the ECML itself, particularly most of those south of Morpeth, were single-storey. North of Morpeth were the striking green stations built in local stone in a Tudor-with-knobs-on style, with semi-dormers, again bay windows at the platform level, catslide shelters, portico entrances, ball finials on the gables, etc. In this style, the most attractive stations throughout the ECML were at Warkworth, Chathill, Beal and Belford—most still survive. Other NER architectural features included, at medium-sized stations, all-over roofs with hipped ends—on the ECML seen only at Alnmouth and the original station at Thirsk—and 'Rialto-shaped' footbridges of decorative woodwork or of elaborate iron-work. Signal boxes on the NER were also unmistakable, featuring wide expanses of multi-paned glazing, low-pitched roofs (at least in later designs) and set sometimes at great elevation on gantries over the tracks.

The small stations of the NBR were on the other hand very undistinguished, particularly those on the ECML between Berwick and Edinburgh. They had a low, single-storey elevation, and most were built of stone with large plain windows near to platform level. They had no embellishments and the most primitive facilities for staff and passengers. NBR signal boxes were solidly built and had sash-windows, but few details to distinguish their pre-Grouping origin.

Almost all the wayside stations on the ECML possessed a goods yard, with goods shed, crane, cattle pen, loading docks and a few sidings; those in the NE Area had the distinctive NER coal-drops for hopper-bottom wagons. They were just like other Victorian local stations, but as they were on a busy main line, most also had at least one refuge siding and often loops to allow freight trains to be overtaken by expresses.

As elsewhere, by the 1930s, with the advent of the bus, lorry and motor car, the wayside station had experienced its best years and outlived its usefulness. On the ECML, they were

Chathill station before Grouping.

fundamentally a nuisance, at least on its preponderant double-track sections, for trains stopping at them severely handicapped the schedules of the fast expresses. Consequently, their train services had become reduced to the level of being of little use to anyone.

The smallest stations between Hitchin and Grantham had in 1939 five to six trains stopping each way on weekdays and on Sundays Tempsford, Offord and Buckden, Abbots Ripton, Yaxley and Farcet, Tallington and Great Ponton had none. Further down, Hougham, Claypole, Carlton-on-Trent, Crow Park, Tuxford North, Barnby Moor and Sutton, Ranskill and Rossington had four to five trains, while Dukeries Junction had one (two on Fridays and Saturdays) and Carlton, Dukeries, Barnby Moor, Ranskill and Rossington were closed on Sundays. The local stations between Doncaster and Selby were similarly served on weekdays but none of them had Sunday trains. The three between Selby and York had as many as six on weekdays, on a stopping service between the two centres, although none on Sundays.

North of York, it was even worse, with the wayside stations between York and Thirsk having on weekdays just two Down trains—three in the case of Alne and Pilmoor. Otterington had a few more by virtue of the Leeds–Teesside service, while beyond Northallerton and on to Durham the service was perhaps one train better. In the Up direction, most of the wayside stations between Darlington and York had just one train early in the morning plus a midday one on Saturdays, and none at the end of the working day. Beningbrough, Tollerton, Raskelf, Pilmoor and Otterington were closed on Sundays. The rest of the local stations had just one train each first thing on Sunday morning.

Durham–Newcastle resembled more a 'suburban' service of stopping trains, as did Newcastle–Alnmouth, while north of the latter and on through Berwick to Dunbar, the wayside stations (other than a few such as Chathill, Belford and Beal) survived on the same ration of two or three trains per day, although as far as Berwick they also had two on Sundays.

During the war, in spite of the virtual absence of personal transport and the proximity to many ECML wayside station of the many military airfields, passenger services were cut even nearer to vanishing point.[2] For example, on weekdays, Tallington and Great Ponton had two Down trains—the second in the early afternoon—and two Up trains, while Hougham, Carlton and Dukeries had just one Down train, although they thrived on two Up trains. Between York and Darlington there were morning and evening all-station trains on the Down, but still only a morning one Up (plus one mid-day Saturday). North of Newcastle, the service was much as pre-war, except that many of the wayside stations were closed for most of the war period.

After the war, services at ECML wayside stations remained scarcely any different from their wartime nadir, and the logical step was taken very soon after Nationalisation of closing several of them. The manoeuvre of taking off services in order to make a station a candidate for closure began long before Dr Beeching's appointment. These apparently useless stations—starting with Barnby Moor and Sutton in 1949 and culminating with the wholesale closures in 1958—occurred before Beeching's survey. In most cases, the stations concerned had first been reduced to having just one train per day—and in some cases in one direction only. As elsewhere on BR in the 1950s, most of them were of more use as railheads for freight (especially coal) and remained open for this purpose for several more years.

Station Closures

There was little modernisation achieved before 1959. This was due to the parlous financial state of BR in general and the failure of successive governments to provide adequate funds for the public purse, as well as the general shortage of materials and labour after the war. The other side to modernisation was the closure of unremunerative branch lines and of many little-used wayside stations, first to passenger services, then to freight.

Closure dates between September 1939 and December 1959 of wayside stations on the ECML are listed here. A number of small stations were demoted to unstaffed halts some time before closure, and this began very early in the 1950s. In many cases where staffed goods facilities were removed, a public delivery siding (PDS) may have remained, or there may have been private sidings left. It will be noted that many of the wayside stations were closed to passengers before the 'Beeching Era'. The first to go was Lamesley (June 1945) and most lost their passenger facilities in the late 1950s when stopping services on the ECML were discontinued, in part to allow accelerated express services. In any case, their chief passenger-rated traffic in most cases was not in people but in parcels, although much of the parcels traffic was being dealt with at principal stations or lost to road services altogether. Goods facilities went later, with the major rationalisation of the 'Re-shaping' era.

Passenger stations closed since 1959 were: Temple Hirst, Tollerton, Croft Spa, Ferryhill, Gateshead West, Heaton, Longhoughton, Belford, Beal, Tweedmouth, Burnmouth, Ayton, Reston, Grantshouse, East Linton, East Fortune, Inveresk, Joppa, Piershill and Abbeyhill.

In the following table:

* = closed temporarily to passengers
** = PDS from September 1958
\# = Private sidings remained open

	Closed to Passengers	Closed to Freight
Three Counties	1/59	1/70
Arlesey & Henlow	1/51[3]	1/60
Tempsford	11/56	3/65#
Offord & Buckden	2/59	4/65#
Abbots Ripton	9/58	10/64
Holme	4/59	10/70#
Yaxley & Farcet	4/59	11/69#
Tallington	6/59	2/66#
Essendine	6/59	3/66#
Little Bytham	6/59	11/65#
Corby (Lincs)[4]	6/59	10/64
Great Ponton	9/58	4/63
Barkston	3/55	7/64
Hougham	9/57	9/57
Claypole	9/57	7/64
Carlton-on-Trent	3/53	12/55
Crow Park	10/58	5/64[5]
Dukeries Junction[6]	6/50	-------
Tuxford North	5/55	6/64
Barnby Moor & Sutton	1/49	-------
Ranskill	10/58	12/64#
Bawtry	10/58	4/71
Rossington	10/58	5/63
Arksey	8/52	12/64
Moss	6/53	-------
Balne	9/58	7/64
Heck	9/58	4/63
Riccall	9/58	7/64**
Escrick	6/53	9/61
Naburn	6/53	7/64
Beningbrough	9/58	7/65**
Alne	5/58	8/64
Raskelf	5/58	8/64
Pilmoor	5/58	9/59
Sessay	9/58	8/64
Otterington	9/58	8/64

Danby Wiske	9/58	9/58
Cowton	9/58	6/64
Aycliffe	3/53	3/53#
Bradbury	1/50	1/50
Plawsworth	4/52	9/63
Birtley	12/55	------
Lamesley	6/45	9/59
Low Fell	4/52	------
Bensham	4/54	------
Forest Hall	9/58	9/58
Killingworth	9/58	6/65[7]
Annitsford	9/58	11/63#
Plessey	9/58	4/62[8]
Stannington	9/58	8/64**
Longhirst	10/51	8/64[9]
Chevington	9/58	8/64
Warkworth	9/58	4/62#
Little Mill	9/58	6/65**
Christon Bank	9/58*	6/65**
Newham	9/50*	9/50
Lucker	2/53*	6/65**
Goswick	9/58*	8.64**
Scremerston	7/51*	7/51
Cockburnspath	9/51	1/65
Innerwick	6/51	8/64
Newhailes	2/50	------

9
ECML Tunnels and Principal Overbridges

The following list was compiled from the bridge registers held by Railtrack, and the information provided is that relevant to the period 1939–59. Bridges over roads and other railways of a total length of more than 40 feet and those over waterways of more than 30 feet in total are listed; in many instances, the crossing was not straight and the width at right angles was less. Heights over waterways are for normal conditions. Distances given are from the buffer-stops at King's Cross and are to the centre of the structure.

Bridge No.	Distance from King's Cross (miles)	Designation	No. of Spa
------	0.5	Gas Works Tunnel	------
------	1.0	Copenhagen Tunnel	------
10	1.7	Holloway Road	2 + 2
------	1.7	------	21
11	1.8	Hornsey Road	1 + 3
11A	2.1	Down Canonbury loop/Highbury Goods	2
12	2.5	Seven Sisters Road	1
16	2.6	Stroud Green Road	1
21	3.3	Tottenham &Hampstead	1
25	4.2	Hornsey Viaduct[2] No. 1	3
		Hornsey Viaduct No. 2	1
		Hornsey Viaduct No. 3	Severa
------	5.5	Wood Green Tunnel	------
32	6.1	North Circular Road	1
------	7.9	Barnet Tunnel	------
43	9.3	East Barnet Lane, New Barnet	1
------	10.2	Hadley South Tunnel	------
------	10.8	Hadley North Tunnel	------
------	11.8	Potters Bar Tunnel	------
49	12.7	Drakes Lane, Potters Bar	1
64	18.7	River Lea	5
65	18.9	Pearts Bridge, Welwyn Garden City	5
69	21.6	Welwyn Viaduct (River Mimram)	40
------	22.2	Welwyn South Tunnel	------
------	23.1	Welwyn North Tunnel	------
72	23.4	Robbery Lane Viaduct, Woolmer	7
82A	26.3	Hertford line fly-under, Langley	1
95	30.0	Wymondley Highway	2
103	32.4	Grove Mill Lane, Hitchin	4
104	32.8	River Hiz	3
105	32.8	Ickleford Bridge, Hitchin	3
116	43.1	Stratford Brook	1
116A	43.1	River Ivel	5
129	47.6	Howitt's Lane, Tempsford	3
130	51.2	Brown's Road, St Neots	3
134	52.5	Gallows Brook St Neots	4
136	53.5	River Lane, Paxton	3
140A	57.8	Over MR Kettering-Huntingdon line	1
141	57.8	Leeds Brook, Huntingdon	4

Construction	Length(s)	Notes
------	1,584 feet	Three bores
------	1,782 feet	Three bores[1]
rders/Brick arches	97 feet + 20 feet 1 inch + 47 feet 3 inches + 20 feet 4 inches	
Brick arches	17 feet each	
Girder	85 feet 6 inches—109 feet	Varied by line
Girders	50 feet—56 feet	
Girders	69 feet 9 inches—86 feet 6 inches	Varied by line
Girders	66 feet 10 inches—71 feet	Varied by line
ought iron girders	55 feet 6 inches—59 feet	Varied by line
rders/Brick arches	45 feet 1 inch—48 feet 6 inches + 28–30 feet	Varied by line[3]
Girder	50 feet	
ler/Concrete/Brick arches	23 feet 10 inches—55 feet 3 inches	Varied by line
------	2,115 feet	Two bores
Girder	83 feet	Built 1931
------	1,815 feet	Two bores
Steel girder	40 feet	Reconstructed 1936-37
------	1,152 feet	Second bore 1959
------	696 feet	Second bore 1959
------	3,642 feet	Second bore 1959
Brick arch	16 feet 6 inches	Reconstructed as Girder (68 feet) 1955
Brick arches	30 feet each	
Brick arches	13 feet each	
Brick arches	30 feet each	
------	1,338 feet	
------	3,138 feet	
Brick arches	21 feet 8 inches each	
Steel girder	68 feet 9 inches	
Steel girders	42 feet 4 inches—44 feet 6 inches	Varied by line
Brick arches	34 feet each	
Brick arches	30 feet each	
Brick arches	22 feet each	
Steel girder	46 feet 9 inches	
Timber[4]	17 feet each	GN&LNW lines
Brick arches	18 feet each	
Brick arches	18 feet each	
Brick arches	21 feet 6 inches each	
Brick arches	25 feet each	
Steel girder	52 feet 11 inches	
Brick arches	26 feet 1 inches	

142	57.9	West Meadows, Huntingdon	3
143	58.1	Flood arches, River Ouse, Huntingdon	7
144	58.2	River Great Ouse	3
145	58.3	Brompton Lane, Huntingdon	3
146	58.7	Nun's Brook	5
149	59.1	Views Common, Huntingdon	3
150	59.4	Ermine Street. Huntingdon	1
151	59.9	Jenkin's Bridge, Huntingdon	3
159	64.8	Wood Walton Bridge, Abbots Ripton	3
160	65.3	Green Lane, Abbots Ripton	3
161	66.4	Sawtry Road, Connington	5
162	66.7	Monks Lode, Connington	3 + 1 +
163	67.1	Black Horse Drain, Connington	3
176	72.3	Pig Water, Yaxley	2 + 1 +
177	72.4	Cattle Arch, Yaxley	3
184	75.7	Nene Viaduct Approach, Peterborough	8
------	75.8	Nene Viaduct over GER and MR lines	1
------	75.9	Nene Viaduct, River Nene	3 + 3
------	75.9	Nene Viaduct Approach	5
190	83.4	South Meadow Drain, Lolham	5
191	83.5	Lolham South Flood Openings	5
192	83.8	Lolham North Flood Openings	4
193	83.8	St John's Flood Arches, Lolham	4
194	84.3	Welland Old River Tallington	3
195	84.4	Mill Stream, Tallington	3
210	92.6	Bytham Road, Little Bytham	3
212	92.8	Bytham Viaduct, Little Bytham	9
215	93.9	Boxer's Bridge Counthorpe	3
216	94.3	Counthorpe Road	3
225	97.3	Corby, occupation arches	3
227	97.9	Colsterworth Viaduct, Corby	3
228	98.4	Easton Bridge, Corby	3
------	100.6	Stoke Tunnel	------
233	102.1	Ponton Viaduct, Great Ponton	3 + 1
236	103.2	Whalebone Bridge, Little Ponton	3
238	104.3	River Witham, Saltersford	3
243	105.7	Melton Road/Wharf Road Grantham	4
245	105.9	Grange Bridge, Grantham	3
247	106.4	Great North Road, Barrowby	3
------	108.1	Peascliffe Tunnel	------
259	110.3	River Witham, Barkston North Junction	3
273	119.4	Clay Lane, Balderton	Seven

Brick arches	20 feet 11 inches each	
Brick arches	18 feet	
Steel girders	75 feet	Reconstructed 1924-1959
Brick arches	18 feet 2 inches each	
Brick arches	30 feet 3 inches	
Brick arches	18 feet each	
Girder	49 feet 8 inches (Down) 73 feet (Up)	
Brick arches	18 feet each	
Brick arches	29 feet 8 inches each	
Brick arches	30 feet	
Brick arches	12 feet each	
Brick arches	19 feet each, centre 53 feet 10 inches	
Brick arches	30 feet 8 inches each	
Brick Arches	14 feet 4 inches each—42 feet 6 inches—14 feet	
Brick arches	20 feet 6 inches	
Brick arches	20 feet each	Varied by line
Trussed girder	110 feet[5]	
Trussed girder/Brick arches	60 feet 6 inches each girder—20 feet each arch	
Brick arches	20 feet each	
Brick arches	12 feet each (cu-waters)	
Brick arches	12 feet each (cu-waters)	
Brick arches	12 feet each	
Brick arches	12 feet each, segmented	
Brick arches	15 feet each, segmented	
Brick arches	15 feet each, segmented	
Brick arches	25 feet each	
Brick arches	10 to 33 feet each	
Brick arches	18 feet each	
Brick arches	18 feet each	
Brick arches	18 feet each	
Brick arches	33 feet each	
Brick arches	25 feet 4 inches each	
------	2,640 feet	
Brick arches	26 feet 11 inches each—33 feet 11 inches	
Brick arches	26 feet each	
Brick arches	45 feet each	
Brick arches	30 feet 6 inches—33 feet 4 inches each	
Brick arches	20 feet each	
Brick arches/Girder	13 feet—44 feet 3 inches—12 feet 9 inches	
------	2,901 feet	
Brick arches	34 feet 9 inches each	
Brick arches	26 to 31 feet each	

278	121.0	Newark Dyke	1
280	121.3	Trent Viaduct	14 + 1 + 5
281	121.5	Trent Flood Openings	6
------	134.4	Askham Tunnel	------
302	138.3	River Idle, Retford	5
307	139.6	Chesterfield Canal, Babworth	1
313	147.2	Bawtry Viaduct	27
314	147.4	New Cut Bridge, Bawtry	1
321	152.0	River Torne, Black Carr Junction	3 + 1
330	156.3	River Dun Navigation, Doncaster	1
332	156.6	River Don, Doncaster	1
333	156.9	Moat Hills Flood Openings, Marshgate	2
334	157.0	Bentley Bank Flood Openings, Marshgate	2
335	157.0	Dock Hills Drain, Bentley	Severa
338	157.6	Bentley Mill Goight	3
342	159.8	Tilts Drain, Shaftholme	4
343	160.1	Shaftholme Flood Openings	2
1A	164.8	Went Bridge, River Went, Balne	1
5	166.8	Aire & Calder Canal, Heck	1
11	168.3	Over LMSR Wakefield-Goole line	1
14	168.7	Weeland Road, Heck	1
18	169.5	River Aire, Temple Hirst	4
21	173.4	Selby Canal	1
25	174.4	Selby Swing Bridge, River Ouse	2 (1 swiv
39	184.2	Naburn Swing Bridge[6], River Ouse	2 (1 swi
12	191.3	Skelton Bridge, River Ouse	4
------	200.5	Kyle Beck, Alne	1
39	207.9	Cod Beck, Thirsk	3
57	217.2	Boroughbridge Road, Northallerton	1
75	223.9	Wiske Bridge, River Wiske, Cowton	1
87	229.0	A167, Croft Spa	1
88	229.2	Tees Bridge, River Tees, Croft Spa	4
100	232.4	Parkgate Bridge, Darlington	3
103	233.5	Skerne Viaduct, River Skerne	5
110	235.4	River Skerne, south of Aycliffe	3
128	237.3	Aycliffe Viaduct	1 +
131	237.7	River Skerne, north of Aycliffe	1

steel-truss girders	262 feet 6 inches	
Brick arches	18 feet each—9 feet 5 inches—40 feet—18 feet each	
Brick arches	10 feet 1 inch each	
------	171 feet	
Brick arches	20 feet each	
Steel girder	47 feet 11 inches	
Brick arches	31–32 feet	
Brick arches	40 feet	
Brick arches	11 feet 6 inches each—35 feet 4 inches	
Steel Truss	80 feet 10½ inches	
Steel Truss	185 feet	
Brick arches	20 feet each	
Brick arches	20 feet each	
Wrought Iron Girders	20 feet 11 inches each	
Girders	19 feet 4 inches—22 feet 8 inches each	
Girders	15 feet 11 inches—24 feet each	
Wrought iron girders	20 feet each	
Brick arches	31 feet 9 inches	
Wrought iron girder	127 feet	
Steel girder	29 feet	
Steel girder	44 feet 9 inches	
Concrete/Wrought iron girders	12 feet 3 inches—15 feet 6 inches—128 feet 6 inches—86 feet 6 inches	
Wrought iron girder	101 feet	
Wrought iron girders	103 feet fixed—119 feet 6 inches swing	80 feet opening. 39 feet 6 inches fixed with signal box above swivel pier
Wrought iron girders	102 feet 6 inches fixed, 172 feet 3 inches swing	Two equal openings
Stone arches	12 feet—66 feet 6 inches—65 feet—66 feet	Additional single line bridge built in 1942 for Down Goods line[7]
Steel girders	32 feet 8 inches	Renewed 1956–58[8]
Stone arches	21 feet 10 inches each	
Steel girder	40 feet 6 inches[9]	
Stone arch	50 feet	
Steel girders	38 feet 4 inches	
Stone arches	59 feet 6 inches each	45 feet 6 inches above water to soffits
Steel box girders	10 feet 8 inches—51 feet 7 inches—10 feet 6 inches[10]	
Stone arches	30 feet each	
Stone arches	34 feet 5 inches	
Stone arches	40 feet + 20 feet each	
Wrought iron lattice girders	64 feet 9 inches	

143	239.9	Preston Bridge, River Skerne	1
167	247.3	Thinford Stream, Tursdale	3
169	247.9	Tursdale Stream	2
176	250.3	Croxdale Viaduct	11
184	252.4	Boyne Road (A690), Relly Mill	1
185	252.6	Langley Moor Viaduct, River Deerness	4 + 2
187	253.4	Relly Mill Viaduct, River Browney	5
190	254.1	Durham Viaduct, River Wear	11
193	254.3	Framwellgate (A691), Durham	2
208	257.2	Chester Low Road, Plawsworth	1
210	257.4	Plawsworth Viaduct (road and Black Dene Stream)	5 + 1
215	259.0	Chester Moor Colliery (road)	1
216	259.1	Chester Moor Viaduct (South Burn)	8
223	260.3	Chester-le-Street Viaduct (Cong Burn)	11
233	262.4	Birtley Colliery lines	1 + 2
251	266.9	Lobley Hill, Bensham	1
258	267.7	King Edward Bridge Approaches	Several
259	267.9	King Edward Bridge, River Tyne	4
260	268.0	King Edward Bridge Approaches (North)	10
261	268.1	Pottery Lane Bridge, Newcastle	1
262	268.1	Over Forth Goods Warehouses, Newcastle	9
3	268.5	Clavering Place, Newcastle	1
5	268.5	------	1
7	268.5	Dean Street, Newcastle	1
8	268.6	Dean Street, Newcastle	6 + 1
9	268.7	Pilgrim Street, Newcastle	3
10	268.7	------	13
11	268.8	Manor Chare, Manors	1
12	268.8	Manor Chare, Manors	4
13	268.8	Manors East, City Road	1
15	268.9	Trafalgar Street, Manors	1
21	269.3	Bermondsey Street, Manors	1
22	269.4	Ouseburn Viaduct (stream and Stepney Road)	9
29	271.1	Benfield Road, Benton Bank	3 + 1
31A	271.4	Benton Hall Bridge (stream)	1
62	280.6	Plessey Viaduct, River Blyth	5
74	286.0	Bothal Viaduct, River Wansbeck	1 + 9
91	298.3	Coquet Viaduct, River Coquet	1 + 9
110	303.9	Alnmouth Viaduct, River Alne	18
189	333.9	Billendean Road, Tweedmouth	3

Steel girder	33 feet 8 inches	
Stone arches	20 feet each	
Stone arches	30 feet—12 feet	
Brick arches	60 feet each	
Steel girder	90 feet 3 inches	
e wrought iron, steel plate	59 feet 6 inches each	59 feet above water
Brick arches	60 feet each	50 feet 6 inches—66 feet 3 inches above water
Stone arches	60 feet each	
rick/stone arches	36 feet each	
steel plate girder	56 feet 6 inches	
Brick arches	55 feet + 34 feet 10 inches	
steel plate girder	40 feet	
Brick arches	60 feet each	40–81 feet above water
Brick arches	60 feet each, semi-elliptical	41–90 feet above water
teel plate girders	12 feet + 46 feet 11 inches	
teel plate girder	37 feet 4 inches	
Stone arches	50 feet	30–70 feet above streets
eel lattice girders	191–300—200–231 feet	83 feet above high water
Stone arches	25 feet each	27 feet 6 inches—33 feet above streets
teel plate girder	35 feet 2 inches	
el girders (mainly)	32 feet 3 inches—50 feet	32 feet 9 inches above roadway
ick (glazed) arch	46 feet	27 feet above street
t-iron arch girders	76 feet	24 feet above street
Stone arch	78 feet	47 feet 6 inches above street
Brick arches	20 feet each + 12 feet	
Stone arches	10 feet—40 feet—10 feet	
Brick arches	20 feet each	
Stone arch	43–49 feet	Varied by line. 50 feet above street
Brick arches	20 feet each	
ought iron girders	65 feet 6 inches—91 feet	Varied by line. 34 feet above street
ought iron girders	70 feet	
Stone arches	24 feet 7 inches—91 feet	Varied by line. 54 feet above street
ought iron lattice girders	42 feet 9 inches—43 feet—2 × 117 feet 6 inches—3 × 119 feet 6 inches—2 × 36 feet	108 feet above water
Steel girders	25 feet—53 feet	
Steel girder	131 feet 2 inches	
Stone arches	55 feet each	96 feet 6 inches above water
Brick arches	12 feet + 50 feet each	34–123 feet high
Brick arches	12 feet + 50 feet each + 12 feet	29 feet 6 inches—89 feet high
Brick arches	30 feet	22 feet—75 feet high
Brick arches	25 feet each	

191	334.2	Great North Road, Tweedmouth	2
194	334.7	Un-named, Tweedmouth	5
195	335.1	Royal Border Bridge, River Tweed	28
118	353.3	Penmanshiel Tunnel[11]	------
109	357.0	Dunglass Viaduct, Cockburnspath	5 + 1
77	366.1	Beltonford Bridge, Great North Road	1
76	366.2	Biel Water, Dunbar	1
67	369.6	Tyne Bridge, East Linton	2 + 1
66	369.7	East Linton (road)	1
28	386.1	Monktonhall Viaduct, River Esk	2
24	385.1	Wallyford (Durmore) Tunnel	------
13	390.2	Brighton Road, Portobello	1
12	390.5	Baileyfield Road, Portobello	1
7	391.7	St Margaret's Tunnel, Edinburgh	------
4	392.2	Milton Street Bridge, Edinburgh	1
------	393.0	Calton Tunnel	------

Borders Flooding

Not listed individually were Bridges Nos 123–127, 130, 133, 137 and 138, between Reston and Grantshouse (between 347.7 and 351.5 miles from King's Cross), all being 21–31 feet long and made from stone or wrought iron.

After the flood disaster of 12 August 1948, temporary military-style trestle bridges were provided and later they were all rebuilt in welded steel. The new bridges (58–62-foot span) were twice as wide as those destroyed and in two instances (Nos 126–7 and 137–8), two bridges were replaced by one. Seven of these bridges were over the Eye Water. Also, a very small (11-foot 7-inch) bridge—No. 116 between Grantshouse and Cockburnspath—was replaced by a culvert.

The Thornton Water bridge (No. 100, 20 feet 2 inches) at Innerwick had been damaged, but did not need replacement. In addition, considerable stretches of the line on embankment and numerous culverts had to be restored. In all, a total length of 1,200 feet of the ECML between Berwick and Dunbar had to be reconstructed, taking into account the embankments and other structures of the line that were washed away.

Brick arches	35 feet—46 feet	
Brick arches	30 feet each	60 feet 6 inches over road
Brick arches	61 feet 6 inches each	77 feet—101 feet 6 inches high
------	978 feet	
Stone arches	30 feet each + 135 feet	111 feet above water
Steel girder	35 feet	
Steel girder	43 feet 4 inches	175 feet over water
Stone arches/wrought iron lattice girder	89 feet	
Steel girder	56 feet 6 inches	
Stone arches	64 feet each	32 feet over water
------	279 feet	Replaced by overbridge 1951
Steel girder	40 feet 9 inches	
Steel girders	57 feet 6 inches—61 feet 6 inches	Varied by line
------	180 feet	
Steel girder	49 feet	49 feet above road
------	1,194 feet (south)—1,422 feet (north)	Two bores

10
Gradients and Speed Restrictions on the ECML

Although lacking severe gradients, the East Coast Main Line was, as were most railways in Britain in general, a switchback. Barely 100 miles of the 393 miles from King's Cross to Edinburgh Waverley consisted of level track: the longest individual level stretch was the 11 miles from a mile north of York to half a mile beyond Alne. On the entire route, there were only a dozen level sections in excess of two miles in length and none were north of Berwick-on-Tweed. There were 395 changes of gradient between King's Cross and Waverley, an average almost exactly of one change per route mile. The steepest was a short fall at 1:78 approaching Waverley station; the longest stretch of constant gradient was the eight miles at 1:200 from midway between Hornsey and Wood Green to Potters Bar. A broad description of the route is included here—without listing all the minute changes, some of which were barely 300–400 yards in length, beginning at the southern end.

The steep climb through Gasworks and Copenhagen Tunnels at 1:107 was followed by a brief level stretch before the 1:440 rise through Finsbury Park to Harringay. Following a brief downhill run through Hornsey, the eight-mile pull at 1:200 to Potters Bar began, after which it was downhill for about 5½ miles to Hatfield, where the station stood on the level. A mile beyond Hatfield was another stretch at 1:200 to Welwyn Viaduct (level), then up again at 1:200 to Woolmer Green box.

After Woolmer Green, the line descended with minor undulations for 33 miles to Offord and Buckden, which included five miles at 1:200 from Stevenage to nearby Three Counties (briefly level at Hitchin), then 1:264/1:400 for 3½ miles to Arlesey. Two miles of level ground from Paxton box (one mile on from Offord) to Huntingdon North was followed by a 1:200 climb of three miles to Leys box, a brief level, then a 1:200 descent of 4½ miles through Abbots Ripton to Connington box, a four-mile level through Holme, thence more minor undulations to Peterborough North.

Leaving Peterborough, the line climbed for a mile at 1:270, levelled at New England North Junction, then went down 1:330 for a mile to a 2½-mile level section accommodating the Werrington water troughs. After that the ascent to Stoke box commenced, gradually at first, with short level sections interspersed with inclines of 1:400/1:563. Two miles after

Tallington, the line steepened to 1:264 for 2½ miles through Essendine, eased for two miles, then for nine miles through Little Bytham and Corby to the summit at Stoke box, it rose at 1:200/1:178, broken by a 1½-mile easement approaching Corby.

From Stoke box through the tunnel, there was a gradual descent all the 20 miles on to Newark, the first five miles nearly to Grantham at 1:200, then essentially level to Peascliffe Tunnel, 1:440 through the tunnel and again 1:200 for about two miles through Barkston, finally slackening off over the last 9½ miles to 1:200/1:550. Newark station was on a short level section, after which the line descended slightly to a 5½-mile level stretch from Muskham water troughs to Crow Park. Then followed a climb of a mile at 1:300 and nearly three miles at 1:200 to Dukeries Junction and after some minor undulations, Askham Tunnel was entered.

The line then descended for 3½ miles at 1:178/1:200 to a level at Retford, whence it continued with only minor rises and falls, all the way to York and beyond as far as Alne. Beyond there, the line rose very gradually at gradients often as low as 1:650, interspersed with level stretches and a very minor dip 2½ miles either side of Croft Spa to Darlington. Generally having to cross the grain of the land across County Durham and Northumberland, the ECML undulated a great deal in the ensuing 100 miles or so, with 71 changes of gradient in the 49 miles through Newcastle-on-Tyne to Alnmouth. In the 10½ miles from Darlington to beyond Bradbury, the line climbed gradually, with stretches of a mile or so at 1:200/203 interspersed with two level stretches of two and three miles respectively.

After Bradbury, it fell for about seven miles, first at 1:528 to level at Ferryhill, then at 1:200/1:158 to Croxdale from where it rose sharply at 1:150/1:163 for the three miles to Relly Mill Junction, then fell more steeply (1:101/1:120) for about 1½ miles through Durham to Newton Hall Junction. Two miles of roughly level track were then succeeded by 2½ miles downhill at 1:150 to Chester-le-Street. Two miles at 1:198 interspersed with short easier stretches than brought the line down to a trough at Ouston Junction.

From there the line climbed almost continuously for 14 miles to Cramlington, usually at moderate grades of around 1:200 while briefly level over the River Tyne at Newcastle and between Killingworth and Annitsford. The undulations continued after Cramlington at grades of 1:200/1:300, but after Alnmouth, there was a 3½-mile climb at 1:170 to Little Mill, after which the line descended with more gentle inclines interspersed with some short level sections to Beal. Two level miles then followed before a climb of nearly three miles at 1:190 from Goswick to beyond Scremerston and a two-mile dip down to the Royal Border Bridge and up into Berwick-on-Tweed.

After Berwick, the same gradient continued for six miles to Burnmouth, whence the line was roughly level for about four miles before resuming upward at 1:200 to a summit just beyond Grantshouse. Commencing through Penmanshiel Tunnel, there followed a steep descent for four miles at 1:96 through Cockburnspath, whence the line continued roughly level, but with some 41 undulations in the next 33 miles to Portobello. From there a mile up at 1:300 to Piershill Junction was followed by a short level section and a mile climb at 1:78 to Abbeyhill Junction, before the line entered Calton Tunnel and finally reached Edinburgh Waverley station.

Permanent Speed Restrictions

In 1939, the following were imposed:

Severe: Peterborough North, Selby, York, Durham, King Edward Bridge Junction (Down trains), Newcastle Central, Manors East, Morpeth.

Moderate: Retford (Down trains), Doncaster, Chaloner's Whin Junction (Down trains), Skelton Junction (Up trains), Alnmouth Junction, Berwick-on-Tweed, Abbeyhill Junction (Up trains).

11

Staff Distribution (October 1939)

Like the other railway companies, the LNER employed a very large labour force. Whether this was too large is certainly arguable, but at the time, the 'Big Four' generally tended to be self sufficient, with little 'out-sourcing', and there was a great amount of clerical work to be performed.[1]

While the general policy of the railway companies during the pre-war/post-Grouping period was a 'DIY' one, it had a number of inconsistencies. For instance, while the 'Big Four' owned collieries or had controlling shares in some, none were involved with steel or paper mills—as the consumption of both was extremely high. They printed their own stationery and tickets, but was a rule not their timetables. Despite their possession of large and well-equipped engineering works, besides a number of smaller establishments, the companies were compelled from time to time to have locomotives, rolling stock and/or other components to be manufactured by contractors. For example, for several years during the 1930s, the shipbuilders Harland and Wolff Ltd held a contract to supply cast-iron brake shoes to the Southern Railway.

There was an incredible amount of clerical work involved in the handling of goods traffic, and to a lesser extent, passenger traffic. For goods traffic—at least as far as the LNER was concerned—this was carried out, in most cases minus the aid of even the basic typewriter. There were three forms to be completed for each freight consignment to any single addressee. First, the consignment note, which was the basis of the contract between the consignor and the railway company, upon which the details of the consignment were entered and the carriage charges calculated. These particulars were then repeated on a second document, the Invoice, which was a company document giving details of the wagon number(s) into which the consignment was loaded, its route (to ensure the maximum percentage of its journey, if bound to a non-LNER destination, should be over LNER metals), the carriage charges and details of any LNER ropes, chains or packing materials used.

On arrival at its destination, a third document, the delivery sheet, had to be prepared in duplicate, yet again listing the relevant particulars of the consignment, for signature by the consignee. Virtually all this work was done with pencil and carbon paper, which itself was frequently worn out to the point of illegibility.

Provision of a single form in triplicate, which needed to be filled in only once, would not have been difficult—but a young clerk at King's Cross who did just that was once told by his immediate boss to mind his own business and not try to put people out of work. This attitude sometimes encountered at the time in the lower echelons of railway service later came to full flowering in the post-Nationalisation years. The figure of employees per route mile of the 'Big Four' provides a useful yardstick to judge the employment situation. They are: LMSR, 33.5; LNER, 27.6; GWR, 26.6; SR, 31.2. By comparison, the Cheshire Lines Committee system, for which its owning companies (LNER and LMSR) provided a large part of the administrative back-up from their own staffs, had only 19.5 employees per route mile.

The LNER as a whole was by no means the most prodigal of the four main line companies as regards staff numbers. Unfortunately, owing to the company's somewhat idiosyncratic system of staff classification, some differences are encountered when attempting to ascertain the numbers employed on the ECML. While the total number of employees in a particular grade in any year can be obtained from the ministry of labour records, it is not now possible to say with any degree of accuracy how many of all grades were employed at individual stations along the ECML. The figures given in National Archive files refer only to operating department staff—stationmasters, yardmasters, shunters, signalmen, porters, etc—and not to members of the passenger or goods manager's departments, i.e. booking office, parcels office, and goods office clerks, all of whom were necessary elements of station staffs, although accountants and general correspondence clerks only appeared at larger stations.

No records of the numbers of such staff members at individual stations appear to have survived. From personal recollections of a former LNER employee at King's Cross goods during the 1930s, some approximate idea of the figures involved can be obtained.

At King's Cross inwards delivery office, there were clerks on shift work round the clock from Sunday evening to the following Saturday midday. The outwards office was staffed from Monday morning to Saturday afternoon. Each of these offices employed some 50–60 men. Women were not employed in either of the two offices, although one young lady typist worked for a time in the inwards delivery office during 1938, but was soon transferred elsewhere as the uninhibited language of the male staff became too much for her.

The inwards and outwards correspondence offices worked on a 9–5 basis, each employing about 25 men and women; the accounts department, also 9–5, about 50–60; a number of miscellaneous small offices—fish, coal, potato market, cartage, pay—overall had a total of 30. Altogether there were about 250–300 clerical staff and these figures would be approximately true for all the other major goods stations along the ECML, such as York, Darlington, Newcastle (Forth) and Edinburgh (Leith Walk).

At Ilford, a medium-sized goods station servicing a moderately industrialised area on the former GER main line to Ipswich and beyond, the normal clerical staff in 1939 numbered eight, plus one extra person drafted in to assist with the work of distributing Anderson air raid shelters in the area. At smaller rural stations such as Rayleigh on the GER London–Southend line, the total station staff comprised the stationmaster (who also held the position at Hockley, the next station on the line), two passenger booking clerks, one full-time goods clerk, with another who worked there mornings only and spent the afternoon at Billericay Goods station, where he relieved the morning clerk who belonged to Brentwood.

There were six passenger station porters and one goods porter also at Rayleigh, and on the payroll were two signalmen and one travelling ticket inspector, who happened to live in the village. The official rat-catching cat—at tenpence halfpenny a week for milk—completed the establishment. An assumption can be made for similar staff numbers being present at stations on the ECML.

Fortunately, precise details of the numbers and distribution of Operating Staff at principal passenger and goods stations on the ECML have survived in National Archive files, which cover the whole of the southern area as of 31 October 1939, when a certain number had also joined HM Forces. These files also contain the names of staff and their salaries, but are incomplete as they do not include the large numbers of office staff—and perhaps others—in the commercial department.

King's Cross Passenger

Stationmaster (H. Ireland, £650 p.a.)	1
Assistant Stationmasters	2
Clerks (Male)	4
Clerks (Female)	1
Yard Inspectors	4
Station Inspectors	6
Goods Inspectors	2
Guards	144
Train Attendants	30
Signalmen	19
Foremen	3
Travelling Ticket Collectors	22
Station Foremen	13
Excess Luggage Collectors	3
Letter Sorters	3
Porters	92
Lost Property Attendants	4
Cloakroom Attendants	9
Telegraph Lads	6
Messenger Lads	6
Station Lamp Men	5
Signal Lamp Men	2
Station Lamp Lads	3
Yard Foremen	3
Shunters	22
Lavatory Attendants	9
Office Cleaners	4

King's Cross Parcels

Inspectors	3
Foremen	11
Leading Parcel Porters	42
Parcels Porters	118
Lad Messengers	5

King's Cross Carriage Cleaning

Foreman	1
Chargemen	3
Cleaners (Male)	44
Cleaners (Female)	11
Lads	2
Total	669 (7 in HM Forces)

King's Cross Goods Management

Goods Agent (F.C. Robbins)	1
Operating Assistant	1
Assistant Yardmasters	3

Staff Office

Clerks (Male)	2
Clerks (Female) (+2 in Armed Forces)	4

Inwards Night Fish Office

Clerk	1

Operating Office

Clerks (Male)	1
Clerks (Female)	2

Granary Staff

Caller-off	1
Porters (one was the Cat-Man)	2
Goods Guards	152

Shunting Staff

Inspectors	5
Foremen	6
Shunters	63
Points men	3
Number-takers	7
Office-Men	4
Messenger	1
Porters	2

Coal Yard Staff

Inspector	1
Shunters	7

Inwards Capstan Staff

Capstan Men	4
Lads	2

Outwards Capstan Staff

Foremen	6
Capstan Men	21

Potato Market Capstan Staff

Capstan Men	6

Inwards Shed Staff

Foremen	7
Working Foremen	4
Tracers	5
Checkers (+1 in HM Forces)	59
Number-takers	3
Loaders	57
Callers-off	57
Office Men	5
Crane Driver	1

Carter	1
Porters	123
Under-man	1
Lad Porters	2

Outwards Shed Staff

Foremen	17
Checkers (+1 in HM Forces)	72
Number-takers	5
Loaders	66
Callers-off	72
Sheeters (+2 in HM Forces)	25
Under-men	3
Porters (+23 in HM Forces)	210
Lad Messenger	1

Mobile Crane Staff

Crane Drivers	6
Checkers	4
Loaders	12

Potato Market Staff

Foremen	2
Checkers	3
Number-takers	3
Sheeters	2
Under-men	2

Miscellaneous Staff

Working Foreman	1
Timekeeper	1
Container-cleaner	1
Stationmaster	1
Chief Clerk	1
Clerks	2

Additional

Special Goods Agent	1
Operating Assistant	1
Assistant Yardmasters	3
Clerks	14
Women Clerks	2
Total	1,164 (29 in HM Forces)

King's Cross Mineral Depot

Foreman	1
Capstan-man	1
Traverser-worker	1
Coal Porters (mostly casual, +1 in HM Forces)	11
Total	14 (+1 in HM Forces)

Holloway, Including East Goods, Ashburton Grove and Cattle Docks

Total	147

Finsbury Park

Stationmaster	1
Clerks (1 Male, 1 Female)	2
Inspectors	3
Signalmen	19
Telegraph Lads	11
Ticket Collectors	13
Parcels Foreman	1
Station Foremen	3
Parcels Porters	8
Station Porters	24
Shunters	6
Cloakroom Attendant	1
Signal Lamp Man	1
Waiting Room Attendant	1
Carriage Cleaners	39
Total	39

Ferme Park Yard

Total	78 (No Guards)

Hornsey Carriage Sidings

Yard Inspector	1
Shunters	6
Foremen, Carriage Cleaning	2
Chargeman	2
Cleaners (Male)	62
Cleaners (Female)	3
Total	76

New Barnet

Total Staff	27

Hatfield

Total Staff	74

Knebworth (Atypical Outer Suburban Station)

Stationmaster	1
Signalmen	6
Porters	3
Lad Porters	2
Goods Porter	1
Total	13

Hitchin

Total	99 (excluding Clerks)

Peterborough North Passenger

Stationmaster	1
Chief Clerk	1
Station Inspectors	3
Station Foremen	3
Signalmen	10
Telegraph Lads	3
Ticket Collectors	2
Parcel Porters	14
Station Porters	16
Station Lamp Men	3
Signal Lamp Man	1
Passenger Guards	14
Chargeman Carriage Cleaners	10
Carriage Cleaners	10
Passenger Shunters	11
Goods Shunters	5
Shunt-Horse Driver	1
Ladies' Room Attendants (+1 Part-time)	1
Total	113 (omitting Passenger Manager's Clerks)

Peterborough North Goods

Total	54

New England Yard

Yardmaster	1
Assistant Yardmaster	1
Yard Inspectors	6
Clerks	4
Timekeepers	2
Signalmen	25
Telegraph Lads	6
Pointsmen	12
Yard Foremen	12
Shunters	48
Number-takers	3
Goods Guards	122
Lad Messengers	3
Signal Lamp Men	1
Station Lamp Men	2
Crossing Keeper	1
Total	249

Grantham Passenger

Stationmaster	1
Clerks (Male)	2
Clerks (Female)	1
Inspectors	3
Signalmen	19
Telegraph Lads	9
Station Foremen	2
Travelling Ticket Collector	1
Parcels Porters	9
Porters	12
Porter Guard	1
Lad Messengers	3
Ladies' Room Attendant	1
Signal Lamp Man	1
Station Lamp Men	3
Passenger Guards	9
Carriage Cleaners	8
Yard Foreman	3
Goods Shunters	11
Passenger Shunters	4
Shunt-Horse Drivers	3
Total	106

Grantham Goods

Total	30

Newark Passenger

Total	62

Newark Goods

Total	21 (plus six on loan from LMSR)

Retford Passenger and Goods

Total	88

Crow Park
(atypical Wayside Station)

Stationmaster	1
Signalmen	3
Porters	2
Crossing Keepers	2
Total	8

Doncaster

District Superintendent's Office

District Superintendent	1
Assistant District Superintendent	1
Special Assistant	1
Chief Clerk	1
Clerks (Male)	30
Clerks (Female)	9
Relief Clerks	9
Chief Controller	1
Deputy Controllers	2
Controllers	27
District Inspectors	3
Rolling Stock Inspector	1
Letter Sorter	1
Female Messenger	1
Office Cleaners	2
Messengers	5
Total	95

Doncaster Central Passenger

Stationmaster	1
Clerks (Male)	3
Clerk (Female	1
Station Inspectors	5
Signalmen	18
Telegraph Lads	13
Crossing Keepers	2
Foreman Ticket Collector	1
Ticket Collectors	11
Porters	20
Porter Guards	2
Parcels Porters	17
Station Foremen	5
Station Lamp Men	3
Signal Lamp Men	1
Passenger Guards	12
Passenger Shunters	14
Chargeman Carriage Cleaner	1
Carriage Cleaners	7
Excess Luggage Collector	1
Messengers	2
Ladies' Room Attendants	2
Cloakroom Attendants	2
Foremen Parcels Porters	2
Parcels Porters	7
Total	153

Doncaster Central Goods

Total	66

Doncaster Yards

Yardmaster	1
Assistant Yardmaster	1
Chief Clerk	1
Clerks (Male)	5
Clerks (Female)	2
Yard Inspectors	7
Yard Foremen	9
Shunters	61
Pointsmen	9
Signalmen	36
Goods Guards	188
Porters	5
Signal Lamp Men	8
Lad Lamp Man	1
Station Lamp Men	2
Messengers	6
Junior Number Taker	1
Telegraph Lads	10
Sheet Man	1
Letter Sorters	2
Crossing Keeper (Female)	1
Total	357

Superintendent, Southern Area

Chief Ticket Inspector	1
Travelling Ticket Inspectors	12
Chief Clerks	3
Clerks	14
Total	30

Endnotes

Chapter 1

1. During the war, stop gates were installed on either side of the canal section over Gas Works Tunnel to guard against flooding in the event the canal was breached by enemy action.
2. The LPTB built a new station at Highgate (opened January 1941), directly underneath the LNER one and rebuilt East Finchley station.
3. British Railways closed the branch in October 1951, but local councils forced the re-opening of the line in January 1952.
4. Originally the Maiden Lane terminus of 1850 before the GNR completed King's Cross station in 1852, it was used by the MR trains which had run up the GNR from Hitchin until the London Extension from Bedford to St Pancras was completed in 1868.
5. Holloway North Down box was rebuilt shortly after the war, superseding a temporary one built after a collision on 2 February 1940.
6. The GNR was unusual in arranging four-track lines on the basis of direction rather than according to the nature of the traffic. Tracks were in the order: Down Slow, Down Fast, Up Fast, Up Slow, rather than: Down Fast, Up Fast, Down Slow, Up Slow. Consequently, the GNR required two sets of signal boxes devoted to Up or Down line trains.
7. In the late 1950s, the dock became the loading point for motor cars on the 'Anglo-Scottish Car Carrier' train.
8. The LPTB paid for the work in recompense to the LNER for taking over Wellington Carriage Sidings at Highgate for Northern Line stock.
9. From 1942, some coal trains were worked from New England to Temple Mills by means of the siding connection, which necessitated splitting the train at Palace Gates.
10. Drivers of trains on the Up main line were instructed always to take water here to obviate the need to do so in London; the instruction was also given to drivers of Down Cambridge services.
11. In the 1950s, some passenger services (in daytime) were permitted on the Down Goods line between Stevenage and Huntingdon.
12. There was a turntable here for LMSR locomotives as the engine shed inherited by the company at Hitchin had been out of use since before Grouping.
13. During the war, freight traffic was swollen by airfields in the vicinity, and connecting buses were employed for many of the passenger services.
14. In 1939, there had been eleven services, with two on Sundays.
15. For a short time during the 1950s, there was a through train from King's Cross to Nottingham.

16 Along with British Marco (a short distance away), these works were heavily involved in the production of military equipment during the war.
17 This loop was passed for block conversion on summer Saturdays before the war, and converted for normal, full block, passenger working in the 1950s. Other goods loops were enabled by clipping the points to receive trains, such as excursions, at times of pressure.
18 Until Nationalisation, the flat crossing was controlled by the LMSR signal box because the MR line antedated the GNR main line when they were built in the 1850s.
19 Trains running direct to Lincoln ceased on closure of the Clarborough Junction–Sykes Junction line in November 1959, after which they went via Gainsborough.
20 On occasion, the line was used to house the Royal Train when their majesties had visited Doncaster Racecourse for the St Leger meeting.
21 Until September 1951, this had a passenger service from Wakefield to Edlington Halt, two miles west of Bessacarr Junction.
22 Up Independent No. 1 served the main Up platform—No. 4.
23 Although latterly fast freight and fish trains followed the direct route through Stamford Bridge, the long way round from Hull to York was preferred because it did not involve reversal and conflicting movements at York. This route was often used by special—and at times regular—passenger trains.
24 This storage of wagons caused much trouble as thieves would jack up the wagons and steal the brass from the axleboxes.
25 The signal box for Naburn was athwart the bridge, controlling the goods yard by a ground frame.
26 In 1961, Dringhouses Up Yard was enlarged by nine roads and provided with a hump, becoming the first marshalling yard in the country to be devoted exclusively to braked freight trains.
27 Until 1938, this box was called North Junction, York Yard North was 'Severus Junction' and Skelton was 'Poppleton Junction'.
28 In the 1950s, a regular monthly excursion ran from Derby to Newcastle behind an LMR locomotive.
29 The line remained open for goods until 1957.
30 Shortly before the war, a major bomb dump was established close to Brafferton station, which was the first one from Pilmoor on the branch. Run by No. 92 Maintenance Unit RAF, the dump supplied five principal Bomber Command airfields in the vicinity (Dishforth, Linton, Leeming, Topcliffe and Tholtorpe) and others at times. Traffic grew during the war to 13,400 wagons inwards in 1944, with two special trains per day (one on Sundays).
31 In the 1950s, a milk train ran on Sundays and was advertised to take passengers.
32 This replaced a manual box of 140 levers, which survived opposite its replacement for many years subsequently.
33 The official spelling is Deerness.
34 An unusual feature on the Up platform was the 'Private Waiting Room' provided for prisoners and escorts for Durham gaol, who still travelled by rail into the 1950s.
35 The well-known daily empty stock train to Holloway also went by this coast route and York.
36 During the war, most of the trains to Alnwick started from Manors North and ran out by the Jesmond Loop and the new Benton North-West Curve to the main line.
37 The Ashington group of collieries dispatched 12,000 tons of coal per day in 1957.
38 This was the only pair signalled for passenger trains, although Dam Dykes, Dudley, was signalled after the war.
39 The loops between Dudley and Dam Dykes were very long and could accommodate up to six full-length goods trains. During the war, trains queued one behind the other in these loops, but in doing so ran the serious risk of running out of water, for there was a water column at Dudley but not at Dam Dykes. At Stannington, Clifton, Beal and Goswick, crews were instructed to back their trains in, so freeing the engines to uncouple and go off for water and coal.

40 This was the first diesel-electric locomotive to work a passenger service.
41 For Viscount Grey of Falloden, foreign secretary 1905–1916, chairman of the NER and later a director of the LNER.

Chapter 2

1 One of the more obvious measures was the erection of protective walls around signal boxes and the fortress-like design of new ones built. There was also the erection of defences and obstacles such as 'dragon's teeth' concrete structures and the placing of demolition charges and decking of bridges to allow passage of road vehicles in an emergency—on the ECML, only Selby and Naburn were so treated.
2 On the LNER, £22,000 was spent on emergency goods depots and those at Finsbury Park, Tufnell Park and Palmers Green (opened March–August 1942) related to the ECML.
3 This was part of the total reconstruction and relocation of King's Cross Metropolitan station, which was eventually completed in March 1941. The new station was west of King's Cross Metropolitan Junction, but after the war, some trains also used the old station.
4 A notable movement occurred on 3 February 1941, when the 18-inch howitzer 'Boche Buster' (and perhaps others) passed through in transit from Catterick to Dover.
5 This line was used more frequently than that to Sandy, as the latter was only used for wagon storage post-war and was taken up in April 1966.
6 Information courtesy John McCrickard.
7 Railwaymen were particularly assisted in this area by servicemen, both skilled and unskilled.
8 The Post Office jealously guarded its monopoly and the LNER had plans for an exchange at Doncaster rejected but did manage to have one at York approved in January 1942, although not completed until September 1943.
9 'C' box survived until 1979.
10 Route-setting was by hand switches, but only from signal to signal, and the switches had to be operated separately. When a train had passed, turning the switch back to normal restored the points on the route. The interlocking prevented conflicting movements by blocking the operation of potentially conflicting switches until the first switch had been returned to normal.

Chapter 6

1 All figures are those current at the time but expressed decimally. Higher figures are for those working in the London area.
2 For example, in October 1942, returns revealed that 93 men from the Royal Corps of Signals were engaged in setting up new telephone links between control offices on the LNER. Forty men of the Pioneer Corps were also helping to build the new Yard at Connington. Many soldiers were also engaged in burying telegraph cables near Airfields. In February 1944, of the 1,001 men made available by the Army, the LNER received 340. Of these, ECML centres engaged 123 with driving experience as firemen, 58 'blockmen' were employed as shunters, and 18 were used as shed labourers, but half had returned to the forces by May 1944.

Chapter 7

1 Closed soon after the war.
2 Replaced by a new power box in March 1955. After the opening of the widened stretch from Greenwood in May 1959, communicated with New Barnet North by Track Circuit Block, Greenwood box being eliminated.
3 When the north to west loop to the LMSR line was opened in 1940, a box was provided at the junction, 1.36 miles north of Sandy box. The junction box (Sandy North) remained in use for some years after the war, although the loop was used only for wagon storage.

4 In 1958, the long section between Abbots Ripton and Connington South was split when a new box was opened at Wood Walton.
5 Renamed Connington South in 1942 when the Down Yard was built, the northern exit of which was controlled by a new box—Connington North—0.94 miles away.
6 Renewed during the war, perhaps when the new Down loop was installed.
7 During the war, and for a few years afterwards, there was a box at Torworth Crossing (0.75 miles south of Ranskill) where the loop from the ROF Ranskill joined the main line.
8 In January 1949, the new power box at Doncaster South (0.33 mile from Bridge Junction box) superseded South Yorkshire Junction and south boxes.
9 In February 1949, the new power box at Doncaster North (0.24 mile from Doncaster South power box) superseded 'A' and 'B' boxes and also Frenchgate and Marshgate Junction boxes, the block section from Doncaster North to Arksey station box now being 1.94 miles.
10 In February 1942, Riccall station box became Riccall South, and extra boxes were built at Riccall North (1.32 miles north) and at Escrick South (a further 0.68 mile on), when new loops were installed between these points; at the same time Escrick station box was renamed Escrick North.
11 Distance from platform box.
12 In connection with wartime widening works, Sessay Wood box became Pilmoor South in 1943 and Pilmoor station box became Pilmoor North. In 1942, a new box was built to replace the ground frame at Sessay station, 1.93 miles north of Pilmoor station (by then north) box.
13 On Sundays, this box was only open for 'theatrical traffic'. It was rebuilt 25 yards to the north in December 1953, and in December 1954, it took over the work of Ferryhill Sidings box; it also ceased to signal the main lines, but still signalled the Leamside (Slow) lines and the platform lines.
14 On the route via the High Level Bridge.
15 Distance via King Edward Bridge.
16 In October 1942, on being rebuilt 0.02 miles further south to control the new Up reception Sidings, 'C' Pit box was renamed Little Benton South; 0.33 miles north, a new box was also built, called Little Benton North.
17 In 1940, a new box, Benton North, was built 0.42 miles north of Benton Quarry box to control the new west to north loop from the Gosforth line, and when it was open, Forest Hall station box functioned as a gate box only.
18 In April 1952, an extra box, Widdrington North, was installed 1.51 miles north of Widdrington station box. It was in fact a second-hand one brought from Stonefall (Starbeck).
19 Alnmouth South was closed in 1951 and its functions were taken over by Alnmouth North, which was renamed 'Alnmouth'.
20 Dunbar West box was reconstructed in massive concrete when the loop lines were extended in 1942.

Chapter 8

1 Not actually a GNR station, but opened by the LNER in 1926.
2 Heck was an exception, having two airfields nearby.
3 Reopened on a slightly different site in October 1988.
4 Corby Glen from 1947.
5 PDS from October 1958.
6 Low Level and High Level closed at the same time.
7 Handled parcels until October 1966.
8 PDS from July 1951.
9 Unstaffed public siding from October 1951.

Chapter 9

1. The goods line tunnel on the west side was at an elevation 12 feet above the other two bores.
2. Three successive bridges, the second over Turnpike Lane and the third over the New River.
3. Down Slow No. 1, Down and Up main, Up slow and Up Goods Nos 1 and 2 on Brick Arches; Down Slow No. 2, Down Goods, Up Coal, reception lines and engine line on Girders.
4. Probably replaced by 1939; LMR viaduct was replaced in 1959.
5. Portion between LMSR line and river on 20-foot brick arches on Up side only.
6. Both Selby and Naburn swing bridges were hydraulically operated.
7. New Bridge was designated 12A and had five spans of second-hand wrought iron: 38 feet 3 inches, 56 feet, 67 feet 3 inches, 56 feet and 38 feet 3 inches.
8. Many other smaller bridges between York and Northallerton were renewed either in 1942 or during the last widening works in 1959–60.
9. This was immediately followed by a shorter girder at a skew over the Low Level lines.
10. Further widened in 1932.
11. Tunnel collapsed in March 1979 and line was diverted to a new course, eliminating the tunnel.

Chapter 11

1. This chapter has contributions from former LNER employee Peter Erwood.

Bibliography

This list includes publications referred to in this work, together with some suggestions for background reading. Unless otherwise stated, the place of publication for all titles is London.

Addyman, J. and Fawcett, B., *The High Level Bridge and Newcastle Central Station: 150 Years across the Tyne* (1999)
Aldcroft, D. H., *British Transport since 1914: An Economic History* (Newton Abbot: David & Charles, 1975)
Allen, C. J., *Locomotive Practice and Performance in the Twentieth Century* (Cambridge: W. Heffer & Sons, 1949); *The Locomotive Exchanges, 1870–1948* (Ian Allan, Second Edition, 1950); *Titled Trains of Great Britain* (Ian Allan, Third Edition, 1954); *The Great Eastern Railway* (Ian Allan, Third Edition, 1961); *The North Eastern Railway* (Ian Allan, 1964); *The London & North Eastern Railway* (Ian Allan, 1966); *Gresley Pacifics of the LNER* (Ian Allan, Second Edition, 1990)
Allen, G. F., *British Railways Today and Tomorrow* (Ian Allan, 1959); *The Eastern Since 1948* (Ian Allan, 1981)
Anderson, P. H., *Forgotten Railways Vol. 2, The East Midlands* (Newon Abbot: David & Charles, Second Edition, 1985)
Appleby, K., *British Rail's Super Centres—York* (Ian Allan, 1993)
Austin, S., *From the Footplate: The Elizabethan* (Ian Allan, 1993)
Bagwell, P. S., *The Railwaymen: The History of the National Union of Railwaymen* (George Allen & Unwin, 1963); *The Transport Revolution from 1770* (Batsford, 1974); *Doncaster: Town of Train Makers, 1853–1990* (Doncaster: Doncaster Books, 1991)
Balfour, G., *The Armoured Train: Its Development and Usage* (Batsford, 1981)
Barnett, A. L., *The Railways of the South Yorkshire Coalfield from 1880* (RCTS, 1984)
Batty, S. R., *Rail Centres: Doncaster* (Ian Allan, 1991)
Behrend, G., *Pullman in Europe* (Ian Allan, 1962)
Bell, R., *History of the British Railways during the War* (Railway Gazette, 1946)
Blakemore, M. (ed.), *The London & North Eastern Railway: Backtrack Special Issue* (Penryn: Atlantic, 2001)
Body, G., *British Rail Routes Past and Present: The East Coast Main Line. King's Cross to Newcastle: The Route of the 'Silver Jubilee'* (Petersborough: Silver Link, 1995)
Bolger, P., *BR Steam Motive Power Depots: ER, ScR, NER* (Ian Allan (three volumes), 1982, 3, and 4)
Bonavia, M. R., *The Organisation of British Railways* (Ian Allan, 1971); *British Rail: The First 25 Years* (Newton Abbot: David & Charles, 1981); *A History of the LNER, Vol. II: The Age of the Streamliners, 1934–1939* (George Allen & Unwin, 1982); *A History of the LNER, Vol. III: The Last Years, 1939–48* (George Allen & Unwin, 1982); *The Cambridge Line* (Ian Allan, 1995)

Boyes, G., Searle, M., and Steggles, D., *Ottley's Bibliography of British Railway History: Second Supplement* (York: National Railway Museum, 1998)

Boyes, G., *A Bibliography of the History of Inland Waterways, Railways & Road Transport in the British Isles. Journal of the Railway & Canal Historical Society* (1996–2002)

Bradshaw's British Railway Guide and Hotel Directory (Henry Blacklock & Co., 1939–1959)

British Railways Board, *The Re-shaping of British Railways* (HMSO, 1963)

British Transport Commission, *Modernisation and Re-Equipment of British Railways* (BTC, 1955)

British Transport Historical Records Collection: A Provisional Guide (Kew Public Record Office, 1977)

Brodribb, J., *LNER County Stations* (Ian Allan, 1988)

Bryan, T., *The Great Western at War, 1939–45* (Sparkford: Patrick Stephens, 1995)

Buck, G. A., *A Pictorial Survey of Railway Stations* (Oxford Publishing, 1992)

Butt, R. V. J., *The Directory of Railway Stations* (Sparkford: Patrick Stephens, 1995)

Calvert, R., *Transport Dis-integrated* (1973)

Carter, C. S., 'LNER Buffet Cars' in *Backtrack*, Vol. 9 (1995), pp. 14–21.

Carter, O., *An Illustrated History of British Railways Hotels, 1838–1983.* (St Michaels, Silver Link, 1990)

Carter, R. S., *British Railways Main-Line Diesels* (Ian Allan, 1963)

Casserley, H. C. and Asher, L. L., *Locomotives of British Railways, London & North Eastern Group: A Pictorial Record* (Dakers, 1958)

Chapman, S. (ed.), *Railway Memories, No. 2 Darlington and South-West Durham* (Todmorden: Bellcode Books, 1990)

Charlton, L. G. and Mountford, C. E., *Industrial Locomotives of Northumberland* (Market Harborough: Industrial Railway Society, 1983)

Clay, J. F. and Cliffe, J., *The LNER 4-6-0 Classes* (Ian Allan, 1975)

Clay, J. F. and Cliffe, J., *The LNER 2-6-0 Classes* (Ian Allan, 1978)

Clinker, C. R., *Clinker's Register of Closed Passenger Stations and Goods Depots in England, Scotland and Wales, 1830–1980* (Weston-super-Mare: Avon-Anglia, 1988)

Conolly, W. P., *British Railways Pre-Grouping Atlas and Gazetteer* (Ian Allan, 1976)

Cookson, P. and Farline, J. E., *LNER Lines in the Yorkshire Ridings* (Oldham: Challenger Press, 1995)

Cox, E. S., *British Railways Standard Steam Locomotives* (Ian Allan, 1966)

Crump, N., *By Rail to Victory: The Story of the LNER in Wartime* (LNER, 1947)

Cupit, J. and Taylor, W., *The Lancashire, Derbyshire & East Coast Railway* (Lingfield, 1966)

Daniels, G. and Dench, L. A., *Passengers No More* (Ian Allan, Second Edition, 1973)

Department of Transport, *Transport Statistics, Great Britain 1992* (HMSO, 1992)

Dow, G., *Great Central Vols I–III* (Locomotive Publishing Co., 1959–65)

Earley, M. W., *The LNER Scene: An Album of Photographs by Maurice W. Earley* (Oxford: Oxford Publishing, 1973)

Earnshaw, A., *Trains in Trouble, Vols V–VIII* (Penryn: Atlantic, 1989–1993); *Britain's Railways at War* (Penryn: Atlantic)

Edwards, C., *Railway Records: A Guide to Sources* (Public Record Office, 2001)

Ellis, C. H., *The North British Railway* (Ian Allan, 1955)

Essery, R. J., Rowland, D. P., and Steel, W. O., *British Goods Wagons from 1887 to the Present Day* (Newton Abbot: David & Charles, 1970)

Fiennes, G. F., *I Tried to Run a Railway* (Ian Allan, 1967)

Franks, D., *The Stamford & Essendine Railway* (Leeds: Turntable Enterprises)

Franks, D. L., *Great Northern and London & North-Western Joint Railway* (Leeds: Turntable Enterprises, 1974)

Fry, E. V. (ed.), *Locomotives of the LNER Parts 1 to 10A* (17 parts) (RCTS, 1963–1990)

Gammell, G. J., *LNER Branch Lines* (Sparkford: Oxford Publishing, 1993)

Goode, C. T., *The Goole & Selby Railway* (Tarrant Hinton: Oakwood Press, 1976); *The Wensleydale Branch* (Trowbridge: Oakwood Press, 1980); *The Hertford Loop Line* (Trowbridge: Oakwood Press, 1980)

Gordon, D. I., *A Regional History of the Railways of Great Britain: Vol. V, The Eastern Counties* (Newton Abbot: David & Charles, 1968)

Goslin, G. W., *Steam on the Widened Lines, Vol. I: The Great Northern and Midland Railways and their Successors* (Connor & Butler, 1997); *Steam on the Widened Lines, Vol. II: Great Western and Southern Companies* (Connor & Butler, 1998); *Goods Traffic on the LNER* (Didcot: Wild Swan Publications, 2002)

Gourvish, T. R., *British Railways 1948–73: A Business History* (Cambridge University Press, 1986)

Griffiths, R. and Hooper, J., *Great Northern Engine Sheds, Vol. I: Southern Area* (Pinner: Irwell Press, 1989); *Great Northern Engine Sheds, Vol. II: The Lincolnshire Loop, Nottinghamshire & Derbyshire* (Oldham: Challenger Publications, 1996); *Great Northern Engine Sheds, Vol. III: Yorkshire and Lancashire* (Nottingham: Challenger Publications/Railbus, Book Law, 2000)

Grinling, C. H., *The History of the Great Northern Railway* (Allen & Unwin, Revised Edition, 1966)

Groundwater, K., *Newcastle's Railways: A View from the Past* (Ian Allan, 1998)

Gwilliam, K. M. and Mackie, P. J., *Economics and Transport Policy* (Allen & Unwin, 1975)

Hajducki, A. M., *The Haddington, Macmerry and Gifford Branch Lines* (Headington: Oakwood Press, 1994)

Hands, P. and Richards, C., *British Railways Steaming on the East Coast Main Line* (Solihull: Defiant, 1986); *British Railways Steaming on the ex-LNER Lines, Vols I–III* (Solihull: Defiant, 1988/91/94); *British Railways Steaming Through Peterborough* (Solihull: Defiant, 1989)

Hardy, R. H. N., *Steam in the Blood* (Ian Allan, 1971); *Beeching: Champion of the Railway?* (Ian Allan, 1989)

Haresnape, B., *Gresley Locomotives: A Pictorial History* (Ian Allan, 1981); *Railway Liveries: London & North Eastern Railway* (Ian Allan, 1984); *Pullman Travelling in Style* (Ian Allan, 1987)

Harris, M., *Gresley's Coaches: Coaches Built for GNR, ECJS and LNER, 1905–53* (Newton Abbot: David & Charles, 1973); *This is York—Major Railway Centres* (Ian Allan, Second Edition, 1983); *LNER Carriages* (Nairn: David St John Thomas, 1994); *LNER Standard Gresley Carriages* (Chertsey: Mallard Books, 1998)

Harris, N. (ed.), *LNER Reflections: A Collection of Photographs from the Hulton Picture Co., Special Anniversary Edition* (Carnforth: Silver Link, 1995)

Harvey, D. W., *Bill Harvey's Sixty Years in Steam* (Newton Abbot: David & Charles, 1986)

Hawkins, C., Hooper, J., and Reeves, G., *British Railways Engine Sheds, No. 1 LNER Inheritance* (Pinner: Irwell Press, 1988); *The Great British Railway Station King's Cross* (Pinner: Irwell Press, 1990)

Henshaw, D., *The Great Railway Conspiracy* (Hawes: Leading Edge, Second Edition, 1994)

Hick, F. L., *That Was My Railway* (Wadenhoe: Silver Link, 1991)

Higgins, R. N., *Over Here: The Story of the United States Army Transportation Corps Class S160 Locomotives* (Rochdale: Big Jim, 1980)

Hodge, P., *The Hertford Loop: The First Hundred Years of a Local Railway* (Southgate: Southgate Civic Trust, 1976)

Hoole, K., *A Regional History of the Railways of Great Britain, Vol. IV: North East England* (Dawlish: David & Charles, 1965); *North Eastern Locomotive Sheds* (Newton Abbot: David & Charles, 1972); *North Eastern Album* (Ian Allan, 1974); *Railways in the Yorkshire Dales* (Clapham (Yorks), Dalesman, 1975); *The East Coast Main Line Since 1925* (Ian Allan, 1977); *North Eastern Branch Lines Since 1925* (Ian Allan, 1978); *North Eastern Stations: A Photographic Collection* (Clapham (Yorks): Dalesman, 1978); *The 4-4-0 Classes of the North Eastern Railway* (Ian Allan, 1979); *Rail Centres: York* (Ian Allan, 1983); *Railways of Tyneside, Vol. I* (Clapham (Yorks), Dalesman, 1983); *North Eastern Branch Lines Past and Present* (Poole: Oxford Publishing, 1984); *Forgotten Railways: North-East England* (Newton Abbot: David & Charles, Second Edition, 1984); *Railway Stations of the North East* (Newton Abbot: David & Charles, 1985); *Rail Centres: Newcastle* (Ian Allan, 1986); *Trains in Trouble, Vols III–IV* (Penryn: Atlantic Publishers, 1982–83)

Hooper, J., *LNER Sheds in Camera* (Yeovil: Oxford Publishing, 1984)

Hornby, F., *London Suburban: An Illustrated History of the Capital's Commuter Lines Since 1948* (Wadenhoe: Silver Link, 1995)

Howat, P., *Railways of Ryedale and the Vale of Mowbray* (Nelson (Lancs.): Henderson, 1988)
Hughes, G. J., *The Gresley Influence* (Ian Allan, 1983); *LNER* (Ian Allan, 1986); *An Economic History of the London & North Eastern Railway* (University of London, 1990); *Sir Nigel Gresley: The Engineer and His Family* (Trowbridge: Oakwood Press, 2001)
Hughes, G. J. (ed.), *A Gresley Anthology* (Didcot: Wild Swan, 1994)
Hunter, M. and Thorne, R. (eds), *Change at King's Cross from 1800 to the Present* (Historical Publications, 1990)
Hurst, G., *Register of Closed Railways, 1948–1991* (Worksop: Milepost, 1992)
Independent Commission of Transport, *Changing Directions: The Report of the Independent Commission on Transport* (Coronet, 1974)
Jackson, A. A., *London's Termini* (Newton Abbot: David & Charles, 1969)
John, E., *Timetable for Victory* (British Railways, 1945)
Johnson, J. and Long, R. A., *British Railways Engineering, 1948–80* (Mechanical Engineering, 1981)
Joy, D., *A Regional History of the Railways of Great Britain, Vol. VIII: South and West Yorkshire* (Newton Abbot: David & Charles, 1975)
Karmel, D. and Beddington, R., The Transport Act 1947 (Butterworth, 1948)
Kay, P. A., *A Guide to Railway Research and Sources for Local History* (Teignmouth: SSG Publications, 1990)
Kingston, P., *Royal Trains* (Newton Abbot: David & Charles, 1985)
Leleux, R., *A Regional History of the Railways of Great Britain, Vo. IX: The East Midlands* (Newton Abbot: David & Charles, 1976)
Meacher, C., *LNER Footplate Memories: A Story of Twenty-Five Years On and Off Shed* (Truro: Bradford Barton, 1985)
Milner, C. and Banks, C., *British Railways Past and Present, No. 10: The East Midlands* (Wadenhoe: Silver Link, 1991)
Ministry of Transport, *Railway Accidents: Reports by HM Inspectorate to the Minister of Transport* (HMSO, 1940–1959)
Ministry of Transport and Civil Aviation, *The British Transport Commission: Re-Appraisal of the Plan for the Modernisation and Re-Equipment of British Railways* (HMSO, 1959)
Morrison, B. and Brunt, K., *British Railways Past and Present: London* (Peterborough: Silver Link, 1991)
Morrison, G., *Gresley A4s: The LNER Streamlined Pacific Locomotives* (Ian Allan, 2000); *The Power of the A1s* (Oxford: Oxford Publishing, 2001); *The Power of the V2s* (Oxford: Oxford Publishing, 2001)
Mountford, C. E. and Charlton, L. G., *Industrial Locomotives of Durham* (Market Harborough: Industrial Railway Society, 1977)
Mullay, A. J., *Non-Stop! London to Scotland Steam* (Gloucester: Alan Sutton, 1989); *Rail Centres: Edinburgh* (Ian Allan, 1991); *Streamlined Steam: Britain's 1930s Luxury Expresses* (Newton Abbot: David & Charles, 1994)
Munby, D. L. and Watson, A. H., *Inland Transport Statistics, Great Britain 1900–1970, Vol. I: Railways, Public Road Passenger Transport, London Transport* (Oxford: Clarendon Press, 1978)
Murphy, B., *ASLEF 1880–1980: A Hundred Years of the Locomen's Trade Union* (ASLEF, 1980)
Nash, C. A., *Public Versus Private Transport* (Macmillan, 1976)
Neve, E., *East Coast from King's Cross* (Ian Allan, 1983)
Nock, O. S., *The Great Northern Railway* (Ian Allan, 1958); *LNER Steam* (Newton Abbot: David & Charles, 1969); *Britain's Railways at War, 1939–1945* (Ian Allan, 1971); *The Gresley Pacifics Vols I and II* (Newton Abbot: David & Charles, 1973–74); *Great Locomotives of the LNER* (Wellingborough: Patrick Stephens, 1988)
Nock, O. S. and Treacy, E., *Main Lines Across the Border* (Nelson, 1960)
Oldham, K., *Steam in Wartime Britain* (Dover: Alan Sutton, 1993)
Ottley, G., *A Bibliography of British Railway History (to 1963)* (Science Museum/National Railway Museum, Second Edition, 1983); *A Bibliography of British Railway History Supplement (1963–1980)* (Science Museum/National Railway Museum, Second Edition, 1983)

Parkin, K., *British Railways Mark 1 Coaches* (Penryn: Atlantic Publishers/Historical Model Railway Society, 1991)
Pike, S. N., *Mile by Mile on the LNER: King's Cross Edition* (1947)
Pollock, D. R. and White, D. E., *The 2-8-0 and 2-10-0 Locomotives of the War Department, 1939–1945* (RCTS, 1946)
Railway Clearing House, *History of the Railways During the War: A Report Prepared by the Railway Operating Superintendents* (not Published, but available at National Archives, Ref: RAIL1085/122. 1946)
Railway Magazine, 'Gradients of the British Main Line Railways' (The Railway Publishing Co., 1938)
Report from the Parliamentary Select Committee on Nationalised Industries: Railways (British Transport Commission, 1960)
Rhodes, J., *The Midland & Great Northern Joint Railway* (Ian Allan, 1982)
Robinson, P. J. and Groundwater, K., *British Railways Past and Present: The North East* (Wadenhoe: Silver Link, 1987)
Rogers, H. C. B., *Thompson & Peppercorn: Locomotive Engineers* (Ian Allan, 1979)
Rose, P., *Railway Memories No. 5: Return to York* (Todmorden: Bellcode Books, 1993)
Rowledge, J. W. P., *Heavy Goods Engines of the War Department, Vol. II: The Stanier 8F 2-8-0* (Poole: Springhead Railway Books, 1977); *Heavy Goods Engines of the War Department, Vol. III: Austerity 2-8-0 and 2-10-0* (Poole: Springhead Railway Books, 1978); *Austerity 2-8-0s and 2-10-0s* (Ian Allan, 1987)
Sanders, K. and Hodgins, D., *British Railways Past and Present No. 9: South East Scotland* (Wadenhoe: Silver Link, 1991)
Sanderson, E., *Railway Memories No. 1: York* (Todmorden: Bellcode Books, 1988)
Sanderson, H. F., *Railway Commercial Practice Vols 1 and 2* (Chapman & Hall, 1952)
Savage, C. I., *History of the Second World War: United Kingdom Civil Series, Inland Transport* (HMSO, 1957); *An Economic History of Transport* (Hutchinson, Second Edition, 1961)
Semmens, P. W. B., *Bill Hoole: Engineman Extraordinary* (Ian Allan, 1966); *North Eastern Engineman: Driver Syd Midgley and Fifty Years of Steam* (Truro: Bradford Barton, 1980); *Speed on the East Coast Main Line: A Century and a Half of Accelerated Services* (Wellingborough: Patrick Stephens, 1990)
Smith, W. A. C. and Anderson, P., *An Illustrated History of Edinburgh's Railways* (Caernarfon: Irwell Press, 1995)
Stephenson, B., *LNER Album, Vols I–III* (Ian Allan, 1970–76)
Stobbs, A. W., *Memories of the LNER: Tyneside* (1988)
Thomas, J., *The North British Railway, Vols I and II* (Newton Abbot: David & Charles, 1969, 1975); *A Regional History of the Railways of Great Britain, Vol. VI: Scotland and the Lowlands and the Borders* (Newton Abbot: David & Charles, 1971)
Thompson, A. R. and Groundwater, K., *British Railways Past and Present No. 11: North Yorkshire Part 1* (Wadenhoe: Silver Link, 1992)
Tomlinson, W. W., *The North Eastern Railway: Its Rise and Development* (Newton Abbot: David & Charles, 1971 (Reprint))
Tourret, R., *Allied Military Locomotives of the Second World War* (Abingdon: Tourret Publishing, 1996)
Townend, P. N., *East Coast Pacifics at Work* (Ian Allan, 1982); *The Colour of Steam Vol. 4: The LNER Pacifics* (Penryn: Atlantic Publishers, 1985); *Top Shed* (Ian Allan, 1989)
Treacy, E., *Lure of Steam* (Ian Allan, 1966)
Trevena, A., *Trains in Trouble, Vols I and II* (Penryn: Atlantic Publishers, 1980–81)
Tufnell, R. M., *The Diesel Impact on British Rail* (Mechanical Engineering Publications, 1979); *The British Railcar: A.E.C. to H.S.T.* (Newton Abbot: David & Charles, 1984)
Tuplin, W. A., *North Eastern Steam* (Allen & Unwin, 1970); *Great Northern Steam* (Ian Allan, 1971)
Walker, G., *Road and Rail: An Enquiry into the Economics of Competition and State Control* (Allen & Unwin, 1942)

Warn, C. R., *Rural Branch Lines of Northumberland* (Newcastle-upon-Tyne: Frank Graham, 1978); *Rails Between Wear and Tyne* (Newcastle-upon-Tyne: Frank Graham, 1982)
Waszak, P., *Rail Centres: Peterborough* (Ian Allan, 1984)
White, H. P., *A Regional History of the Railways of Great Britain, Vol. III: Greater London* (Phoenix House, 1963)
White, P. R., *Planning for Public Transport* (Hutchinson, 1976)
Whitehouse, P. and Powell, J., *Treacy's Routes North* (Newton Abbot: David & Charles, 1985)
Whitehouse, P. and Thomas, D. St J., *LNER 150: The London & North Eastern Railway A Century and a Half of Progress* (Newton Abbot: David & Charles, 1985)
Whitehouse, P. and Jenkinson, D., *From BR to Beeching Vol. III: The Routes of the Thompson and Peppercorn Pacifics* (Penryn: Atlantic Publishers, 1990)
Whiteley, J. S. and Morrison, G. W., *Profile of the Deltics* (Oxford: Oxford Publishing, 1980); *Profile of the A1s, A2s and A3s* (Oxford: Oxford Publishing, 1982); *Profile of the A4s* (Poole: Oxford Publishing, 1985)
Whittle, G., *The Railways of Consett and North-West Durham* (Newton Abbot: David & Charles, 1971); *The Newcastle & Carlisle Railway* (Newton Abbot: David & Charles, 1979)
Wignall, C. J., *Complete British Railways Maps and Gazetteer, 1830–1981* (Poole: Oxford Publishing, 1983)
Williams, S. C. S. and Short, E., *Railways, Roads and the Public* (Eyre & Spottiswood, 1939)
Wilmot, G. F. A., *The Railway in Finchley: A Study of Suburban Development* (Finchley Public Libraries Committee, 1962)
Woodward, G. S., *The Hatfield, Luton & Dunstable Railway, and on to Leighton Buzzard* (Tarrant Hinton: Oakwood Press, 1977)
Wooler, N., *Dinner in the Diner* (Newton Abbot: David & Charles, 1987)
Wright, C., 'Conflicts, Accidents, Catastrophes and Chaos: Road Transport in the Twenty-First Century' (*Journal of the Royal Society of Medicine*, Vol. 87, pp. 403–407)
Wrottesley, A. J. F., *The Midland & Great Northern Joint Railway* (Newton Abbot: David & Charles, 1970); *The Great Northern Railway, Vols I–III* (Batsford, 1979–81)
Yeadon, W. B., *Yeadon's Register of LNER Locomotives Vols I–IX* (Various, 1990–1996)
Young, J. N., *Great Northern Suburban* (Newton Abbot: David & Charles, 1977)

For Articles and Notes

First and foremost, *The Railway Observer*, the monthly journal of the RCTS. Also, *The Railway Gazette, The Railway Magazine*, and *Modern Railways*; *Trains Illustrated* and *Railway World*; *Steam World*; *Steam Days*; *Backtrack*; *British Railways Illustrated*: *LNER Magazine*; and *British Railways Eastern Region Magazine*.

The primary source of information and reference has been the archives held in the National Archives, Kew. The files that have been particularly useful include: RAIL390-401 (LNER files); Rail 900-999 (timetables); Rail 1000-1165 (General and Miscellaneous); AN2 and AN3 (REC 1939-47); AN4 onwards (British Railways after Nationalisation, with Eastern and North Eastern Region files concentrated in AN 23-29 (Scottish Region records are mainly held at the Scottish Record Office, Edinburgh); MT6, MT9 and certain other MT classes.

Extensive records are also held at the National Railway Museum, York, and there are many regional sources for records. Additionally, specialist societies are a valuable fount of details, including: Railway Correspondence & Travel Society (RCTS); Stephenson Locomotive Society (SLS); Railway & Canal Historical Society; the Signalling Record Society; North Eastern Railway Society; and North British Railway Study Group.